ILLUSTRATED SERIES™

COMPREHENSIVE

MICROSOFT® OFFICE 365®
ACCESS® 2019

LISA FRIEDRICHSEN

Australia • Brazil • Canada • Mexico • Singapore • United Kingdom • United States

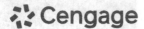

Illustrated Series™ Microsoft® Office 365®
Access® 2019 Comprehensive
Lisa Friedrichsen

SVP, GM Skills & Global Product Management: Jonathan Lau

Product Director: Lauren Murphy

Product Assistant: Veronica Moreno-Nestojko

Executive Director, Content Design: Marah Bellegarde

Director, Learning Design: Leigh Hefferon

Associate Learning Designer: Courtney Cozzy

Vice President, Marketing—Science, Technology, and Math: Jason R. Sakos

Senior Marketing Director: Michele McTighe

Marketing Manager: Timothy J. Cali

Director, Content Delivery: Patty Stephan

Content Manager: Grant Davis

Digital Delivery Lead: Laura Ruschman

Designer: Lizz Anderson

Text Designer: Joseph Lee, Black Fish Design

Cover Template Designer: Lisa Kuhn, Curio Press, LLC www.curiopress.com

For product information and technology assistance, contact us at **Cengage Customer & Sales Support, 1-800-354-9706 or support.cengage.com.**

For permission to use material from this text or product, submit all requests online at **www.copyright.com.**

Library of Congress Control Number: 2019939825

Student Edition ISBN: 978-0-357-02569-7
Looseleaf available as part of a digital bundle

Cengage
200 Pier 4 Boulevard
Boston, MA 02210
USA

Cengage is a leading provider of customized learning solutions with employees residing in nearly 40 different countries and sales in more than 125 countries around the world. Find your local representative at **www.cengage.com.**

To learn more about Cengage platforms and services, register or access your online learning solution, or purchase materials for your course, visit **www.cengage.com.**

Printed in the United States of America
Print Number: 03   Print Year: 2022

Brief Contents

Contents

Access 2019

Getting to Know Microsoft Office Versions

Cengage is proud to bring you the next edition of Microsoft Office. This edition was designed to provide a robust learning experience that is not dependent upon a specific version of Office.

Microsoft supports several versions of Office:

- **Office 365:** A cloud-based subscription service that delivers Microsoft's most up-to-date, feature-rich, modern productivity tools direct to your device. There are variations of Office 365 for business, educational, and personal use. Office 365 offers extra online storage and cloud-connected features, as well as updates with the latest features, fixes, and security updates.

- **Office 2019:** Microsoft's "on-premises" version of the Office apps, available for both PCs and Macs, offered as a static, one-time purchase and outside of the subscription model.

- **Office Online:** A free, simplified version of Office web applications (Word, Excel, PowerPoint, and OneNote) that facilitates creating and editing files collaboratively.

Office 365 (the subscription model) and Office 2019 (the one-time purchase model) had only slight differences between them at the time this content was developed. Over time, Office 365's cloud interface will continuously update, offering new application features and functions, while Office 2019 will remain static. Therefore, your onscreen experience may differ from what you see in this product. For example, the more advanced features and functionalities covered in this product may not be available in Office Online or may have updated from what you see in Office 2019.

For more information on the differences between Office 365, Office 2019, and Office Online, please visit the Microsoft Support site.

Cengage is committed to providing high-quality learning solutions for you to gain the knowledge and skills that will empower you throughout your educational and professional careers.

Thank you for using our product, and we look forward to exploring the future of Microsoft Office with you!

Using SAM Projects and Textbook Projects

SAM and *MindTap* are interactive online platforms designed to transform students into Microsoft Office and Computer Concepts masters. Practice with simulated SAM Trainings and MindTap activities and actively apply the skills you learned live in Microsoft Word, Excel, PowerPoint, or Access. Become a more productive student and use these skills throughout your career.

If your instructor assigns SAM Projects:

1. Launch your SAM Project assignment from SAM or MindTap.
2. Click the links to download your **Instructions file**, **Start file**, and **Support files** (when available).
3. Open the Instructions file and follow the step-by-step instructions.
4. When you complete the project, upload your file to SAM or MindTap for immediate feedback.

To use SAM Textbook Projects:

1. Launch your SAM Project assignment from SAM or MindTap.
2. Click the links to download your **Start file** and **Support files** (when available).
3. Locate the module indicated in your book or eBook.
4. Read the module and complete the project.

Open the Start file you downloaded.

Save, close, and upload your completed project to receive immediate feedback.

IMPORTANT: To receive full credit for your Textbook Project, you must complete the activity using the Start file you downloaded from SAM or MindTap.

Using SAM Projects and Textbook Projects

SAM and MindTap are interactive online platforms designed to transform students into Microsoft Office and Computer Concepts masters. Practice with simulated SAM Trainings and MindTap activities and actively apply the skills you learned live in Microsoft Word, Excel, PowerPoint, or Access. Become a more productive student and use these skills throughout your career.

If your instructor assigns SAM Projects:

1. Launch your SAM Project assignment from SAM or MindTap.
2. Click the links to download your instructions file, **Start file**, and **Support files** (when available).
3. Open the instructions file and follow the step-by-step instructions.
4. When you complete the project, upload your file to SAM or MindTap for immediate feedback.

To use SAM Textbook Projects:

1. Launch your SAM Project assignment from SAM or MindTap.
2. Click the links to download your **Start file** and **Support files** (when available).
3. Locate the module indicated in your book or eBook.
4. Read the module and complete the project.

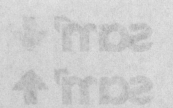

sam ↓   Open the start file you downloaded.

sam ↑   Save, close, and upload your completed project to receive immediate feedback.

IMPORTANT: To receive full credit for your Textbook Project, you must complete the activity using the Start file you downloaded from SAM or MindTap.

Getting Started with Access

Lydia Snyder is the vice president of operations for JCL Talent, a company that provides recruitment and employment services for employers and job seekers. You will work with Lydia to use Microsoft Access 2019 to store, maintain, and analyze job placement data.

Module Objectives

After completing this module, you will be able to:

- Understand relational databases
- Open and explore a database
- Navigate and enter data
- Edit existing data
- Create a table
- Modify fields
- Create a query

- Create a form
- Create a report
- Save and share a database with OneDrive
- Create a new database
- Compact and back up a database

Files You Will Need

IL_AC_1-1.accdb

Support_IL_AC_1_Employees.xlsx

IL_AC_1-2.accdb

Support_IL_AC_1_StatesAndProvs.xlsx

IL_AC_1-3.accdb

IL_AC_1-4.accdb

Learning
Outcomes
• Describe relational
  database concepts
• Explain when to
  use a database
• Compare a
  relational database
  to a spreadsheet

Understand Relational Databases

Microsoft Access 2019 is relational database software that runs on the Windows operating system. You use **relational database software** to manage data organized into lists, such as information about customers, products, vendors, employees, projects, or sales. Some companies track lists of information in a spreadsheet program such as Microsoft Excel. Although Excel offers some list management features, Access provides many more tools and advantages for managing data. Access uses a relational database model to manage data, whereas Excel manages data as a single list. **TABLE 1-1** compares the two programs.

CASE   *Lydia has noticed that JCL Talent manages multiple copies of several lists of data in Excel. She asks you to help her review the advantages of managing data in a relational database model used by Access as compared to the single list spreadsheet approach used by Excel.*

DETAILS

The advantages of using Access for database management include the following:

• **Duplicate data is minimized**

  FIGURES 1-1 and **1-2** compare how you might store data in a single list in an Excel spreadsheet versus managing the same data using three tables in an Access relational database. With Access, you enter company data only once no matter how many jobs that company has to offer.

• **Information is more accurate, reliable, and consistent because duplicate data is minimized**

  When data is not duplicated, it is more accurate, reliable, and consistent.

• **Data entry is faster and easier using Access forms**

  Data entry forms (screen layouts) make data entry faster, easier, and more accurate than entering data in a spreadsheet.

• **Information can be viewed and sorted in many ways using Access queries, forms, and reports**

  In Access, you can save multiple queries (questions about the data), data entry forms, and reports, allowing different users to view the same data in different ways.

• **Information is more secure using Access forms, passwords, and security features**

  Access databases can be encrypted and password protected. Forms can be created to protect and display specific data.

• **Several users can share and edit information at the same time**

  Unlike spreadsheets or word-processing documents, more than one person can enter, update, and analyze data in an Access database at the same time. This also means that you are not tempted to create copies that inevitably become inaccurate because of the difficulties of updating multiple copies of the same data. Having all users work on the same, single set of data at the same time is enormously accurate and reliable.

FIGURE 1-1: Using a spreadsheet to organize data

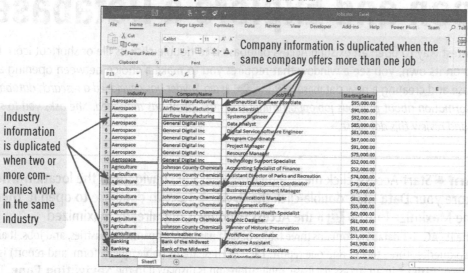

Company information is duplicated when the same company offers more than one job

Industry information is duplicated when two or more companies work in the same industry

FIGURE 1-2: Using a relational database to organize data

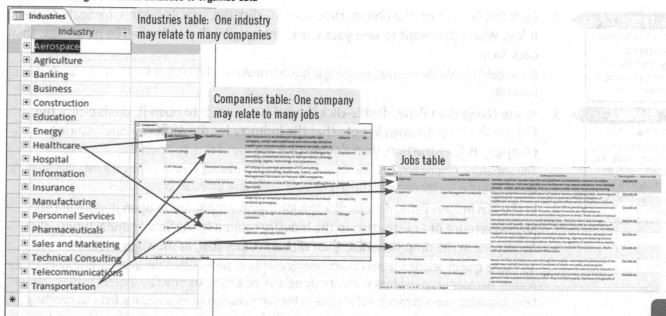

Industries table: One industry may relate to many companies

Companies table: One company may relate to many jobs

Jobs table

TABLE 1-1: Comparing Excel with Access

feature	Excel	Access
Data entry	Provides only one spreadsheet layout	Provides the ability to create an unlimited number of data entry forms
Storage	Restricted to a single file's limitations	Virtually unlimited when coupled with the ability to use Microsoft SQL Server to store data
Data model	Manages single lists of information	Manages data in a relational database with related tables, which tremendously reduces data redundancy and improves data integrity
Reporting	Provides a printout of the spreadsheet	Provides the ability to create and save an unlimited number of reports that summarize and organize data in different ways
Security	Limited to file security options such as marking the file "read-only" or protecting a range of cells	When used with SQL Server, provides extensive security down to the user and data level
Multiuser capabilities	Limited to one user at a time	Allows multiple users to simultaneously enter and update data

Open and Explore a Database

The fastest way to open an existing Access database is to double-click its file or shortcut icon. If you start Access on its own, you see a window that requires you to make a choice between opening an existing database and creating a new database. **CASE** ▶ *Lydia Snyder has developed a research database containing information about previous job opportunities that JCL Talent has managed. She asks you to start Access 2019 and review this database.*

STEPS

1. **sam** ⬇ **Start Access, click the Open Other Files link, navigate to the location where you store your Data Files, double-click the IL_AC_1-1.accdb database to open it, then click the Maximize button ☐ if the Access window is not already maximized**

   The IL_AC_1-1 database contains three tables of data named Companies, Industries, and Jobs. It also includes two queries, three forms, and one report. Each of these items (table, query, form, and report) is a different type of **object** in an Access database application and is displayed in the **Navigation Pane**. The purpose of each object is defined in **TABLE 1-2**.

TROUBLE
If a yellow Security Warning bar appears below the ribbon, click Enable Content.

2. **Click the File tab on the ribbon, click Save As, click the Save As button, navigate to the folder where you want to save your work, enter IL_AC_1_Jobs in the File name box, then click Save**

   If you need to redo the exercises, return to this step to make another copy of the IL_AC_1-1.accdb starting Data File.

TROUBLE
If the Navigation Pane is not open, click the Shutter Bar Open/Close button ⟪ to open it and view the database objects.

3. **In the Navigation Pane, double-click the Industries table to open it, double-click the Companies table to open it, note that the Industry for the Airflow Manufacturing company is Construction, then double-click the Jobs table to open it**

   The Industries, Companies, and Jobs tables each open in Datasheet View to display the data they store. An Access **table** is the fundamental building block of a relational database because tables store all the data.

4. **In the Navigation Pane, double-click the JobsByIndustry query to open it, double-click any occurrence of Construction in the Industry column for Airflow Manufacturing, click Aerospace in the drop-down list, then click any other row, as shown in FIGURE 1-3**

   An Access **query** selects a subset of data from one or more tables. Given the Industry field value for the Airflow Manufacturing company is stored only once in the Airflow Manufacturing record in the Companies table, changing one occurrence of that value in the query changes all records that select that company.

5. **Double-click the CompanyEntry form in the Navigation Pane to open it, then click the Next button in the upper-right corner of the form three times**

   An Access **form** is a data entry screen that often includes command buttons to make common tasks such as moving between records easy to perform. Forms are the most common way to enter and edit data. Note that Airflow Manufacturing's Industry value is Aerospace, which reflects the change you made to Airflow Manufacturing in the JobsByIndustry query.

6. **Double-click the JobsByHighestSalary report in the Navigation Pane to open it, then scroll down to see Airflow Manufacturing**

   An Access **report** is a professional printout that can be distributed electronically or on paper. The Aerospace update to Airflow Manufacturing carried through to the report, demonstrating the power and productivity of a relational database.

7. **Right-click each object tab (except for the Companies table), click Close on the shortcut menu, notice that the Industry for Airflow Manufacturing is now set to Aerospace in the Companies table, then close it**

   Changes to data are automatically saved as you work.

FIGURE 1-3: IL_AC_1_Jobs.accdb database

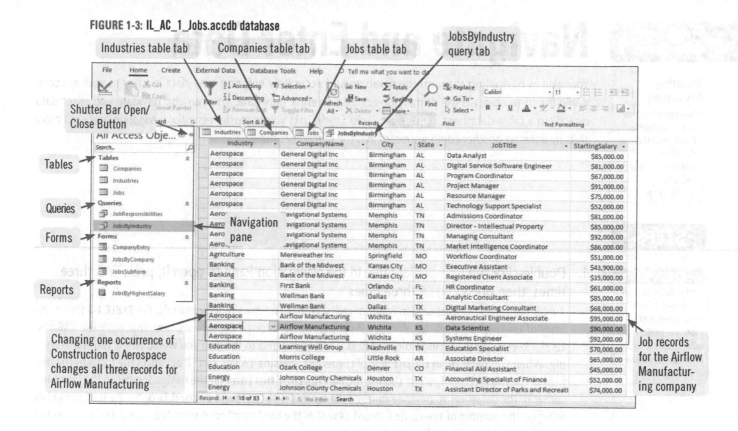

TABLE 1-2: Access objects and their purpose

object	icon	purpose
Table		Contains all the data within the database in a spreadsheet-like view called **Datasheet View**; tables are linked with a common field to create a relational database
Query		Allows you to select a subset of fields or records from one or more tables; create a query when you have a question about the data
Form		Provides an easy-to-use data entry screen
Report		Provides a professional presentation of data with headers, footers, graphics, and calculations on groups of records

Access

Navigate and Enter Data

Learning Outcomes
- Navigate records in a datasheet
- Enter records in a datasheet
- Define essential database terminology

Your skill in navigating through the database and accurately entering new data is a key to your success. While the form object is the primary object used to enter new data, you can also navigate and enter data directly in a table datasheet. **CASE** *Lydia Snyder asks you to master essential navigation and data entry skills by entering another company record into the Companies table.*

STEPS

1. **Double-click the Companies table in the Navigation Pane to open it, press TAB three times, then press ENTER three times**

   A table datasheet presents data in columns called **fields** and rows called **records**. See **TABLE 1-3** for a summary of essential database terminology. As you navigate through the records, note that both the TAB and ENTER keys move the focus to the next field. The **focus** refers to the data you would edit if you started typing. When you navigate to the last field of the record, pressing TAB or ENTER advances the focus to the first field of the next record. You can also use the **navigation buttons** on the navigation bar in the lower-left corner of the datasheet to navigate through the records. The **Current record box** on the navigation bar tells you the number of the current record as well as the total number of records in the datasheet. You use the navigation bar to practice record navigation.

2. **Click the Next record button ▶ on the navigation bar, click the Previous record button ◀, click the Last record button ▶|, click the First record button |◀, then click the New (blank) record button ▶⁎ on the navigation bar to move to a new record**

   You navigate to and enter new records at the end of the datasheet. A complete list of navigation keystrokes is shown in **TABLE 1-4**.

3. **At the end of the datasheet, enter the new record, as shown in FIGURE 1-4**
   The CompanyName is Jigsaw Company, **the Industry is** Information, **the Description is** Jigsaw provides big data mining, analytics, and forecasting tools and services, **the City is** Dayton, **and the State is** OH

   The **edit record symbol** 🖉 appears to the left of the record you are currently editing. When you move to a different record, Access automatically saves the data.

   Your CompanyID value might differ from the one in **FIGURE 1-4**. The CompanyID field is an **AutoNumber** field, which means that Access automatically enters the next consecutive number into the field as it creates the record. If you delete a record or are interrupted when entering a record, Access discards the value in the AutoNumber field and does not reuse it. Therefore, AutoNumber values do not represent the number of records in your table. Instead, they only provide a unique value per record.

Changing from Navigation mode to Edit mode

If you navigate to another area of the datasheet by clicking with the mouse pointer instead of pressing TAB or ENTER, you change from Navigation mode to Edit mode. In Edit mode, Access assumes that you are making changes to the current field value, so keystrokes such as CTRL+END, CTRL+HOME, ◀—, and —▶ move the insertion point within the field. To return to Navigation mode, press TAB or ENTER (thus moving the focus to the next field), or press ↑ or ↓ (thus moving the focus to a different record).

FIGURE 1-4: Adding a new record to the Companies table

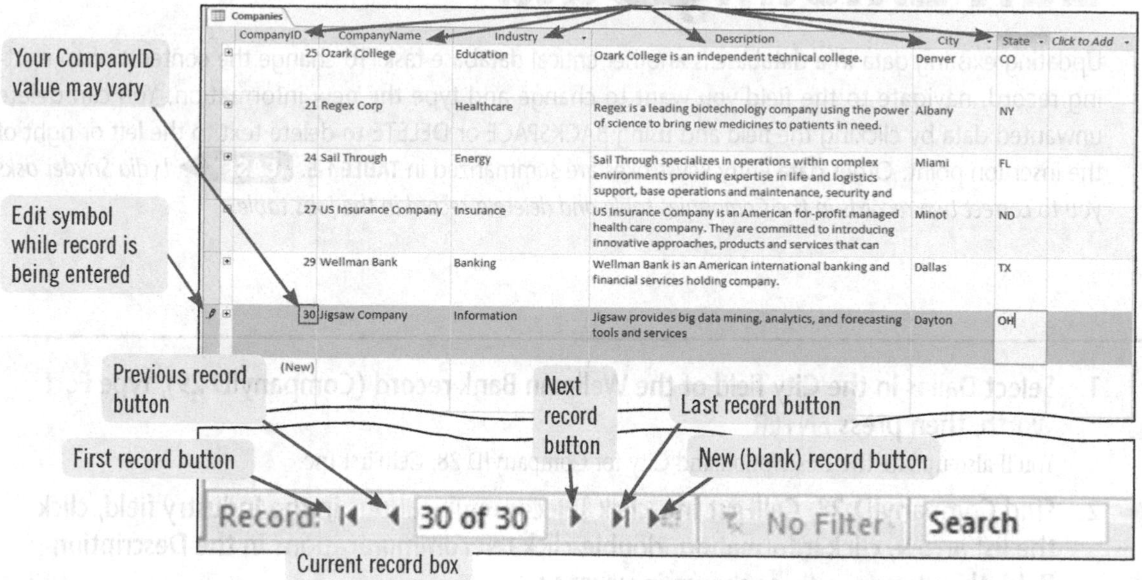

Fields

Your CompanyID value may vary

Edit symbol while record is being entered

Previous record button

First record button

Next record button

Last record button

New (blank) record button

Record: 14 ◀ 30 of 30 ▶ ▶I ▶⊞ No Filter Search

Current record box

TABLE 1-3: Essential database terminology

term	description
Field	A specific piece or category of data such as a company name, first name, last name, city, state, or phone number
Record	A group of related fields that describes a person, place, thing, or transaction such as a company or job
Primary key field	A field that contains unique information for each record, such as a CompanyID value for a company
Table	A collection of records for a single subject such as Industries, Companies, or Jobs
Relational database	Multiple tables that are linked together to address a business process such as managing industries, companies, and jobs at JCL Talent
Objects	The parts of an Access database that help you view, edit, manage, and analyze the data; Access has six major objects: tables, queries, forms, reports, macros, and modules

TABLE 1-4: Navigation mode keyboard shortcuts

shortcut key	moves to the
TAB, ENTER, or →	Next field of the current record
SHIFT+TAB or ←	Previous field of the current record
HOME	First field of the current record
END	Last field of the current record
CTRL+HOME or F5	First field of the first record
CTRL+END	Last field of the last record
↑	Current field of the previous record
↓	Current field of the next record

Resizing and moving datasheet columns

You can resize the width of a field in a datasheet by dragging the column separator, the thin line that separates the field names to the left or right. The pointer changes to ‡ as you make the field wider or narrower. Release the mouse button when you have resized the field. To adjust the column width to accommodate the widest entry in the field, double-click the column separator. To move a column, click the field name to select the entire column, then drag the field name left or right.

Edit Existing Data

Learning Outcomes
• Edit data in a datasheet
• Delete records in a datasheet
• Preview and print a datasheet

Updating existing data in a database is another critical database task. To change the contents of an existing record, navigate to the field you want to change and type the new information. You can delete unwanted data by clicking the field and using BACKSPACE or DELETE to delete text to the left or right of the insertion point. Other data entry keystrokes are summarized in **TABLE 1-5.** **CASE** ▶ *Lydia Snyder asks you to correct two records in the Companies table and delete a record in the Jobs table.*

STEPS

1. **Select** Dallas **in the City field of the Wellman Bank record (CompanyID 29), type** Fort Worth, **then press** ENTER

   You'll also update the Description and City for CompanyID 28, CellFirst Inc.

QUICK TIP
The ScreenTip for the Undo button ↶ displays the action you can undo.

2. **Find CompanyID 28, CellFirst Inc, click** Telecommunications **in the Industry field, click the** list arrow, **click** Information, **double-click** telecommunications **in the Description field, then type** media **as shown in FIGURE 1-5**

   While editing a field value, you press ESC once to remove the current field's editing changes, and twice to remove all changes to the current record. When you move to another record, Access saves your edits, so you can no longer use ESC to remove editing changes to the current record. You can, however, click the Undo button ↶ on the Quick Access Toolbar to undo the last saved action.

3. **Double-click the** Jobs table **in the Navigation Pane to open it in Datasheet View, click the** record selector **for the second record (JobID 2, Alark Inc, Care Management Associate), click the** Delete button **in the Records group, then click** Yes

QUICK TIP
If requested to print the Companies or Jobs datasheet by your instructor, click the Print button, then click OK.

   A message warns that you cannot undo a record deletion. The Undo button ↶ is dimmed, indicating that you cannot use it. The Jobs table now has 82 records. The first four are shown in **FIGURE 1-6.**

4. **Click the** File tab, **click** Print, **then click** Print Preview **to preview the printout of the Jobs table before printing**

QUICK TIP
It's a good idea to close the objects if you are not currently working with them.

5. **Click the** Close Print Preview button, **then right-click each** table tab **and click** Close

FIGURE 1-5: Editing records in the Companies table

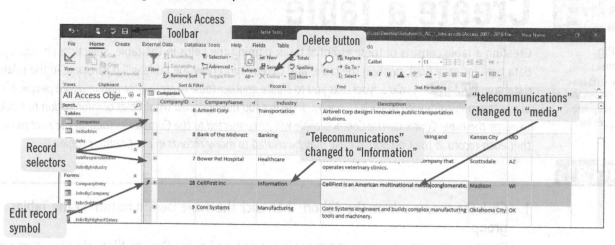

FIGURE 1-6: Deleting a record in the Jobs table

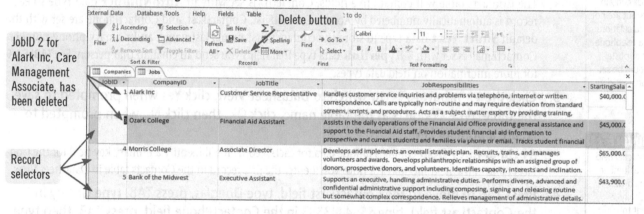

TABLE 1-5: Edit mode keyboard shortcuts

editing keystroke	action
BACKSPACE	Deletes one character to the left of the insertion point
DELETE	Deletes one character to the right of the insertion point
F2	Switches between Edit and Navigation mode
ESC	Undoes the change to the current field
ESC, ESC	Undoes all changes to the current record
F7	Starts the spell-check feature
CTRL+'	Inserts the value from the same field in the previous record into the current field
CTRL+;	Inserts the current date in a Date field

Create a Table

Learning
Outcomes
• Create a table in
Table Design View
• Set appropriate
data types for
fields

Creating a table consists of these essential tasks: naming the fields in the table, selecting an appropriate data type for each field, naming the table, and determining how the table will participate in the relational database. **CASE** *Lydia Snyder asks you to create another table to store information about people JCL regularly communicates with at each company. Together you have decided what fields of information to track and to name the table Contacts. The Contacts table will be connected to the Companies table in the next module so that each record in the Companies table may be related to many records in the Contacts table.*

STEPS

1. **Click the Create tab on the ribbon, then click the Table Design button in the Tables group**

   You can create a table in either Datasheet View or Design View, but **Design View** gives you more control over the characteristics called **field properties** of each field in the table.

QUICK TIP
Fields that contain numbers but are not used in calculations such as a telephone number or postal code should be set as a Short Text data type.

2. **Enter the Field Names and Data Types for each field as shown in FIGURE 1-7**

   The Contacts table will contain five fields. ContactID is set with an **AutoNumber** data type so each record is automatically numbered by Access. ContactFirst, ContactLast, and ContactPhone are set with the default **Short Text** data type to store the contact's first name, last name, and primary phone number. ContactEmail is set with a **Hyperlink** data type that helps you send an email to that person. See **TABLE 1-6** for more information on field data types.

3. **Click the View button to switch to Datasheet View, click Yes when prompted to save the table, type Contacts as the table name, click OK, then click No when prompted to create a primary key**

   A **primary key field** contains unique data for each record. You'll identify a primary key field for the Contacts table in the next module. For now, you'll enter the first record in the Contacts table in Datasheet View.

TROUBLE
The ContactID field is an AutoNumber field, which will automatically increment to provide a unique value. If the number has already incremented beyond 1 for the first record, it doesn't matter.

4. **Press TAB to move to the ContactFirst field, type Douglas, press TAB, type Griffey in the ContactLast field, type 5554443333 in the ContactPhone field, press TAB, then type dgriffey@accentgroup.com**

   Right now, you have not identified Douglas Griffey's company affiliation. After you relate the tables in the next module, Access will make it easy to relate each contact to the correct company.

5. **Point to the divider line after the ContactEmail field name, then double-click the column resize pointer ↔ to widen the ContactEmail field to read the entire email value, as shown in FIGURE 1-8**

6. **Right-click the Contacts table tab, then click Save to save the table**

Creating a table in Datasheet View

You can also create a new table in Datasheet View using the commands on the Fields tab of the ribbon. However, if you use Design View to design your table before entering data, you will probably avoid some common data entry errors because Design View helps you focus on the appropriate data type for each field.

Selecting the best data type for each field before entering any data into that field helps prevent incorrect data and unintended typos. For example, if a field has a Number, Currency, or Date/Time data type, you will not be able to enter text into that field by mistake.

FIGURE 1-7: Creating a table in Design View

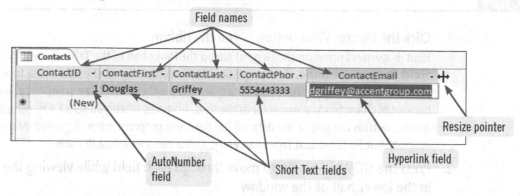

Create these field names →

Set these data types →

Field Name	Data Type
ContactID	AutoNumber
ContactFirst	Short Text
ContactLast	Short Text
ContactPhone	Short Text
ContactEmail	Hyperlink

FIGURE 1-8: Entering a new record in Datasheet View

Field names

ContactID	ContactFirst	ContactLast	ContactPhor	ContactEmail
1	Douglas	Griffey	5554443333	dgriffey@accentgroup.com
(New)				

Resize pointer

AutoNumber field

Short Text fields

Hyperlink field

TABLE 1-6: Data types

data type	description of data
Short Text	Text or numbers not used in calculations such as a name, postal code, or phone number fewer than 255 characters
Long Text	Lengthy text greater than 255 characters, such as comments or notes
Number	Numeric data that can be used in calculations, such as quantities
Large Number	Provides additional analytical capability and deepens the integration experience when users are importing or linking to BigInt data
Date/Time	Dates and times
Currency	Monetary values
AutoNumber	Sequential integers controlled by Access
Yes/No	Yes or No or Null (neither Yes nor No)
OLE Object	OLE (Object Linking and Embedding) objects such as an Excel spreadsheet or Word document
Hyperlink	Web and email addresses or links to local files
Attachment	Files such as .jpg images, spreadsheets, and documents
Calculated	Result of a calculation based on other fields in the table
Lookup Wizard	The Lookup Wizard is not a data type even though it is on the Data Type list. It helps you set Lookup properties, which display a drop-down list of values for the field. After using the Lookup Wizard, the final data type for the field is either Short Text or Number depending on the type of data in the drop-down list.

Object views

Each object has a number of views that allow you to complete different tasks. For example, to enter and edit data into the database using a table or query, use Datasheet View. To enter and edit data in a form, use Form View. To see how a report will appear on a physical piece of paper, use Print Preview. To see all the available views for an object, click the arrow at the bottom of the View button on the Home tab.

Modify Fields

Field properties are the characteristics that describe each field, such as the Field Name, Data Type, Field Size, Format, Input Mask, Caption, or Default Value. These properties help ensure database accuracy and clarity because they restrict the way data is entered, stored, and displayed. You can modify most field properties in Table Datasheet View and all field properties in Table Design View. **CASE** ▶ *After reviewing the Contacts table with Lydia Snyder, you decide to change several Short Text field properties.*

STEPS

1. **Click the** Design View button ☒ **on the ribbon**

   Field properties appear on the General tab on the lower half of the Table Design View window called the **Field Properties pane**. Field properties change depending on the field's data type. For example, when you select a field with a Short Text data type, you see the **Field Size property**, which determines the number of characters you can enter in the field. However, when you select a Hyperlink or Date/Time field, Access controls the size of the data, so the Field Size property is not displayed. Many field properties are optional, but for those that require an entry, Access provides a default value.

2. **Press the** DOWN ARROW **to move through each field while viewing the field properties in the lower half of the window**

   The **field selector** button to the left of the field indicates which field is currently selected.

3. **Click the** ContactFirst **field name, double-click** 255 **in the Field Size property text box, type** 20, **right-click the** Contacts **tab, click** Save **on the shortcut menu, then click** Yes

   The default value for the Field Size property for a Short Text field is 255, but you want to make the Field Size property for Short Text fields only as large as needed to accommodate the longest reasonable entry. In some cases, shortening the Field Size property helps prevent typographical errors. For example, you should set the Field Size property for a State field that stores two-letter state abbreviations to 2 to prevent typos such as TXX.

4. **Click the** ContactLast **field name, double-click** 255 **in the Field Size property text box, type** 20, **right-click the** Contacts **tab, click** Save **on the shortcut menu, then click** Yes

   No existing entries are greater than the new Field Size values, so no data is lost. Table Design View of the Contacts table should look like **FIGURE 1-9**.

5. **Right-click the** Contacts table tab, **then click** Close

FIGURE 1-9: Modifying field properties

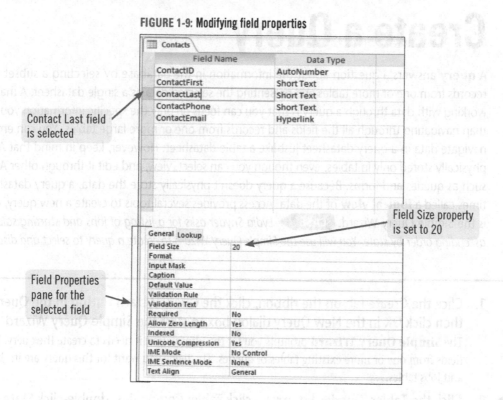

Contact Last field is selected

Field Size property is set to 20

Field Properties pane for the selected field

Field properties

Properties are the characteristics that define the field. Two properties are required for every field: Field Name and Data Type. Many other properties, such as Field Size, Format, Caption, and Default Value, are defined in the Field Properties pane in the lower half of a table's Design View. Many common properties can also be accessed on the Fields tab of the ribbon in Table Datasheet View. As you add more property entries, you are generally restricting the amount or type of data that can be entered in the field, which increases data entry accuracy. For example, you might change the Field Size property for a State field to 2 to eliminate an incorrect entry such as FLL. Field properties change depending on the data type of the selected field. For example, Date/Time, Currency, and Yes/No fields do not have a Field Size property because Access controls the size of fields with those data types.

Create a Query

Learning Outcomes
- Describe the purpose for a query
- Create a query with the Simple Query Wizard

A **query** answers a question about the information in the database by selecting a subset of fields and records from one or more tables and presenting the selected data as a single datasheet. A major benefit of working with data through a query is that you can focus on only the specific information you need, rather than navigating through all the fields and records from one or more large tables. You can enter, edit, and navigate data in a query datasheet just like a table datasheet. However, keep in mind that Access data is physically stored only in tables, even though you can select, view, and edit it through other Access objects such as queries and forms. Because a query doesn't physically store the data, a query datasheet is sometimes called a **logical view** of the data. Access provides several tools to create a new query, one of which is the Simple Query Wizard. **CASE** *Lydia Snyder asks for a listing of jobs and starting salaries sorted in ascending order by state. You will use the Simple Query Wizard to create a query to select and display this data.*

STEPS

1. **Click the** Create tab **on the ribbon, click the** Query Wizard button **in the Queries group, then click** OK **in the New Query dialog box to start the Simple Query Wizard**

   The **Simple Query Wizard** prompts you for the information it needs to create the query. You can select fields from one or more existing tables or queries. The fields you want for this query are in the Companies and Jobs tables.

2. **Click the** Tables/Queries list arrow, **click** Table: Companies, **double-click** State **in the Available Fields list to move it to the Selected Fields list, click the** Tables/Queries list arrow, **click** Table: Jobs, **double-click** JobTitle, **then double-click** StartingSalary **as shown in FIGURE 1-10**

   You've selected three fields for this query from two different tables.

3. **Click** Next, **click** Next **to select Detail, select** Companies Query **in the title text box, type** JobsByState **as the name of the query, then click** Finish

   The JobsByState datasheet opens, displaying one field from the Companies table (State) and two from the Jobs table (JobTitle and StartingSalary). To sort the records by JobTitle within State, you'll select those two fields and use the Ascending button on the Home tab.

4. **Use the column selector pointer ↓ to drag across the field names of** State **and** JobTitle **to select both columns, click the** Home tab **on the ribbon, then click the** Ascending button **in the Sort & Filter group**

   The JobsByState datasheet is sorted in ascending order by the State field, and then in ascending order by the JobTitle field within each state, as shown in **FIGURE 1-11**.

5. **Right-click the** JobsByState tab, **click** Close, **then click** Yes **when prompted to save the query**

Simple Query Wizard

The **Simple Query Wizard** is a series of dialog boxes that prompt you for the information needed to create a Select query. A **Select query** selects fields from one or more tables in your database and is by far the most common type of query.

The other query wizards—Crosstab, Find Duplicates, and Find Unmatched—are used to create queries that do specialized types of data analysis and are covered in Module 5.

FIGURE 1-10: Using the Simple Query Wizard

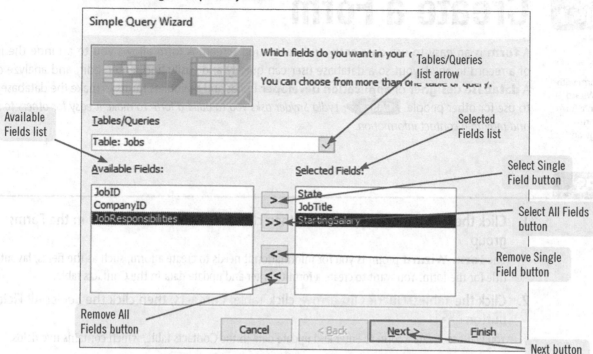

FIGURE 1-11: Sorting a query datasheet

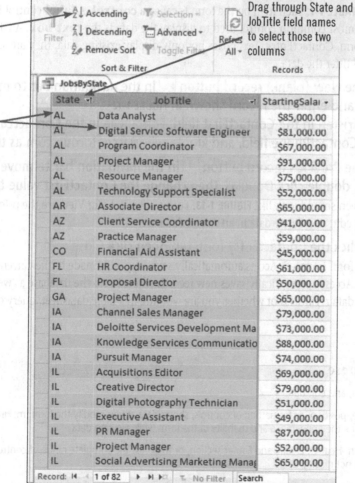

Access

Create a Form

Learning Outcomes
- Create a form with the Form Wizard
- Sort data in a form
- Describe form terminology and views

A **form** is an easy-to-use data entry and navigation screen. A form allows you to arrange the fields of a record in any layout so a database user can quickly and easily find, enter, edit, and analyze data. A **database designer** or **application developer** builds and maintains forms to make the database easy to use for other people. **CASE** ▶ *Lydia Snyder asks you to build a form to make it easy for others to enter and maintain contact information.*

STEPS

1. **Click the** Create tab **on the ribbon, then click the** Form Wizard button **in the Forms group**

    The **Form Wizard** prompts you for information it needs to create a form, such as the fields, layout, and title for the form. You want to create a form to enter and update data in the Contacts table.

2. **Click the** Tables/Queries list arrow, **click** Table: Contacts, **then click the** Select All Fields **button** `>>`

    You want to create a form to enter and update data in the Contacts table, which contains five fields.

3. **Click** Next, **click the** Columnar option button, **click** Next, **modify Contacts to** ContactEntry **for the title, then click** Finish

    The ContactEntry form opens in **Form View**. Access provides three different views of forms, as summarized in **TABLE 1-7**. Each item on the form is called a **control**. A **label** control is used to describe the data, and the most common control used to display the data is the **text box**. A label is also used for the title of the form, ContactEntry. Text boxes not only display existing data, they are also used to enter, edit, find, sort, and filter the data.

4. **Click the** New (blank) record button `▶*` **in the navigation bar to move to a new, blank record and enter the record shown in FIGURE 1-12**

    Enter Kristen **in the ContactFirst field,** Fontanelle **in the ContactLast field,** 5556667777 **in the ContactPhone field, and** kfontanelle@accentgroup.com **as the ContactEmail value**

5. **Click the** Previous record button `◀` **in the navigation bar to move back to the first record, double-click** Douglas, **then change the ContactFirst value to** Doug

    Your screen should look like **FIGURE 1-13**. Forms open in Form View are the primary tool for database users to enter, edit, and delete data in an Access database.

6. **Right-click the** ContactEntry form tab, **then click** Close

    When a form is closed, Access automatically saves any edits made to the current record. As you have experienced, Access automatically saves new records entered into the database as well as any edits you make to existing data regardless of whether you are working in a table datasheet, query datasheet, or form.

TABLE 1-7: Form views

view	primary purpose
Form	To find, sort, enter, and edit data
Layout	To modify the size, position, or formatting of controls; shows data as you modify the form, making it the tool of choice when you want to change the appearance and usability of the form while viewing data
Design	To modify the Form Header, Detail, and Footer section, or to access the complete range of controls and form properties; Design View does not display data

FIGURE 1-12: Entering a new record in a form

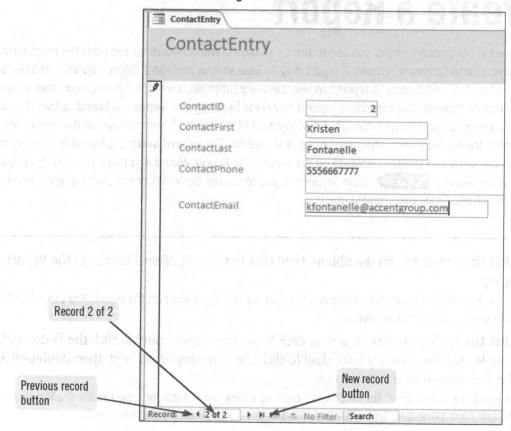

Record 2 of 2

Previous record button

New record button

FIGURE 1-13: Editing an existing record in a form

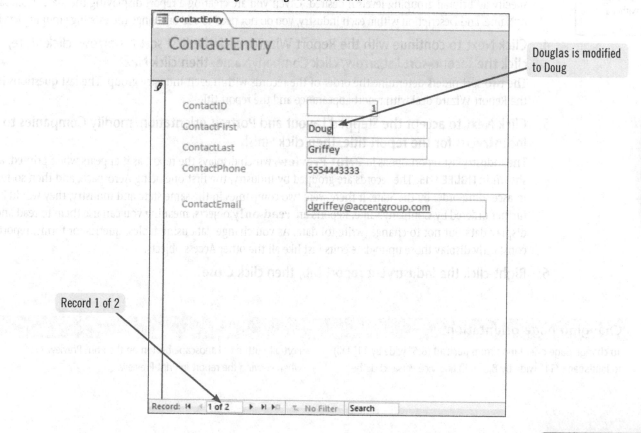

Douglas is modified to Doug

Record 1 of 2

Create a Report

Learning
Outcomes
• Create a report
  with the Report
  Wizard
• Change page
  orientation

A **report** is the primary object you use to print database content because it provides the most formatting, layout, and summary options. A report may include various fonts and colors, clip art and lines, and multiple headers and footers. A report can also calculate subtotals, averages, counts, and other statistics for groups of records. You can create reports in Access by using the **Report Wizard**, a tool that asks questions to guide you through the initial development of the report. Your responses to the Report Wizard determine the record source, style, and layout of the report. The **record source** is the table or query that defines the fields and records displayed on the report. The Report Wizard also helps you sort, group, and analyze the records. **CASE** *Lydia Snyder asks you to use the Report Wizard to create a report to display company information within each industry.*

STEPS

1. **Click the** Create tab **on the ribbon, then click the** Report Wizard button **in the Reports group**

    The Report Wizard starts, prompting you to select the fields you want on the report. You can select fields from one or more tables or queries.

2. **Click the** Tables/Queries list arrow, **click** Table: Companies, **double-click the** State field, **double-click the** Industry field, **double-click the** CompanyName field, **then double-click the** Description field

    As you have experienced, the first step of creating a new query, form, or report using the Simple Query Wizard, Form Wizard, or Report Wizard is to select the desired fields for the new object.

3. **Click** Next **to advance to the report grouping options, as shown in** FIGURE 1-14

    The Report Wizard automatically wants to group the records by Industry and gives you the opportunity to specify additional grouping levels if desired. Given you are creating a report displaying the State, CompanyName, and Description within each Industry, you do not need to add or change the existing grouping level.

4. **Click** Next **to continue with the Report Wizard, click the** first sort list arrow, **click** State, **click the** second sort list arrow, **click** CompanyName, **then click** Next

    The two sort orders determine the order of the records within each Industry group. The last questions in the Report Wizard deal with report appearance and the report title.

5. **Click** Next **to accept the Stepped Layout and Portrait orientation, modify Companies to** IndustryList **for the report title, then click** Finish

    The IndustryList report opens in **Print Preview**, which displays the report as it appears when printed, as shown in **FIGURE 1-15**. The records are grouped by Industry, the first one being Aerospace, and then sorted in ascending order by the State. If there were two companies in the same state and industry, they would be further ordered by CompanyName. Reports are **read-only** objects, meaning you can use them to read and display data but not to change (write to) data. As you change data using tables, queries, or forms, reports constantly display those up-to-date edits just like all the other Access objects.

6. **Right-click the** IndustryList report tab, **then click** Close

---

Changing page orientation

To change page orientation from **portrait** (8.5" wide by 11" tall) to **landscape** (11" wide by 8.5" tall) and vice versa, click the Portrait button or Landscape button on the Print Preview tab when viewing the report in Print Preview.

FIGURE 1-14: Setting report grouping fields

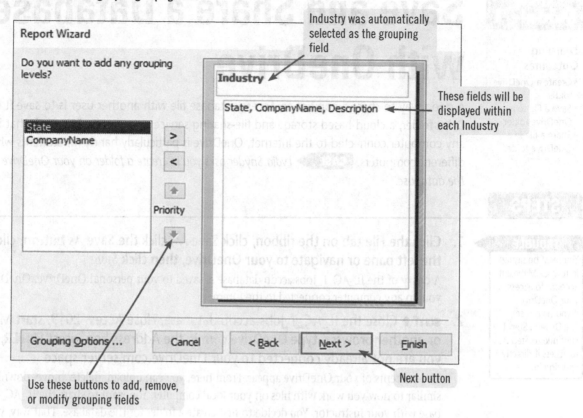

Industry was automatically selected as the grouping field

These fields will be displayed within each Industry

Next button

Use these buttons to add, remove, or modify grouping fields

FIGURE 1-15: Previewing a report

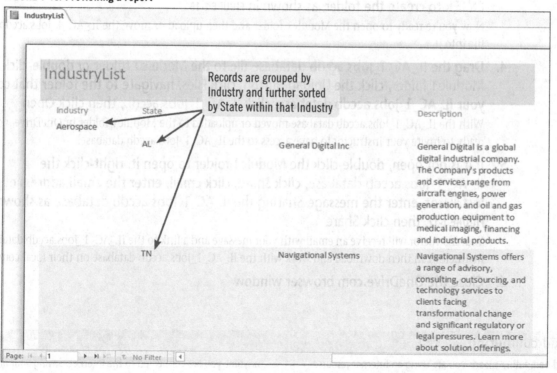

Records are grouped by Industry and further sorted by State within that Industry

Save and Share a Database with OneDrive

Learning Outcomes
- Create a OneDrive folder
- Save a file to a OneDrive folder
- Share a file in a OneDrive folder

A good way to share a copy of an Access database file with another user is to save it to a shared One-Drive folder, a cloud-based storage and file-sharing service provided by Microsoft that is accessible from any computer connected to the Internet. OneDrive is particularly handy for students who work on many different computers. **CASE** *Lydia Snyder asks you to create a folder on your OneDrive to save and share the database.*

STEPS

1. **Click the** File tab **on the ribbon, click** Save As, **click the** Save As button, **click** OneDrive **in the left pane or navigate to your OneDrive, then click** Save

   A **copy** of the IL_AC_1_Jobs.accdb database is saved to your personal OneDrive. OneDrive is available to you on any computer connected to the Internet.

2. **sam⬆ Close the** IL_AC_1_Jobs.accdb database, **close** Access 2019, **start** Microsoft Edge **or another browser, type** OneDrive.com **in the Address box, press** ENTER, **then sign in if you are not already connected to your OneDrive.com server space**

   The contents of your OneDrive appear. From here, you can upload, delete, move, download, or copy files, similar to how you work with files on your local computer. You want to share the IL_AC_1_Jobs.accdb database with your instructor. You decide to first create a folder for the database. That way, your OneDrive will stay more organized.

3. **Click the** New button, **click** Folder, **type** Module1 **as the new folder name, then press** ENTER **to create the folder, as shown in** FIGURE 1-16

   Now you're ready to open the Module1 folder and then upload or move the IL_AC_1_Jobs.accdb database file into it.

4. **Drag the** IL_AC_1_Jobs.accdb database file **to the** Module1 folder *or* double-click the Module1 folder, **click the** Upload button, **click** Files, **navigate to the folder that contains your** IL_AC_1_Jobs.accdb database, **click** IL_AC_1_Jobs.accdb, **then click** Open

   With the IL_AC_1_Jobs.accdb database moved or uploaded to the Module1 folder in OneDrive, you're now ready to invite your instructor to have access to the IL_AC_1_Jobs.accdb database.

5. **If it is not open, double-click the** Module1 folder **to open it, right-click the** IL_AC_1_Jobs.accdb database, **click** Share, **click** Email, **enter the** email address of your instructor, **enter the message** Sharing the IL_AC_1_Jobs.accdb database **as shown in** FIGURE 1-17, **then click** Share

   Your instructor will receive an email with your message and a link to the IL_AC_1_Jobs.accdb database. Your instructor can then download and work with the IL_AC_1_Jobs.accdb database on their local computer.

6. **Close the OneDrive.com browser window**

Cloud computing

Cloud computing means you are using an Internet resource to complete your work. Using **OneDrive**, a free service from Microsoft, you can store files in the "cloud" and retrieve them anytime you are connected to the Internet. Saving your files to the OneDrive is one example of cloud computing.

FIGURE 1-16: Creating a new folder in OneDrive

New button   Upload button

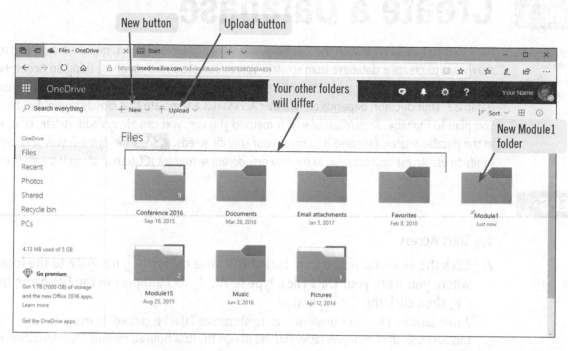

Your other folders will differ

New Module1 folder

FIGURE 1-17: Sharing a database with OneDrive

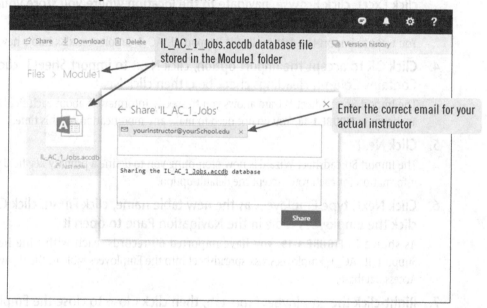

IL_AC_1_Jobs.accdb database file stored in the Module1 folder

Enter the correct email for your actual instructor

Access is a local application

Unlike Word and Excel, Access does not have an online version of itself. Access is a **local application** that runs from the hard drive of a local Windows machine. You can share a copy of a database with others using OneDrive, but remember that saving a database to OneDrive creates a **copy** of the database. For multiple people to work in the same database at the same time, the database must be located in a shared folder on a local file server.

Access

Create a Database

Learning Outcomes
• Create a database
• Import data from Excel

Now that you are familiar with the four main objects of a database (tables, queries, forms, and reports), you may want to create a database from scratch. You can create a new database using an Access **template**, a sample database provided within the Microsoft Access program, or you can start with a completely blank database. Your decision depends on whether Access has a template that closely resembles the type of data you plan to manage. Regardless of which method you use, you can always add, delete, or modify objects in the database later, tailoring it to meet your specific needs. **CASE** *Lydia Snyder sees another opportunity to use Access and asks you to create a new database to track JCL technical support calls from employees.*

STEPS

1. **Start Access**

2. **Click the** Blank database icon, **click the** Browse button , **navigate to the location where you store your Data Files, type** IL_AC_1_TechSupport **in the File name box, click** OK, **then click the** Create button

   A new database file with a single table currently named Table1 is created. To create the first table needed for this database, the Employees table, you will import the data from an existing Excel spreadsheet.

3. **Right-click the** Table1 tab, **click** Close, **click the** External Data tab **on the ribbon, click the** New Data Source button **in the Import & Link group, point to** From File, **click** Excel, **click** Browse, **navigate to the location where you store your Data Files, click** Support_IL_AC_1_Employees.xlsx, **then click** Open

   You want to import the data in the file Support_IL_AC_1_Employees.xlsx into a new table.

4. **Click** OK **to accept the import option, click** Next **to import Sheet1, click the** First Row Contains Column Headings check box, **then click** Next

   The Import Spreadsheet Wizard allows you to specify information about each field that you are importing as shown in **FIGURE 1-18**. You do not need to make any modifications at this time.

5. **Click** Next

   The Import Spreadsheet Wizard is now prompting you to define a primary key field which contains unique information for each row. Accept the default option.

6. **Click** Next, **type** Employees **as the new table name, click** Finish, **click** Close, **then double-click the** Employees table **in the Navigation Pane to open it**

   As shown in **FIGURE 1-19**, you have imported 60 records, each with nine fields of data from the Support_IL_AC_1_Employees.xlsx spreadsheet into the Employees table in the IL_AC_1_TechSupport.accdb Access database.

7. **Right-click the** Employees table tab, **then click** Close to close the Employees table

FIGURE 1-18: Using the Import Spreadsheet Wizard

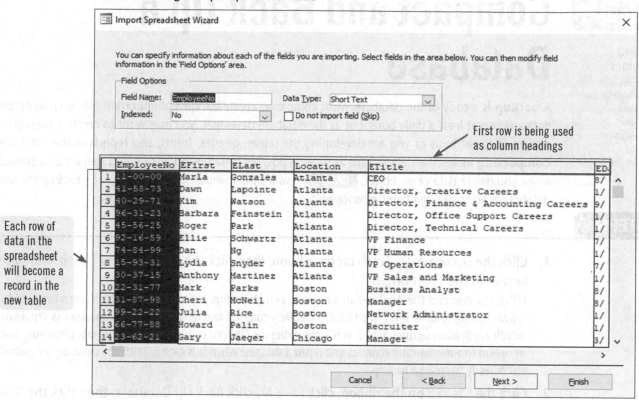

FIGURE 1-19: Employees table in Datasheet View

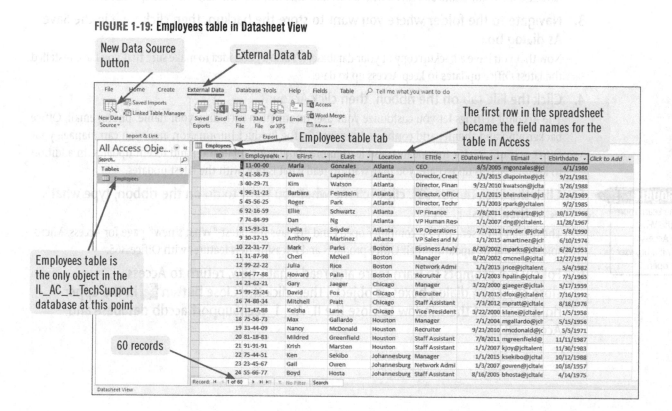

Compact and Back Up a Database

**Learning
Outcomes**
• Compact and
repair a database
• Back up a
database
• View Account
settings
• Use the Tell Me
box

A **backup** is a copy of the database. Most companies create backups of important files such as Access databases on at least a daily basis, but as the database developer, you may want to create a backup on a more frequent basis as you are developing the tables, queries, forms, and reports in the database. **Compacting** makes the database file as small as possible by removing any unused space that is created when you delete data or an object. **CASE** *Lydia Snyder would like you to frequently back up the new database as you make significant enhancements.*

STEPS

1. **Click the** Database Tools tab **on the ribbon, then click the** Compact and Repair Database button **in the Tools group**

   When you compact the database, an automatic **repair** feature is also initiated, which helps keep hidden system files up to date. It is a good idea to regularly compact and repair your databases. **Access Options**, default application settings, which you access using the Options command on the File tab, allow you to set an option to automatically compact and repair a database when it is closed. With the database compacted, you're ready to create a backup.

2. **Click the** File tab **on the ribbon, click** Save As, **click** Back Up Database, **then click the** Save As button

   Although any copy of the database can serve as a backup, when you use the Back Up Database option, the database file is automatically saved with a filename that includes the date the backup was made.

3. **Navigate to the folder where you want to store the backup, then click** Save **in the Save As dialog box**

   Now that you have a backup copy of your database, it's also a good idea to make sure that you have installed the latest Office updates to keep Access up to date.

4. **Click the** File tab **on the ribbon, then click** Account

   The Account settings let you customize your user information including your name, photo, email, Office background and theme, and connected services. In the Product Information area, you can manage your Office account, check for updates, and learn more about your application and recent updates. In addition to keeping Access up to date, you may want to read what is new with the latest updates.

5. **Click the** Back button ⊖, **click** Tell me what you want to do **on the ribbon, type** what's new, **then press** ENTER

   The default browser on your computer opens and displays the latest "What's new" page for Access. Microsoft is constantly updating their Office products and releasing new features with Office 365.

6. **Follow the prompts to learn more and read what's new, return to Access, close any open dialog boxes or objects, then click the** Close button ✕ **in the upper-right corner of the window to close the IL_AC_1_TechSupport.accdb database and Access 2019**

Practice

Concepts Review

Label each element of the Access window shown in FIGURE 1-20.

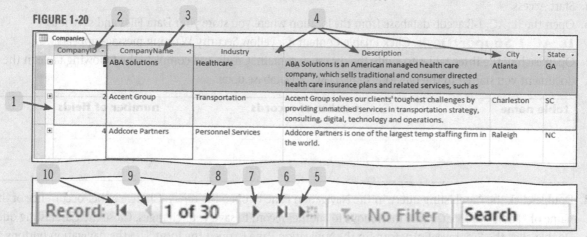

FIGURE 1-20

Match each term with the statement that best describes it.

11. Field
12. Record
13. Table
14. Datasheet
15. Query
16. Form
17. Report

a. A subset of data from one or more tables
b. A collection of records for a single subject, such as all the customer records
c. A professional printout of database information
d. A spreadsheet-like grid that displays fields as columns and records as rows
e. A group of related fields for one item, such as all the information for one customer
f. A category of information in a table, such as a company name, city, or state
g. An easy-to-use data entry screen

Select the best answer from the list of choices.

18. Which Access object cannot be used to enter or edit data?
   a. Report
   b. Table
   c. Query
   d. Form

19. Which of the following is *not* an advantage of managing data with relational database software such as Access versus spreadsheet software such as Excel?
   a. Allows multiple users to enter data simultaneously
   b. Uses a single table to store all data
   c. Reduces duplicate data entry
   d. Provides data entry forms

20. Which of the following is *not* a typical benefit of relational databases?
   a. Minimized duplicate data entry
   b. Tables automatically create needed relationships
   c. More accurate data
   d. More consistent data

Skills Review

1. **Understand relational databases.**
   a. In a Word document, enter your name and the current date.
   b. Using a bulleted list, identify five advantages of managing database information in Access versus using a spreadsheet.
   c. Write a sentence to explain how the terms *field*, *record*, *table*, and *relational database* relate to one another.
   d. Save the document with the name **IL_AC_1_Database** then close it and close Word.

2. **Open and explore a database.**
   a. Start Access.
   b. Open the IL_AC_1-2.accdb database from the location where you store your Data Files and save it as **IL_AC_1_SupportDesk**. Click Enable Content if a yellow Security Warning message appears.
   c. Open each of the three tables to study the data they contain. Create and complete the following table in the document you started in the previous step, IL_AC_1_Database.docx.

table name	number of records	number of fields

   d. Double-click the CaseListing query in the Navigation Pane to open the query. Change either occurrence of the last name of "Poole" to **Fredrick** then move to another record to save your changes. Close the CaseListing query.
   e. Double-click the EmployeeEntry form in the Navigation Pane to open the form. Use the navigation buttons to navigate through the 20 records to observe each employee's cases. When you reach the Lisa Fredrick record (record 17 of 20), change her extension value to **8686**. Close the EmployeeEntry form.
   f. Double-click the CallLog report in the Navigation Pane to open the report. The records are listed in ascending order by employee last name. Scroll through the report to find the "Fredrick, Lisa" record. Close the CallLog report. Note that both the edit to Lisa's last name and the change to her extension value in previous steps are reflected in the report.
   g. In your IL_AC_1_Database.docx document, add one more sentence to explain why the edits to Lisa's record in previous steps carried through to the CallLog report. Check the spelling, save your changes, then close the IL_AC_1_Database.docx document.

3. **Navigate and enter data.**
   a. Double-click the Employees table to open it, then enter the following record for a new employee:
      EmployeeID: (AutoNumber)
      LastName: Curtiss
      FirstName: Pamela
      Extension: 8181
      Department: Marketing
   b. Close the Employees table.

4. **Edit existing data.**
   a. Double-click the Cases table to open it, click the ResolvedDate field for CaseID 1, then enter **4/3/21**. Note that you can use the automatic Calendar Picker that assists you when you are entering or updating data in a field with a Date/Time data type. You can also type a date using a month/day/year format.
   b. Click the ResolvedDate field for the record with CaseID 5 and enter today's date. Note that you can enter today's date from the keyboard or use the CTRL+; shortcut. (*Hint*: Press and hold the CTRL key while pressing the semicolon ; key.)
   c. Edit the CaseTitle value for CaseID 23 to include the word **automatically** as in "Excel formulas are not automatically updating".
   d. Close the Cases table.

Skills Review (continued)

5. Create a table.

a. Click the Create tab on the ribbon, click the Table Design button in the Tables group, then create a new table with the following three fields and data types:

field name	data type
StateName	Short Text
StateAbbreviation	Short Text
Capital	Short Text

b. Save the table with the name **States**. Click No when asked if you want Access to create the primary key field.

6. Modify fields.

a. In Design View of the States table, change the Field Size property for the StateName and Capital fields to **25**, and the StateAbbreviation field to **2**.

b. Enter an Input Mask property of **LL;;*** for the StateAbbreviation field. (*Hint*: Do not use the Input Mask Wizard. Enter the property directly into the Input Mask property box.)

c. Change the Field Name of the StateAbbreviation field to **StateAbbrev**.

d. Save the States table, then test the Input Mask by entering the first record into the table for Alabama using the following information:

StateName	StateAbbrev	Capital
Alabama	AL	Montgomery

e. Use the Tell Me (Search) box to read about the three parts of an Input Mask property and the meaning of the L character.

f. Close the States table.

7. Create a query.

a. Use the Simple Query Wizard to create a new query with the following fields in the following order: LastName and FirstName from the Employees table, CaseTitle from the Cases table, and CallDateTime from the Calls table.

b. Select a detail query, and title the query **CallListing**.

c. Display the query datasheet, and change the last name of Mindi Meyers to **Perez**. Notice that both records that display Mindi's name change to Perez when you move to a new record. Her name was stored only once in the Employees table but selected twice for this query because she has taken two calls.

d. Save and close the CallListing query.

8. Create a form.

a. Use the Form Wizard to create a new form based on all the fields in the Employees table. Use a Columnar layout and title the form **EmployeeMaster**.

b. Use the record navigation buttons to navigate to the third record to confirm that Mindi Meyers has been changed to Mindi Perez.

c. Save and close the EmployeeMaster form.

9. Create a report.

a. Use the Report Wizard to create a new report based on all the fields of the Employees table.

b. Group the records by Department, and sort them in ascending order by LastName and then FirstName.

c. Use a stepped layout and a landscape orientation.

d. Title the report **EmployeeMasterList**, and preview it as shown in **FIGURE 1-21**.

e. Use the navigation buttons to locate the Mindi Perez record (in the Research department) to confirm that the report is also based on the updated data.

f. Save and close the EmployeeMasterList report.

EmployeeMasterList

EmployeeMasterList

Department	LastName	FirstName	EmployeeID	Extension
Accounting				
	Calderon	Sean	29	6788
	Hoover	Carlos	12	3557
	Rivas	Philip	32	3322
	Serrano	Craig	24	7621
Executive				
	Carson	Victor	16	9862
	Holloway	Martin	19	9682
Human Resources				
	Fuentes	Eugene	9	2002
	Guerra	Chris	33	4411
Marketing				
	Carey	Alan	26	7958
	Mckenzie	Jesse	23	2879
	Short	Peggy	15	1366

10. **Save and share a database with OneDrive.**
    a. Close the IL_AC_1_SupportDesk.accdb database.
    b. Log into your Microsoft OneDrive.com account.
    c. Create a Module1 folder (if you have not already done so).
    d. Upload the IL_AC_1_SupportDesk.accdb database to the Module1 folder.
    e. Through email, share the IL_AC_1_SupportDesk.accdb database with your instructor.

11. **Create a new database.**
    a. Start Access and use the Blank desktop database to create a new database named **IL_AC_1_CustomerSurvey** in the folder where you store your Data Files.
    b. Close the Table1 table without saving it.
    c. Build the first table by importing a listing of states and provinces from an existing Excel spreadsheet named **Support_IL_AC_1_StatesAndProvs**.
    d. The first row contains column headings. Accept the default field options, but choose StateAbbrev as the primary key field.
    e. Name the new table **StatesAndProvs**, and do not save the import steps.
    f. Open the StatesAndProvs table in Datasheet View to confirm that 64 records were imported, then close the StatesAndProvs table.

12. **Compact and back up a database.**
    a. On the Database Tools tab, compact and repair the IL_AC_1_CustomerSurvey.accdb database.
    b. Create a backup of the IL_AC_1_CustomerSurvey.accdb database in the folder where you store your Data Files. Be sure to use the Back Up Database option so that the current date is automatically appended to the filename.
    c. View your Account settings, and in a Word document, note your existing Connected Services.
    d. Using the Tell me what you want to do feature, research Connected Services and pick one of the services to explore further. Identify which Connected Service you chose in your Word document, write at least one sentence explaining why you chose it and one sentence describing the features it offers. Save the document with the name **IL_AC_1_AccessConnectedServices**.
    e. Close the IL_AC_1_CustomerSurvey.accdb database and Access.

Independent Challenge 1

It's important to think about how to set up proper fields for a table before working in Access. Consider the following twelve subject areas:

- Contacts
- Islands of the Caribbean
- Members of the U.S. House of Representatives
- College course offerings
- Physical activities
- Ancient wonders of the world
- Restaurant menu
- Shopping catalog items
- Vehicles
- Conventions
- Party guest list
- Movie listings

a. For each subject, create a table in a single Word document named **IL_AC_1_SampleTables**. The table should contain four to seven columns and three rows. In the first row, enter appropriate field names that you would expect to see in a table used to manage that subject. Note the guidelines for proper field construction below.

b. In the second and third rows of each table, enter two realistic records. The first subject, Contacts, is completed as an example to follow.

TABLE: Contacts

FirstName	LastName	Street	Zip	Phone
Marco	Lopez	100 Main Street	88715	555-612-3312
Christopher	Stafford	253 Maple Lane	77824	555-612-1179

c. Use the following guidelines as you build each table in Word:

- Make sure each record represents one item in that table. For example, in the Restaurant Menu table, the following table is a random list of categories of food. These records do not represent one item in a restaurant menu.

Beverage	Appetizer	Meat	Vegetable	Dessert
Milk	Chicken wings	Steak	Carrots	Chocolate cake
Tea	Onion rings	Salmon	Potato	Cheesecake

A better example of records that describe an item in the restaurant menu would be the following:

Category	Description	Price	Calories	Spicy
Appetizer	Chicken wings	$10	800	Yes
Beverage	Milk	$2	250	No

- Do not put first and last names in the same field. This prevents you from easily sorting, filtering, or searching on either part of the name later.
- Break street, city, state, zip, and country data into separate fields for the same reasons.
- Do not put values and units of measure such as 5 minutes, 4 lbs., or 6 square miles in the same field. This also prevents you from sorting and calculating on the numeric part of the information.
- Make your field names descriptive such as TimeInMinutes or AreaInSquareMiles so that each record's entries are consistent.
- Remember that this exercise is a conceptual exercise on creating proper fields for a particular subject. Putting all these tables in one Access database would be analogous to putting a letter to your Congressman, a creative poem, and a cover letter to a future employer all in the same Word file. Use Word for this exercise to focus on the concepts of creating appropriate fields and records for a subject.

d. Save and close the IL_AC_1_SampleTables Word document.

Independent Challenge 2

You are working for a city to coordinate a series of community-wide preparedness activities. You have started a database to track the activities and volunteers who are attending them.

a. Start Access, then open the IL_AC_1-3.accdb database from the location where you store your Data Files. Save it with the name **IL_AC_1_Volunteers** and then enable content if prompted.

b. Open each table's datasheet to study the number of fields and records per table.

c. In a Word document named **IL_AC_1_VolunteerTables**, re-create the following table and fill in the blanks:

table name	number of records	number of fields

d. Close all open tables, then use the Simple Query Wizard to create a query using the following fields in the following order: FirstName and LastName from the Volunteers table, and ActivityName, ActvityDate, and ActivityHours from the Activities table. Show detail records, name the query **VolunteerActivity**, then open it in Datasheet View.

e. In the ActivityName field, change any occurrence of Shelter Fundamentals to **Outdoor Shelter Fundamentals**, then click any other record to save the change, as shown in FIGURE 1-22. Save and close the VolunteerActivity query.

f. Use the Form Wizard to create a new form based on all the fields in the Activities table. Use a columnar layout, title the form **ActivityEntry**, and view it in Form View. The Outdoor Shelter Fundamentals record should be the first record in the form. Save and close the ActivityEntry form.

FIGURE 1-22

FirstNa	LastNar	ActivityName	ActivityDate	ActivityHour
Rhea	Alman	Outdoor Shelter Fundamentals	7/31/2021	8
Micah	Ati	Managing Volunteers	8/27/2021	8
Young	Bogard	Outdoor Shelter Fundamentals	7/31/2021	8
Andrea	Collins	First Aid	8/1/2021	8
Gabriel	Hammer	Outdoor Shelter Fundamentals	7/31/2021	8
Evan	Bouchart	Forklift Training	8/14/2021	6
Ann	Bovier	Outdoor Shelter Fundamentals	7/31/2021	8
Gabriel	Hammer	Warehouse Logistics	8/19/2021	4
Forrest	Browning	Forklift Training	8/14/2021	6
Patch	Bullock	Cardiopulmonary resuscitation CPR	8/28/2021	4
Student Fi	Student Lε	Community Preparedness	8/7/2021	16
Denice	Custard	Water Safety	8/4/2021	6
Angela	Cabriella	Water Safety	8/4/2021	6
Gina	Daniels	Livestock in Disasters	8/22/2021	0
Quentin	Garden	Personal Safety and Security	8/15/2021	6
Heidi	Kalvert	Grief Counseling	8/6/2021	8
Helen	Hubert	Automated External Defibrillator AED	8/5/2021	4
Jeremiah	Hopper	Hurricane Preparedness	8/26/2021	6
Loraine	Goode	Outdoor Shelter Fundamentals	7/31/2021	8
Karla	Larson	Animals in Disasters	8/8/2021	4
Katrina	Margolis	Incident Management	8/11/2021	4
Harvey	McCord	Food Service	8/13/2021	6
Sally	Olingback	Community Preparedness	8/7/2021	16
Mallory	Olson	Basic Life Support BLS	8/25/2021	4

Record: I◄ ◄ 2 of 76 ► ►I ►≡ No Filter   Search

Getting Started with Access

Independent Challenge 2 (continued)

g. Use the Report Wizard to create a new report based on the following fields in the following order: ActivityName from the Activities table and LastName from the Volunteers table. View the data by ActivityName then sort the records in ascending order by the LastName. Use a stepped layout and a portrait orientation. Title the report **ActivityRoster** and preview the report.

h. Close the IL_AC_1_Volunteer.accdb database, then exit Access.

Visual Workshop

Open the IL_AC_1-4.accdb database from the location where you store your Data Files and save it as
IL_AC_1_CollegeCourses, then enable content if prompted. Use the Simple Query Wizard to create the query
shown in **FIGURE 1-23** that contains the ClassNo, Description, and Credits fields from the Classes table, and the SectionNo,
MeetingDay, and Time fields from the Sections table. Name the query **DepartmentOfferings**.

FIGURE 1-23

ClassNo	Description	Credits	SectionNo	MeetingDay	Time
ACCT109	Basics of Income Taxes	3	52	M	10:00 AM
ACCT111	Small Business Accounting	3	51	T	8:00 AM
ACCT121	Accounting I	3	48	W	10:00 AM
ACCT121	Accounting I	3	49	H	12:00 PM
ACCT121	Accounting I	3	50	M	1:00 PM
ACCT122	Accounting II	3	47	T	11:00 AM
ACCT135	Computerized Accounting Applications	3	44	W	9:00 AM
ACCT135	Computerized Accounting Applications	3	45	W	8:00 AM
ACCT135	Computerized Accounting Applications	3	46	M	9:00 AM
ACCT145	Accounting for Nonprofits	3	43	H	8:00 AM
ACCT155	Cost Accounting	3	42	T	9:00 AM
ACCT165	Managerial Accounting	3	41	W	1:00 PM
ACCT201	Fraud Examination	3	40	H	9:00 AM
BUS120	Managerial Attitudes	3	39	M	2:00 PM
BUS121	Introduction to Business	3	38	T	2:00 PM
BUS123	Personal Finance	3	37	H	1:00 PM
BUS123	Personal Finance	3	36	W	10:00 AM
BUS140	Principles of Supervision	3	34	T	9:00 AM
BUS140	Principles of Supervision	3	35	M	8:00 AM
CIS134	Programming Fundamentals	4	6	M	3:00 PM
CIS134	Programming Fundamentals	4	7	T	6:00 PM
CIS134	Programming Fundamentals	4	8	M	8:00 AM
CIS134	Programming Fundamentals	4	9	T	8:00 AM
CIS162	Database Programming	4	5	W	8:00 AM

Record: ◄ ◄ 1 of 59 ► ►I ►☐ ⦰ No Filter   Search

Building Tables and Relationships

CASE At JCL Talent, you are working with Lydia Snyder, vice president of operations, to continue developing the Access database that tracks job placement data. You will improve the individual tables in the database and then link them together to create a relational database.

Module Objectives

After completing this module, you will be able to:

- Import data from Excel
- Modify fields in Datasheet View
- Modify Number and Currency fields
- Modify Short Text fields
- Modify Date/Time fields

- Create primary key fields
- Design related tables
- Create one-to-many relationships
- Work with subdatasheets

Files You Will Need

IL_AC_2-1.accdb
Support_IL_AC_2_States.xlsx
Support_IL_AC_2_Provs.xlsx
IL_AC_2-2.accdb
Support_IL_AC_2_Departments.xlsx
Support_IL_AC_2_Employees.xlsx
IL_AC_2-3.accdb

IL_AC_2-4.accdb
IL_AC_2-5.accdb
Support_IL_AC_2_Majors.xlsx
Support_IL_AC_2_Classes.xlsx
Support_IL_AC_2_Enrollments.xlsx
Support_IL_AC_2_Sections.xlsx
Support_IL_AC_2_Students.xlsx

Import Data from Excel

Learning Outcomes
- Import data from Excel
- Describe other file formats that work with Access

Importing enables you to quickly copy data from an external file into an Access database. You can import data from many sources, such as another Access database; Excel spreadsheet; SharePoint site; Outlook email; or text files in an HTML, XML, or delimited text file format. In a **delimited text file**, data is separated by a common character, the **delimiter**, such as a comma, tab, or dash. A **CSV (comma-separated value)** file is a common example of a delimited text file. An **XML file** contains the data surrounded by **Extensible Markup Language (XML)** tags that identify field names and data. The most common file format for importing data into an Access database is **Microsoft Excel**, the spreadsheet program in the Microsoft Office suite. **CASE** *Lydia Snyder gives you two Excel spreadsheets that list information for USA states and Canadian provinces and asks you to import the data into the database.*

STEPS

QUICK TIP
Updates to linked data made in the original data source are reflected in the Access database, but linked data cannot be changed in Access.

1. **sam↓ Start Access, open the** IL_AC_2-1.accdb database **from the location where you store your Data Files, save it as** IL_AC_2_Jobs, **enable content if prompted, click the** External Data tab, **click the** New Data Source button **in the Import & Link group, point to** From File, **click** Excel, **click the** Browse button, **navigate to the location where you store your Data Files, then double-click** Support_IL_AC_2_States.xlsx

   The **Get External Data - Excel Spreadsheet** dialog box opens, as shown in **FIGURE 2-1**. You can **import** the records to a new table, **append** the records to an existing table, or **link** to the data source. Both importing and appending create a copy of the data in the database. **Linking** means that the data is not copied into Access; it is only stored in the original data source. See **TABLE 2-1** for more information on file formats that can share data with Access.

2. **Click** OK

   The **Import Spreadsheet Wizard** helps you import data from Excel into Access and presents a sample of the data to be imported, as shown in **FIGURE 2-2**.

QUICK TIP
You can save the choices you made while importing if you need to repeat the steps regularly.

3. **Click the** First Row Contains Column Headings check box, **click** Next, **click** Next **to accept the default field options, click the** Choose my own primary key option button, **click the** StateName list arrow, **click** StateAbbrev **to choose it as the primary key field, click** Next, **type** States **as the new table name, click** Finish, **then click** Close

   The **primary key field** stores unique data for each record. The two-character state abbreviation is unique for each state and will be used later to connect to other tables. You also want to import more data that represents the 13 provinces in Canada.

4. **Click the** New Data Source button, **point to** From File, **click** Excel, **click the** Browse button, **navigate to the location where you store your Data Files, then double-click** Support_IL_AC_2_Provs.xlsx

TROUBLE
If a "Subscript out of range" error message appears, close the database, reopen it, then repeat Steps 4 and 5.

5. **Click the** Append option button **in the Get External Data – Excel Spreadsheet dialog box, click the** Companies list arrow, **click** States, **click** OK, **click** Next, **click** Finish, **then click** Close

   In order to append data to an existing table, the column names of the Excel spreadsheet must match the field names in the Access table.

6. **Double-click the** States table **to view the imported data, note 64 in the record selector box at the bottom of the datasheet, then close the States table**

   A better name for the table would be StatesAndProvinces.

TROUBLE
An object must be closed before you can rename it.

7. **Right-click the** States table **in the Navigation Pane, click** Rename, **type** StatesAndProvinces **as the new name, then press ENTER**

FIGURE 2-1: Get External Data – Excel Spreadsheet dialog box

Import to a new table

Append to an existing table

Link to the data

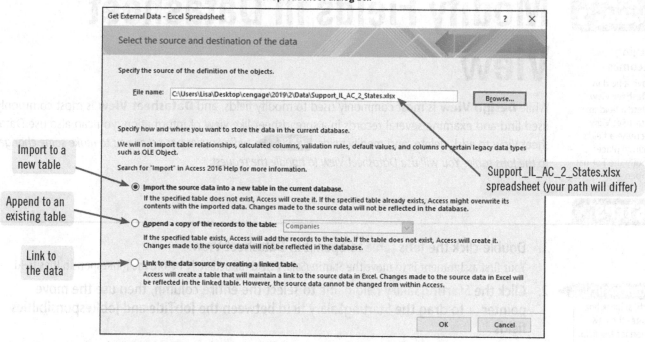

Support_IL_AC_2_States.xlsx spreadsheet (your path will differ)

FIGURE 2-2: Import Spreadsheet Wizard

First Row Contains Column Headings check box

First row

Records of data

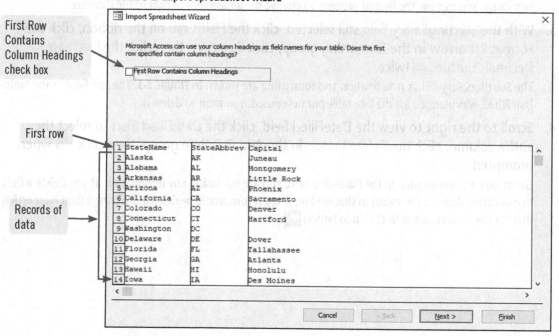

TABLE 2-1: File formats that Access can link to, import, and export

file format	import	link	export
Access	✓	✓	✓
Excel	✓	✓	✓
Word			✓
SharePoint site	✓	✓	✓
Email file attachments			✓
Outlook folder	✓	✓	
ODBC database (such as SQL Server)	✓	✓	✓

file format	import	link	export
dBASE	✓	✓	✓
HTML document	✓	✓	✓
PDF or XPS file			✓
Text file (delimited or fixed width)	✓	✓	✓
XML file	✓		✓

Modify Fields in Datasheet View

Learning
Outcomes
• Move a field in
  Datasheet View
• Delete a field in
  Datasheet View
• Decrease a field's
  decimal places
• Modify the Format
  property

While **Design View** is most commonly used to modify fields, and **Datasheet View** is most commonly used find and examine several records in a spreadsheet-like view of information, you can also use Datasheet View to add, delete, and modify fields. **CASE** *Lydia Snyder has asked you to make some changes to the Jobs table. You will use Datasheet View to handle the request.*

STEPS

1. **Double-click the** Jobs table **to open it in Datasheet View**

   Your first assignment is to move the StartingSalary field immediately before the JobResponsibilties field.

2. **Click the** StartingSalary field name **to select the entire column, then use the move pointer** ⍟ **to drag the** StartingSalary field **between the JobTitle and JobResponsibilties fields**

   The StartingSalary field was created using a Number data type, but you want to display the data as a monetary value. You can use the Format property to change the appearance of data in the datasheet.

3. **With the** StartingSalary field **still selected, click the** Fields tab **on the ribbon, click the** Format list arrow **in the Formatting group, click** Currency, **then click the** Decrease Decimals button **twice**

   The StartingSalary field's new position and formatting are shown in **FIGURE 2-3**. The last field in the table, DateFilled, was planned for the Jobs table but never used. You want to delete it.

4. **Scroll to the right to view the DateFilled field, click the** DateFilled field **to select the entire column, click the** Delete button **in the Add & Delete group, then click** Yes **when prompted**

   Given no data was entered in the DateFilled field, you are not losing any information. If you delete a field that contains data, all the values in that field for every record would be deleted. Deleting a field is an action that cannot be reversed with the Undo button ⤺.

FIGURE 2-3: StartingSalary field in the Jobs table has been moved and formatted

JobID	CompanyID	JobTitle	StartingSalar	Responsibilities
1	Alark Inc	Customer Service Representative	$40,000	Handles customer service inquiries and problems via telephone, internet or written correspondence. Calls are typically non-routine and may require deviation from standard screens, scripts, and procedures. Acts as a subject matter expert by providing training.
3	Ozark College	Financial Aid Assistant	$45,000	Assists in the daily operations of the Financial Aid Office providing general assistance and support to the Financial Aid staff. Provides student financial aid information to prospective and current students and families via phone or email. Tracks student financial
4	Morris College	Associate Director	$65,000	Develops and implements an overall strategic plan. Recruits, trains, and manages volunteers and awards. Develops philanthropic relationships with an assigned group of donors, prospective donors, and volunteers. Identifies capacity, interests and inclination.
5	Bank of the Midwest	Executive Assistant	$43,900	Supports an executive, handling administrative duties. Performs diverse, advanced and confidential administrative support including composing, signing and releasing routine but somewhat complex correspondence. Relieves management of administrative details.
6	Bank of the Midwest	Registered Client Associate	$35,000	Provides dedicated operational and sales support to multiple Financial Advisors. Works with all applications in the Microsoft Office suite.
7	Bower Pet Hospital	Client Service Coordinator	$41,000	Drives the flow of clients and pets through the hospital, maximizes the productivity of the veterinary medical team (in terms of numbers of clients and pets), ensures good communication with associates and clients, and coordinates the care of clients and pets in
8	Bower Pet Hospital	Practice Manager	$59,000	Develops associates and fosters an engaging team environment. Ensures that clients and patients have a positive experience when they visit the hospital. Optimizes the growth of our businesses.
9	Johnson County Chemicals	Planner of Historic Preservation	$51,000	Provides advanced technical assistance and analysis related to planning initiatives and land development applications. Reviews and processes various land development applications. Prepares plans, reports, studies, and analyses pertaining to long-range

Record: 1 of 82   No Filter   Search

Currency versus Number data type

In general, if a number represents a **fractional** value (such as dollars and cents, not a whole number), choose Currency for its data type. The underlying reason that all fractional values should be given a Currency data type is that a computer works with numbers using a binary system (1s and 0s), which cannot accurately store decimal fractions such as 0.1 or 0.01. The system can lead to rounding errors that all programming languages must address. In Access, the Currency data type includes special code to avoid these errors. If you are working with **integer** (a whole number, not a fraction) data, however, the Number data type provides faster performance. Whether you choose the Currency or Number data type, you can format the data to look as desired.

Modify Number and Currency Fields

Learning Outcomes
• Add a Currency field
• Add a Number field
• Modify the Field Size property for a Number field
• Modify the Decimal Places property

Number and Currency fields have similar properties because they both contain numeric values. The **Currency** data type is best applied to fractional values such as those that represent money down to the cent. The **Number** data type is best used to represent integer values, whole numbers such as quantities, measurements, and scores. **CASE** *Lydia asks you to add two new fields to the Jobs table. The first field named Fee represents money in dollars and cents, so you will use the Currency data type. The second field named Applicants represents the total number of people who applied for the job, which is never a fraction, so you will use the Number data type.*

STEPS

QUICK TIP
Scroll to the right side of the datasheet to find the Click to Add field name placeholder.

1. **Click the** Click to Add field name placeholder, **click** Currency, **type** Fee, **then press** ENTER
   The Fee field has been added as a new Currency field in the Jobs table. It will store monetary data in dollars and cents.

2. **Click the** Click to Add field name placeholder, **click** Number, **type** Applicants, **then press** ENTER
   The Applicants field has been added as a new Number field in the Jobs table. Test your new fields with sample data.

3. **Click the** Fee field **for the first record, type** 25.25, **press** TAB, **type** 50, **then click the second record to see the data you've entered, as shown in** FIGURE 2-4
   Access automatically formatted the value in the Fee field as $25.25. Some field properties can be set in both Datasheet View and Design View.

4. **Click the** Fee field, **click the** Fields tab **on the ribbon if not already selected, click the** Default Value button **in the Properties group, type** 50.25, **click** OK **in the Expression Builder dialog box, click the** Applicants field, **then click the** Increase Decimals button **in the Formatting group**
   The **Default Value** property automatically enters the property value, in this case 50.25, for all new records. The **Decimal Places** property displays the value with the given number of digits to the right of the decimal point. Because the Applicants field will store only whole numbers, showing the decimal place does not make good sense. You will switch to Table Design View to see how the same property can be modified in both views, then change the Decimal Places property value for the Applicants field back to 0.

5. **Right-click the** Jobs table tab, **click** Design View, **make sure the** Applicants field **is selected, click the** Decimal Places property box, **change the value to** 0, **then press** ENTER
   Table Design View gives you access to *all* field properties and as such, is generally the preferred way of changing field properties.
   The **Field Size** property determines the size or length of the maximum value for that field. Choosing the smallest Field Size for your Number fields helps improve database performance. See TABLE 2-2 for more information on Number Field Size property options. The Integer Field Size is large enough to hold any potential entry in the Applicants field.

QUICK TIP
Double-click a property name to toggle through the choices.

6. **With the** Applicants field **still selected, click the** Field Size property, **click the** Field Size list arrow, **then click** Integer
   Your Table Design View should look like FIGURE 2-5.

7. **Save the Jobs table then close it**

FIGURE 2-4: Adding a Currency field and a Number field

Fee Currency field

Applicants Number field

JobTitle	StartingSalary	JobResponsibilities	Fee	Applicants	Click to A
Customer Service Representative	$40,000	Handles customer service inquiries and problems via telephone, internet or written correspondence. Calls are typically non-routine and may require deviation from standard screens, scripts, and procedures. Acts as a subject matter expert by providing training,	$25.25	50	
Financial Aid Assistant	$45,000	Assists in the daily operations of the Financial Aid Office providing general assistance and support to the Financial Aid staff. Provides student financial aid information to prospective and current students and families via phone or email. Tracks student financial			
Associate Director	$65,000	Develops and implements an overall strategic plan. Recruits, trains, and manages volunteers and awards. Develops philanthropic relationships with an assigned group of donors, prospective donors, and volunteers. Identifies capacity, interests and inclination.			
Executive Assistant	$43,900	Supports an executive, handling administrative duties. Performs diverse, advanced and confidential administrative support including composing, signing and releasing routine but somewhat complex correspondence. Relieves management of administrative details.			

FIGURE 2-5: Modifying Number Field properties in Table Design View

Applicants field is selected

Fee field has a Currency Data Type

Applicants field has a Number Data Type

Field Size property

Decimal Places property

Field Size list arrow

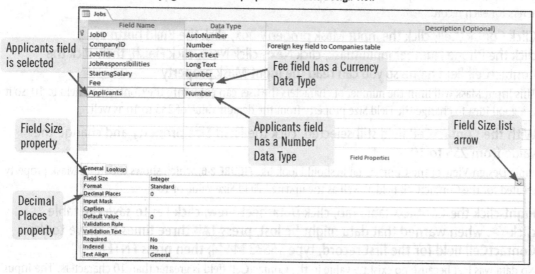

TABLE 2-2: Number Field Size property options

property	description
Byte	Stores numbers from 0 to 255 (no fractions)
Integer	Stores numbers from –32,768 to 32,767 (no fractions)
Long Integer	Stores numbers from –2,147,483,648 to 2,147,483,647 (no fractions)
Single	Stores numbers (including fractions with six digits to the right of the decimal point) times 10 to the –38th to +38th power
Double	Stores numbers (including fractions with more than 10 digits to the right of the decimal point) in the range of 10 to the –324th to +324th power

Modify Short Text Fields

Learning Outcomes
- Modify the Input Mask property
- Enter data using an input mask
- Modify the Field Size property

Short Text is the most common and therefore the default field data type. Short Text is used for any field that stores letters and any field that contains numbers that do not represent quantities such as a zip code, telephone number, or product number. Short Text fields have some additional properties unique to textual data such as Input Mask. Modifying the properties of a Short Text field helps ensure database accuracy and clarity because properties can restrict the way data is entered, stored, and displayed. See **TABLE 2-3** for more information on Short Text field properties. **CASE** *After reviewing the Contacts table with Lydia, you decide to modify the Input Mask and Field Size properties for the ContactCell field. You will work in Table Design View to make the changes.*

STEPS

1. **Right-click the** Contacts table **in the Navigation Pane, then click** Design View **on the shortcut menu**

   The **Input Mask** property provides a visual guide for users as they enter data. The ContactCell field is a good candidate for an Input Mask because phone numbers are consistently entered with 10 numeric characters for each record.

2. **Click** ContactCell, **click the** Input Mask **property box, click the** Build button ..., **click the** Phone Number input mask, **click** Next, **click** Next, **click** Finish, **then click the** ContactCell field name **so you can read the Input Mask property**

   This Input Mask will limit the number of characters the user can enter into the ContactCell field to 10, so it is a good idea to change the Field Size property from the default value of 255 to 10 as well.

3. **With the** ContactCell field **still selected, click the** Field Size property **and change the value from 255 to** 10

   Table Design View of the Contacts table should look like **FIGURE 2-6**, which shows the Input Mask property created for the ContactCell field as well as the updated Field Size value of 10.

4. **Right-click the** Contacts table tab, **click** Datasheet View, **click** Yes **to save the table, click** Yes **when warned that data might be lost, press** TAB **three times to move to the** ContactCell field **for the first record, type** 5553334444, **then press** ENTER

   No data was lost because no existing value in the ContactCell field is greater than 10 characters. The Input Mask property creates an easy-to-use visual guide to facilitate accurate and consistent data entry for the ContactCell field.

   Your screen should look like **FIGURE 2-7**.

5. **Right-click the** Contacts table tab, **then click** Close

FIGURE 2-6: Modifying the Input Mask property

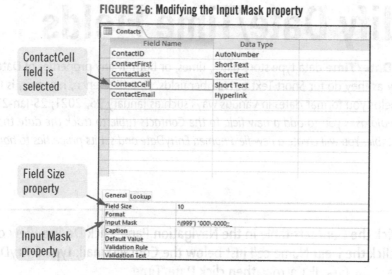

ContactCell field is selected

Field Size property

Input Mask property

FIGURE 2-7: Entering data with an input mask

Data entered with an input mask

ContactID	ContactFirst	ContactLast	ContactCell	ContactEmail
1	Doug	Griffey	(555) 333-4444	dgriffey@accentgroup.com
2	Kristen	Fontanelle	(555) 666-7777	kfontanelle@accentgroup.cc
(New)				

TABLE 2-3: Common Short Text field properties

property	description	sample field	sample property entry
Field Size	Controls how many characters can be entered into the field	State	2
Format	Controls how information will be displayed and printed	State	> (displays all characters in uppercase)
Input Mask	Provides a pattern for data to be entered	Phone	!(999) 000-0000;1;_
Caption	Describes the field in the first row of a datasheet, form, or report; if the Caption property is not entered, the field name is used to label the field	EmpNo	Employee Number
Default Value	Displays a value that is automatically entered in the given field for new records	City	Des Moines
Required	Determines if an entry is required for this field	LastName	Yes

Working with the Input Mask property

The Input Mask property provides a **pattern** for data to be entered, using three parts, each separated by a ; (semicolon). The first part provides a pattern for what type of data can be entered. For example, **9** represents an optional number, **0** a required number, **?** an optional letter, and **L** a required letter. The second part determines whether all displayed characters (such as dashes in a phone number) are stored in the field. For the second part of the input mask, a 0 entry stores all characters, such as 555-1199, and a 1 entry stores only the entered data, 5551199. The third part of the input mask determines which character Access uses to guide the user through the mask. Common choices are the asterisk (*), underscore (_), or pound sign (#).

Modify Date/Time Fields

Learning Outcomes
• Modify the Format property
• Modify the Default Value property
• Modify the Required property

Fields with a **Date/Time** data type store dates, times, or both. Many properties of Date/Time fields work the same way as they do for Short Text or Number fields. One difference, however, is the **Format** property, which helps you format dates in various ways such as January 25, 2021; 25-Jan-21; or 01/25/2021.

CASE *Lydia asks you to add a new field to the Contacts table to track the date that the contact was added to the table. You will create a new field named EntryDate and set its properties to handle this request.*

STEPS

1. **Right-click the** Contacts table **in the Navigation Pane, click** Design View **on the shortcut menu, click the** Field Name cell **just below the ContactEmail, type** EntryDate, **press** TAB, **click the** Data Type list arrow, **then click** Date/Time

   With the field name and data type set, you use field properties to further describe the field.

2. **With the EntryDate field still selected, click the** Format property box, **click the** Format list arrow, **then click** Medium Date

   The **Format** property changes the way the data is displayed *after it is entered*. All dates in Access are *entered* in a month/day/year pattern.

3. **With the EntryDate field still selected, click the** Default Value property box, **then type** =Date()

   The Default Value property automatically enters a value in all new records. The equal sign = indicates that you are using a calculated expression, and **Date()** is an Access function that returns the current date.

   The updated Table Design View for the Contacts table is shown in **FIGURE 2-8**.

TROUBLE
The current date will obviously be the date you perform these steps.

4. **Right-click the** Contacts table tab, **click** Save, **right-click the** Contacts table tab **again, then click** Datasheet View

   Note that the current date is already entered in the EntryDate field for the new record. To change the value, you can enter dates from the keyboard using a month/day/year pattern or pick a date from a pop-up calendar using the **Date Picker**.

5. **Press** TAB **five times to move to the** EntryDate field, **click the** Date Picker icon ▦, **click the current date on the pop-up calendar, click the** EntryDate field **for the second record, click the** Date Picker icon ▦, **then click the current date on the calendar for the second record as well**

   With valid dates in the EntryDate field of both records, you can set the Required property to Yes for the EntryDate field.

6. **Click the** EntryDate field name, **click the** Fields tab **on the ribbon, then click the** Required check box **as shown in FIGURE 2-9**

   The **Required** property will create an error message if the user attempts to enter a record in the database without a date in the EntryDate field.

7. **Close the Contacts table**

FIGURE 2-8: Creating a Date/Time field

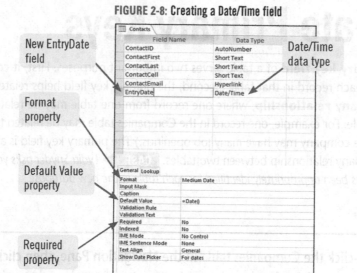

- New EntryDate field
- Format property
- Default Value property
- Required property
- Date/Time data type

FIGURE 2-9: Working with dates

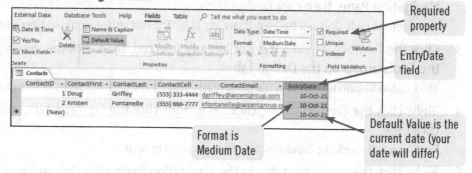

- Required property
- EntryDate field
- Format is Medium Date
- Default Value is the current date (your date will differ)

Entering dates

If you type the date for a Date/Type field instead of choosing a date from the pop-up calendar, Access assumes that years entered with two digits from 30 to 99 refer to the years 1930 through 1999, and 00 to 29 refers to the years 2000 through 2029. To enter a year before 1930 or after 2029, you must type all four digits of the year.

Using Smart Tags

Smart Tags are buttons that automatically appear in certain conditions. They provide a small menu of options to help you work with the task at hand. For example, in Table Design View, Access provides the **Property Update Options** Smart Tag to help you quickly apply property changes to other objects of the database that use the field. Another Smart Tag, the **Error Indicator** helps identify potential errors.

Create Primary Keys

The **primary key field** of a table serves two important purposes. First, it contains data that uniquely identifies each record in that table. Second, the primary key field helps relate one table to another in a **one-to-many relationship**, where one record from one table may be related to many records in the second table. For example, one record in the Companies table may be related to many records in the Jobs table. (One company may have many job openings.) The primary key field is always on the "one" side of a one-to-many relationship between two tables. **CASE** ▶ *Lydia Snyder asks you to confirm that a primary key field has been appropriately identified for each table in the new database.*

STEPS

1. **Right-click the** Companies table **in the Navigation Pane, then click** Design View
   The CompanyID AutoNumber field has been set as the primary key field as evidenced by the **key symbol** to the left of the field name. A field with the AutoNumber data type is a good candidate for the primary key field in a table because it automatically contains a unique number for each record.

2. **Right-click the** Companies table tab, **click** Close, **right-click the** Contacts table **in the Navigation Pane, then click** Design View
   The Contacts table does not have a primary key field. The best choice would be the ContactID field.

3. **Click the** ContactID field **if it is not already selected, then click the** Primary Key button **in the Tools group on the Design tab**
   The ContactID field is now set as the primary key field for the Contacts table, as shown in **FIGURE 2-10**.

4. **Right-click the** Contacts table, **click** Save, **right-click the** Contacts table tab **again, then click** Close
   Next, you will check the Industries table for a primary key field.

5. **Right-click the** Industries table **in the Navigation Pane, click** Design View, **observe that the Short Text Industry field is set as the primary key field, right-click the** Industries table tab, **then click** Close
   Next, check the Jobs table.

6. **Right-click the** Jobs table **in the Navigation Pane, click** Design View, **observe that the AutoNumber JobID field is set as the primary key field, right-click the** Jobs table tab, **then click** Close
   Next, check the StatesAndProvinces table.

7. **Right-click the** StatesAndProvinces table **in the Navigation Pane, click** Design View, **observe that the Short Text StateAbbrev field is set as the primary key field as shown in** FIGURE 2-11, **right-click the** StatesAndProvinces table tab, **then click** Close
   Often, the primary key field is the first field in the table, but that is not a requirement. If you do not make any design changes to an object, you are not prompted to save it when you close it.
   Now that you have confirmed that each table in the database has an appropriate primary key field, you are ready to link the tables together to create a relational database. The primary key field plays a critical role in this process.

FIGURE 2-10: Setting the primary key field in Design View of the Contacts table

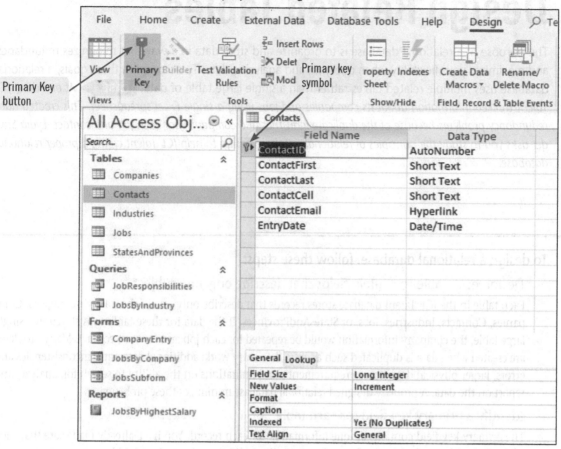

FIGURE 2-11: Design View of the StatesAndProvinces table

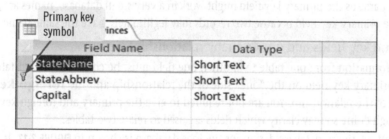

Design Related Tables

Learning
Outcomes
• Understand the
terminology used
when creating a
relational database
• Understand the
steps to create a
relational database
• Analyze one-to-
many relationships

The purpose of a relational database is to organize and store data in a way that minimizes redundancy and maximizes your flexibility when querying and analyzing data. To accomplish these goals, a relational database uses multiple related tables rather than a single large table of data. **CASE** *At one time, JCL Talent tracked information about its companies and jobs using a single Excel spreadsheet. This created data redundancy problems because of the duplicate industries and companies for each job and contact. Lydia Snyder asks you to study the principles of relational database design to help JCL Talent create a proper relational database.*

DETAILS

To design a relational database, follow these steps:

• **Design each table to contain fields that describe only one subject**

Each table in the JCL Talent database stores records that describe only one of the following subjects: Companies, Contacts, Industries, Jobs, or StatesAndProvinces. If the data for these tables was stored in a single large table, the company information would be repeated for each job and for each contact. Many problems are created when data is duplicated such as extra data entry work; additional data entry inconsistencies and errors; larger physical data storage requirements; and limitations on the ability to search for, analyze, and report on the data. A properly designed relational database minimizes these problems.

• **Identify a primary key field for each table**

The primary key field contains unique information for each record. You have already made sure that each of the five tables has a proper primary key field. Generally the primary key field has a numeric data type such as AutoNumber (automatically increments) or Number (user controlled), but sometimes Short Text fields serve this purpose such as the StateAbbrev field in the StatesAndProvinces table. Although using a contact's last name as the primary key field might work in a very small database, names are generally a poor choice for the primary key field because two records may legitimately have the same name.

• **Build foreign key fields and one-to-many relationships**

To tie the information from one table to another, one field must be common to each table. This linking field is the primary key field on the "one" side of the relationship and the **foreign key field** on the "many" side of the relationship. You are not required to give the primary and foreign key fields the same name, although doing so may clarify which fields are used to relate two tables.

The current relational database design for the Jobs database is shown in **FIGURE 2-12**. It is only partially completed. Currently, one record in the Industries table is related to many records in the Companies table using the common Industry field. One record in the Companies table is related to many records in the Jobs tables using the common CompanyID field. The StatesAndProvinces as well as the Contacts tables are not currently participating in the relational database, but you will correct that in the next lesson. See **TABLE 2-4** for a summary of important relational database terminology.

TABLE 2-4: Terminology used when creating a relational database

term	definition
Field	An individual column of information in a table. A field should not contain more than one piece of data. For example, always separate first and last names into two fields to preserve your ability to sort, filter, or find either name. Do not enter numbers and units of measurement such as *10 minutes* or *5 hours* into a single field. Doing so prevents you from easily sorting and calculating on the numeric part of the information.
Record	A group of related fields that describes a person, place, thing, or transaction such as a company or a job; a row

term	definition
Table	A collection of records for a single subject such as Industries, Companies, Jobs, Contacts, or StatesAndProvinces
Primary key field	A field that contains unique data for each record. Often an AutoNumber or Number field, a primary key field may also have a Short Text data type. The primary key field may also be used on the parent table ("one" table) side of a one-to-many relationship.
Foreign key field	A field in the child table ("many" table) that connects each record to the appropriate record in the parent table ("one" table)
Parent table	The table on the "one" side of a "one-to-many" relationship
Parent record	A record in the parent table
Child table	The table on the "many" side of a "one-to-many" relationship
Child record	A record in the child table
One-to-many relationship	A link between two tables that relates one record in the parent table to many records in the child table. For example, one record in the Industries table can be related to many records in the Companies table. One record in the Companies table can be related to many records in the Jobs table. One record in the Companies table can be related to many records in the Contacts table.
One-to-one relationship	A link between two tables that relates one record in the parent table to one record in the child table. One-to-one relationships are rare because this relationship can be simplified by moving all the fields into a single table.
Many-to-many relationship	If two tables have a many-to-many relationship, it means that one record in one table may be related to many records in the other table and vice versa. You cannot directly create a many-to-many relationship between two tables in Access. To connect two tables with this relationship, you must establish a third table called a **junction table** and create two one-to-many relationships from the original two tables using the junction table as the child table for both relationships. For example, at a school, the Students and Classes tables have a many-to-many relationship because one student can be in many classes and one class can have many students. To connect the Students and Classes tables, you would have to create a third table, perhaps called Enrollments, as the junction table. One student can be enrolled in many classes. One class can have many enrollments.
Junction table	The table between two tables that have a many-to-many relationship; the junction table is a child table to both of the other two tables.
Referential integrity	A set of rules that helps eliminate the creation of orphan records in a child ("many") table. For example, with referential integrity enforced, you cannot enter a value in a foreign key field of the child ("many") table that does not have a match in the linking field of the parent ("one") table. Referential integrity also prevents you from deleting a record in the parent ("one") table if a matching entry exists in the foreign key field of the child ("many") table.
Orphan record	A record in a child ("many") table that has no match in the parent ("one") table. Orphan records cannot be created in a child table if referential integrity is enforced.
Scrubbing or data cleansing	The process of removing and fixing orphan records in a relational database

FIGURE 2-12: Initial relational design for the Jobs database

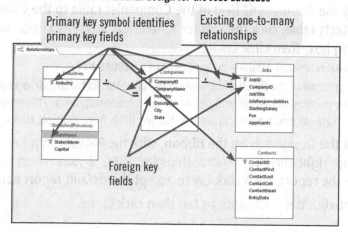

Access

Create One-to-Many Relationships

Learning Outcomes
• Create a foreign key field
• Create one-to-many relationships
• Set referential integrity
• Create a Relationship report

You must connect the tables in your database in proper one-to-many relationships to enjoy the benefits of a relational database. You use a common field in each table to create one-to-many relationships between the tables. The common field is always the primary key field in the parent ("one") table and is called the foreign key field in the child ("many") table. **TABLE 2-5** includes a few common one-to-many relationships.

CASE *Lydia Snyder asks you to complete the relational database by connecting the StatesAndProvinces and Contacts tables with one-to-many relationships.*

STEPS

1. **Click the** Database Tools tab **on the ribbon, click the** Relationships button, **then drag the** StatesAndProvinces table **from the Navigation Pane to the Relationships window**

   Each table in the database is represented by a small **field list** window that displays the table's field names. A **key symbol** identifies the primary key field in each table. To relate the two tables in a one-to-many relationship, you connect them using a common field, which is always the primary key field on the parent ("one") side of the relationship.

2. **Drag the** StateAbbrev field **in the StatesAndProvinces table to the** State field **in the Companies table**

   The Edit Relationships dialog box opens, as shown in **FIGURE 2-13**, which provides information about the tables and fields that will participate in the relationship and the option to enforce referential integrity.

3. **Click the** Enforce Referential Integrity check box, **then click** Create

   A **one-to-many line** appears between the StatesAndProvinces table and the Companies table. The parent ("one") side, as indicated by the "1" symbol on the line, identifies the primary key field used in the relationship. The child ("many") side, as indicated by the **infinity symbol**, identifies the foreign key field used in the relationship.

   The Contacts table does not have a corresponding foreign key field, which you need to create a one-to-many relationship.

4. **Right-click the** Contacts table field list, **click** Table Design, **click the blank** Field Name cell **just below the EntryDate field, type** CompanyID, **click the** Data Type list arrow, **click** Number, **right-click the** Contacts table tab, **click** Save, **right-click the** Contacts table tab **again, then click** Close

   Now you are ready to connect the Contacts table to the Companies table.

5. **Drag the** CompanyID field **in the Companies table to the** CompanyID field **in the Contacts table, click the** Enforce Referential Integrity check box **in the Edit Relationships dialog box, then click** Create

   The final relational database design is shown in **FIGURE 2-14**.

   A printout of the Relationships window, called the **Relationship report**, includes table names, field names, primary key fields, and one-to-many relationship lines. This printout is a helpful resource as you later create queries, forms, and reports that use fields from multiple tables.

6. **Click the** Design tab **on the ribbon, click the** Relationship Report button **in the Tools group, right-click the** Relationships for IL_AC_2_Jobs report tab, **click** Close, **click** Yes **to save the report, then click** OK **to accept the default report name**

7. **Right-click the** Relationships tab **then click** Close

FIGURE 2-13: Edit Relationships dialog box

FIGURE 2-14: Final Relationships window

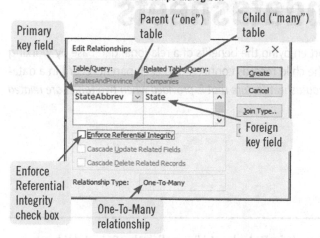

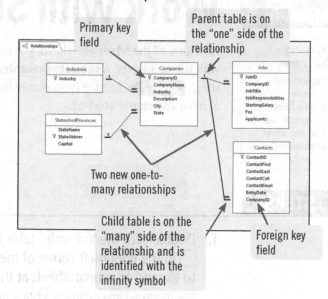

TABLE 2-5: Common one-to-many relationships

table on "one" side	table on "many" side	linking field	description
Products	Sales	ProductID	A ProductID field must have a unique entry in a Products table, but it is listed many times in a Sales table
Students	Enrollments	StudentID	A StudentID field must have a unique entry in a Students table, but it is listed many times in an Enrollments table as the student enrolls in multiple classes
Employees	Promotions	EmployeeID	An EmployeeID field must have a unique entry in an Employees table, but it is listed many times in a Promotions table as the employee is promoted to new job positions over time

Specifying the data type of the foreign key field

The foreign key field in the child table must have the same data type (Short Text or Number) as the primary key it is related to in the parent table. An exception to this rule is when the primary key field in the parent table has an AutoNumber data type. In this case, the linking foreign key field in the child table must have a Number data type. Also note that a Number field used as a foreign key field must have a Long Integer Field Size property to match the Field Size property of the AutoNumber primary key field.

Cascade options

Cascade Update Related Fields means that if a value in the primary key field (the field on the "one" side of a one-to-many relationship) is modified, all values in the foreign key field (the field on the child ("many") side of a one-to-many relationship) are automatically updated as well. **Cascade Delete Related**

Records means that if a record on the parent ("one") side of a one-to-many relationship is deleted, all related records in the child ("many") table are also deleted. Because both of these options automatically change or delete data in the child ("many") table behind the scenes, they should be used with caution.

Work with Subdatasheets

Learning Outcomes
• Expand and collapse subdatasheets
• Work with data in a subdatasheet
• Customize the status bar

Now that all the tables are related, you can start enjoying the benefits of a relational database by working with subdatasheets. A **subdatasheet** shows the child records connected to each parent record in a datasheet. **CASE** *You and Lydia explore the subdatasheet feature that is provided when two tables are related in a one-to-many relationship.*

STEPS

1. **Double-click the** Industries table **to open it in Datasheet View, click the** Select All button ☐ **in the upper-left corner of the Industries datasheet, then click any** Expand button ⊞ **to expand all subdatasheets at the same time, as shown in** FIGURE 2-15

   The Industries and Companies tables are linked in a one-to-many relationship, so the subdatasheet for each industry record displays related child records from the Companies table.

   Note that the records in the subdatasheet also have Expand buttons.

2. **Click the** Expand button ⊞ **to the left of the Navigational Systems record (the second record in the Aerospace subdatasheet)**

   The Companies table participates as the parent table in two different one-to-many relationships, so you are presented with the Insert Subdatasheet dialog box, asking which child table you want to select.

3. **Click** Jobs **in the Insert Subdatasheet dialog box**

   Notice that the CompanyID field is automatically added to the Link Child Fields and Link Master Fields boxes, as shown in **FIGURE 2-16**, because it is the field that connects the Companies and Jobs tables.

4. **Click** OK **in the Insert Subdatasheet dialog box**

   The four records in the Jobs table are linked to the Navigational Systems record in the Companies table and are now displayed in the Navigational Systems subdatasheet. You can use subdatasheets to enter and edit data.

5. **Enter** 50.25 **as the Fee field value for each of the four job records in the Navigational Systems subdatasheet, click the** Select All button ☐ **in the upper-left corner of the Industries datasheet, click the** Collapse button ⊟ **to the left of the Aerospace record, right-click the** Industries table tab, **click** Close, **then click** No **when asked to save changes to the Companies table**

6. **Double-click the** Jobs table **to open it in Datasheet View, scroll down to the records for the Navigational Systems company (JobIDs 23 through 26), then scroll to the right to view the 50.25 entries you previously made to the Fee field in a subdatasheet**

   When working with data in Datasheet View, subdatasheets make it easy to view child records.

   As you are working with Access, you may notice messages and indicators that appear in the status bar, the bottom bar in the application window. See **TABLE 2-6** for information on status bar indicators. You may turn these indicators on and off by right-clicking the status bar and selecting the indicator that you want to change. Most of the indicator messages appear in the right corner of the status bar.

7. **sam↑** **Right-click the** Jobs table tab, **click** Close, **click the** Database Tools tab, **click the** Compact and Repair Database button, **then close Access**

FIGURE 2-15: Expanding subdatasheets for the Industries table

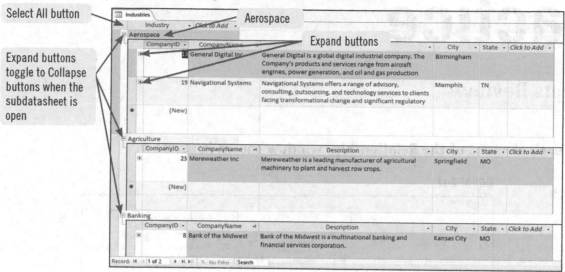

Select All button

Expand buttons toggle to Collapse buttons when the subdatasheet is open

Aerospace

Expand buttons

FIGURE 2-16: Insert Subdatasheet dialog box

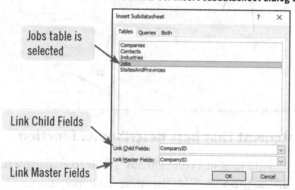

Jobs table is selected

Link Child Fields

Link Master Fields

TABLE 2-6: Status bar indicators

status bar indicator	displays
Caps Lock	**Caps Lock** in the status bar when the Caps Lock is toggled on
Kana Mode	Short for Katakana, which is a Japanese language; you must have a special installation of Access to enter these characters
Num Lock	**Num Lock** in the status bar when the Num Lock is toggled on.
Scroll Lock	**Scroll Lock** in the status bar when the Scroll Lock is toggled on
Overtype	**Overtype** in the status bar when Overtype mode (vs. Insert mode) is toggled on
Filtered	**Filtered** in the status bar when using the filter features
Move Mode	**Move Mode** in the status bar when using customized insertion point and key behaviors
Extended Selection	**Extended Selection** in the status bar when using extend mode, a feature that allows you to more easily select text without using a mouse
View Shortcuts	**View shortcut icons**

Practice

Concepts Review

Identify each element of the Relationships window shown in FIGURE 2-17.

FIGURE 2-17

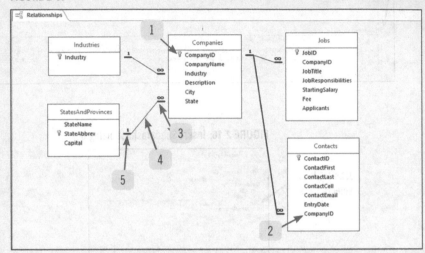

Match each term with the statement that best describes its function.

6. **Subdatasheet**
7. **Currency data type**
8. **Importing**
9. **Foreign key field**
10. **Referential integrity**
11. **Primary key field**
12. **Number data type**
13. **Integer**
14. **Linking**

a. Field used in a child ("many") table to establish a one-to-many relationship
b. Use this with fields that store fractional values.
c. A whole number
d. A way to copy information from another database, spreadsheet, or file format into an Access database
e. Use this with fields that store integers.
f. A way to connect to data in an external source without copying it
g. A field that contains unique information for each record in that table
h. Shows related records from a child ("many") table
i. A set of rules that prevent the creation of orphan records in the child ("many") table

Select the best answer from the list of choices.

15. What would be the best data type for a field that stores prices in dollars and cents?
    a. Short Text
    b. Currency
    c. Number
    d. AutoNumber

16. What would be the best data type for a field that stores the quantity of various car parts in inventory?
    a. Short Text
    b. Currency
    c. Number
    d. AutoNumber

17. Which of the following is *not* a file format that Access can import?
    a. Access
    b. Word
    c. Excel
    d. HTML

18. **Which of the following properties would you use to create a visual guide for data entry?**
   a. Format
   b. Default Value
   c. Field Size
   d. Input Mask

19. **Which is *not* true about enforcing referential integrity?**
   a. It is required for all one-to-many relationships.
   b. It prevents orphan records.
   c. It prevents records from being deleted on the "one" side of a one-to-many relationship that have matching records on the "many" side.
   d. It prevents records from being created on the "many" side of a one-to-many relationship that do not have a matching record on the "one" side.

20. **Which of the following is *not* true about linking?**
   a. Access can link to data in an Excel spreadsheet.
   b. Linking copies data from one data file to another.
   c. Access can link to data in an HTML file.
   d. You can edit linked data in Access.

Skills Review

1. **Import data from Excel.**
   a. Start Access.
   b. Open the IL_AC_2-2.accdb database from the location where you store your Data Files and save it as **IL_AC_2_SupportDesk**. Click Enable Content if a yellow Security Warning message appears.
   c. Import the **Support_IL_AC_2_Departments.xlsx** spreadsheet, located where you store your Data Files, to a new table in the current database using the Import Spreadsheet Wizard. Make sure that the first row is specified as a column heading, and do not create or select a primary key field. Name the table **Departments** and do not save the import steps.
   d. Open the Departments table in Table Datasheet View to confirm that the import worked properly. The Departments table should have seven records. Close the Departments table.
   e. Append the records from the **Support_IL_AC_2_Employees.xlsx** spreadsheet, located where you store your Data Files, to the existing Employees table. (*Hint*: If a "Subscript out of range" error appears, close the database, reopen it, then repeat Step 1e.)
   f. Open the Employees table in Table Datasheet View to confirm that the append process worked properly. The Employees table should have 26 records. Close the Employees table.

2. **Modify Datasheet View.**
   a. Open the Calls table in Datasheet View and delete the last field, CallPriority, which currently has no data.
   b. Move the CallMinutes field between the CallDateTime and CallNotes fields.
   c. Decrease decimals on the CallMinutes field to **0** and make sure the Format property is set to **Standard**.
   d. Save and close the Calls table.

3. **Modify Number and Currency fields.**
   a. Open the Employees table in Datasheet View and after the Department field, add a new field named **Salary** with a Currency data type.
   b. After the Salary field, add another field named **Dependents** with a Number data type.
   c. Enter **55000** for the Salary field and **3** for the Dependents field for the first employee (Aaron Cabrera, EmployeeID 3).
   d. Decrease the decimals for the Salary field to **0**.
   e. Make the Default Value for the Dependents field **1**.
   f. Save and close the Employees table.

Skills Review (continued)

4. Modify Short Text fields.

a. Open the Employees table in Design View and after the Dependents field, add a new field named **EmergencyPhone** with a Short Text data type.

b. Use the Input Mask Wizard to add a Phone Number input mask. Use the asterisk (*) as the Placeholder character and accept the other default settings.

c. Change the Field Size property of the EmergencyPhone field to **10**.

d. Change the Field Size property of the Department field to **15**.

e. Save the Employees table and click **Yes** when prompted. No data will be lost because no existing entries exceed the new Field Size property limits you have set.

f. Display the Employees table in Datasheet View, tab to the EmergencyPhone field for the first record (Aaron Cabrera EmployeeID 3), then type **5552227777** to experience the value of the Input Mask property.

g. Close the Employees table.

5. Modify Date/Time fields.

a. Open the Cases table in Design View and change the Format property for both the OpenedDate and the ResolvedDate fields to **Short Date**.

b. Change the Default Value for the OpenedDate field to **=Date()** to provide today's date.

c. Change the Required Value for the OpenedDate field to **Yes**.

d. Save the table, click Yes when prompted to test the data, then close the Cases table.

6. Create primary key fields.

a. Open the Departments table in Table Design View and set the Department field as the primary key field. Save and close the Departments table.

b. Open each of the other tables, Calls, Cases, and Employees, in Design View to view and confirm that they have a primary key field. In each case, the first field is designated as the primary key field and has an AutoNumber data type. A field with an AutoNumber data type will automatically increment to the next number as new records are entered into that table.

7. Design related tables.

a. Open the Relationships window to study the existing relationships between the tables.

b. Drag the edges of the field lists so that all fields are clearly visible and drag the field list title bars as needed to clearly position the tables so that the Calls table is to the right of the Cases table and the Cases table is to the right of the Employees table.

c. Be ready to discuss these issues in class or in an online discussion thread.
- Why is it important to relate tables in the first place?
- What relationships exist in this database?
- What role does the primary key field in each table play in the relationships identified in Step 7a?
- What is the foreign key field in each of the relationships?
- What parent ("one") tables exist in this database?
- What child ("many") tables exist in this database?
- What do the "1" and infinity symbols tell you about the relationship?

d. Save the Relationships window.

8. Create one-to-many relationships.

a. Add the Departments table to the Relationships window. Position it to the left of the Employees table.

b. Create a one-to-many relationship between the Departments table and the Employees table using the common Department field.

c. Enforce referential integrity on the relationship.

d. Save the Relationships window, as shown in **FIGURE 2-18**, then close it.

Skills Review (continued)

9. **Work with subdatasheets.**

   a. Open the Departments table in Datasheet View. Expand the Accounting Department's subdatasheet to display the employees who work in that department.

   b. Change the Extension value of EmployeeID 24 (Craig Serrano) from 7621 to **7766** in the subdatasheet.

FIGURE 2-18

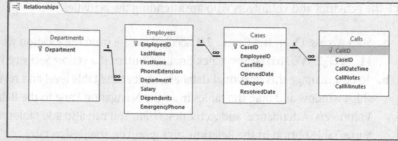

   c. Expand the subdatasheet for EmployeeID 24 (Craig Serrano) to see the cases that are linked to that employee.

   d. Expand the subdatasheet for CaseID 22 (Email attachment problem) to see what calls are linked to that case.

   e. Collapse all subdatasheets and close the Departments table.

   f. Compact and repair the database and close Access.

Independent Challenge 1

As the manager of Riverwalk, a multi-specialty health clinic, you have created a database to manage the schedules that connect each healthcare provider with the nurses that provider needs to efficiently handle patient visits. In this exercise, you create the primary keys and relationships required to create a relational database.

   a. Start Access. Open the IL_AC_2-3.accdb database from the location where you store your Data Files and save it as **IL_AC_2_Riverwalk**. Click Enable Content if a yellow Security Warning message appears.

   b. Open the Relationships window. Drag the ScheduleItems table from the Navigation Pane to the Relationships window, positioning it between the existing four tables. (*Hint:* You can also add tables to the Relationships window by clicking the Show Table button in the Relationships group on the Design tab.)

   c. Now that all four tables are in the Relationships window, notice that each table has a primary key field except for the ScheduleItems table. Open the ScheduleItems table in Design View, set the TransactionNo field as the primary key field, then save and close the table to return to the Relationships window.

   d. To connect the tables, you have to decide how "one" record in a parent table relates to "many" records in a child table. In this case, the ScheduleItems table is the child table to each of the four other tables. Therefore, build four one-to-many relationships with referential integrity as follows:

   • Drag the ScheduleNo field from the ScheduleDate table to the ScheduleNo field of the ScheduleItems table.

   • Drag the LocationNo field from the Locations table to the LocationNo field of the ScheduleItems table.

   • Drag the DoctorNo field from the Providers table to the DoctorNo field of the ScheduleItems table.

   • Drag the NurseNo field from the Nurses table to the NurseNo field of the ScheduleItems table.

   e. Be sure to enforce referential integrity on each relationship. Doing so will add the "1" and "infinity" symbols to the relationship line. If they are missing, double-click the relationship line to open the Edit Relationships dialog box, where you can check the Enforce Referential Integrity check box.

   f. Click the Relationship Report button in the Tools group on the Design tab to create a relationships report, as shown in **FIGURE 2-19**.

   g. Save and close the report with the default name of **Relationships for IL_AC_2_ Riverwalk**, then save and close the Relationships window.

   h. Compact and repair the database then close Access.

FIGURE 2-19

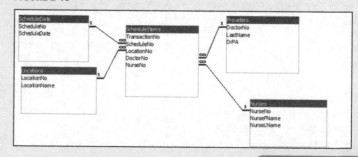

Access

Independent Challenge 2

You are working for a city to coordinate a series of community-wide preparedness activities. You have started a database to track the activities and volunteers who are attending the activities.

a. Start Access. Open the IL_AC_2-4.accdb database from the location where you store your Data Files and save it as **IL_AC_2_Volunteers**. Click Enable Content if a yellow Security Warning message appears.

b. To best manage this relational database, start at the table level and review the table relationships. Open the Relationships window and drag the tables from the Navigation Pane to the Relationships window in this order: Zipcodes, Volunteers, Attendance, and Activities. (*Hint*: You can also add tables to the Relationships window by clicking the Show Table button in the Relationships group on the Design tab.)

c. Some of the relationships are more obvious than others. For example, one record in the Zipcodes table may be related to many records in the Volunteers table. To establish this relationship, drag the Zip field from the Zipcodes table to the Zipcode field in the Volunteers table and enforce referential integrity on the relationship.

d. The Volunteers, Attendance, and Activities tables are more difficult to analyze because one volunteer may be related to many activities and one activity may have many volunteers. This many-to-many relationship is resolved with the Attendance table, which serves as the junction table between the Volunteers and Activities tables. Open the Attendance table in Design view and add two foreign key fields named **VolunteerID** and **ActivityID**, each with a Number data type. Save and close the Attendance table and return to the Relationships window.

e. With the foreign key fields in the Attendance table established, you are ready to link the Volunteers, Attendance, and Activities tables by building these two relationships:

  • Drag the VolunteerID field from the Volunteers table to the VolunteerID field in the Attendance table. Enforce referential integrity on the relationship.

  • Drag the ActivityID field from the Activities table to the ActivityID field in the Attendance table. Enforce referential integrity on the relationship.

f. The final Relationships window should look like **FIGURE 2-20**. Save and close the Relationships window.

g. Open the Zipcodes table to review its one-to-many relationship with the Volunteers table by working in Table Datasheet View.

h. Expand the subdatasheet for the 64145 Springfield KS record, change Micah Ati's name to *your name*, then close the Zipcodes table.

i. Compact and repair the database and close Access.

FIGURE 2-20

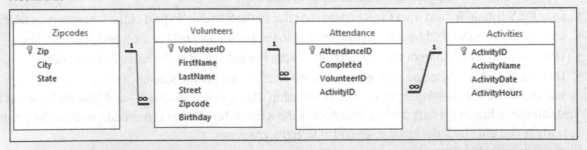

Building Tables and Relationships

Visual Workshop

Open the IL_AC_2-5.accdb database from the location where you store your Data Files and save it as **IL_AC_2_CollegeCourses**, then enable content if prompted. Import the **Support_IL_AC_2_Majors.xlsx** Excel spreadsheet and append the records to the Departments table. Do not save the import steps.

Import the following spreadsheets as new tables with the following names. For each import, use the first row as the column headings and other default options of the Import Spreadsheet Wizard. Do not save the import steps.

Import **Support_IL_AC_2_Classes.xlsx** as **Classes** and set ClassNo as the primary key field.

Import **Support_IL_AC_2_Enrollments.xlsx** as **Enrollments** and set EnrollmentID as the primary key field.

Import **Support_IL_AC_2_Sections.xlsx** as **Sections** and set SectionNo as the primary key field.

Import **Support_IL_AC_2_Students.xlsx** as **Students** and set StudentID as the primary key field.

In the Relationships window, relate the tables in one-to-many relationships using **FIGURE 2-21** as a guide. Enforce referential integrity on each relationship. Save and close the Relationships window.

FIGURE 2-21

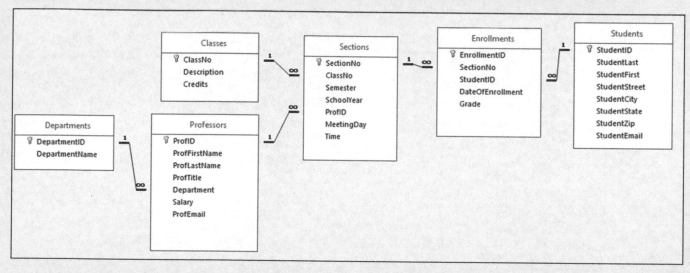

Creating Queries

CASE ▶ Now that you've updated the tables in the database for JCL Talent and linked them in one-to-many relationships to create a relational database, you're ready to mine the data for information. You'll develop queries to provide Lydia Snyder, vice president of operations, with fast and accurate answers.

Module Objectives

After completing this module, you will be able to:

- Work in Query Datasheet View
- Work in Query Design View
- Work in SQL View
- Sort data
- Find and replace data
- Filter data

- Enter and save criteria
- Apply AND criteria
- Apply OR criteria
- Create calculated fields
- Format a datasheet

Files You Will Need

IL_AC_3-1.accdb

IL_AC_3-2.accdb

IL_AC_3-3.accdb

IL_AC_3-4.accdb

IL_AC_3-5.accdb

Work in Query Datasheet View

Learning Outcomes
- Edit and delete records
- Hide and unhide columns
- Freeze and unfreeze columns

A **query** answers a question about the information in the database by allowing you to select a subset of fields and records from one or more tables and present them in a single datasheet. You can enter, edit, and navigate data in **Query Datasheet View**, which displays each field as a column and each record as a row just like Table Datasheet View. Given all data is stored only in tables, any edits, additions, or deletions made in Query Datasheet View are automatically reflected elsewhere in the database. **CASE** *Lydia asks you to change some data that is currently organized in a query. You'll work in Query Datasheet View to make the updates.*

STEPS

1. **sam ↓ Start Access, open the** IL_AC_3-1.accdb database **from the location where you store your Data Files, save it as** IL_AC_3_Jobs, **enable content if prompted, then double-click the** JobsByIndustry query **to open it in Datasheet View**

   Each time a query is opened, it shows a current view of the data. Notice that the datasheet displays one record for every job and that one company may be connected to many jobs.

   The records for General Digital Inc in Birmingham do not have a value in the State field. Although data is stored in tables, you can edit data in Query Datasheet View.

2. **Click the** State field cell **for any General Digital Inc record, type** AL, **then click any other record**

   All records for General Digital Inc in this query update to show AL (Alabama) in the State field because General Digital Inc is related to six records in the Jobs table.

3. **Click the** record selector **to the left of the twelfth record (CompanyID 8 and JobTitle of Executive Assistant), click the** Delete button **in the Records group, then click** Yes

   You can delete records from a query datasheet the same way you delete them from a table datasheet. Notice that the navigation bar now indicates that you have 81 records in the datasheet as shown in **FIGURE 3-1**.

   In large datasheets, you may want to freeze certain fields so that they remain on the screen at all times.

   QUICK TIP
   To unfreeze a field, right-click any field name, then click Unfreeze All Fields on the shortcut menu.

4. **Right-click the** CompanyName field name **to select the entire column, click** Freeze Fields **on the shortcut menu, press** TAB **as needed to move to the** Applicants field **for the first record, then type** 15

   Notice that the CompanyName field is now positioned as the first field in the datasheet and doesn't scroll off the screen as you press TAB.

   In large datasheets, you may also want to hide fields.

   QUICK TIP
   To unhide a field, right-click any field name, click Unhide Fields on the shortcut menu, click the check box beside the field that you want to unhide, then click Close.

5. **Press** TAB **as needed to move to the** Description field, **right-click the** Description field name **to select the entire column, as shown in** FIGURE 3-2, **then click** Hide Fields **on the shortcut menu**

   Hiding a field in a query datasheet doesn't remove it from the query, it merely hides it on the datasheet.

6. **Right-click the** JobsByIndustry tab, **click** Save, **right-click the** JobsByIndustry tab, **then click** Close

   Saving your changes to this query saves the changes you made to freeze the CompanyName field and to hide the Description field. Edits to data are automatically saved as you work.

FIGURE 3-1: Editing data in Query Datasheet View

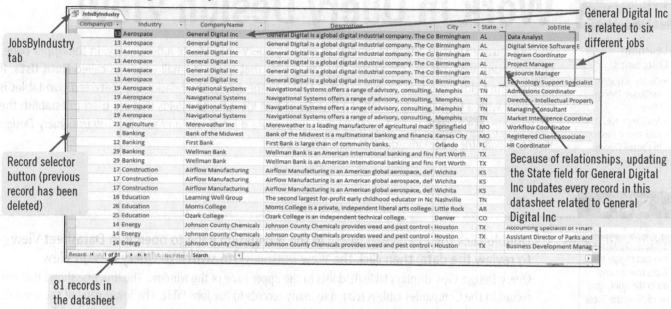

JobsByIndustry tab
Record selector button (previous record has been deleted)
81 records in the datasheet
General Digital Inc is related to six different jobs
Because of relationships, updating the State field for General Digital Inc updates every record in this datasheet related to General Digital Inc
CompanyID
Industry
CompanyName
Description
City
State
JobTitle

FIGURE 3-2: Freezing and hiding columns in Query Datasheet View

Freeze the CompanyName field
Description field name
Hide and Unhide Fields
Freeze Fields and Unfreeze All Fields
Sort A to Z
Sort Z to A
Copy
Paste
Field Width
Hide Fields
Unhide Fields
Freeze Fields
Unfreeze All Fields

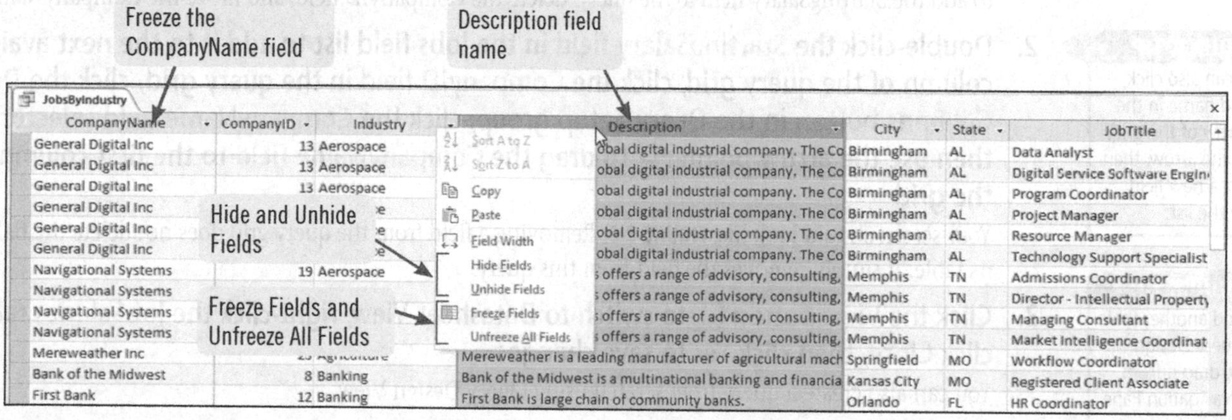

Work in Query Design View

You use **Query Design View** to modify an existing query or to create a new query. In the upper pane, Query Design View presents the fields you can use for that query in small windows called **field lists**. If you use the fields from two or more related tables in the query, the relationship between two tables is displayed with a **join line** (also called a **link line**) that identifies the fields that are used to establish the relationship. **CASE** *Lydia Snyder asks you to produce a list of jobs and salaries. You use Query Design View to modify the JobSalaries query to meet her request.*

STEPS

1. **Double-click the** JobSalaries query **in the Navigation Pane to open it in Datasheet View to review the data, then click the** View button ☒ **to switch to Query Design View**

   Query Design View displays table field lists in the upper pane of the window. The link line shows that one record in the Companies table is related to many records in the Jobs table. The lower pane of the window, called the **query design grid** (also called the **QBE**, **query by example grid**, or **query grid** for short), displays the field names, sort orders, and criteria used within the query. The JobSalaries query selects the Industry and CompanyName fields from the Companies table and three fields from the Jobs table. You want to add the StartingSalary field to the query, delete the CompanyID field, and move the CompanyName field.

2. **Double-click the** StartingSalary field **in the Jobs field list to add it to the next available column of the query grid, click the** CompanyID field **in the query grid, click the** Delete Columns button **in the Query Setup group, click the** CompanyName field selector, **then use the arrow pointer** ⤆ **to drag the** CompanyName field **to the first column of the grid**

   Your screen should look like **FIGURE 3-3**. Removing a field from the query grid does not delete the field from its table. It simply removes the field from this query.

3. **Click the** View button ▦ **to switch to Datasheet View, right-click the** JobSalaries tab, **click** Close, **then click** Yes **to save changes**

   You can also create a query from scratch using Query Design View.

4. **Click the** Create tab **on the ribbon, click the** Query Design button **in the Queries group, double-click** Jobs **in the Show Table dialog box, double-click** Companies, **then click** Close

   For this query, you want to include three fields. You can drag fields from the field lists to any column to position them in the query. Any existing fields will move to the right to accommodate the new field.

5. **Drag the** StartingSalary field **to the first column of the grid, drag the** JobTitle field **to the first column of the grid, then drag the** CompanyName field **to the first column of the grid**

   Your screen should look like **FIGURE 3-4**.

6. **Click the** Datasheet View button ▦ **to run the query**

   For a **select query**, a query that selects fields and records, you can **run** the query by clicking either the Datasheet View button or the Run button. In an **action query**, clicking the Run button starts a process that modifies all of the selected records. Because the Datasheet View button never changes data regardless of what type of query you are building, it is a safe way to run a select query or view selected fields and records for an action query. In later modules, you will learn about action queries that change data.

7. **Right-click the** Query1 tab, **click** Save, **type** CompanyJobs **as the new query name, then click** OK

Creating Queries

FIGURE 3-3: Adding and removing fields in Query Design View

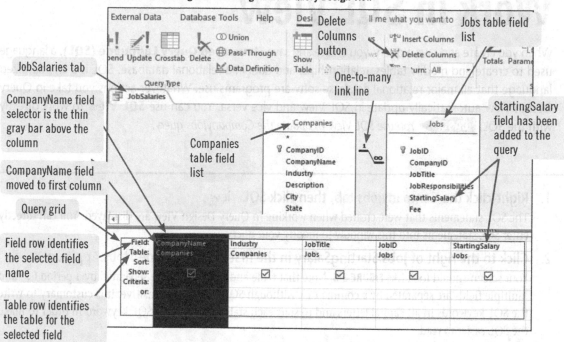

FIGURE 3-4: Creating a new query in Query Design View

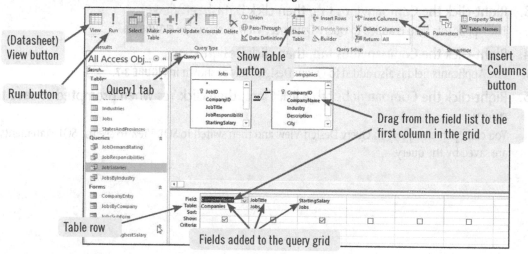

Adding or deleting a table in Query Design View

You might want to add a table's field list to the upper pane of Query Design View to select fields from that table for the query. To add a new table to Query Design View, drag it from the Navigation Pane to Query Design View, or click the Show Table button in the Query Setup group on the Design tab. To delete an unneeded table from Query Design View, click its title bar, then press DELETE.

Linking tables in Query Design View

If tables are joined in the Relationships window, they are automatically joined in Query Design View. If tables are not joined in the Relationships window, you can join them in Query Design View by dragging the linking field from one field list to another. However, you cannot enforce referential integrity on a relationship created in Query Design View. Also, a relationship created in Query Design View is established for that query only. Creating one-to-many relationships for the database in the Relationships window provides tremendous productivity and application performance benefits over relating tables within individual queries.

Work in SQL View

**Learning
Outcomes**
• Modify a query in
  SQL View
• Learn common
  SQL keywords

When you create and save a query, you create and save **Structured Query Language (SQL)**, a language used to create and modify tables, relationships, and data in a relational database. SQL is a standardized language that all major relational database software programs use. Whatever actions you take in Query Design View automatically update in SQL View and vice versa. You can use **SQL View** to work directly with the SQL. **CASE** ▶ *You use SQL View to update the CompanyJobs query.*

STEPS

1. **Right-click the** CompanyJobs tab, **then click** SQL View

   The SQL statements that were created when working in Query Design View are displayed. You can directly enter SQL statements into this window to modify your query.

2. **Click to the right of Jobs.StartingSalary in the first line, then type** , Jobs.Applicants

   Your screen should look like **FIGURE 3-5**. Note that table and field names are separated by a period (.) and multiple fields are separated by a comma (,). Although SQL is not case sensitive, it is customary to write the SQL keywords in all capital letters and to start each statement with an SQL keyword in order to make the SQL easier to read.

   A select query starts with the SQL keyword **SELECT**. Some of the most common SQL keywords are shown in **TABLE 3-1**.

TROUBLE
If you receive an
error message,
make sure you have
used a comma
(,) to separate the
new field name and
spelled the table and
field name correctly.

3. **Right-click the** CompanyJobs tab, **then click** Datasheet View

   The Applicants field is added to Query Datasheet View as shown in **FIGURE 3-6**.

4. **Right-click the** CompanyJobs tab, **then click** Design View

   The Applicants field is also added to Query Design View as shown in **FIGURE 3-7**.

5. **Right-click the** CompanyJobs tab, **click** Close, **then click** Yes **when prompted to save the query**

   You can open any query in Query Design View and then switch to SQL View to see the SQL statements that are saved by the query.

FIGURE 3-5: Adding the Applicants field in SQL View

CompanyJobs tab

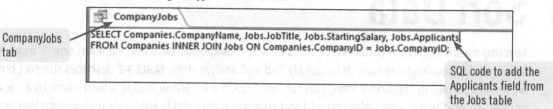

CompanyJobs

SELECT Companies.CompanyName, Jobs.JobTitle, Jobs.StartingSalary, Jobs.Applicants
FROM Companies INNER JOIN Jobs ON Companies.CompanyID = Jobs.CompanyID;

SQL code to add the Applicants field from the Jobs table

FIGURE 3-6: Viewing the Applicants field in Query Datasheet View

CompanyJobs

CompanyName	JobTitle	StartingSalar	Applicants
ABA Solutions	Project Manager	$65,000	31
Accent Group	Customer Service	$65,000	4
Accent Group	Operations Project Specialist	$69,000	25
Accent Group	Client Product Support Associate	$72,000	31
AIT Group	Microsoft PowerPoint specialist	$49,000	22
Addcore Partners	Program Manager	$72,000	16

Applicants field from the Jobs table added to the datasheet

FIGURE 3-7: Viewing the Applicants field in Query Design View

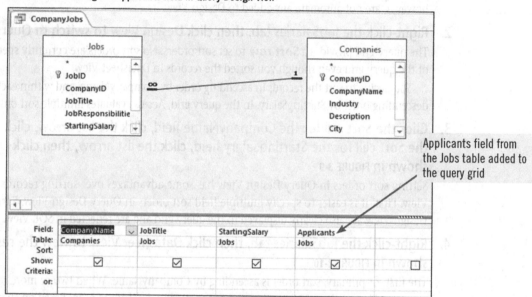

CompanyJobs

Jobs

* JobID
CompanyID
JobTitle
JobResponsibilitie
StartingSalary

∞   1

Companies

* CompanyID
CompanyName
Industry
Description
City

Applicants field from the Jobs table added to the query grid

Field:	CompanyName	JobTitle	StartingSalary	Applicants	
Table:	Companies	Jobs	Jobs	Jobs	
Sort:					
Show:	☑	☑	☑	☑	☐
Criteria:					
or:					

TABLE 3-1: Common SQL keywords

keyword	identifies...
SELECT	which fields you want to include in a select query
FROM	what tables contain the fields you have selected
WHERE	criteria used to limit the number of records selected
ORDER BY ... ASC (DESC)	sort order for the records; ASC means ascending, DESC means descending
INNER JOIN ... ON	which records will be selected when choosing fields from more than one table (there must be a match in both tables)
INSERT	the data and fields used when adding a new record
UPDATE...SET	the data and fields used when updating specific records
DELETE	records to delete

Sort Data

Learning Outcomes
- Sort records in Query Datasheet View
- Sort records in Query Design View

Sorting means to order records in ascending or descending order based on values in one or more fields. Sorting helps you organize records to quickly find and analyze data. TABLE 3-2 describes the Sort buttons on the Home tab. In Datasheet View, you can also click the list arrow beside a field name to access sort options. Query Design View helps you add and save sort orders and is especially useful when you want to sort on multiple fields. **CASE** *Lydia Snyder asks you to sort the JobSalaries query to more clearly show the records with a high starting salary.*

STEPS

1. **Double-click the** JobSalaries query **in the Navigation Pane to open it in Datasheet View, click the** StartingSalary field, **click the** Descending button **in the Sort & Filter group, then use the column resize pointer ↔ to widen the StartingSalary field as shown in** FIGURE 3-8

   The JobSalaries query now displays the records from highest StartingSalary to lowest, and the StartingSalary field displays a small descending sort indicator by the field name. Sort orders applied to Datasheet View, however, are not automatically added to Design View.

2. **Right-click the** JobSalaries tab, **then click** Design View **to switch to Query Design View**

   The query grid provides a **Sort row** to set sort orders. No sort orders are currently specified in the Sort row of the query grid even though you sorted the records in Datasheet View.

   You decide to sort the records in ascending order by CompanyName, and within each CompanyName, in descending order by StartingSalary. In the query grid, Access evaluates multiple sort orders from left to right.

3. **Click the** Sort cell for the CompanyName field, **click the** list arrow, **click** Ascending, **click the** Sort cell for the StartingSalary field, **click the** list arrow, **then click** Descending **as shown in** FIGURE 3-9

   Setting sort orders in Query Design View has some advantages over sorting records in Query Datasheet View. First, it is easier to specify multiple field sort orders in Query Design View. Sort orders set in Query Design View are also clearly displayed in the query grid and are reflected in SQL View.

4. **Right-click the** JobSalaries tab, **then click** Datasheet View **to view the resorted records as shown in** FIGURE 3-10

   The first, or primary, sort order is ascending by CompanyName. When two or more records have the same CompanyName value, the records are further sorted in descending order based on the StartingSalary field.

5. **Right-click the** JobSalaries tab, **click** Close, **then click** Yes **when prompted to save changes**

   Sort orders set in Query Design View are always saved with the query.

FIGURE 3-8: Sorting in Query Datasheet View

Ascending button Descending button Remove Sort button

JobSalaries tab

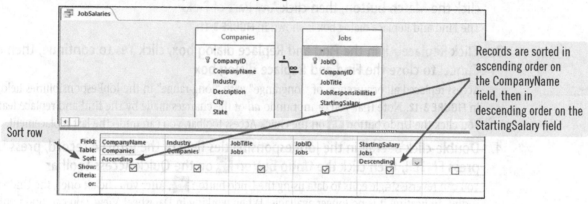

StartingSalary list arrow and sort indicator

Records are sorted in descending order based on the StartingSalary field

FIGURE 3-9: Sorting by multiple fields in Query Design View

Sort row

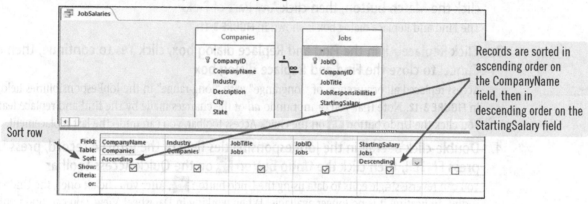

Records are sorted in ascending order on the CompanyName field, then in descending order on the StartingSalary field

FIGURE 3-10: Final JobSalaries datasheet

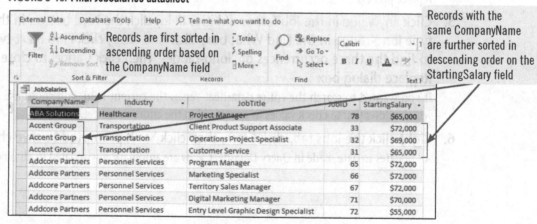

Records are first sorted in ascending order based on the CompanyName field

Records with the same CompanyName are further sorted in descending order on the StartingSalary field

TABLE 3-2: Datasheet View Sort buttons

name	button	purpose
Ascending		Sorts records based on the selected field in ascending order (0 to 9, A to Z)
Descending		Sorts records based on the selected field in descending order (Z to A, 9 to 0)
Remove Sort		Removes the current sort order

Access

Find and Replace Data

Access provides some excellent tools to help you find and replace data in Query Datasheet View. **TABLE 3-3** describes the Find buttons on the Home tab. **CASE** *Lydia Snyder asks you to find and replace all occurrences of "longrange" in the JobResponsibilities field of the Jobs table with the correct spelling of the word, "long-range".*

STEPS

1. **Double-click the** Jobs table **to open it in Datasheet View**

   The sort and find features work the same way in Table and Query Datasheet View.

2. **Click** any value in the JobResponsibilities field, **click the** Replace button **in the Find group, type** longrange **in the Find What box, click in the** Replace With box, **type** long-range, **click the** Match button, **then click** Any Part of Field

   The Find and Replace dialog box is shown in **FIGURE 3-11**.

3. **Click** Replace All **in the Find and Replace dialog box, click** Yes **to continue, then click** Cancel **to close the Find and Replace dialog box**

   Access replaced all occurrences of "longrange" with "long-range" in the JobResponsibilities field, as shown in **FIGURE 3-12**. Note that you cannot undo *all* of the changes made by the find and replace feature, but if you click the Undo button 🔄 on the Quick Access toolbar, you can undo the last replacement.

4. **Double-click** overall **in the JobResponsibilities field of the JobID 4 record, press DELETE, press ENTER, then click the** Undo button 🔄 **on the Quick Access toolbar**

   You can reverse single edits to data using the Undo button 🔄. After you click it once, the Undo button 🔄 is dim, indicating it is no longer available. When working in Datasheet View, you can undo only the *most recent* edit. Use the Find feature to find and review all of the replacements that were made with the find and replace process.

5. **Click** any value in the JobResponsibilities field, **click the** Find button **in the Find group, type** long-range **in the Find What box, click** Find Next, **click** Find Next two more times **to find the three occurrences of "long-range," then click** Cancel **to close the Find and Replace dialog box**

   If you wanted to search the entire datasheet versus the current field, you could use the Look In option, which allows you to check values in every field in the entire datasheet.

6. **Right-click the** Jobs tab, **click** Close, **then click** Yes **if prompted to save changes**

   All updates to data made in Query Datasheet View are automatically updated in all objects.

FIGURE 3-11: Find and Replace dialog box

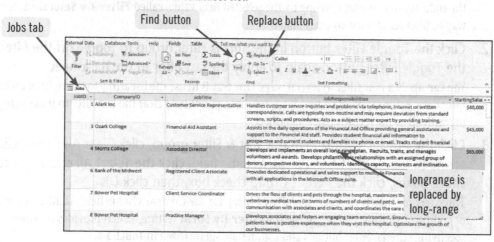

Find What box → Find What: longrange
Replace With box → Replace With: long-range
Look In Current Field → Look In: Current field
Match Any Part of Field → Match: Any Part of Field
Search: All
☐ Match Case   ☑ Search Fields As Formatted

Find Next
Cancel
Replace
Replace All ← Replace All button

FIGURE 3-12: Jobs table in Datasheet View

Jobs tab   Find button   Replace button

JobID	CompanyID	JobTitle	JobResponsibilities	StartingSalary
1 Alark Inc		Customer Service Representative	Handles customer service inquiries and problems via telephone, Internet or written correspondence. Calls are typically non-routine and may require deviation from standard screens, scripts, and procedures. Acts as a subject matter expert by providing training.	$40,000
3 Ozark College		Financial Aid Assistant	Assists in the daily operations of the Financial Aid Office providing general assistance and support to the Financial Aid staff. Provides student financial aid information to prospective and current students and families via phone or email. Tracks student financial	$45,000
4 Morris College		Associate Director	Develops and implements an overall long-range plan. Recruits, trains, and manages volunteers and awards. Develops philanthropic relationships with an assigned group of donors, prospective donors, and volunteers. Identifies capacity, interests and inclination.	$65,000
6 Bank of the Midwest		Registered Client Associate	Provides dedicated operational and sales support to multiple Financial with all applications in the Microsoft Office suite.	
7 Bower Pet Hospital		Client Service Coordinator	Drives the flow of clients and pets through the hospital, maximizes the veterinary medical team (in terms of numbers of clients and pets), ens communication with associates and clients, and coordinates the care	
8 Bower Pet Hospital		Practice Manager	Develops associates and fosters an engaging team environment. Ensure patients have a positive experience when they visit the hospital. Optimizes the growth of our businesses.	

longrange is replaced by long-range

TABLE 3-3: Find buttons

Find	🔍	Opens the Find and Replace dialog box to find data
Replace	ᵃᵇ⁄ₐc	Opens the Find and Replace dialog box to find and replace data
Go To	→	Helps you navigate to the first, previous, next, last, or new record
Select	⌖	Helps you select a single record or all records in a datasheet

Filter Data

Filtering a datasheet *temporarily* displays records that match given criteria. **Criteria** are limiting conditions you set. For example, you might want to show only jobs with a starting salary greater than a certain value or those companies in a particular state. Although filters provide a quick and easy way to display a temporary subset of records in the current datasheet, they are not as powerful or flexible as queries. The most important difference is that a query is a saved object within the database, whereas a filter is removed when you close the datasheet. **TABLE 3-4** compares filters and queries. **CASE** ▶ *Lydia Snyder asks several questions about the JobsByIndustry query. You will use filters to answer these questions.*

STEPS

1. **Double-click the** JobsByIndustry query **to open it, click any occurrence of** Energy **in the Industry field, click the** Selection button **in the Sort & Filter group, then click** Equals "Energy"

   Nine records from two companies are selected, as shown in **FIGURE 3-13**. A filter icon appears to the right of the Industry field name. Filtering by the selected field value, called **Filter By Selection**, is a fast and easy way to filter records for an exact match.

2. **Click the** Toggle Filter button **in the Sort & Filter group to toggle off the filter, then click the** Toggle Filter button **again to apply the last filter to the datasheet**

   You can apply a new filter in several ways. One way is to use the list arrow to the right of each field name to filter data. Before applying a new filter, however, you should clear the last filter to make sure you are working with all of the records in the datasheet.

3. **Click the** Advanced button **in the Sort & Filter group, click** Clear All Filters, **click the list arrow to the right of the CompanyName field, click the** Select All check box **to clear all check boxes, click the** Accent Group check box, **then click** OK

   Three records match the criteria of *Accent Group* for the CompanyName field. To filter for multiple criteria or comparative data, you might use the **Filter By Form** feature, which provides maximum flexibility for specifying criteria. Filter buttons and features are summarized in **TABLE 3-5**.

4. **Click the** Advanced button **in the Sort & Filter group, click** Clear All Filters, **click the** Advanced button **again, then click** Filter By Form

   After clearing all filters, the Filtered/Unfiltered button to the right of the navigation buttons at the bottom of the datasheet displays "No Filter" to indicate that all previous filters have been cleared. The Filter by Form window opens.

5. **Scroll to the right, click the** StartingSalary cell, **type** >=50000, **click the** Applicants cell, **then type** <=10 **as shown in FIGURE 3-14**

   If more than one criterion is entered, a record must satisfy the requirements for each criterion to be selected.

6. **Click the** Toggle Filter button **in the Sort & Filter group**

   The datasheet selects 14 records that match both of the filter criteria, as shown in **FIGURE 3-15**. Note that filter icons appear next to the StartingSalary and Applicants field names.

7. **Right-click the** JobsByIndustry tab, **click** Close, **then click** Yes **if prompted**

   Filters are *temporary* views of the data. Filters are *not* saved with a table or query datasheet after you close the datasheet even if you save the datasheet. If you want to save criteria, create a query.

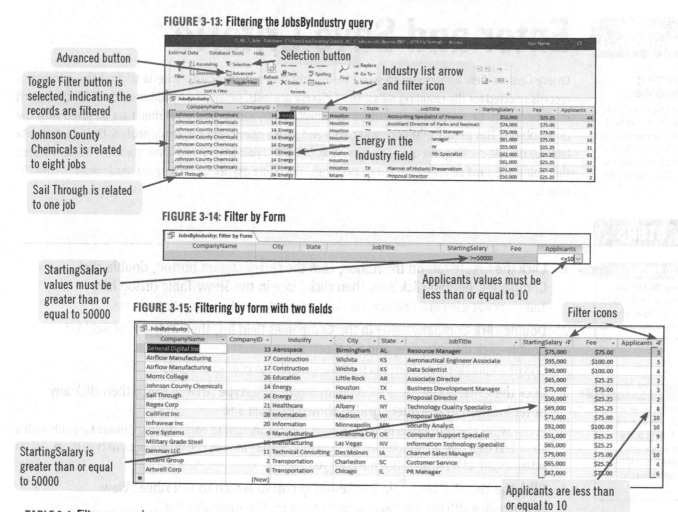

FIGURE 3-13: Filtering the JobsByIndustry query

Advanced button

Toggle Filter button is selected, indicating the records are filtered

Johnson County Chemicals is related to eight jobs

Sail Through is related to one job

Selection button

Industry list arrow and filter icon

Energy in the Industry field

FIGURE 3-14: Filter by Form

StartingSalary values must be greater than or equal to 50000

Applicants values must be less than or equal to 10

FIGURE 3-15: Filtering by form with two fields

Filter icons

StartingSalary is greater than or equal to 50000

Applicants are less than or equal to 10

TABLE 3-4: Filters vs. queries

characteristic	filters	queries
Are saved as an object in the database		•
Can be used to select a subset of records in a datasheet	•	•
Can be used to select a subset of fields in a datasheet		•
Resulting datasheet used to enter and edit data	•	•
Resulting datasheet used to sort, filter, and find records	•	•
Commonly used as the source of data for a form or report		•
Can calculate sums, averages, counts, and other types of summary statistics across records		•
Can be used to create calculated fields		•

TABLE 3-5: Filter buttons

name	button	purpose
Filter	▼	Provides a list of values in the selected field that can be used to customize a filter
Selection	▼	Filters records that equal, do not equal, or are otherwise compared with the current value
Advanced	▦	Provides advanced filter features such as Filter By Form, Save As Query, and Clear All Filters
Toggle Filter	▼	Applies or removes the current filter

Access

Enter and Save Criteria

Learning Outcomes
- Add a criterion to a Short Text field
- Add a criterion to a Number field
- Add a criterion to a Date/Time field

Query Design View allows you to select fields, add sort orders, or add criteria to limit the number of records selected for the resulting datasheet. **Criteria** are tests, or limiting conditions, for which the record must be true to be selected for the query datasheet. Fields, sort orders, and criteria are all saved with the query object. This means that once you create and save a query, you can easily analyze the selected data later by double-clicking the query to open it. **CASE** *Lydia Snyder asks some questions about the data that you suspect will be reviewed on a regular basis. You create queries for these questions in order to save the criteria.*

STEPS

QUICK TIP

Drag the bottom edge of a field list to resize it to display all fields.

1. **Click the Create tab on the ribbon, click the Query Design button, double-click Companies, double-click Jobs, then click Close in the Show Table dialog box**

   This query will select one field from the Companies table and three from the Jobs table.

2. **Double-click CompanyName in the Companies field list, then in the Jobs field list double-click JobTitle, Fee, and FirstPosted**

   Criteria are limiting conditions you set in the query design grid.

QUICK TIP

Query criteria are not case sensitive, but using proper uppercase and lowercase text makes criteria easier to read.

3. **Click the Criteria cell for the CompanyName field, type Artwell Corp, then click any other location in the query grid as shown in FIGURE 3-16**

   Access assists you with **criteria syntax**, rules that specify how to enter criteria. Criteria for fields with a Short Text data type are surrounded by "quotation marks" though you do not need to type them. Access automatically adds the quotation marks for you.

4. **Click the View button 🔲 in the Results group to switch to Datasheet View**

   Eight records match the criterion of Artwell Corp in the CompanyName field.

5. **Click the View button 🔲 to switch to Design View, delete the "Artwell Corp" criterion in the CompanyName field, click the Fee Criteria cell, type 75, then click the View button 🔲**

   Criteria in Number, Currency, and Yes/No fields are not surrounded by any characters. Thirty records are selected where the Fee field equals 75.

6. **Click the View button 🔲, delete the 75 criterion in the Fee field, click the FirstPosted Criteria cell, type 1/4/21, then click in any other location in the query grid as shown in FIGURE 3-17**

   Criteria for fields with a Date/Time data type are surrounded by #pound signs# though you do not need to type them. The pound sign symbol (#) is also known as the number sign, hashtag, and octothorpe.

7. **Click the View button 🔲**

   Seven records are selected where the FirstPosted field equals 1/4/21.

8. **Right-click the Query1 tab, click Save, type FirstPostedJan4, click OK, right-click the FirstPostedJan4 tab, then click Close**

   The query is saved with the new name, FirstPostedJan4, as a new query object in the database. Criteria entered in Query Design View are saved with the query.

FIGURE 3-16: Entering text criteria

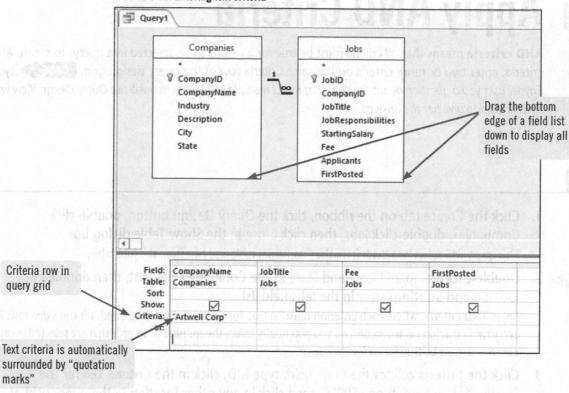

Drag the bottom edge of a field list down to display all fields

Criteria row in query grid

Text criteria is automatically surrounded by "quotation marks"

FIGURE 3-17: Entering date criteria

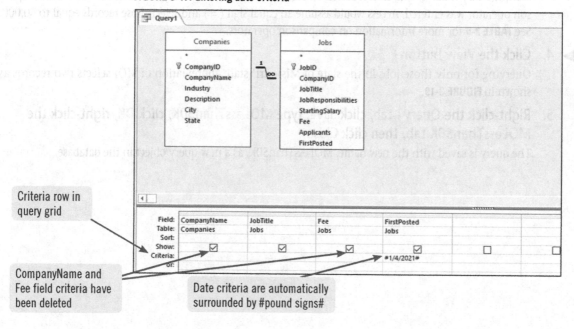

Criteria row in query grid

CompanyName and Fee field criteria have been deleted

Date criteria are automatically surrounded by #pound signs#

Creating Queries

Apply AND Criteria

Learning
Outcomes
• Enter AND criteria
  in a query
• Use comparison
  operators

AND criteria means that *all* criteria must be true for a record to be selected in a query. To create AND criteria, enter two or more criteria on the *same* Criteria row of the query design grid. **CASE** ▸ *Lydia Snyder asks you a question about the data that meets multiple conditions. You will use Query Design View with AND criteria to give her the answer.*

STEPS

1. **Click the Create tab on the ribbon, click the Query Design button, double-click Companies, double-click Jobs, then click Close in the Show Table dialog box**
   This query will select two fields from the Companies table and two from the Jobs table.

2. **Double-click CompanyName and State in the Companies field list, then double-click JobTitle and StartingSalary in the Jobs field list**
   Enter AND criteria, where each criterion must be true for the record to be selected, on the *same* row. For every new criterion on the same row, you potentially *reduce* the number of records that are selected because the record must be true for *each* criterion.

3. **Click the Criteria cell for the State field, type MO, click in the Criteria cell for the StartingSalary field, type <50000, then click in any other location in the query grid as shown in FIGURE 3-18**
   The less than symbol (<) is a **comparison operator** that compares the criterion to the values in the StartingSalary field. In this case, it selects all records with a StartingSalary less than 50,000. If no comparison operator was entered, Access would assume an equal sign (=) and select those records equal to 50,000. See **TABLE 3-6** for more information on comparison operators.

4. **Click the View button 🔳**
   Querying for only those jobs in the state of Missouri (state abbreviation of MO) selects two records as shown in **FIGURE 3-19**.

5. **Right-click the Query1 tab, click Save, type MOLessThan50K, click OK, right-click the MOLessThan50K tab, then click Close**
   The query is saved with the new name, MOLessThan50K, as a new query object in the database.

FIGURE 3-18: Query Design View with AND criteria

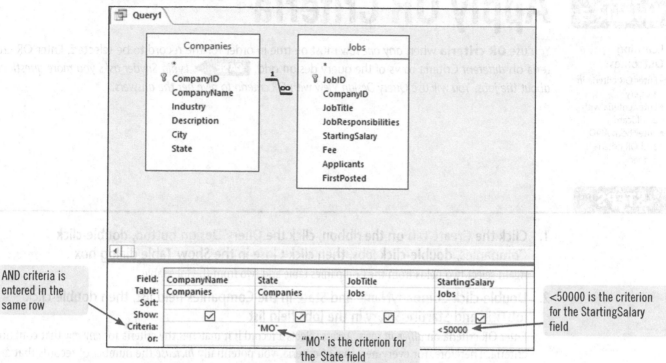

AND criteria is entered in the same row

"MO" is the criterion for the State field

<50000 is the criterion for the StartingSalary field

FIGURE 3-19: Final datasheet of MOLessThan50K query

CompanyName	State	JobTitle	StartingSalaı
Alark Inc	MO	Customer Service Representative	$40,000
Bank of the Midwest	MO	Registered Client Associate	$35,000

Records meet both criteria:
State = "MO"
StartingSalary <50000

TABLE 3-6: Comparison operators

operator	description	expression	meaning
>	Greater than	>500	Numbers greater than 500
>=	Greater than or equal to	>=500	Numbers greater than or equal to 500
<	Less than	<"Elder"	Names from A to Elder, but not Elder
<=	Less than or equal to	<="Langguth"	Names from A through Langguth, inclusive
<>	Not equal to	<>"Fontanelle"	Any name except for Fontanelle
=	Equal to	="Eagan" =500	Equal to Eagan Equal to 500. Note that the equal sign is assumed when no other comparison operator is used.

Searching for blank fields

Is Null and Is Not Null are two other types of common criteria. The **Is Null** criterion finds all records where no entry has been made in the field. **Is Not Null** finds all records where there is any entry in the field, even if the entry is 0. Primary key fields cannot have a null entry.

Access

Apply OR Criteria

Learning
Outcomes
• Enter OR criteria in
  a query
• Enter criteria with
  a wildcard
• Enter both AND
  and OR criteria in
  a query

You use **OR criteria** when *any one row* must be true in order for the record to be selected. Enter OR criteria on *different* Criteria rows of the query design grid. **CASE** ▶ *Lydia Snyder asks you more questions about the jobs. You will use Query Design View with OR criteria to give her the answers.*

STEPS

1. **Click the Create tab on the ribbon, click the Query Design button, double-click Companies, double-click Jobs, then click Close in the Show Table dialog box**

   Again select two fields from the Companies table and two from the Jobs table.

2. **Double-click CompanyName and State in the Companies field list, then double-click JobTitle and StartingSalary in the Jobs field list**

   Enter OR criteria on *different* rows. Access selects a record if it matches the criteria for *any row* that contains criteria. Therefore, for every new row of criteria, you potentially *increase* the number of records that are selected.

QUICK TIP
The query grid
provides eight
criteria rows by
default, but you can
add more by clicking
the Insert Rows
button in the Query
Setup group on the
Design tab.

3. **Click the Criteria cell for the State field, type MO, click the or Criteria cell for the State field, type TX, then click any other location in the query grid as shown in FIGURE 3-20**

   Every Criteria row below the first row is considered an "or" row. Access selects records that match the criterion in *any* row that contains criteria.

4. **Click the View button 🔲**

   Fourteen records meet the State criteria of MO or TX. In addition, you want to select only those records with the word "Manager" in the JobTitle field. You use asterisk characters (*) to help select records that have the word "Manager" in any position in the JobTitle field value.

5. **Click the View button 🔍, click the Criteria cell for the JobTitle field, type *Manager*, then click 🔲**

   Twelve records meet the State criteria of MO with the word "Manager" in the JobTitle field or the State criteria of TX. But *all* TX records are still selected.

6. **Click 🔍, click the second Criteria cell for the JobTitle field, type *Manager*, then click any other location in the query grid as shown in FIGURE 3-21**

   Access adds the **Like** keyword to criteria that contain the asterisk (*) wildcard character.

7. **Click 🔲 to switch to Datasheet View**

   Three records meet the State criteria of MO or the State criteria of TX with the word "Manager" in the JobTitle field, as shown in **FIGURE 3-22**.

8. **Right-click the Query1 tab, click Save, type MOTXManager, click OK, right-click the MOTXManager tab, then click Close**

   You can also use **AND OR** SQL keywords in your criteria. But a simpler approach is to remember these rules: Criteria on a *single row must all be true* for a record to be selected. Criteria on *different rows constitute separate tests* that the record may satisfy in order to be selected.

FIGURE 3-20: Query Design View with OR criteria

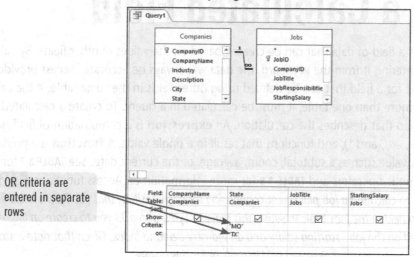

OR criteria are entered in separate rows

FIGURE 3-21: Query Design View with AND and OR criteria

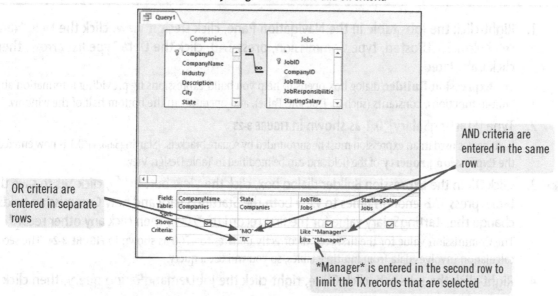

OR criteria are entered in separate rows

AND criteria are entered in the same row

Manager is entered in the second row to limit the TX records that are selected

FIGURE 3-22: Final datasheet of MOTXManager query

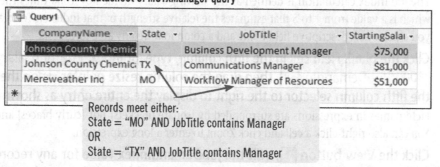

CompanyName	State	JobTitle	StartingSalaı
Johnson County Chemic	TX	Business Development Manager	$75,000
Johnson County Chemic	TX	Communications Manager	$81,000
Mereweather Inc	MO	Workflow Manager of Resources	$51,000
*			

Records meet either:
State = "MO" AND JobTitle contains Manager
OR
State = "TX" AND JobTitle contains Manager

Using wildcard characters

To search for a pattern, you can use a wildcard character to represent any character in the condition entry. Use a question mark (?) to search for any single character and an asterisk (*) to search for any number of characters. Access uses the **Like** keyword when your criterion contains wildcard characters. For example, the criterion Like "12/*/21" finds all dates in December of 2021, and the criterion Like "F*" finds all values that start with the letter F.

Create a Calculated Field

A **calculated field** is a field of data that can be created based on the values of other fields. By calculating the data versus entering it from the keyboard, the data will always be accurate. Access provides the **Calculated** data type for a field that can be defined using other fields in the *same* table. If the calculation uses fields from more than one table, it must be calculated in a query. To create a calculated field, you enter an expression that describes the calculation. An **expression** is a combination of field names, **operators** (such as +, –, /, and *), and functions that result in a single value. A **function** is a predefined formula that returns a value such as a subtotal, count, average, or the current date. See **TABLE 3-7** for more information on arithmetic operators and **TABLE 3-8** for more information on Access functions. **CASE** *Lydia Snyder asks you to calculate a job placement commission for each position that JCL Talent helps fill. You will create a Calculated field in the Jobs table to satisfy this request. Lydia also asks you to create an internal job rating calculation based on the job's starting salary and an industry demand index. Given that data is stored in two different tables, you will create a calculated field in a query for this answer.*

STEPS

1. **Right-click the** Jobs table **in the Navigation Pane, click** Design View, **click the** Field Name cell below FirstPosted, **type** Commission, **press** TAB, **click the** Data Type list arrow, **then click** Calculated

   The **Expression Builder** dialog box opens to help you build expressions by providing information about built-in functions, constants (such as True and False), and operators in the bottom half of the window.

2. **Type** [StartingSalary]*0.1 **as shown in FIGURE 3-23**

   Field names used in an expression must be surrounded by square brackets. [StartingSalary]*0.1 is now entered in the **Expression property** of the field and can be modified in Table Design View.

3. **Click** OK **in the Expression Builder dialog box, click the** View button ▦, **click** Yes **to save the table, press** TAB **enough times to view both the StartingSalary and new Commission fields, change the StartingSalary value for the first record to** 47000, **then click any other record**

   The Commission value for the first record correctly updates to 4700 as shown in **FIGURE 3-24**. The second calculation involves data from multiple tables, so you will use a query.

4. **Right-click the** Jobs tab, **click** Close, **right-click the** JobDemandRating query, **then click** Design View

   The Job Index calculation is defined as the starting salary divided by 1000 times the job demand index, which is a value from 1 to 5 that estimates the relative strength of that industry. To create a calculated field, you enter a new descriptive field name and a colon followed by an expression.

5. **Click the** blank Field cell **in the fifth column, type** JobIndex: [StartingSalary] /1000*[JobDemandIndex], **then drag the column resize pointer ↔ on the right edge of the fifth column selector to the right to display the entire entry as shown in FIGURE 3-25**

   Field names in expressions are surrounded by [square brackets] not {curly braces} and not (parentheses). You can also right-click a cell and click Zoom to enter a long expression.

6. **Click the** View button ▦, **edit the** JobDemandIndex **value for any record with the Industry value of Personnel Services from 3 to** 4, **then click any other record**

   The JobIndex value for all jobs within the industry of Personnel Services automatically recalculated when you changed the JobDemandIndex value used in the expression for that calculated field.

7. **Click the** Save button ▤ **on the Quick Access toolbar, right-click the** JobDemandRating tab, **then click** Close

   Some database experts encourage you to create all calculations using queries because the Calculated field data type doesn't convert well to other relational database systems.

FIGURE 3-23: Creating a Calculated field in Table Design View

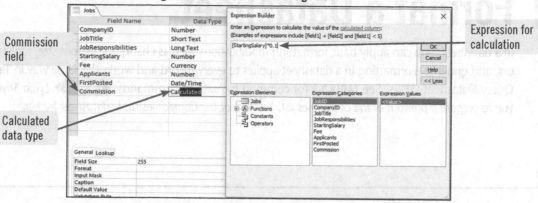

Commission field

Calculated data type

Expression for calculation

FIGURE 3-24: Calculated field in Table Datasheet View

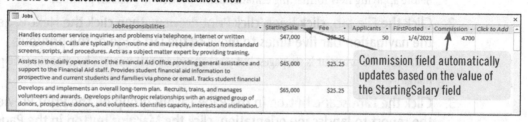

Commission field automatically updates based on the value of the StartingSalary field

FIGURE 3-25: Creating a calculated field in Query Design View

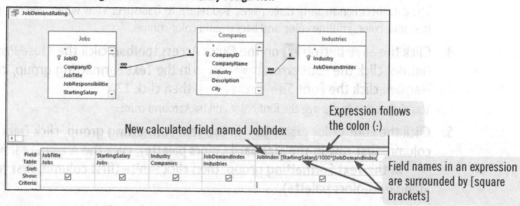

New calculated field named JobIndex

Expression follows the colon (:)

Field names in an expression are surrounded by [square brackets]

TABLE 3-7: Arithmetic operators	
operator	description
+	Addition
−	Subtraction
*	Multiplication
/	Division
^	Exponentiation

TABLE 3-8: Common functions	
function	sample expression and description
DATE	DATE()-[BirthDate] Calculates the number of days between today and the date in the BirthDate field; Access expressions are not case sensitive, so DATE()-[BirthDate] is equivalent to date()-[birthdate] and DATE()-[BIRTHDATE]; therefore, use capitalization in expressions in any way that makes the expression easier to read
PMT	PMT([Rate],[Term],[Loan]) Calculates the monthly payment on a loan where the Rate field contains the monthly interest rate, the Term field contains the number of monthly payments, and the Loan field contains the total amount financed
LEFT	LEFT([LastName],2) Returns the first two characters of the entry in the LastName field
RIGHT	RIGHT([PartNo],3) Returns the last three characters of the entry in the PartNo field
LEN	LEN([Description]) Returns the number of characters in the Description field

Format a Datasheet

Learning
Outcomes
• Change page
orientation
• Change margins
• Format a
datasheet

In a datasheet, you can apply basic formatting modifications such as changing the font size, font face, colors, and gridlines. Formatting in a datasheet applies to every record and works the same way in Table and Query Datasheet Views. See **TABLE 3-9** for common formatting commands. **CASE** *Lydia Snyder asks you to prepare a printout of the companies list. You format the Companies table datasheet for her.*

STEPS

1. **Double-click the** Companies table **to open it in Datasheet View**
   Before applying new formatting enhancements, preview the default printout.

2. **Click the** File tab, **click** Print, **click** Print Preview, **then click the** Next Page button ▶ **in the navigation bar five times to move to the last page of the printout**
   Currently, the printout is six pages, but you can reduce that number by changing the page orientation and margin.

3. **Click the** Landscape button **in the Page Layout group on the Print Preview tab to switch the report to landscape orientation, click the** Margins button **in the Page Size group, click** Narrow, **then click the** Previous Page button ◀ **twice to display the first page**
   The datasheet is now only three pages. You return to Datasheet View where you can make font face, font size, font color, gridline color, and background color choices.

4. **Click the** Save button 🖫 **on the Quick Access toolbar, click the** Close Print Preview **button, click the** Font arrow Calibri (Body) ▾ **in the Text Formatting group, click** Arial Narrow, **click the** Font Size arrow 11 ▾ , **then click** 12
   You also decide to change the font color and background color.

5. **Click the** Font Color arrow 🄰 ▾ **in the Text Formatting group, click** Dark Blue **(fourth column, first row in the Standard Colors palette), click the** Alternate Row Color arrow 🎟 ▾ **in the Text Formatting group, then click** White **(first column, first row in the Standard Colors palette)**

6. **Click the** File tab, **click** Print, **click** Print Preview, **then click the** preview **to zoom in and out**
   Your Companies datasheet should look like **FIGURE 3-26**. The preview is three pages, and in landscape orientation, it is easier to read.

7. **sam↑ Right-click the** Companies tab, **click** Close, **click** Yes **when prompted to save changes, then click the** Close button ✕ **on the title bar to close the database and Access 2019**

FIGURE 3-26: Formatted Companies datasheet

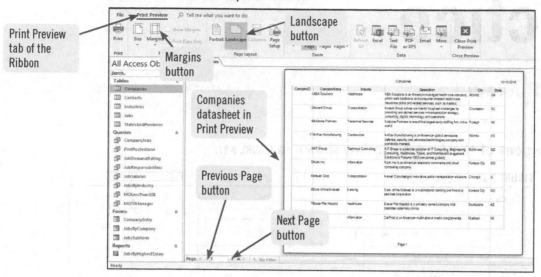

TABLE 3-9: Useful formatting commands

button	button name	description
Calibri (Body) ▾	Font	Changes the font face of the data
11 ▾	Font Size	Changes the font size of the data
B	Bold	Toggles bold on or off
I	Italic	Toggles italic on or off
U	Underline	Toggles underline on or off
A	Font Color	Changes the font color of the data
(icon)	Background Color	Changes the background color
(icon)	Align Left	Left-aligns the data
(icon)	Center	Centers the data
(icon)	Align Right	Right-aligns the data
(icon)	Alternate Row Color	Changes the background color of alternate records
(icon)	Gridlines	Changes the gridlines

Practice

Concepts Review

Label each element of the Access window shown in FIGURE 3-27.

FIGURE 3-27

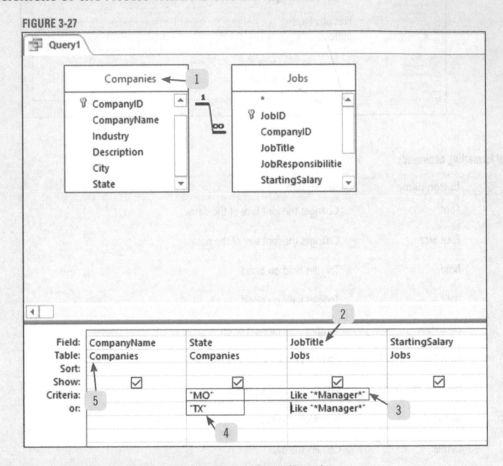

Match each term with the statement that best describes it.

6. **Query grid**   a. A fast and easy way to filter the records for an exact match

7. **Field selector**   b. Limiting conditions used to restrict the number of records that are selected in a query

8. **Filter**   c. The thin gray bar above each field in the query grid

9. **Filter By Selection** d. Creates a temporary subset of records

10. **Field lists**   e. Small windows that display field names

11. **Sorting**   f. Rules that determine how criteria are entered

12. **Join line**   g. Used to search for a pattern of characters

13. **Criteria**   h. The lower pane in Query Design View

14. **Syntax**   i. Identifies which fields are used to establish a relationship between two tables

15. **Wildcard**   j. Putting records in ascending or descending order based on the values of a field

Select the best answer from the list of choices.

16. **AND criteria:**
    a. Determine sort orders.
    b. Help set link lines between tables in a query.
    c. Must all be true for the record to be selected.
    d. Determine fields selected for a query.

17. **SQL stands for which of the following?**
    a. Simple Query Listing
    b. Structured Query Language
    c. Standard Query Language
    d. Special Query Listing

18. **Which of the following is *not* true about a calculated field?**
    a. You can create some calculated fields in a table.
    b. You can create all calculated fields in a query.
    c. Some database experts encourage all calculated fields be created in a query.
    d. Once the expression for a calculated field is created, it cannot be changed.

19. **Which of the following describes OR criteria?**
    a. Use two or more rows of the query grid to select only those records that meet given criteria.
    b. Select a subset of fields and/or records to view as a datasheet from one or more tables.
    c. Reorganize the records in either ascending or descending order based on the contents of one or more fields.
    d. Use multiple fields in the query design grid.

20. **Which of the following is *not* true about a query?**
    a. A query can select fields from one or more tables in a relational database.
    b. A query is the same thing as a filter.
    c. A query can be used to enter and edit data.
    d. An existing query can be modified in Query Design View.

Skills Review

1. **Work in Query Datasheet View.**
   a. Open the IL_AC_3-2.accdb database from the location where you store your Data Files and save it as **IL_AC_3_SupportDesk**. Click Enable Content if a yellow Security Warning message appears.
   b. Open the CaseDetails query in Datasheet View and change Cabrera to **Douglas** in the LastName field of either the first or second record.
   c. Delete the third record (EmployeeID 6, Tony Roth).
   d. Hide the Dependents field.
   e. Freeze the first three fields: EmployeeID, FirstName, and LastName in their current positions in the datasheet. (*Hint*: Select all three fields by dragging through their field names before selecting the Freeze Fields option.)
   f. Save and close the CaseDetails query.

2. **Work in Query Design View.**
   a. Create a new query in Query Design View. Add the Cases and Calls tables.
   b. Select the CaseTitle and Category fields from the Cases table. Select the CallDateTime and CallNotes from the Calls table.
   c. Save the query with the name **CallListing**, then view it in Datasheet View to observe that one case may have many calls over a period of several dates in the CallDateTime field.

Skills Review (continued)

3. Work in SQL View.

a. Open the CallListing query in SQL View.

b. Add the CallMinutes field to the query after the CallNotes field.

c. Save the query then view it in Datasheet View to make sure your SQL statement was entered correctly. Save and close the CallListing query.

4. Sort data.

a. Open the EmployeeCalls query in Datasheet View, sort the records in ascending order by the LastName field, then save and close the query.

b. Open the EmployeesByDepartment query in Design View, then add an ascending sort order to the Department, LastName, and FirstName fields.

c. Save the EmployeesByDepartment query, then view it in Datasheet View.

d. Be prepared to discuss this question in class on in a discussion thread: Were all three sort fields used to determine the order of the records? If so, where?

e. Close the EmployeesByDepartment query.

5. Find and replace data.

a. In Datasheet View of the Cases table, click any value in the Category field, then search for all occurrences of "Office" and replace it with **Microsoft Office** using the Whole Field match.

b. Click the Undo button on the Quick Access toolbar and note that you can undo your last replacement, but not all replacements.

c. Edit the Category entry in the last record (CaseID 23) to be **Microsoft Office** versus Office.

d. Save and close the Cases table datasheet.

6. Filter data.

a. Open the CaseDetails query and filter for all records where the Department is **Accounting** and the CallMinutes is **greater than or equal to 30**. Your datasheet should show five records that meet this criteria.

b. There are several ways to apply a filter, including the filter buttons in the Sort & Filter group of the ribbon, the Filter by Form feature, and the options listed in the sort and filter menu when you click the list arrow to the right of the field name in the datasheet. In class or in a discussion group, be prepared to explain which technique you chose to apply the filter.

c. Save and close the CaseDetails query. Reopen it to see that all records are shown. In class or in a discussion group be prepared to explain why the filter criteria was not reapplied to the query.

7. Enter and save criteria.

a. Create a query in Query Design View with the Cases and Employees tables.

b. Add the following fields, in this order: CaseID and Category from the Cases table, LastName and FirstName from the Employees table.

c. Add criteria to select only those records with **Internet** in the Category field.

d. Save the query with the name **InternetCases**, display it in Datasheet View to make sure you have selected the correct records, and then close the InternetCases query.

8. Apply AND criteria.

a. Right-click the InternetCases query, copy it, and then paste it as **InternetAccountingCases**.

b. Add the Department field to the InternetAccountingCases query, then add criteria to select all of the records **Internet** in the Category field and **Accounting** in the Department field.

c. Display the results in Datasheet View as shown in FIGURE 3-28, then save and close the query.

FIGURE 3-28

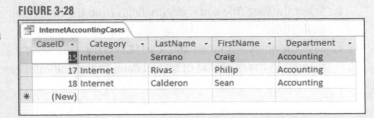

CaseID	Category	LastName	FirstName	Department
15	Internet	Serrano	Craig	Accounting
17	Internet	Rivas	Philip	Accounting
18	Internet	Calderon	Sean	Accounting
(New)				

Skills Review (continued)

9. Apply OR criteria.

   a. Copy the InternetAccountingCases, then paste it as **InternetAccountingProductionCases**.

   b. Open the InternetAccountingProductionCases query in Design View, then add criteria to select the records in either the Departments of **Accounting** or **Production** with a Category value of **Internet**.

   c. Display the results in Datasheet View as shown in **FIGURE 3-29**, then save and close the query.

FIGURE 3-29

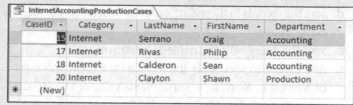

CaseID	Category	LastName	FirstName	Department
15 Internet	Internet	Serrano	Craig	Accounting
17 Internet		Rivas	Philip	Accounting
18 Internet		Calderon	Sean	Accounting
20 Internet		Clayton	Shawn	Production
* (New)				

10. Create Calculated fields.

   a. Open the Employees table in Design View then add field named **Monthly** with a Currency format and Calculated data type.

   b. Use the expression **[Salary]/12** to calculate the values for the new Monthly field.

   c. Save the Employees table and display it in Datasheet View.

   d. Change the salary for Mindi Perez from $70,000 to **80000** then click anywhere else in the datasheet to observe the automatic update to the Monthly field.

   e. Save and close the Employees table.

   f. Create a new query in Query Design View with the Employees, Cases, and Calls tables.

   g. Add the LastName field from the Employees table, the CaseTitle field from the Cases table, and the CallMinutes field from the Calls table.

   h. Add a calculated field to the fourth column of the query grid with the following field name and expression: **TotalTime: [CallMinutes]+10** which estimates the total time required per call for assuming a five-minute gap before and after each call.

   i. Save the query with the name **TotalCallMinutes** and display the datasheet. Change the CallMinutes value for the first "Google doesn't look right" record from 40 minutes to 45 minutes, then click anywhere else in the datasheet. The TotalTime value should automatically update to 55.

   j. Save and close the TotalCallMinutes datasheet.

   k. In class or in a discussion group, be prepared to discuss the TotalTime calculated field in the TotalCallMinutes query. What are the advantages and disadvantages of creating this field in a query versus in the Calls table?

11. Format a datasheet.

   a. In the Cases table datasheet, apply the Georgia font and a **12**-point font size.

   b. Change the alternate row color to Light Blue 1 (fifth column, second row in the Standard Colors palette), and the gridlines to None.

   c. Display the Cases datasheet in Print Preview, then switch the orientation to Landscape, and the margins to Narrow. The datasheet should now fit on a single sheet of paper.

   d. Save the Cases datasheet, and then close it.

   e. Close Access 2019.

Independent Challenge 1

As the manager of Riverwalk, a multi-specialty health clinic, you have created a database to manage the schedules that connect each healthcare provider with the nurses that provider needs to efficiently handle patient visits. In this exercise, you will create a query to answer a special scheduling question at the clinic.

   a. Start Access. Open the IL_AC_3-3.accdb database from the location where you store your Data Files and save it as **IL_AC_3_Riverwalk**. Click Enable Content if a yellow Security Warning message appears.

   b. Create a new query in Query Design View with the Locations, ScheduleItems, ScheduleDate, and Nurses tables.

Independent Challenge 1 (continued)

c. Add the following fields to the query in this order: LocationName from the Locations table, ScheduleDate from the ScheduleDate table, and NurseLName and NurseFName from the Nurses table.

d. Sort the records in ascending order by ScheduleDate, then NurseLName.

e. Save the query with the name **NorthSouth**.

f. Add criteria to select only the records for a LocationName of **North** or **South**, a NurseLName value of **Washington** or **Fredrick**, and a ScheduleDate **on or after 12/1/2021** as shown in **FIGURE 3-30**.

g. Close the NorthSouth query, then close the database and exit Access 2019.

FIGURE 3-30

LocationNan ⌄	ScheduleDat ⌄	NurseLNam⌄	NurseFNam⌄
North	12/6/2021	Fredrick	Sam
South	12/6/2021	Washington	Dana
North	12/9/2021	Fredrick	Sam
South	12/9/2021	Washington	Dana
North	12/10/2021	Fredrick	Sam
South	12/10/2021	Washington	Dana
North	12/11/2021	Fredrick	Sam
North	12/11/2021	Washington	Dana
North	12/12/2021	Fredrick	Sam
South	12/12/2021	Washington	Dana
North	12/13/2021	Fredrick	Sam
South	12/13/2021	Washington	Dana
North	12/16/2021	Fredrick	Sam
South	12/16/2021	Washington	Dana

Independent Challenge 2

You are working for a city to coordinate a series of community-wide preparedness activities. You have created a database to track the activities and volunteers who are attending the activities. In this exercise you will create a query to answer a special activities question at the city.

a. Start Access. Open the IL_AC_3-4.accdb database from the location where you store your Data Files and save it as **IL_AC_3_Volunteers**. Click Enable Content if a yellow Security Warning message appears.

b. Create a new query in Query Design View with the Volunteers, Attendance, and Activities tables.

c. Add the following fields to the query in this order: FirstName and LastName from the Volunteers table, Completed field from the Attendance table, ActivityName and ActivityHours from the Activities table.

d. Sort the records in ascending order on LastName.

e. Add criteria to select only those records with **CPR** anywhere in the ActivityName field and an ActivityHours value **greater than or equal to 7**.

f. Add a calculated field with the following name and expression to estimate the value of the volunteer's time within that activity: **Labor: [ActivityHours]*15**

g. Save the query with the name **LaborCalculation**, display it in Datasheet View, then change the record for William Wilberforce to have your first and last names, as shown in **FIGURE 3-31**.

h. Close the database and exit Access 2019.

FIGURE 3-31

FirstNa ⌄	LastNar ⌄	Completed ⌄	ActivityName ⌄	ActivityHour ⌄	Labor ⌄
Rhea	Alman	☑	First Aid and CPR	8	120
Young	Bogard	☑	First Aid and CPR	8	120
Forrest	Browning	☑	First Aid and CPR	8	120
Patch	Bullock	☑	First Aid and CPR	8	120
Angela	Cabriella	☑	First Aid and CPR	8	120
Herman	Cain	☑	First Aid and CPR	8	120
Gina	Daniels	☑	First Aid and CPR	8	120
Quentin	Garden	☑	First Aid and CPR	8	120
Loraine	Goode	☑	First Aid and CPR	8	120
Loraine	Goode	☑	CPR and Automated External Defibrillator AED	7	105
Karla	Larson	☑	First Aid and CPR	8	120
Karla	Larson	☑	CPR and Automated External Defibrillator AED	7	105
Aaron	Love	☑	CPR and Automated External Defibrillator AED	7	105
Aaron	Love	☑	First Aid and CPR	8	120
Katrina	Margolis	☑	CPR and Automated External Defibrillator AED	7	105
Katrina	Margolis	☑	First Aid and CPR	8	120
Jaye	Mati	☑	First Aid and CPR	8	120
Jaye	Mati	☑	CPR and Automated External Defibrillator AED	7	105
Jon	Maxim	☑	First Aid and CPR	8	120
Jon	Maxim	☑	CPR and Automated External Defibrillator AED	7	105
Sindy	Russo	☑	First Aid and CPR	8	120
StudentFi	StudentLa	☑	First Aid and CPR	8	120

Record: I◄ ◄ 1 of 22 ► ►I ►* ⌐ No Filter Search

Visual Workshop

Open the IL_AC_3-5.accdb database from the location where you store your Data Files and save it as **IL_AC_3_CollegeCourses**, then enable content if prompted. Create a query in Query Design View based on the Classes, Professors, Sections, Enrollments, and Students tables with the fields shown in **FIGURE 3-32**. Add criteria to select only those records where Grade field value is **A** or **B** and the Credits field value equals **4**. Display the query in Datasheet View, widen the columns to display all of the data, and save it with the name **4CreditsAB**. Close the 4CreditsAB query then exit Access 2019.

FIGURE 3-32

StudentLast	StudentFirst	Description	Credits	Grade	ProfLastName
Mitchell	Irma	Programming Fundamentals	4	B	Zimmerman
Davis	Timothy	Programming Fundamentals	4	A	Zimmerman
Bennet	Domenico	Programming Fundamentals	4	A	Zimmerman
Snow	Frederick	Programming Fundamentals	4	A	Zimmerman
Gregory	Roger	Programming Fundamentals	4	A	Zimmerman
Simmons	Michael	Programming Fundamentals	4	B	Zimmerman
Owen	Leo	Programming Fundamentals	4	B	Zimmerman
Amstell	Mark	Database Programming	4	B	Quinn
Willis	Carl	Database Programming	4	A	Douglas
Cooper	Yehudah	Mobile Application Development	4	B	Quinn
Gallow	Taiichi	Mobile Application Development	4	B	Quinn
Noble	Hector	Database Management	4	B	Zimmerman
Noble	Hector	Engineering Graphics	4	B	Rosenbaum
Cooper	Yehudah	Engineering Graphics	4	B	Rosenbaum
Bennet	Domenico	Engineering Graphics	4	A	Rosenbaum
Dow	Johann	Engineering Graphics	4	A	Rosenbaum
Gregory	Roger	Engineering Graphics	4	A	Rosenbaum
Gallow	Taiichi	Engineering Graphics	4	B	Rosenbaum
Owen	Leo	Engineering Graphics	4	B	Rosenbaum

Record: 1 of 19   No Filter   Search

Working with Forms and Reports

CASE Lydia Snyder, vice president of operations at JCL Talent, asks you to create forms to make job and company information easier to access, enter, and update. She also wants you to create some reports that will provide a professional presentation and analysis of selected data.

Module Objectives

After completing this module, you will be able to:

- Work in Form View
- Work in Form Layout View
- Work in Form Design View
- Work in Report Layout View
- Work in Report Design View
- Add conditional formatting
- Use the Format Painter and themes

Files You Will Need

IL_AC_4-1.accdb

IL_AC_4-2.accdb

IL_AC_4-3.accdb

IL_AC_4-4.accdb

IL_AC_4-5.accdb

Work in Form View

Learning
Outcomes
• Navigate records
  in a form
• Enter records in
  a form

A form allows you to arrange the fields of a record in any layout so a database **user** can quickly and easily find, enter, edit, and analyze data. You can use several different tools to create forms, as shown in TABLE 4-1. Each form has three views, and each view has a primary purpose, as described in TABLE 4-2, although you can complete some tasks in multiple views. **Form View** gives a user an easy-to-use data entry and navigation screen. **CASE** *Lydia Snyder asks you to find and enter company data in the database. You will use a form to complete the work.*

STEPS

1. **saⁿf↓ Start Access, open the IL_AC_4-1.accdb database from the location where you store your Data Files, save it as IL_AC_4_Jobs, enable content if prompted, then double-click the CompanyEntry form to open it in Form View**

   The CompanyEntry form organizes all the fields of the Companies table to clearly display the data from one record at a time. Forms contain **controls** such as labels to describe information, text boxes and combo boxes to help you enter information, and command buttons to help you work with the form. Forms also provide **navigation buttons** in the lower-left corner, which help you navigate through the data.

2. **Click the Next record button ▶ in the navigation bar three times to navigate to the fourth record**

   The **Current Record box** identifies what record you are currently viewing as well as the total number of records. The navigation buttons also provide a way to move to the first or last record in the form very quickly.

3. **Click the Last record button ▶| in the navigation bar**

   To move to a prior record, you use the Previous record and First record buttons.

4. **Click the Previous record button ◀ in the navigation bar, then click the First record button |◀ to return to the first record**

   In addition, you can type any number in the Current Record box to quickly move to that record.

5. **Click the Current Record box, type 17, press ENTER, then change the Industry field value to Aerospace**

   Changes are saved as you move from record to record and new records are always entered at the end.

6. **Click the New (blank) record button ▶* , then enter a new company record, as shown in FIGURE 4-1 and described below**

Company ID:	TAB (AutoNumber field that automatically increments)
Company Name:	Heritage Computing Inc
Industry:	Information
Description:	Database modeling, management, warehousing and analytics.
City:	Springfield
State:	MO

7. **Right-click the CompanyEntry tab, then click Close**

   When you close a form, Access automatically saves data in the current record.

FIGURE 4-1: Adding a new record to the CompanyEntry form in Form View

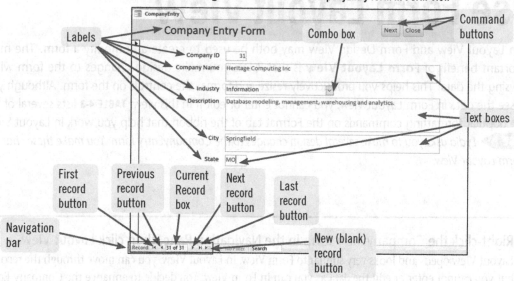

TABLE 4-1: Form creation tools

tool	icon	creates a form
Form		with one click based on the selected table or query
Form Design		from scratch in Form Design View
Blank Form		from scratch in Form Layout View
Form Wizard		by answering a series of questions provided by the Form Wizard dialog boxes
Navigation		to navigate or move between different areas of the database
More Forms		for Multiple Items, Datasheet, Split Form, or Modal Dialog arrangements
Split Form		with two panes, the upper showing one record at a time and the lower displaying a datasheet of many records

TABLE 4-2: Form views

view	primary purpose
Form	To find, sort, enter, and edit data
Layout	To modify the size, position, or formatting of controls; shows data as you modify the form, making it the tool of choice when you want to change the appearance and usability of the form while viewing data
Design	To modify the Form Header, Detail, and Footer section, to work with form rulers and gridlines, or to access the complete range of controls and form properties; Design View does not display data

Access

Use Form Layout View

Learning
Outcomes
• Format controls in
Form Layout View
• Edit labels in Form
Layout View

Form Layout View and Form Design View may both be used to create and modify a form. The most important benefit of **Form Layout View** is that it lets you make design changes to the form while browsing the data. This helps you productively resize and format the controls on the form. Although you can see the data in Form Layout View, you cannot enter or edit it in this view. **TABLE 4-3** lists several of the most popular formatting commands on the Format tab of the ribbon that help you work in Layout View.
CASE ➤ *Lydia asks you to make several design changes to the CompanyEntry form. You make these changes in Form Layout View.*

STEPS

1. **Right-click the** CompanyEntry form **in the Navigation Pane, then click** Layout View
   Layout View opens and looks very similar to Form View. In Layout View, you can move through the records, but you cannot enter or edit the data as you can in Form View. You decide to enhance the Company Entry Form label at the top of the form.

   > **QUICK TIP**
   > You can also apply formatting commands in Form Design View.

2. **Click the** Company Entry Form label **in the Form Header section, click the** Format tab **on the ribbon, click the** Bold button B **, click the** Font Color list arrow ▲ ⁃ **, click** Dark Blue **(fourth column, first row of the Standard Colors palette), click the** Font Size arrow 11 ⁃ **, then click** 24
   You often use Layout View to make minor design changes, such as editing labels and changing formatting characteristics.

3. **Click the** Industry label **to select it, click the** Industry label **again to position the insertion point within the label, edit the text to be** Primary Industry **, then press** ENTER
   Your users do not need the Next button because they use the buttons in the navigation bar, so you can delete the Next command button.

4. **Click the** Next command button, **then press** DELETE
   You change the style, shape, and outline of the Close button.

   > **QUICK TIP**
   > You can undo multiple formatting actions by clicking the Undo button ↺ on the Quick Access toolbar.

5. **Click the** Close command button, **click the** Quick Styles button, **click the** Colored Fill – Blue, Accent 1 option **(second column, second row), click the** Change Shape button, **click the** Oval shape, **click the** Shape Outline button, **then click** Transparent **near the bottom of the menu**
   You decide to make one other small change. You feel that the data in the Company ID text box would be easier to read if it were centered.

   > **TROUBLE**
   > Be sure to modify the text box instead of the Company ID label on the left.

6. **Click** 1 **in the box to the right of the Company ID label, then click the** Center button ≣
   Your CompanyEntry form should look like **FIGURE 4-2**. The form label is more pronounced, the Close button is styled, and the Company ID data is easier to read.

FIGURE 4-2: Modifying controls in Form Layout View

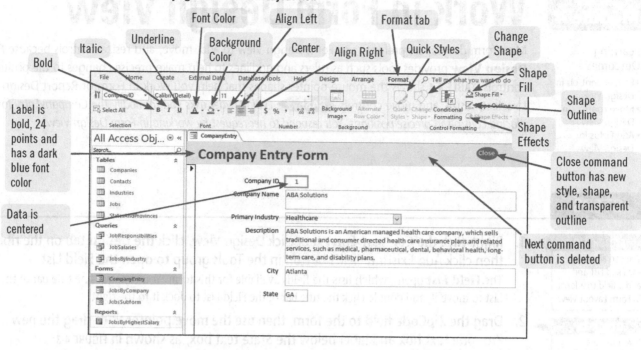

TABLE 4-3: Useful formatting commands

button	button name	description
B	Bold	Toggles bold on or off for the selected control(s)
I	Italic	Toggles italic on or off for the selected control(s)
U	Underline	Toggles underline on or off for the selected control(s)
A	Font Color	Changes the text color of the selected control(s)
⬚	Background Color or Shape Fill	Changes the background color of the selected control(s)
≡	Align Left	Left-aligns the selected control(s) within its own border
≡	Center	Centers the selected control(s) within its own border
≡	Align Right	Right-aligns the selected control(s) within its own border
⊞	Alternate Row Color	Changes the background color of alternate records in the selected section
✎	Shape Outline	Changes the border color, thickness, or style of the selected control(s)
◻	Shape Effects	Changes the special visual effect of the selected control(s)

Work in Form Design View

**Learning
Outcomes**
• Format controls in
  Design View
• Move controls in
  Design View
• Add Fields in
  Design View

Most form developers prefer to use Form Design View to add, move, and resize controls because **Form Design View** provides tools such as rulers and gridlines to help make precise changes to the position of controls. TABLE 4-4 shows the mouse pointer shapes that help you work in Form or Report Design View to select, resize, and move controls. **CASE** *Lydia Snyder asks you to modify the CompanyEntry form by placing controls in precise positions. You respond to her request by working in Form Design View.*

STEPS

1. **Right-click the** CompanyEntry **tab, click** Design View, **click the** Design tab **on the ribbon, then click** Add Existing Fields button **in the Tools group to open the Field List**

   The **Field List** opens, which lists the fields available for this form. You can drag the title bar of the Field List to move it, and double-click the title bar of the Field List to dock it to the right.

2. **Drag the** ZipCode field **to the form, then use the move pointer** ⊹ **to drag the new** ZipCode **text box and label below the State text box, as shown in** FIGURE 4-3

   When you add the ZipCode field to the form, two controls are added: a label and a text box. The **label** on the left describes the data. By default, the label displays the field name, though you can modify it as desired. The **text box** on the right displays the data from the field. It *must* contain the actual field name to stay connected (also called "**bound**") to the data.

3. **Click the** ZipCode label, **click the** ZipCode label **a second time to place the insertion point in the text, modify the text to be** ZIP, **press** ENTER, **click the** Format tab **on the ribbon, click the** Font Color arrow ▲▾, **then click** Automatic

   You also want to align and format the new controls.

4. **Click the** ZIP label, **click the** Align Right button ▤, **press and hold** CTRL, **click the** State label **to select both labels at the same time, click the** Arrange tab **on the ribbon, click the** Align button, **then click** Right

   You right-aligned the ZIP text within the label, then you right-aligned the right edges of the ZIP label with the State label above it. Now left-align the edges of the State and ZipCode text boxes.

5. **Click the** State text box, **press and hold** CTRL, **click the** ZipCode text box, **click the** Align button, **then click** Left

   The new controls for the ZipCode field are now added, moved, and aligned on the form. As a final touch, you want to add a label to the Form Footer section with the text "JCL Talent".

6. **Drag the bottom of the** Form Footer bar **down about 0.5", click the** Design tab **on the ribbon, click the** Label button 𝐴𝑎, **click at about the 1" mark in the Form Footer section, type** JCL Talent, **then press** ENTER

   You are ready to review the final CompanyEntry form in Form View.

7. **Right-click the** CompanyEntry **tab, click** Save, **right-click the** CompanyEntry **tab again, then click** Form View **as shown in** FIGURE 4-4

   In general, it is common to use Form Layout View for formatting changes and Form Design View to add and position new controls. However, much of the functionality between the two views overlaps.

8. **Right-click the** CompanyEntry **tab, then click** Close

FIGURE 4-3: Adding, moving, and aligning controls in Form Design View

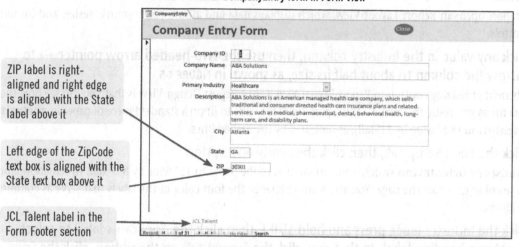

FIGURE 4-4: Final CompanyEntry form in Form View

ZIP label is right-aligned and right edge is aligned with the State label above it

Left edge of the ZipCode text box is aligned with the State text box above it

JCL Talent label in the Form Footer section

TABLE 4-4: Mouse pointer shapes in Form or Report Design View

shape	when does this shape appear?	action
⩕	When you point to any unselected control on the form (the default mouse pointer)	Single-clicking with this mouse pointer selects a control
✥	When you point to the upper-left corner or edge of a selected control in Form Design View or the middle of the control in Form Layout View	Dragging with this mouse pointer moves the selected control(s)
↕ ↔ ⤢ ⤡	When you point to any sizing handle (except the larger one in the upper-left corner in Form Design View)	Dragging with one of these mouse pointers resizes the control

---

Bound versus unbound controls

Controls are either bound or unbound. **Bound controls** display values from a field such as text boxes and combo boxes. The most common bound control is the text box. **Unbound controls** describe data or enhance the appearance of the form. Labels are the most common type of unbound control, but other types include lines, images, tabs, and command buttons. Another way to distinguish bound from unbound controls is to observe the form as you move from record to record. Because bound controls display data, their contents change as you move through the records, displaying data from the field of the current record. Unbound controls such as labels, lines, and command buttons do not change as you move through the records in a form.

Access

Work in Report Layout View

**Learning
Outcomes**
• Create a report
with the Report
tool
• Move, resize, and
format controls
in Report Layout
View
• Change page
orientation

Reports allow you to organize, group, sort, and subtotal records for professional presentations of data. Reports can be created with multiple tools and have multiple views just like forms. See TABLE 4-5 for more information on report creation tools and TABLE 4-6 for more information on report views. Although you use forms for data entry and reports for data distribution, many of the same tasks such as formatting, moving, and resizing controls work similarly between the two objects. For example, **Report Layout View** is very similar to Form Layout View. CASE ▸ *Lydia Snyder asks you to create a specific report. You create the report and then use Report Layout View to modify it.*

STEPS

1. **Click the** JobSalaries query, **click the** Create tab **on the ribbon, then click the** Report **button**

   A report opens in Report Layout View, which displays data and allows you to move, resize, and format controls.

2. **Click any value in the** Industry column, **then use the two-headed arrow pointer ↔ to narrow the column to about half its size, as shown in** FIGURE 4-5

   A benefit of resizing controls in Report Layout View versus Report Design View is that you can see how the data fits as you resize the control. The report is still too wide to fit on a standard piece of paper in **portrait orientation** (8.5" wide by 11" tall), as indicated by the dashed lines.

3. **Click the** Page Setup tab, **then click the** Landscape button

   Landscape orientation switches the orientation of the paper to 11" wide by 8.5" tall, which allows for more columns across the page. You also want to change the font color of the labels that serve as column headings.

4. **Click the** Industry label, **press and hold** SHIFT, **then click the** Applicants label **to select all column heading labels in that row, click the** Format tab **on the ribbon, click the** Font Color arrow ▣ ▾, **then click** Automatic

   Your last change is to move the StartingSalary column to the far right.

5. **Click the** StartingSalary label, **press and hold** SHIFT, **click** any value **in the StartingSalary column, then use the move pointer ⌖ to drag the column to the right of the Applicants column**

   The final JobSalaries report is shown in FIGURE 4-6.

6. **Right-click the** JobSalaries tab, **click** Save, **click** OK **to accept the default name, right-click the** JobSalaries tab, **click** Print Preview **to preview the report as it would fit on a piece of paper, right-click the** JobSalaries tab, **then click** Layout View **to return to Layout View**

FIGURE 4-5: Resizing a column in Report Layout View

Resizing the Industry column

Dashed line indicates the right edge of the paper

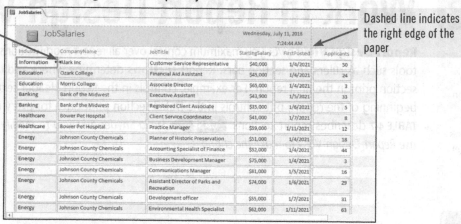

FIGURE 4-6: Final JobSalaries report in Report Layout View

Labels used as column headings have an Automatic font color

StartingSalary column moved to the end

Dashed line in landscape orientation

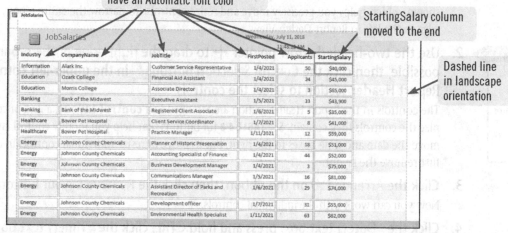

TABLE 4-5: Report creation tools

tool	icon	creates a report
Report		with one click based on the selected table or query
Report Design		from scratch in Report Design View
Blank Report		from scratch in Report Layout View
Report Wizard		by answering a series of questions provided by the Report Wizard dialog boxes
Labels		by answering a series of questions provided by the Label Wizard dialog boxes

TABLE 4-6: Report views

view	primary purpose
Report View	To quickly review the report without page breaks
Print Preview	To review each page of an entire report as it will appear if printed
Layout View	To modify the size, position, or formatting of controls; shows live data as you modify the report, making it the tool of choice when you want to change the appearance and positioning of controls on a report while also reviewing live data
Design View	To work with report sections or to access the complete range of controls and report properties; Design View does not display data

Work in Report Design View

Learning Outcomes
- Modify controls in Report Design View
- Group and ungroup controls in Report Design View
- Change report width

Report Design View gives you maximum control over all report modifications by providing extra design tools such as rulers and section bars. Report **sections** determine where and how often controls in that section print in the final report. For example, controls in the Report Header section print only once at the beginning of the report, but controls in the Detail section print once for every record the report displays. **TABLE 4-7** describes report sections. **CASE** ▸ *Lydia Snyder asks you to modify the JobSalaries report. You use Report Design View to make the changes.*

STEPS

1. **Right-click the** JobSalaries tab, **then click** Design View

   Five report **section bars** are displayed that identify the report sections. The **horizontal ruler** is also shown, which helps you precisely move and resize controls. To narrow the entire report, you drag the right edge to the left in Report Design View.

   QUICK TIP
   If a report is too wide to fit on a piece of paper, a green error indicator appears in the upper-left corner of the report.

2. **Use the two-headed arrow pointer ╋ to drag the** right edge of the report **as far left as possible, then click the** Control Selection button ⊞ **in the upper-left corner of the Report Header section to select the controls**

   The controls in the Report Header section are arranged in a **control layout**, a grid of cells that help organize the controls they contain. See **TABLE 4-8** for buttons that help you modify control layouts. You want to move the date and time boxes to the right, but to move or resize individual controls in a layout, you must first remove the layout.

3. **Click the** Arrange tab **on the ribbon, then click the** Remove Layout button

   Now you can work with the individual controls.

4. **Click the** =Date() text box, **press and hold** CTRL, **click the** =Time() text box, **click the** Size/Space button, **click** Group, **then press** RIGHT ARROW **enough times to position the right edge of the controls at the 9" mark on the horizontal ruler**

   Your screen should look like **FIGURE 4-7**. You can also use the mouse to move controls in Report or Form Design View, though the arrow keys allow you to precisely position the selected controls. You also want to make some formatting changes to the title of the report.

5. **Click the** JobSalaries label **in the Report Header, click the** Format tab **on the ribbon, click the Font Color arrow** ▲ ▾ **click** Automatic, **click the Font Size arrow** 11 ▾, **click** 24, **click the** JobSalaries label **again to place the insertion pointer in the text, then add a space so that the label reads** Job Salaries

   Your final modification will be to change the background color of the StartingSalary data.

   QUICK TIP
   Labels are edited and controls are formatted the same way in Form Design View and Form Layout View.

6. **Click the** StartingSalary text box **in the Detail section, click the** Background Color arrow ▨ ▾, **then click the** Green 2 box **(seventh column, third row in the Standard Colors palette)**

   The final Report Design View should look like **FIGURE 4-8**. To review your modifications, show the report in Print Preview.

7. **Right-click the** JobSalaries tab, **click** Save, **right-click the** JobSalaries tab, **click** Print Preview, **click the** Next Page button ▸ **to navigate through the pages of the report, right-click the** JobSalaries tab, **then click** Close

   Previewing each page of the report helps you confirm that no blank pages are created and allows you to examine how the different report sections print on each page.

FIGURE 4-7: Working in Report Design View

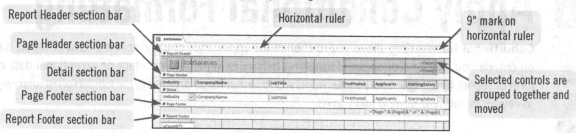

Report Header section bar
Page Header section bar
Detail section bar
Page Footer section bar
Report Footer section bar

Horizontal ruler

9" mark on horizontal ruler

Selected controls are grouped together and moved

FIGURE 4-8: Final JobSalaries report in Report Design View

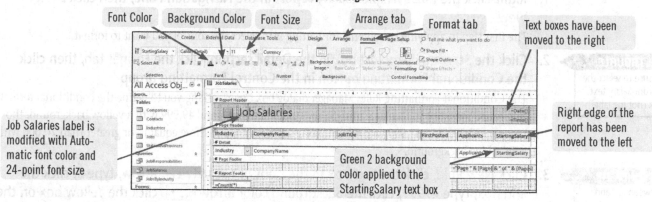

Font Color   Background Color   Font Size   Arrange tab   Format tab   Text boxes have been moved to the right

Job Salaries label is modified with Automatic font color and 24-point font size

Right edge of the report has been moved to the left

Green 2 background color applied to the StartingSalary text box

TABLE 4-7: Report sections

section	where does this section print?
Report Header	At the top of the first page
Page Header	At the top of every page (but below the Report Header on the first page)
Detail	Once for every record
Page Footer	At the bottom of every page
Report Footer	At the end of the report

TABLE 4-8: Control layout buttons

button		description	button		description
Gridlines		Applies gridlines in different colors, widths, and borders to the cells of the control layout	Select Layout		Selects the entire layout
			Select Column		Selects a single column of a layout
Stacked		Applies a vertical layout with labels on the left and text boxes on the right	Select Row		Selects a single row of a layout
			Merge		Merges cells in a layout
Tabular		Applies a horizontal layout similar to a spreadsheet	Split Vertically		Splits cells into two rows
Remove Layout		Removes a layout	Split Horizontally		Splits cells into two columns
Insert Above		Inserts a row above the layout	Move Up		Moves cells into the section above the current section
Insert Below		Inserts a row below the layout	Move Down		Moves cells into the section below the current section
Insert Left		Inserts a column to the left of the layout			
Insert Right		Inserts a column to the right of the layout			

Apply Conditional Formatting

Conditional formatting allows you to change the appearance of a control on a form or report based on criteria you specify. Conditional formatting helps you highlight important or exceptional data on a form or report. **CASE** ▶ *Lydia Snyder wants you to format the salary data in the JobsByHighestSalary report to emphasize different starting salary levels.*

STEPS

1. **Right-click the** JobsByHighestSalary report **in the Navigation Pane, then click** Design View

   The first step in applying conditional formatting is to select the control you want to format.

TROUBLE
Be sure to select the
StartingSalary text
box (not the label).

2. **Click the** StartingSalary text box **in the Detail section, click the** Format tab, **then click the** Conditional Formatting button **in the Control Formatting group**

   The Conditional Formatting Rules Manager dialog box opens, asking you to define the conditional formatting rules. You want to format StartingSalary values between 0 and 49,999 with a yellow background, those between 50,000 and 69,999 with a light green background, and those equal to or greater than 70,000 with a light blue background.

QUICK TIP
Between . . . and
criteria include both
values in the range.

3. **Click** New Rule, **click the** text box to the right of the between arrow, **type** 0, **click the** and box, **type** 49999, **click the** Background color arrow ▦ ▾, **click the** Yellow box **on the bottom row, then click** OK

   You add the second conditional formatting rule.

4. **Click** New Rule, **click the** text box to the right of the between arrow, **type** 50000, **click the** and box, **type** 69999, **click the** Background color arrow ▦ ▾, **click the** Light Green box **on the bottom row, then click** OK

   You add the third conditional formatting rule.

5. **Click** New Rule, **click the** between arrow, **click** greater than or equal to, **click the** value box, **type** 70000, **click the** Background color arrow ▦ ▾, **click the** Light Blue box **on the bottom row, then click** OK

   The Conditional Formatting Rules Manager dialog box with two rules should look like **FIGURE 4-9**.

QUICK TIP
Conditional
formatting works the
same way in Form
and Report Layout
and Design Views.

6. **Click** OK **in the Conditional Formatting Rules Manager dialog box, right-click the** JobsByHighestSalary tab, **then click** Print Preview

   Conditional formatting rules applied a yellow, light green, or light blue background color to the StartingSalary text box for each record, as shown in **FIGURE 4-10**.

7. **Right-click the** JobsByHighestSalary tab, **click** Save, **right-click the** JobsByHighestSalary tab, **then click** Close

FIGURE 4-9: Conditional Formatting Rules Manager dialog box

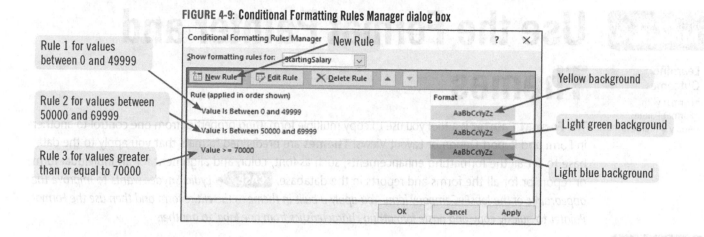

Rule 1 for values between 0 and 49999

Rule 2 for values between 50000 and 69999

Rule 3 for values greater than or equal to 70000

New Rule

Yellow background

Light green background

Light blue background

FIGURE 4-10: Conditional formatting applied to the JobsByHighestSalary report

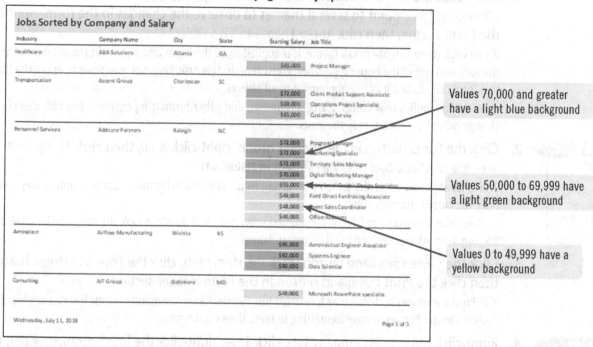

Values 70,000 and greater have a light blue background

Values 50,000 to 69,999 have a light green background

Values 0 to 49,999 have a yellow background

Access

Access
Module 4

Learning
Outcomes
• Format with
  Format Painter
• Apply a theme

Use the Format Painter and Themes

The **Format Painter** is a tool you use to copy multiple formatting properties from one control to another in Form and Report Design or Layout Views. **Themes** are predefined formats that you apply to the database to set all the formatting enhancements, such as font, color, and alignment for an individual form or report or for all the forms and reports in the database. **CASE** ▶ *Lydia Snyder wants to improve the appearance of the JobsByCompany form. You apply a built-in theme to the entire form and then use the Format Painter to quickly copy and paste formatting characteristics from one label to another.*

STEPS

1. **Right-click the** JobsByCompany form **in the Navigation Pane, click** Design View, **click the** Themes button, **point to several themes to observe the changes in the form, right-click the** Facet theme, **then click** Apply Theme to This Object Only

   If you click (versus right-click) a theme, it is applied to all the forms and reports in the database. This keeps the look and feel of the entire application consistent. In this case, however, you want to apply the theme to this form only to test it before applying it to all objects.

   A theme applies new colors, fonts, alignment, and other formatting options. You can also choose to change only the colors or only the fonts.

QUICK TIP
You can apply themes, theme fonts, or theme colors in Form and Report Layout and Design views.

2. **Click the** Fonts button **in the Themes group, right-click** Arial, **then click** Apply Font Scheme to This Object Only **as shown in FIGURE 4-11**

   The current theme fonts change for the current form. The Colors button works in a similar way, changing only the current theme's colors.

   The Print command button was formatted previously and does not look the same as the Close button. To copy formats quickly, you use the Format Painter.

3. **Click the** Close command button, **click the** Home tab, **click the** Format Painter button, **then click the** Print command button **in the Form Header section**

   The Print command button is now formatted just like the Close command button. You can double-click the Format Painter button to copy formatting to more than one control.

QUICK TIP
The Format Painter works the same way in Form and Report Layout and Design Views.

4. **Right-click the** JobsByCompany tab, **click** Save, **right-click the** JobsByCompany tab, **then click** Form View **to review the changes shown in FIGURE 4-12**

5. **Click the** Close command button **to close the CompanyJobs form, click the** Database Tools tab, **then click the** Compact and Repair Database button

6. **sam↑** Close the database and exit Access 2019

FIGURE 4-11: Applying themes

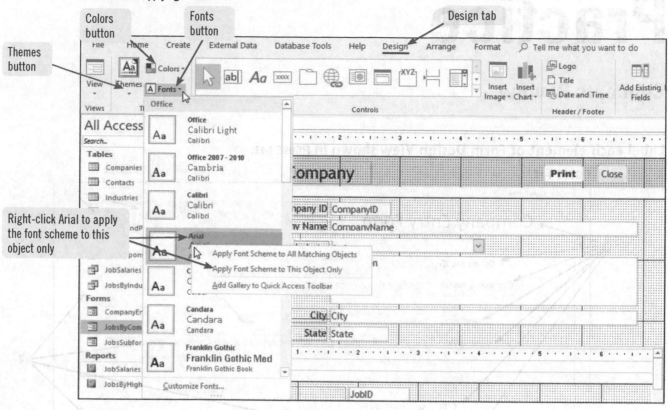

FIGURE 4-12: Final CompanyJobs form

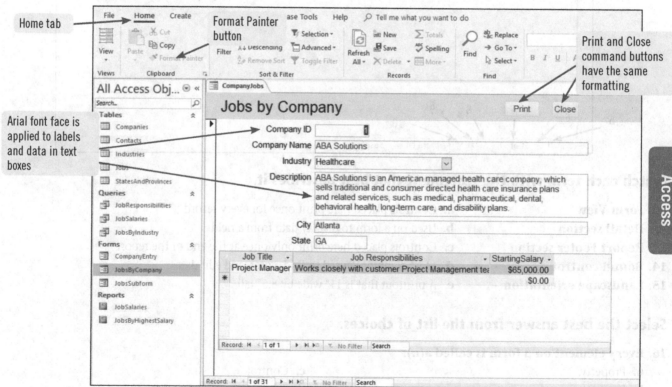

Practice

Concepts Review

Label each element of Form Design View shown in FIGURE 4-13.

FIGURE 4-13

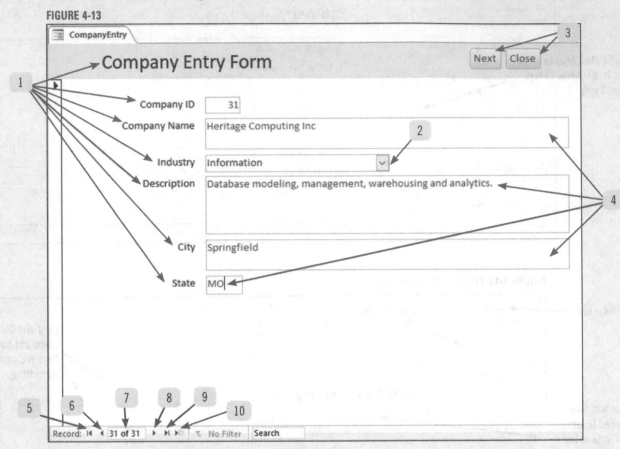

Match each term with the statement that best describes it.

11. Form View
12. Detail section
13. Report Footer section
14. Bound control
15. Landscape orientation

   a. Controls placed here print once for every record
   b. Used on a form to display data from a field
   c. Controls placed here print only once at the end of the report
   d. Most commonly used to find, enter, and edit data
   e. A printout that is 11" wide by 8.5" tall

Select the best answer from the list of choices.

16. Every element on a form is called a(n):
   a. Property.
   b. Item.
   c. Control.
   d. Tool.

17. Which of the following may *not* be used to format controls?
   a. Form View
   b. Form Layout View
   c. Report Design View
   d. Report Layout View

18. The most common bound control is the:
   a. Combo box.
   b. Label.
   c. List box.
   d. Text box.

19. The most common unbound control is the:
   a. Text box.
   b. Combo box.
   c. Label.
   d. Command button.

20. Which view does not show data?
   a. Form Layout View
   b. Form Design View
   c. Print Preview
   d. Report Layout View

Skills Review

1. **Work in Form View.**
   a. Start Access, open the IL_AC_4-2.accdb database from the location where you store your Data Files, save it as **IL_AC_4_SupportDesk**, then enable content if prompted.
   b. Open the EmployeeMaster form in Form View.
   c. Find the record for Peggy Short and change the LastName value to **Hopper**
   d. Add a new record with your name in the LastName and FirstName fields, and **Executive** in the Department field.
   e. Save the EmployeeMaster form.

2. **Work in Form Layout View.**
   a. Open the EmployeeMaster in Layout View.
   b. Modify the label in the Form Header section to have a space between the words to read: **Employee Master**
   c. Modify the labels on the left in the Detail section to have spaces between the words to read: **Employee ID**, **Last Name**, and **First Name**
   d. Modify the labels on the left in the Detail section to be right-aligned.
   e. Change the font color for all labels to Automatic (black).
   f. Save the EmployeeMaster form.

3. **Work in Form Design View.**
   a. Open the EmployeeMaster form in Design View.
   b. Move the Department label and Department combo box up to fill the blank space after the FirstName controls.
   c. Open the Field List, then add the Salary field to the form.
   d. Align the right edge of the Salary label with the labels above it and change the font color for the Salary label to Automatic (black).
   e. Align the left edge of the Salary text box with the combo box and text boxes above it.
   f. Save the EmployeeMaster form and open it in Form View as shown in **FIGURE 4-14**.
   g. Close the EmployeeMaster form.

4. **Work in Report Layout View.**
   a. Use the Report tool to create a new report on the Cases table.
   b. In Layout View of the new report, resize the Category column to be about half of its current size.
   c. In Layout View of the new report, expand the CaseTitle column to be about 50 percent wider than its current size.
   d. Switch the report to landscape orientation.
   e. Move the OpenedDate column, both the label and the text box, to be the third column in the report.

FIGURE 4-14

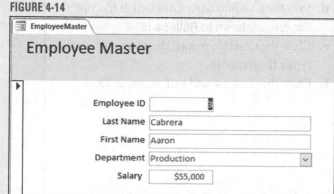

Skills Review (continued)

    f. Modify the font color of the Cases label in the Report Header section to Dark Blue (second to the last button in the last row of the Standard Colors palette) and the font size to **24**.

    g. Delete the date and time controls in the Report Header section.

    h. Modify the font color of the labels that identify every column heading to also be Dark Blue.

    i. Save the report with the name **CaseInfo**.

5. Work in Report Design View.

    a. Switch the CaseInfo report to Report Design View.

    b. Narrow the report to the 10" mark on the horizontal ruler.

    c. Remove the control layout from the controls in the Page Header, Detail, Page Footer, and Report Footer sections. (*Hint*: Click the Control Selection button in the upper-left corner of the section to select the control layout.)

    d. Resize the =Count(*) text box in the Report Footer to be tall enough so that the entire expression is shown. (*Hint*: This expression was created by the Report tool when the report was initially created. It calculates the total number of records in the report.)

    e. Move and align the =Count(*) text box in the Report Footer section so that its top edge is touching the Report Footer section bar and its left edge is aligned with the left edge of the text box in the Page Footer section that contains the page number expression.

    f. Delete any extra space in the Report Footer section by dragging the bottom of the report up as far as possible.

    g. Select all the labels in the Page Header section and group them together so that they will move as a group should you want to reposition them later.

    h. Save the CaseInfo report.

6. Add conditional formatting.

    a. With the CaseInfo report still in Report Design View, add a conditional formatting rule to the Category text box. If the field value is equal to **"MS Office"** change the font color to Red (second column, last row of Standard Colors palette).

    b. Add a second conditional formatting rule to the Category text box. If the field value is equal to **"Internet"** change the font color to Green (sixth column, last row of Standard Colors palette).

    c. Save the CaseInfo report, switch to Print Preview to make sure the conditional formats are applied correctly, then return to Report Design View.

7. Use the Format Painter and themes.

    a. In Report Design View, use the Format Painter to copy the format from the page expression text box in the Page Footer section to the =Count(*) control in the Report Footer section.

    b. Apply the Franklin Gothic theme font to the CaseInfo report object only.

    c. Apply the Blue Warm theme color to the CaseInfo report object only.

    d. Save the CaseInfo report and switch to Print Preview, as shown in **FIGURE 4-15**.

    e. Close the CaseInfo report, then compact and repair the database.

    f. Close the database and exit Access 2019.

FIGURE 4-15

CaseID	EmployeeID	OpenedDate	CaseTitle	Category	ResolvedDate
1	3	4/1/2021	User got the blue screen of death	Computer	4/3/2021
2	5	4/1/2021	I can't log in.	Local Network	
3	6	4/2/2021	I accidentally deleted some files. Can I get them back?	Computer	
5	7	4/3/2021	My computer is too slow.	Computer	8/19/2021
6	9	4/4/2021	My computer is too slow.	Computer	
7	12	4/4/2021	My computer shut down for no good reason.	Computer	
8	14	4/5/2021	The printer won't work.	Printer	
9	15	4/5/2021	I can't see the comments in my Word document.	MS Office	
10	18	4/5/2021	There are little black symbols on my Word document.	MS Office	
11	19	4/8/2021	The wireless network keeps kicking me off.	Local Network	
12	20	4/9/2021	My computer won't recognize my USB device.	Computer	
13	20	4/10/2021	I can't log in.	Local Network	
14	28	4/11/2021	I can't log in.	Local Network	
15	24	4/12/2021	Downloads are taking forever	Internet	
16	33	4/12/2021	My machine keeps restarting	Computer	
17	32	4/12/2021	Pop-up ads are appearing on my desktop	Internet	
18	29	4/13/2021	Google doesn't look right	Internet	
19	28	4/16/2021	My Wi-Fi keeps disconnecting	Local Network	
20	27	4/16/2021	I keep seeing "There is a problem with this website's security certificate"	Internet	4/17/2021
21	26	4/17/2021	Printer problems	Printer	4/18/2021
22	34	4/18/2021	Email attachment problem	MS Office	4/20/2021
23	25	4/18/2021	Excel formulas are not automatically updating	MS Office	4/20/2021

22

Page 1 of 1

Independent Challenge 1

As the manager of Riverwalk, a multispecialty health clinic, you have created a database to manage the schedules that connect each healthcare provider with the nurses that provider needs to efficiently handle patient visits. In this exercise, you will modify a form to help users find, enter, and edit data.

a. Start Access. Open the IL_AC_4-3.accdb database from the location where you store your Data Files and save it as **IL_AC_4_Riverwalk**. Click Enable Content if a yellow Security Warning message appears.

b. Open the ScheduleDate form in Form Design View.

c. Change the font face for all controls in the Detail section, including those in the subform, to Calibri (Detail) and a **10**-point font size. (*Hint*: This form contains a subform, the ScheduleItemsSubform. You can change the font face and font size for the controls directly in Form Design View of the ScheduleDate form, or you can close the ScheduleDate form and apply the formats to the ScheduleItemsSubform in Form Design View.)

d. Modify the Work Schedule label in the Form Header section to read **Doctor and Nurse Schedule**. Change the font size to be **16** and resize the label as needed to display it clearly.

e. There are four command buttons in the Detail section with the following Captions: Day, Nurse, by Location, and by Nurse. Format the Day command button with the Rectangle: Rounded Corners shape, and the Colored Fill – Olive Green, Accent 3 quick style.

f. Use the Format Painter to copy the formatting from the Day command button to the Nurse, by Location, and by Nurse command buttons.

g. Save the ScheduleDate form and switch to Form View.

h. Click the Nurse command button, then click the New (blank) record button to position your insertion point at a new record at the end of the form. Enter your name as a new record.

i. Close the Nurse Entry form, then reopen the ScheduleDate form.

j. Move to the first record in the ScheduleDate form, then add a new record in the subform for LocationNo **East**, DoctorNo **Samuelson**, and your name in the NurseNo field, as shown in **FIGURE 4-16**.

k. Save and close the ScheduleDate form, and compact and repair the database.

l. Close the database, then exit Access 2019.

FIGURE 4-16

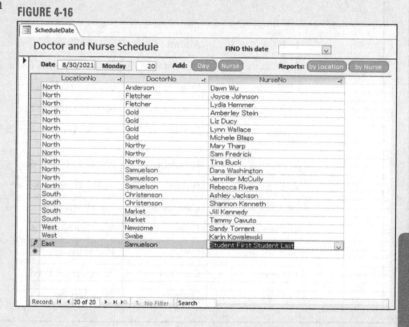

Independent Challenge 2

You are working for a city to coordinate a series of community-wide preparedness activities. You have created a database to track the activities and volunteers who are attending the activities. In this exercise, you will create and modify a report to analyze data.

a. Start Access, open the IL_AC_4-4.accdb database from the location where you store your Data Files, save it as **IL_AC_4_Volunteers**, then enable content if prompted.

b. Use the Report tool to create a new report on the Volunteers table.

c. In Report Layout View, resize the FirstName and LastName columns to be about half as wide.

d. In Report Layout View, resize the Street column to be slightly narrower so that the entire report fits within the dashed line that indicates the right side of the paper in portrait orientation.

Independent Challenge 2 (continued)

e. Switch to Report Design View and remove the control layout from the controls in the Report Header section.

f. Select and then delete the report image to the left of the Volunteers label in the Report Header section. Select and then delete the =Time() text box in the Report Header section.

g. Group the remaining two controls in the Report Header section, then move them to the left edge of the report.

h. Delete the =Count(*) text box in the Report Footer section.

i. Move the text box that contains the page number expression to the left edge of the report.

j. Drag the right edge of the report as far to the left as possible to narrow the report.

k. Apply the Century Schoolbook theme font to this report only.

l. Save the report with the name **VolunteerList**, then display it in Print Preview, as shown in **FIGURE 4-17**.

m. Save and close the VolunteerList report, then compact and repair the database.

n. Close the database and exit Access 2019.

FIGURE 4-17

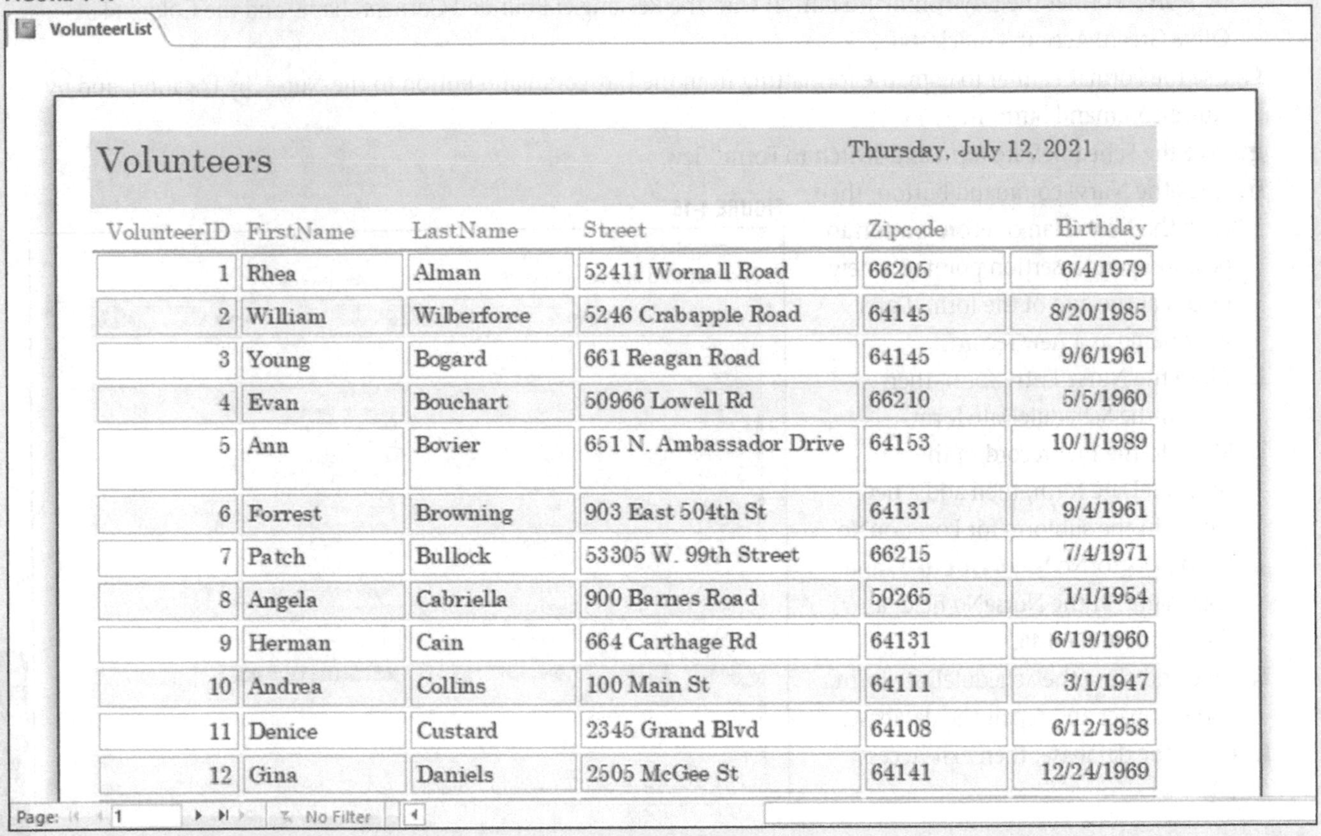

VolunteerList

Volunteers				Thursday, July 12, 2021	
VolunteerID	FirstName	LastName	Street	Zipcode	Birthday
1	Rhea	Alman	52411 Wornall Road	66205	6/4/1979
2	William	Wilberforce	5246 Crabapple Road	64145	8/20/1985
3	Young	Bogard	661 Reagan Road	64145	9/6/1961
4	Evan	Bouchart	50966 Lowell Rd	66210	5/5/1960
5	Ann	Bovier	651 N. Ambassador Drive	64153	10/1/1989
6	Forrest	Browning	903 East 504th St	64131	9/4/1961
7	Patch	Bullock	53305 W. 99th Street	66215	7/4/1971
8	Angela	Cabriella	900 Barnes Road	50265	1/1/1954
9	Herman	Cain	664 Carthage Rd	64131	6/19/1960
10	Andrea	Collins	100 Main St	64111	3/1/1947
11	Denice	Custard	2345 Grand Blvd	64108	6/12/1958
12	Gina	Daniels	2505 McGee St	64141	12/24/1969

Page: 1 ▶ ▶ No Filter ◀

Working with Forms and Reports

Visual Workshop

Start Access, open the IL_AC_4-5.accdb database from the location where you store your Data Files, save it as **IL_AC_4_CollegeCourses**, then enable content if prompted.

In Query Design View, create a query with the following fields from the following tables:

- Description from the Classes table
- ClassNo from the Sections table
- Grade from the Enrollments table
- StudentFirst and StudentLast from the Students table

Save the query with the name **StudentGrades**, display it in Datasheet View, change any occurrence of Carl Willis to *your name*, then close the StudentGrades query.

Use the Report tool to create a report on this query.

Use Report Layout View to narrow the ClassNo, Grade, StudentFirst, and StudentLast columns. Move the Grade column to be the last. Modify the report title to be **Student Grade Listing**.

Use Report Design View to delete all the controls in the Page Footer and Report Footer sections. Delete the text boxes in the Report Header section that calculate the current date and the current time. Also use Report Design View to narrow the width of the report to 8" or less. Save the report with the name **StudentGradeListing** and preview it in Print Preview, as shown in **FIGURE 4-18**. Compact and repair the database, then close the database and exit Access 2019.

FIGURE 4-18

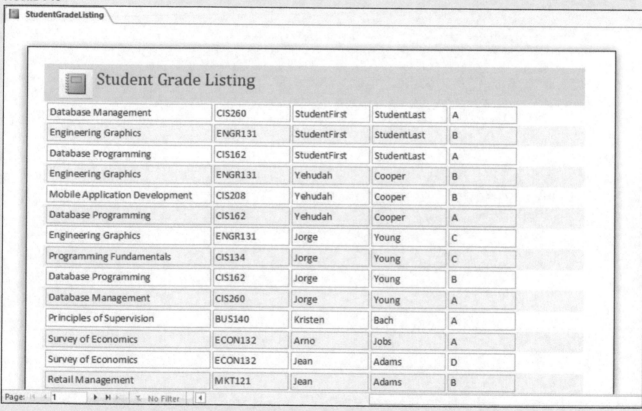

Improving Tables and Creating Advanced Queries

CASE You are working with Lydia Snyder, vice president of operations at JCL Talent, to build a research database to manage industry, company, and job data. In this module, you'll improve tables and build advanced queries.

Module Objectives

After completing this module, you will be able to:

- Create Lookup fields
- Modify Lookup fields
- Modify Validation and Indexed properties
- Create Attachment and Hyperlink fields
- Create Long Text fields
- Create Top Values queries

- Create parameter queries
- Set properties in queries
- Find unmatched records
- Create summary queries
- Create crosstab queries

Files You Will Need

IL_AC_5-1.accdb

Support_AC_5_aba.png

IL_AC_5-2.accdb

Support_AC_5_employee.jpg

IL_AC_5-3.accdb

Support_AC_5_nurse.png

IL_AC_5-4.accdb

IL_AC_5-5.accdb

Create Lookup Fields

Learning
Outcomes
• Create a Lookup
field
• Edit data in a
Lookup field

Lookup fields provide a list of values for a field. The values can be stored in another table or entered in the **Row Source** Lookup property of the field. Fields that are good candidates for Lookup properties are those that contain a defined set of values such as State, Gender, or Department. You can set Lookup properties for a field in Table Design View using the **Lookup Wizard.** **CASE** ▶ *The names and two-character postal abbreviations for the 50 United States, 13 Canadian provinces, and Washington, D.C., are stored in the StatesAndProvinces table. You will use the Lookup Wizard to look up information from this table for the State field in the Companies table.*

STEPS

1. **sanf ↓ Start Access, open the** IL_AC_5-1.accdb database **from the location where you store your Data Files, save it as** IL_AC_5_Jobs, **enable content if prompted, right-click the Companies table** in the Navigation Pane, then click Design View

   The Lookup Wizard is included in the Data Type list.

2. **Click the** Short Text data type **for the State field, click the** Data Type list arrow, **then click** Lookup Wizard

   The Lookup Wizard starts and prompts you for information about where the Lookup column will get its values. You want to look up values from an existing table.

3. **Click** Next, **click** Table: StatesAndProvinces, **click** Next, **click the** Select All Fields button >> , **click** Next, **click the** first field sort arrow, **click** StateAbbrev, **click** Next, **click the** Hide key column check box **to uncheck it, click** Next, **click** Next **to accept the StateAbbrev field to store, click the** Enable Data Integrity check box, **click** Finish **to complete the Lookup Wizard, then click** Yes **to save the table and relationship**

   Note that the data type for the State field is still Short Text. The Lookup Wizard is a process for setting Lookup property values for a field, not a data type itself. The last dialog box of the Lookup Wizard established a one-to-many relationship between the StatesAndProvinces and the Companies tables using the common State field.

4. **Click the** Lookup tab **in the Field Properties pane to observe the new Lookup properties for the State field, as shown in** FIGURE 5-1

   The Lookup Wizard helped you enter Lookup property values for the State field.

5. **Click the** View button ▦ **to switch to Datasheet View, press** TAB **five times to move to the State field, then click the** State list arrow, **as shown in** FIGURE 5-2

   The State field now provides a list of values from the StatesAndProvinces table. The first column with the two-character state or province abbreviation contains the data that is saved in the State field of the Companies table. Note that the first column is wider than needed. You will modify Lookup field properties such as column widths in the next lesson.

6. **Navigate to the record for CompanyID 8 (Bank of the Midwest), click the** State list arrow, **click** MO **for Missouri, then close the Companies table**

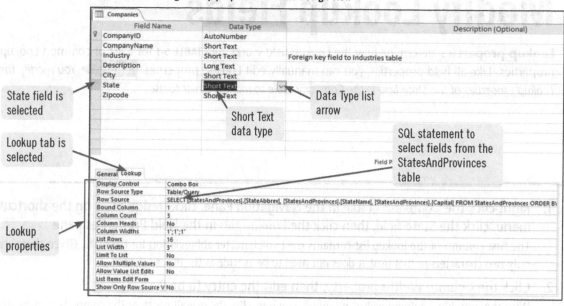

FIGURE 5-1: Viewing Lookup properties in Table Design View

State field is selected

Lookup tab is selected

Lookup properties

Data Type list arrow

Short Text data type

SQL statement to select fields from the StatesAndProvinces table

Field Name	Data Type	Description (Optional)
CompanyID	AutoNumber	
CompanyName	Short Text	
Industry	Short Text	Foreign key field to Industries table
Description	Long Text	
City	Short Text	
State	Short Text	
Zipcode	Short Text	

General Lookup

Display Control	Combo Box
Row Source Type	Table/Query
Row Source	SELECT [StatesAndProvinces].[StateAbbrev], [StatesAndProvinces].[StateName], [StatesAndProvinces].[Capital] FROM StatesAndProvinces ORDER BY
Bound Column	1
Column Count	3
Column Heads	No
Column Widths	1";1";1"
List Rows	16
List Width	3"
Limit To List	No
Allow Multiple Values	No
Allow Value List Edits	No
List Items Edit Form	
Show Only Row Source V	No

FIGURE 5-2: Using a Lookup field in a datasheet

Row Source property selects three fields from the StatesAndProvinces table and sorts the records in ascending order on the StateAbbrev field

CompanyID	CompanyName	Industry	Description	City	State	Zipcode	Click to Add
1	ABA Solutions	Healthcare	ABA Solutions is an American managed health care company, which sells traditional and consumer directed health care insurance plans and related services, such as	Atlanta	GA	30301	
2	Accent Group	Transportation	Accent Group solves our clients' toughest challenges by providing unmatched services in transportation strategy, consulting, digital, technology and operations.	Charlesto	GA HI IA IN	30301 Georgia / Hawaii / Iowa / Idaho	Atlanta Honolulu Des Moines Boise
3	AIT Group	Consulting	AIT Group is a premier provider of IT Consulting Engineering Cons... Management Solu...	Baltimor	IL IN KS	Illinois Indiana Kansas	Springfield Indianapolis Topeka
4	Addcore Partners	Personnel Services	Addcore Partners the world.	Raleigh	KT LA MA	Kentucky Louisiana Massachusetts	Frankfort Baton Rouge Boston
5	Alark Inc	Information	Alark Inc is an Am... computing compa...	Kansas C	MB MD ME	Manitoba Maryland Maine	Winnepeg Annapolis Augusta
6	Artwell Corp	Transportation	Artwell Corp desig... solutions.	Chicago	MI MN MO	Michigan Minnesota Missouri	Lansing St. Paul Jefferson Ci
7	Bower Pet Hospital	Healthcare	Bower Pet Hospital is a privately owned company that operates veterinary clinics.	Scottsdale	AZ	85252	
8	Bank of the Midwest	Banking	Bank of the Midwest is a multinational banking and financial services corporation.	Kansas City	MO	64102	

Record: 1 of 30   No Filter   Search

Multivalued fields

In a datasheet or form, a **multivalued field** presents check boxes next to the values in the list. The check boxes allow you to select more than one value to store in the field. The drawback, however, is that it is more difficult to find and filter for individual values when more than one value is stored in the same field. Many relational database designers prefer to create a child table with a one-to-many relationship to the parent table to store multiple values for a field rather than using a multivalued field. To create a multivalued field, enter Yes in the **Allow Multiple Values** Lookup property.

Access

Modify Lookup Fields

Learning
Outcomes
• Modify Lookup
  properties
• Modify the
  Caption property

Lookup properties determine how the Lookup field works. See TABLE 5-1 for a list of common Lookup properties. Like all field properties, you can manually edit Lookup properties. **CASE** *You modify the Lookup properties of the State field in the Company table to make it easier to use.*

STEPS

1. **Right-click the Companies table in the Navigation Pane, click Design View on the shortcut menu, click the State field, then click the Lookup tab in the Field Properties pane**
   The first column of the lookup list contains the two-character abbreviation for the state. Given there are only two characters in that field, it does not need to be as wide as the other columns.

2. **Click the Column Widths property, then edit the entry to be** 0.5"; 2"; 1.5"
   With the individual column widths modified, you'll modify the overall width of the combo box using the List Width property.

3. **Click the List Width property, then edit the entry to be** 4"
   You also want to show more than 16 rows in the list, which will reduce the amount of scrolling for users.

4. **Click the List Rows property, then edit the entry to be** 30
   You decide to show the field names as column headings in the list.

5. **Double-click the Column Heads property to change the value from No to Yes, as shown in FIGURE 5-3, click the Property Update Options button ⬚, click Update all lookup properties everywhere State is used, then click OK**
   It is best to set all field properties in Table Design View before building queries, forms, and reports, but if you revise a field's properties after creating other objects, the **Property Update Options button ⬚** appears to help you propagate property changes to other objects that use that field.

   You also want to modify the **Caption** property of the CompanyName field to shorten it to "Company" when the field appears in a datasheet, form, or report.

6. **Click the CompanyName field, click the General tab in the Field Properties pane, click the Caption property, then type** Company
   With the modifications made to the Companies table, you are ready to work with the data.

7. **Click the View button ▦ to switch to Datasheet View, click Yes when prompted to save the table, press TAB five times to move to the State field, then click the State list arrow, as shown in FIGURE 5-4**

8. **Close the Companies table**

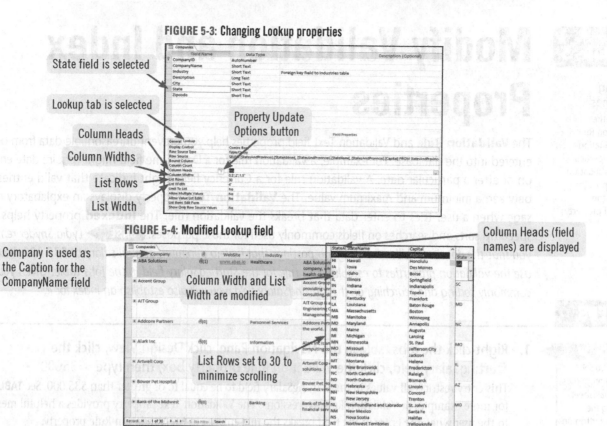

FIGURE 5-3: Changing Lookup properties

State field is selected

Lookup tab is selected

Column Heads

Column Widths

List Rows

List Width

Property Update Options button

FIGURE 5-4: Modified Lookup field

Company is used as the Caption for the CompanyName field

Column Width and List Width are modified

List Rows set to 30 to minimize scrolling

Column Heads (field names) are displayed

TABLE 5-1: Common Lookup properties

property name	description	property values
Display Control	Determines the type of control used to display this field on forms	Text Box, List Box, or Combo Box; if set to Text Box, all other Lookup properties are removed
Row Source Type	Identifies the type of source for the control's data	Table/Query, Value List, or Field List
Row Source	Identifies the source of the control's data	Table name, query name, or SQL statement
Bound Column	Identifies the list column that is bound to the Lookup field	1 by default, but can be set to any number based on the number of fields selected in the Row Source
Column Count	Identifies the number of columns to display in the list	1 by default, but can be set to any number based on the number of fields selected in the Row Source
Column Heads	Determines whether to display field names as the first row in the list	Yes or No; No by default
Column Widths	Sets the column widths in the list	1" by default, but if the Row Source identifies more than one column, column widths are separated by semicolons such as: 1"; 1"; 1"
List Rows	Sets the number of rows to display in the list	16 by default, but can be set to any number
List Width	Sets the overall width of the list	1" by default
Limit To List	Determines whether you can enter a new value into the field or whether the entries are limited to the drop-down list	Yes or No. No by default
Allow Multiple Values	Determines whether you can select more than one value for a field	Yes or No; No by default
Allow Value List Edits	Determines whether users can add or edit the list	Yes or No; No by default
List Items Edit Form	Identifies the name of the form to open and use if allowing users to edit the values in the list	The form name of a form saved in the current database
Show only Row Source Values	Shows only values that match the current row source when Allow Multiples Values is set to Yes	Yes or No; No by default

Access

Modify Validation and Index Properties

Learning
Outcomes
• Modify the
  Validation Rule
  and Validation
  Text properties
• Define Validation
  Rule expressions
• Modify the
  Indexed property

The **Validation Rule** and Validation Text field properties help you prevent unreasonable data from being entered into the database. For example, a validation rule for a Date/Time field might require date entries on or after a particular date. A validation rule for a Currency field might indicate that valid entries fall between a minimum and maximum value. The **Validation Text** property displays an explanatory message when a user tries to enter data that breaks the validation rule. The **Indexed** property helps you speed up sorts and searches on fields commonly used for those purposes. **CASE** *Lydia Snyder reminds you that the database will be tracking job postings that have a minimum annual salary of $35,000. You can use the validation properties to establish this rule for the StartingSalary field in the Jobs table. Given you are commonly sorting and searching on the StartingSalary field, you will also establish an index for it.*

STEPS

QUICK TIP
You can also set validation properties in Table Datasheet View using the Validation button on the Fields tab.

1. **Right-click the** Jobs table **in the Navigation Pane, click** Design View, **click the** StartingSalary field, **click the** Validation Rule property box, **then type** >=35000

   This entry restricts all values in the StartingSalary field to be equal to or greater than $35,000. See **TABLE 5-2** for more examples of Validation Rule expressions. The Validation Text property provides a helpful message to the user when the entry in the field breaks the rule entered in the Validation Rule property.

QUICK TIP
The Test Validation Rules button tests the Validation Rule, Required, and Allow Zero Length properties.

2. **Click the** Validation Text box, **then type** Value must be greater than or equal to $35,000

   Design View of the Jobs table should now look like **FIGURE 5-5**.

3. **Save the table, then click** Yes **when asked to test the existing data with new data integrity rules**

   Because no values in the StartingSalary field are less than $35,000, Access finds no errors in the current data and saves the table.

QUICK TIP
Click the Indexes button on the Design tab to view, add, or modify the indexes for the fields in that table.

4. **Double-click the** Indexed property **to change the value from No to** Yes (Duplicates OK)

   An **index** on a field will speed up the sort and search process for that field. Because the indexing process takes some overhead, be careful to add an index to only those fields that are commonly used for sorting and searching. The Indexed property is automatically set to Yes (No Duplicates) for the primary key field in the table and Yes (Duplicates OK) for other fields in the table that end in "ID".

5. **Click the** View button 🔳 **to display the datasheet, click** Yes **when prompted to save the table, press** TAB **four times to move to the StartingSalary field, type** 29000, **then press** TAB

   Because you tried to enter a value that evaluated false for the Validation Rule expression in the StartingSalary field, a dialog box opens and displays the Validation Text entry, as shown in **FIGURE 5-6**.

6. **Click** OK **to close the validation message, press** ESC **to reject the invalid entry in the** StartingSalary field, **then close the** Jobs table

FIGURE 5-5: Setting Validation and Indexed properties

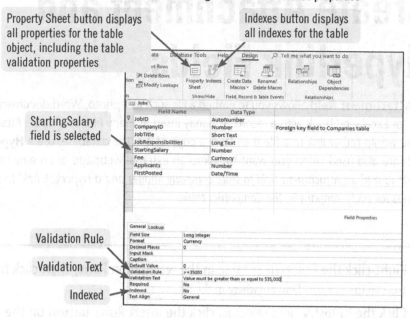

Property Sheet button displays all properties for the table object, including the table validation properties

Indexes button displays all indexes for the table

StartingSalary field is selected

Validation Rule

Validation Text

Indexed

FIGURE 5-6: Validation Text message

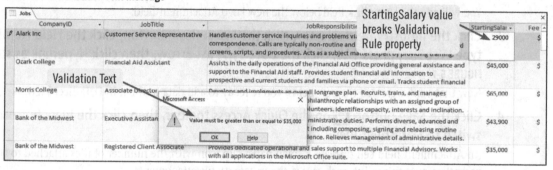

StartingSalary value breaks Validation Rule property

Validation Text

Value must be greater than or equal to $35,000

TABLE 5-2: Validation Rule expressions

data type	validation rule expression	description
Number or Currency	>0	Number must be positive
Number or Currency	>10 And <100	Number must be greater than 10 and less than 100
Number or Currency	10 Or 20 Or 30	Number must be 10, 20, or 30
Short Text	"AZ" Or "CO" Or "NM"	Entry must be AZ, CO, or NM
Date/Time	>=#7/1/19#	Date must be on or after 7/1/2019
Date/Time	>#1/1/10# And <#1/1/30#	Date must be greater than 1/1/2010 and less than 1/1/2030

Table validation properties

If your validation rule includes more than one field, open the Property Sheet for the table by clicking the Properties button on the Design tab in Table Design View. Enter the validation rule expression in the table's Validation Rule property. For example, a validation rule that includes two fields might be [ShipDate]>=[SaleDate], and the accompanying Validation Text property might be "The ShipDate value must be greater than or equal to the SaleDate value".

Improving Tables and Creating Advanced Queries

Learning
Outcomes
• Create an
  Attachment field
• Attach and
  view a file in an
  Attachment field
• Create a Hyperlink
  field
• Enter a webpage
  address in a
  Hyperlink field

Create Attachment and Hyperlink Fields

An **Attachment field** allows you to embed a file such as a photo, Word document, PowerPoint presentation, or Excel workbook with a record. You may insert as many files to a single Attachment field as desired. If you would rather link to a file than store a copy of it in the database, use a **Hyperlink field**. Hyperlink fields are also used when you want to link to an external webpage or an email address. **CASE** ▶ *You decide to add an Attachment field to store company images and a Hyperlink field to store the home webpage address for each company in the Companies table.*

STEPS

QUICK TIP
You can drag the
field selectors to the
left of the field name
to reorder your fields
in Table Design View.

1. **Right-click the** Companies table **in the Navigation Pane, then click** Design View

   You can insert a new field anywhere in the list.

2. **Click the** Industry field selector, **click the** Insert Rows button **on the Design tab, click the** Field Name cell, **type** Logo, **press TAB, click the** Data Type list arrow, **then click** Attachment

   You will add the Hyperlink field below the new Logo Attachment field.

3. **Click the** Industry field selector, **click the** Insert Rows button, **click the** Field Name cell, **type** WebSite, **press TAB, click the** Data Type list arrow, **then click** Hyperlink **as shown in** FIGURE 5-7

   Now that you've created the new fields, you're ready to add data to them in Datasheet View.

4. **Click the** Save button 🖫 **on the Quick Access toolbar, then click the** View button 🏢 **to switch to Datasheet View**

   An Attachment field cell displays a small paper clip icon with the number of files attached to the field in parentheses. At this point, each record shows zero (0) file attachments.

5. **Double-click the** attachment icon 🗓 **for the first record (CompanyID 1 ABA Solutions) to open the Attachments dialog box, click** Add, **navigate to the location where you store your Data Files, double-click** Support_AC_5_aba.png, **then click** OK

   The Support_AC_5_aba.png file is now included with the first record, and the Attachment field reflects that one (1) file has been added. You can attach more than one file and different types of files to the same field. Some file types, such as .png or .jpg files, automatically display their contents (an image) in forms and reports.

6. **Double-click the** attachment icon 🗓 **for the ABA Solutions record to open the Attachments dialog box shown in** FIGURE 5-8, **then click** Open

   The image opens in the program that is associated with the .png extension on your computer such as Windows Photos.

QUICK TIP
Right-click a
Hyperlink field, point
to Hyperlink, then
click Edit Hyperlink
to open the Insert
Hyperlink dialog box
for more hyperlink
options.

7. **Close the window that displays the Support_AC_5_aba.png image, click** Cancel **in the Attachments dialog box, press TAB to move to the WebSite field, type** www.abas.example.com, **then close the Companies table**

   Hyperlink fields store paths to files and webpages, not the files or webpages themselves. If you click www.abas.example.com (or any hyperlink) in the datasheet, your computer attempts to open that link, which in this case would be a website.

FIGURE 5-7: Adding Attachment and Hyperlink fields

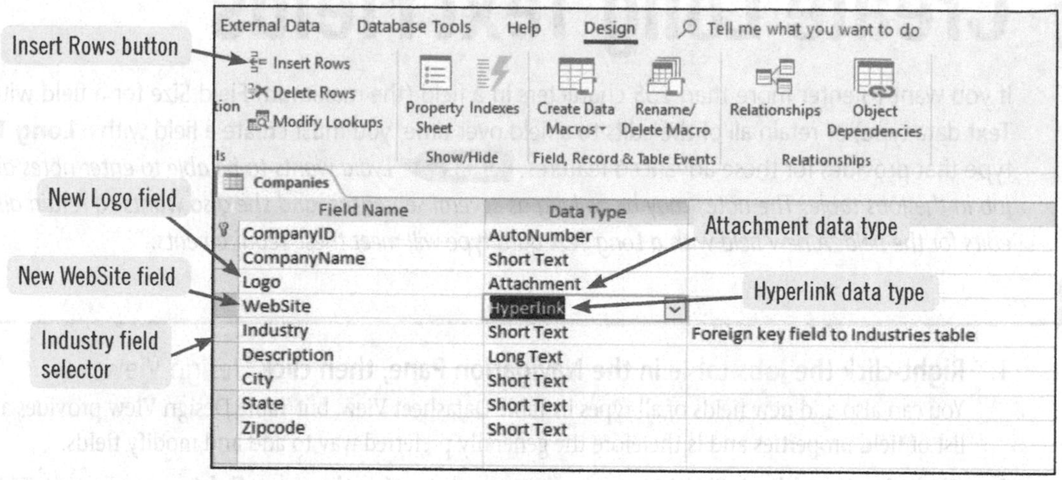

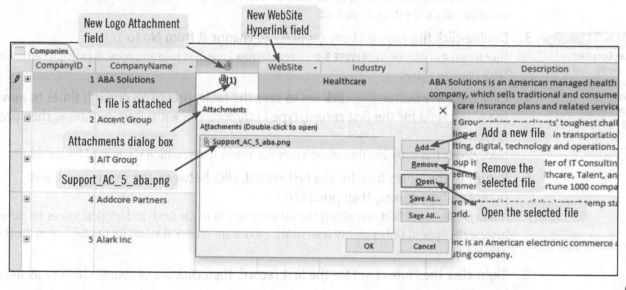

Insert Rows button

New Logo field

New WebSite field

Industry field selector

Attachment data type

Hyperlink data type

Foreign key field to Industries table

FIGURE 5-8: Opening an attached file

New Logo Attachment field

New WebSite Hyperlink field

1 file is attached

Attachments dialog box

Support_AC_5_aba.png

Add a new file

Remove the selected file

Open the selected file

Create Long Text Fields

Learning
Outcomes
• Create a Long Text field
• Set the Append Only property

If you want to enter more than 255 characters in a field (the maximum Field Size for a field with a Short Text data type) or retain all of the edits to a field over time, you must create a field with a **Long Text** data type that provides for these advanced features. **CASE** ▶ *Lydia wants to be able to enter notes about each job in the Jobs table. The notes may be as long as several sentences, and she also wants to retain all historical edits for the field. A new field with a Long Text data type will meet these requirements.*

STEPS

1. **Right-click the** Jobs table **in the Navigation Pane, then click** Design View

   You can also add new fields of all types in Table Datasheet View, but Table Design View provides a complete list of field properties and is therefore the generally preferred way to add and modify fields.

2. **Click the first blank** Field Name cell, **type** Notes **for the new field name, press** TAB, **click the** Data Type arrow, **then click** Long Text

   The Field Properties pane at the bottom of Table Design View changes to display properties associated with a Long Text field such as the **Append Only** property. Setting the Append Only property to Yes retains all historical edits and entries to the field.

QUICK TIP
In Table Datasheet View, use the Memo Settings button on the Fields tab to change the Append Only property for a Long Text field.

3. **Double-click the** Append Only property **to change it from No to** Yes

   Your screen should look like **FIGURE 5-9**. To test the new Long Text field and Append Only property, work in Table Datasheet View.

4. **Click the** View button 📰, **click** Yes **to save the table, press** TAB **enough times to move to the** Notes field **for the first record, type** Entry level job with great potential, **then press** ENTER

   Next, modify this entry and then observe how the historical information is preserved for the field.

5. **Return to the** Notes field **for the first record, click between the words** great **and** potential, **type** career, **then press** ENTER

   Although the Notes field only shows the last entry or edit to the field, all historical values are preserved because the Append Only property is set to Yes. To view the historical values for the field, open the History window.

6. **Right-click the** Notes field **for the first record, then click** Show column history **as shown in FIGURE 5-10**

   Each time you change the Notes field, a new line is added to the History for Notes dialog box to time-stamp the new field value.

7. **Click** OK **in the History for Notes dialog box, then close the** Jobs table

FIGURE 5-9: Creating a Long Text field

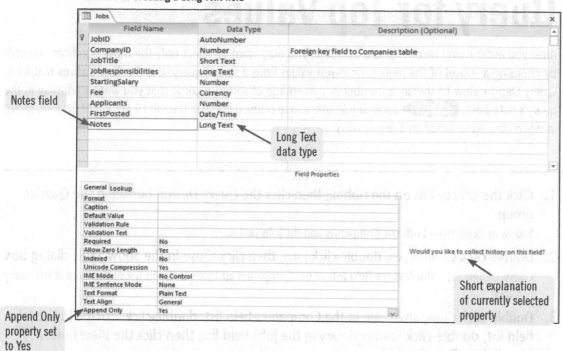

Notes field

Long Text data type

Would you like to collect history on this field?

Short explanation of currently selected property

Append Only property set to Yes

FIGURE 5-10: Viewing the History for a Long Text field

Notes field

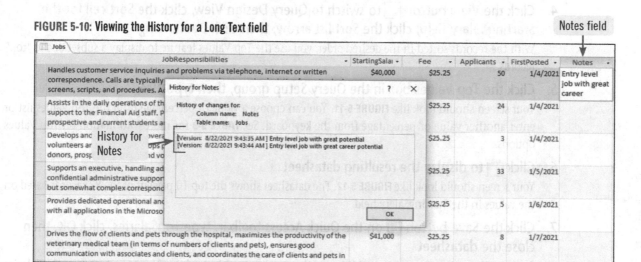

History for Notes

Allow Zero Length property

The **Allow Zero Length** property is available for both Short Text and Long Text fields. Yes is the default value and means that the field will accept an **intentional zero length value** when you enter two consecutive quotation marks (""). You may want to enter an intentional zero length value in a table that stores client information. For example, some clients may not want to provide personal information such as their phone number or email address. To indicate that those fields are intentionally blank, you'd enter an intentional zero length value, "". Intentional zero length values are often confused with **null** values, which mean that the field is empty for no particular reason. Both intentional zero length and null values appear blank, which can create confusion in a query. You query for intentional zero length values using two consecutive quotation marks "" as the criterion. You query for null values using **Is Null** as the criterion.

Query for Top Values

After you enter many records into a database, you may want to select only the most significant records by choosing a subset of the highest or lowest values from a sorted query. Use the **Top Values** feature in Query Design View to specify a number or percentage of sorted records that you want to display in the query's datasheet. **CASE** *Lydia Snyder asks you to create a listing of the top 10 percent of the jobs, sorted in descending order based on StartingSalary.*

STEPS

1. **Click the** Create tab **on the ribbon, then click the** Query Design button **in the Queries group**
   You want fields from both the Companies and the Jobs tables.

2. **Double-click** Companies, **double-click** Jobs, **then click** Close **in the Show Table dialog box**
   Query Design View displays the field lists of the Companies and Jobs tables in the upper pane of the query window.

3. **Double-click** CompanyName **in the Companies field list, double-click** JobTitle **in the Jobs field list, double-click** StartingSalary **in the Jobs field list, then click the** View button 🔲 **to switch to Datasheet View**
   The datasheet shows 82 total records. You want to know the top 10 percent of jobs based on the highest starting salaries. The next task in a Top Values query is to sort the records in the desired order.

4. **Click the** View button 🔲 **to switch to Query Design View, click the** Sort cell for the StartingSalary field, **click the** Sort list arrow, **then click** Descending
   With the records sorted in the desired order, you use the Top Values feature to display a subset of the "top" records.

5. **Click the** Top Values box **in the Query Setup group, then type** 10%
   Your screen should look like **FIGURE 5-11**. You can choose a value or percentage from the Top Values list or enter another value or percentage from the keyboard. See **TABLE 5-3** for more information on Top Values options.

6. **Click** 🔲 **to display the resulting datasheet**
   Your screen should look like **FIGURE 5-12**. The datasheet shows the top 10 percent of the 82 records based on the values in the StartingSalary field.

7. **Click the** Save button 🔲 **on the Quick Access toolbar, type** TopSalaries, **click OK, then close the datasheet**
   As with all queries, if you enter additional job records into this database, the statistics in the TopSalaries query are automatically updated.

FIGURE 5-11: Creating a Top Values query

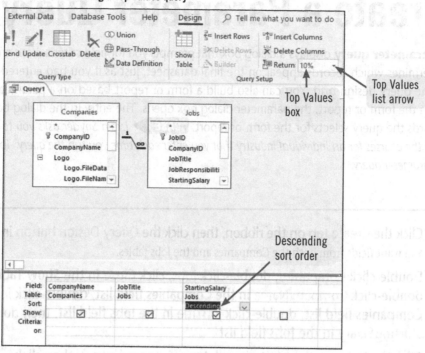

FIGURE 5-12: Top Values datasheet

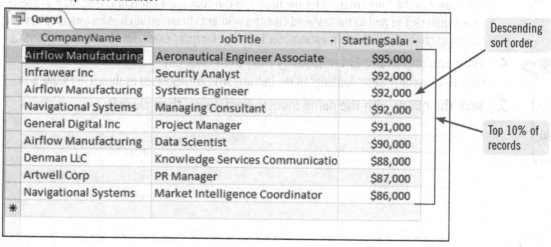

TABLE 5-3: Top Values options

action	displays
Click 5, 25, or 100 in the Top Values list	Top 5, 25, or 100 records
Enter a number, such as 10, in the Top Values box	Top 10, or whatever value is entered, records
Click 5% or 25% in the Top Values list	Top 5 percent or 25 percent of records
Enter a percentage, such as 10%, in the Top Values text box	Top 10 percent, or whatever percentage is entered, of records
Click All	All records

Create a Parameter Query

Learning
Outcomes
• Enter parameter
  criteria
• Describe Like
  operator criteria

A **parameter query** displays a dialog box that prompts you for field criteria. Your entry in the dialog box determines which records appear on the final datasheet, just as if you had entered that criteria directly in the query design grid. You can also build a form or report based on a parameter query. When you open the form or report, the parameter dialog box opens. The entry in the dialog box determines which records the query selects for the form or report. **CASE** ▶ *Lydia Snyder asks you to create a query to display the courses for an individual industry that you enter each time you run the query. To do so, you will create a parameter query.*

STEPS

QUICK TIP
You can also drag
a table from the
Navigation Pane into
Query Design View.

1. **Click the Create tab on the ribbon, then click the Query Design button in the Queries group**
   You want fields from both the Companies and the Jobs tables.

2. **Double-click Companies, double-click Jobs, click Close in the Show Table dialog box, double-click CompanyName in the Companies field list, double-click Industry in the Companies field list, double-click JobTitle in the Jobs field list, then double-click StartingSalary in the Jobs field list**

QUICK TIP
To enter a long
criterion, right-click
the Criteria cell, then
click Zoom.

3. **Click the Industry field Criteria cell, type [Enter industry:], then click ▦ to display the Enter Parameter Value dialog box, as shown in FIGURE 5-13**
   In Query Design View, you enter each parameter criterion within [square brackets], and it appears as a prompt in the Enter Parameter Value dialog box. The entry you make in the Enter Parameter Value dialog box is used as the final criterion for the field. You can combine logical operators such as greater than (>) or less than (<) as well as the keyword Like and wildcard characters such as an asterisk (*) with parameter criteria to create flexible search options. See **TABLE 5-4** for more examples of parameter criteria.

QUICK TIP
Query criteria are
not case sensitive,
so "banking,"
"Banking," and
"BANKING" all yield
the same results.

4. **Type Banking in the Enter industry box, then click OK**
   Only those records with "Banking" in the Industry field are displayed as shown in **FIGURE 5-14**.

5. **Save the query with the name IndustryParameter, then close it**

FIGURE 5-13: Creating a parameter query

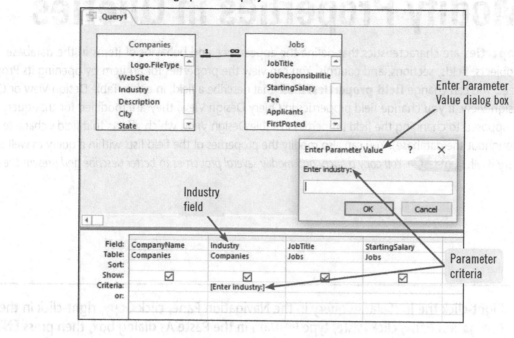

Industry field

Enter Parameter Value dialog box

Parameter criteria

FIGURE 5-14: Running a parameter query

Only records with "Banking" in the Industry field are selected

CompanyName	Industry	JobTitle	StartingSalar
Bank of the Midwest	Banking	Executive Assistant	$43,900
Bank of the Midwest	Banking	Registered Client Associate	$35,000
First Bank	Banking	HR Coordinator	$61,000
Wellman Bank	Banking	Digital Marketing Consultant	$68,000
Wellman Bank	Banking	Analytic Consultant	$85,000

TABLE 5-4: Examples of parameter criteria

field data type	parameter criteria	description
Date/Time	>=[Enter start date:]	Searches for dates on or after the entered date
Date/Time	>=[Enter start date:] and <=[Enter end date:]	Prompts you for two date entries and searches for dates on or after the first date and on or before the second date
Short Text	Like [Enter the first character of the last name:] & "*"	Searches for any name that begins with the entered character
Short Text	Like "*" & [Enter any character(s) to search by:] & "*"	Searches for words that contain the entered characters anywhere in the field

Modify Properties in Queries

Learning
Outcomes
• Copy and paste a
  query
• Modify query
  Description
  and Recordset
  properties
• Modify a field's
  Caption and
  Format properties
  in a query
• Modify a field list's
  Alias property

Properties are characteristics that define the appearance and behavior of items in the database, such as objects, fields, sections, and controls. You can view the properties for an item by opening its Property Sheet. You can change **field properties**, those that describe a field, in either Table Design View or Query Design View. If you change field properties in Query Design View, they are modified for that query only (as opposed to changing the field properties in Table Design View, which affects that field's characteristics throughout the database). You can also modify the properties of the field lists within a query as well as the query itself. **CASE** *You copy a query and modify several properties to better describe and present the data.*

STEPS

1. **Right-click the** JobSalaries query **in the Navigation Pane, click** Copy, **right-click in the** Navigation Pane, **click** Paste, **type** JobData **in the Paste As dialog box, then press** ENTER
   Copying and pasting a query is a fast way to build a new, similar query.

2. **Right-click the** JobData query, **click** Design View, **click the** Property Sheet button **in the Show/Hide group, then click in the upper portion of Query Design View (but not on a field list)**
   The Property Sheet dialog box opens to show you the properties that describe the entire query.

3. **Click the** Description property, **type** For Lydia's weekly meeting, **click** Dynaset **in the Recordset Type property, click the** Recordset Type list arrow, **then click** Snapshot **as shown in** FIGURE 5-15
   The **Description** property allows you to document the content, purpose, or author of a query. The Description property also appears on **Database Documenter** reports, a feature on the Database Tools tab that helps you create reports with information about the database.
      The **Recordset Type** property has two common choices: Snapshot and Dynaset. **Snapshot** locks the recordset, which prevents the data from being updated using this query. **Dynaset** is the default value and allows updates to data in this query.

QUICK TIP
"Selection type"
at the top of the
Property Sheet
indicates what
properties you are
viewing.

4. **Click the** FirstPosted field **in the query grid, click the** Caption property **in the Property Sheet, type** Posted, **click the** Format property, **click the** Format property list arrow, **then click** Medium Date
   If you modify the field properties in a table, the properties apply to all objects in the database. You can override those settings by changing the properties for a field in a query, but property updates to a field made in a query apply to that query only.

5. **Click the** title bar of the Companies field list, **double-click** Companies **in the Alias property in the Property Sheet, then type** Organizations **as shown in** FIGURE 5-16
   The **Alias** property renames the field list in Query Design View. The Alias property doesn't change the actual name of the underlying table, but it can be helpful when you are working with a database that uses technical or outdated names for tables or queries.

QUICK TIP
To add a description
to an object in the
Navigation Pane,
right-click the object,
then click View
Properties on the
shortcut menu.

6. **Save and close the** JobData query

FIGURE 5-15: Setting query properties

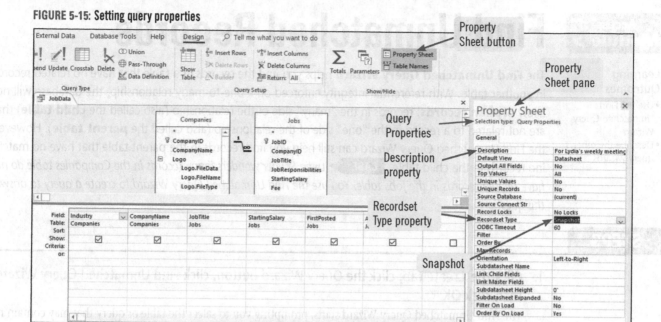

FIGURE 5-16: Setting field list properties

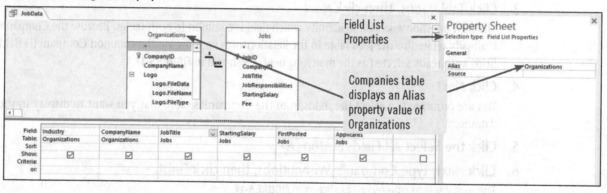

Find Unmatched Records

Learning Outcomes
• Use the Find Unmatched Query Wizard
• Describe the other query wizards

The **Find Unmatched Query Wizard** helps you find the records in a table that have no related records in another table. With referential integrity enforced on a one-to-many relationship, the database will not allow **orphan records**, records in the "many" side of the relationship (also called the **child table**) that are not related to a record in the "one" side of the relationship (also called the **parent table**). However, the Find Unmatched Query Wizard can still help you find records in the parent table that have no matching records in the child table. **CASE** *Lydia Snyder wonders if any records in the Companies table do not have related records in the Jobs table. You use the Find Unmatched Query Wizard to create a query to answer this question.*

STEPS

1. **Click the** Create tab, **click the** Query Wizard button, **click** Find Unmatched Query Wizard, **then click** OK

   The Find Unmatched Query Wizard starts, prompting you to select the table or query that may contain no related records. **TABLE 5-5** describes the other query wizards. All queries may be modified in Query Design View regardless of whether they are initially created with a wizard or directly in Query Design View.

2. **Click** Table: Companies, **then click** Next

   You want to find which companies have no related records in the Jobs table.

3. **Click** Table: Jobs, **then click** Next

   The next question asks you to identify which field is common to both tables. Because the Companies table is already related to the Jobs table in the Relationships window via the common CompanyID field, those fields are already selected as the matching fields, as shown in **FIGURE 5-17**.

4. **Click** Next

   You are prompted to select the fields from the Companies table that you want to display in the query datasheet.

5. **Click the** Select All Fields button >>

6. **Click** Next, **type** CompaniesWithoutJobs, **then click** Finish

   The query selects one record as shown in **FIGURE 5-18**.

7. **Save and close the CompaniesWithoutJobs query**

FIGURE 5-17: Find Unmatched Query Wizard

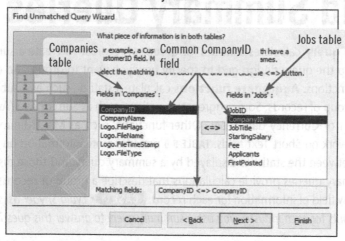

FIGURE 5-18: CompaniesWithoutJobs query in Datasheet View

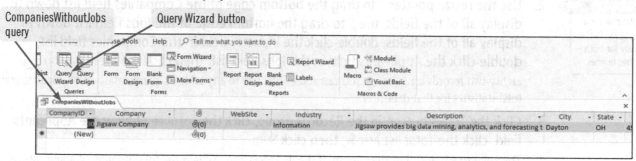

TABLE 5-5: Query wizards

name	description
Simple Query Wizard	Helps you build a select query
Crosstab Query Wizard	Helps you build a crosstab query
Find Duplicates Query Wizard	Helps you find duplicate records in a table
Find Unmatched Query Wizard	Helps you find records in one table that have no related records in another table

Reviewing referential integrity

Recall that you can establish, or enforce, **referential integrity** between two tables when joining tables in the Relationships window. Referential integrity applies a set of rules to the relationship that ensures that no orphaned records currently exist, are added to, or are created in the database. A table has an **orphan record** when information in the foreign key field of the "many"

table doesn't have a matching entry in the primary key field of the "one" table. The term "orphan" comes from the analogy that the "one" table contains **parent records**, and the "many" table contains **child records**. Referential integrity means that a Delete query would not be able to delete records in the "one" (parent) table that has related records in the "many" (child) table.

Build Summary Queries

Learning
Outcomes
• Create a summary
  query
• Define aggregate
  functions

A **summary query** calculates statistics for groups of records. To create a summary query, you add the **Total row** to the query design grid to specify how you want to group and calculate the records using aggregate functions. **Aggregate functions** calculate a statistic such as a subtotal, count, or average on a field in a group of records. Some aggregate functions, such as Sum or Avg (Average), work only on fields with Number or Currency data types. Other functions, such as Min (Minimum), Max (Maximum), or Count, also work on Short Text fields. TABLE 5-6 provides more information on aggregate functions. A key difference between the statistics displayed by a summary query and those displayed by calculated fields is that summary queries provide calculations that describe a group of records, whereas calculated fields provide a new field of information for each record. **CASE** *Lydia Snyder asks you to summarize the number of applicants for each industry. You use a summary query to answer this question.*

STEPS

1. Click the Create tab on the ribbon, click the Query Design button, double-click Companies, double-click Jobs, then click Close in the Show Table dialog box

2. Use the resize pointer ↕ to drag the bottom edge of the Companies field list down to display all of the fields, use ↕ to drag the bottom edge of the Jobs field list down to display all of the fields, double-click the Industry field in the Companies field list, double-click the Applicants field in the Jobs field list, then click the View button ▦

   Eighty-two records are selected. You can add a Total row to any table or query datasheet to calculate grand total statistics for that datasheet.

3. Click the Totals button in the Records group, click the Total cell below the Applicants field, click the Total list arrow, then click Sum

   The Total row is added to the bottom of the datasheet and displays the total number of applicants for all jobs, 1,715. Other Total row statistics include Average, Count, Maximum, Minimum, Standard Deviation, and Variance. To create subtotals per industry, you need to group the records with the same Industry value together, a task you complete in Query Design View.

4. Click the View button ▨ to return to Query Design View, click the Totals button in the Show/Hide group, click Group By in the Applicants column, click the Group By list arrow, click Sum, double-click the JobID field in the Jobs table to add it to the grid, click Group By in the JobID column, click the Group By list arrow, then click Count

   The Total row is added to the query grid below the Table row. To calculate summary statistics for each industry, the Industry field is the Group By field, as shown in FIGURE 5-19. You are also subtotaling the Applicants field using the Sum operator and counting the JobID field using the Count operator to calculate the number of jobs in each industry.

5. Click ▦ to display the datasheet, use the column resize pointer ↔ to widen each column as needed to view all field names, click in the Total row for the SumOfApplicants field, click the list arrow, click Sum, click in the Total row for the CountOfJobID field, click the list arrow, then click Sum

   The Energy industry leads all others with a count of 238 applicants. There are still 1,715 total applicants for 82 different jobs, as shown in FIGURE 5-20, but now each record represents a subtotal for all of the jobs in each industry instead of one record per job.

6. Click the Save button ▣ on the Quick Access toolbar, type IndustryApplicants, click OK, then close the query

FIGURE 5-19: Building a summary query

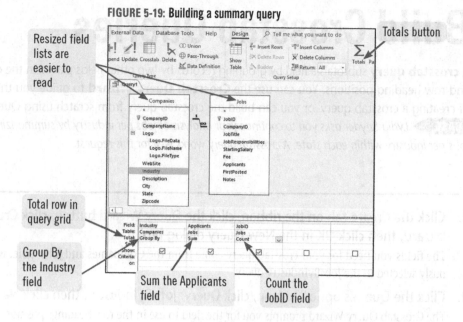

- Resized field lists are easier to read
- Totals button
- Total row in query grid
- Group By the Industry field
- Sum the Applicants field
- Count the JobID field

FIGURE 5-20: Summary query in Datasheet View

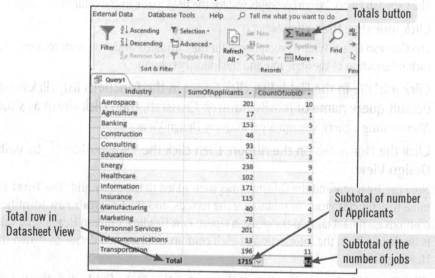

- Totals button
- Total row in Datasheet View
- Subtotal of number of Applicants
- Subtotal of the number of jobs

TABLE 5-6: Aggregate functions

aggregate function	used to find the...
Sum	Total of values in a field
Avg	Average of values in a field
Min	Minimum value in a field
Max	Maximum value in a field
Count	Number of values in a field (not counting null values)
StDev	Standard deviation of values in a field
Var	Variance of values in a field
First	Field value from the first record in a table or query
Last	Field value from the last record in a table or query

Build Crosstab Queries

Learning
Outcomes
• Create a crosstab
  query
• Modify a crosstab
  query

A **crosstab query** subtotals a field by grouping records by two other fields placed in the column heading and row heading positions. You can use the **Crosstab Query Wizard** to guide you through the steps of creating a crosstab query, or you can build the crosstab query from scratch using Query Design View.
CASE *Lydia Snyder asks you to continue your analysis of jobs per industry by summarizing the number of jobs per industry within each state. A crosstab query works well for this request.*

STEPS

1. **Click the** Create tab **on the ribbon, click the** Query Wizard button, **click** Crosstab Query Wizard, **then click** OK **in the New Query dialog box**
   The fields you need for your crosstab query come from the Companies and Jobs table, which were previously selected in the JobsByIndustry query.

2. **Click the** Queries option button, **click** Query: JobsByIndustry, **then click** Next
   The Crosstab Query Wizard prompts you for the field to use in the row headings position.

3. **Double-click** State, **then click** Next
   The Crosstab Query Wizard prompts you for the field to use in the column headings position.

4. **Click** Industry, **then click** Next
   The Crosstab Query Wizard prompts you for the calculated field. You want to count the number of jobs for each intersection of the State row and the Industry column.

5. **Click** JobTitle **in the Fields list, click** Count **in the Functions list, click** Next, **accept the default query name of** JobsByIndustry_Crosstab, **then click** Finish **as shown in** FIGURE 5-21
   After creating a query, you modify it in Query Design View.

6. **Click the** Home tab **on the ribbon, then click the** View button ☒ **to switch to Query Design View**
   Note the Total row and the Crosstab rows were added to the query grid. The **Total row** helps you determine which fields group or summarize the records, and the **Crosstab row** identifies which of the three positions each field takes in the crosstab report: Row Heading, Column Heading, or Value. The **Value field** is the field within the intersection of each column and row. You decide to switch the Row and Column Heading fields.

7. **Click** Row Heading **in the Crosstab row for the State field, click the** list arrow, **click** Column Heading, **click** Column Heading **in the Crosstab row for the Industry field, click the** list arrow, **then click** Row Heading **as shown in** FIGURE 5-22

8. **Click** ▦ **to review the new crosstab datasheet**
   The updated datasheet summarizes the same records but the Column Heading and Row Heading fields have been switched.

9. **saⁿf⬆ Save and close the** JobsByIndustry_Crosstab query, **compact and close the** IL_AC_5_Jobs.accdb database, **then close Access**
   Crosstab queries appear with a crosstab icon to the left of the query name in the Navigation Pane.

FIGURE 5-21: JobsByIndustry_Crosstab query in Datasheet View

State field is in the Row Heading position

Industry field is in the Column Heading position

Aerospace

Education

Count of JobTitle for entire row (all industries) for TN is 5

JobTitle field is also counted in the Row Heading position, which subtotals each row

Count of JobTitle in the Aerospace industry for TN is 4

Count of JobTitle in the Education industry for TN is 1

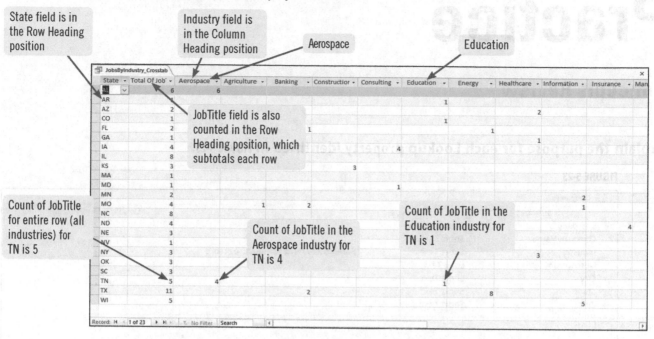

State	Total Of Job	Aerospace	Agriculture	Banking	Construction	Consulting	Education	Energy	Healthcare	Information	Insurance	Man
AL	6	6										
AR	1											
AZ	2								2			
CO	1						1					
FL	2			1				1				
GA	1								1			
IA	4					4						
IL	8				3							
KS	3											
MA	1						1					
MD	1											
MN	2									2		
MO	4		1	2						1		
NC	8											
ND	4											4
NE	3											
NV	1											
NY	3									3		
OK	3											
SC	3											
TN	5	4					1					
TX	11		2					8				
WI	5									5		

Record: 1 of 23 · No Filter · Search

FIGURE 5-22: JobsByIndustry_Crosstab query in Design View

Crosstab query button is selected

Crosstab row

State field switched to the Column Heading position

Industry field switched to the Row Heading position

JobTitle field is counted in the Value (intersection) position of the crosstab query

JobTitle field is also counted in the Row Heading position (appears as the second column in **FIGURE 5-21**)

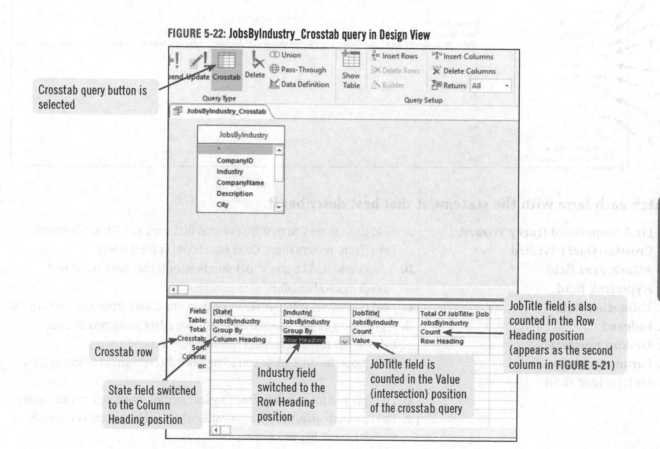

Field:	[State]	[Industry]	[JobTitle]	Total Of JobTitle: [Job
Table:	JobsByIndustry	JobsByIndustry	JobsByIndustry	JobsByIndustry
Total:	Group By	Group By	Count	Count
Crosstab:	Column Heading	Row Heading	Value	Row Heading
Sort:				
Criteria:				
or:				

Access

Practice

Concepts Review

Explain the purpose for each Lookup property identified in FIGURE 5-23.

FIGURE 5-23

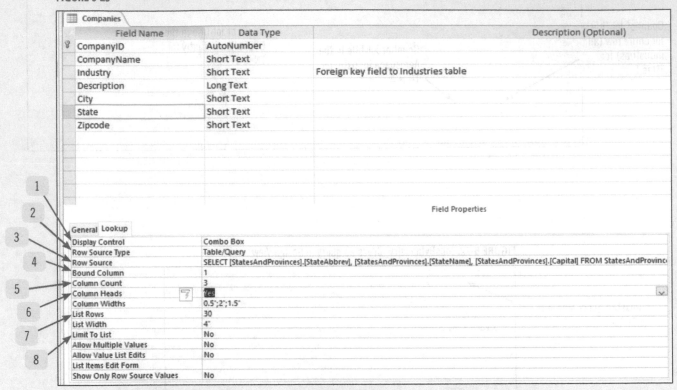

Match each term with the statement that best describes it.

9. **Find Unmatched Query Wizard**

10. **Crosstab Query Wizard**

11. **Attachment field**

12. **Hyperlink field**

13. **Validation Rule**

14. **Indexed**

15. **Lookup properties**

16. **Parameter criteria**

17. **Multivalued field**

a. Field that allows you to store external files such as a Word document, PowerPoint presentation, Excel workbook, or JPEG image

b. A process to build a query that selects records that have no related records in another table

c. Field that allows you to make more than one choice from a drop-down list

d. A process to build a query that summarizes data using two different fields in the row and column heading positions

e. Field properties that allow you to supply a drop-down list of values for a field

f. Prompts you for an entry used to select records when you run the query

g. Field property that should be considered for fields that are commonly used for searching and sorting

h. Field property that prevents unreasonable data entries for a field by testing the entry against an expression

i. Field that links to external resources such as webpages

Select the best answer from the list of choices.

18. **Which of the following fields is a good candidate for a Long Text data type?**
    a. Comments
    b. LastName
    c. City
    d. Department

19. **Which of the following is *not* true about queries?**
    a. New queries can be created in Query Design View or with a Query Wizard.
    b. Existing queries can be modified in Query Design View or with a Query Wizard.
    c. Existing queries can be copied and pasted to create a new query.
    d. New queries can be created on existing queries.

20. **What is the purpose of enforcing referential integrity?**
    a. To require an entry for each field of each record
    b. To prevent incorrect entries in the primary key field
    c. To prevent orphan records from being created
    d. To force the application of meaningful validation rules

Skills Review

1. **Create Lookup fields.**
   a. Start Access, open the IL_AC_5-2.accdb database from the location where you store your Data Files, and save it with the name **IL_AC_5_SupportDesk**. Enable content if prompted.
   b. Open the Employees table in Design View, then start the Lookup Wizard for the Department field.
   c. The lookup field will get its values from the Departments table. Select the Department field and do not specify a sort field.
   d. Do not adjust column widths. Use the default Department label, click the Enable Data Integrity check box, click Finish to finish the Lookup Wizard, then click Yes to save the table.
   e. Display the Employees table in Datasheet View, then add a new record with *your name* in the LastName and FirstName fields, **7700** in the Phone Extension field, **Marketing** in the Department Lookup field, **$55,000** in the Salary field, **1** in the Dependents field, and **(555) 111-1234** in the EmergencyPhone field.
   f. Save and close the Employees table.

2. **Modify Lookup fields.**
   a. Open the Departments table in Datasheet View and add a new record with the Department value of **Information Systems**.
   b. Add a new field named **Extension** with a Short Text data type and the values shown in FIGURE 5-24.
   c. Save and close the Departments table, then open the Employees table in Table Design View.
   d. Click the Department field, click the Lookup tab in the Field Properties pane, then modify the following properties:
      - Row Source: **SELECT Departments.Department, Departments.Extension FROM Departments;** (*Hint*: You can edit the SQL SELECT statement directly in the property or click the Build button and add the Extension field to the query.)
      - Column Count: **2**
      - Column Heads: **Yes**
      - Column Widths: **1.5"; 0.5"**
      - List Width: **2"**
      - Limit to List: **Yes**
   e. Save the Employees table, switch to Datasheet View, then modify the Department value for your name from Marketing to **Information Systems**.
   f. Close the Employees table.

FIGURE 5-24

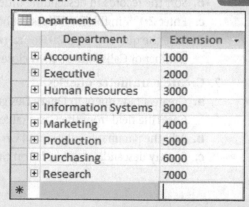

Departments	
Department	Extension
⊞ Accounting	1000
⊞ Executive	2000
⊞ Human Resources	3000
⊞ Information Systems	8000
⊞ Marketing	4000
⊞ Production	5000
⊞ Purchasing	6000
⊞ Research	7000
*	

Skills Review (continued)

3. Modify validation and index properties.

  a. Open the Calls table in Design View.

  b. Click the CallMinutes field name, then type **>=1** in the Validation Rule box.

  c. Click the Validation Text box, then type **CallMinutes value must be greater than or equal to 1** as the Validation Text.

  d. Save and test the changes, then open the Calls table in Datasheet View.

  e. Test the Validation Text and Validation Rule properties by tabbing to the CallMinutes field and entering **0**. Click OK when prompted with the Validation Text message, then press ESC to remove the invalid CallMinutes field entry.

  f. Return to Table Design View, then double-click the Indexed property for the CallMinutes field to toggle it from No to Yes (Duplicates OK).

  g. Click the Indexes button in the Show/Hide group to display all of the indexes for the table. Given you do not often search or sort on the CaseID field, click the selector button to the left of the first index named CaseID, which is set on the CaseID field, then press DELETE.

  h. Click the Indexes button to toggle off the Indexes dialog box, then save and close the Calls table.

4. Create Attachment and Hyperlink fields.

  a. Open the Employees table in Design View, then add a new field after the EmergencyPhone field with the field name **Photo** and an Attachment data type. Enter **Company photo for ID badge** for the field's Description.

  b. Add another new field after the Photo field with the field name **Email** and a Hyperlink data type.

  c. Save the Employees table, display it in Datasheet View, then attach a .jpg or .png file of yourself to the Attachment field for the record with your name or use the **Support_AC_5_employee.jpg** file provided in the location where you store your Data Files.

  d. Enter your school email address in the Email field for the record that contains your name. Close the Employees table.

  e. Use the Form Wizard to create a form based on all of the fields in the Employees table. Use a Columnar layout, and title the form **Employees Entry Form**.

  f. Navigate to the last record that contains your information, and if requested by your instructor, print only that record, then close the Employees Entry Form.

5. Create Long Text fields.

  a. Open the Cases table in Table Design View.

  b. Add a new field named **Comments** with a Long Text data type just below the ResolvedDate field.

  c. Modify the Allow Zero Length property for the Comments field from Yes to **No**.

  d. Modify the Append Only property for the Comments field from No to **Yes**.

  e. Save and close the Cases table.

6. Create Top Values queries.

  a. Create a new query in Query Design View with the CallID and CallMinutes fields from the Calls table and the CaseTitle and Category fields from the Cases table.

  b. Sort the records in descending order by the CallMinutes field.

  c. Enter **20%** in the Top Values list box to display the top 20% of records with the largest values in the CallMinutes field.

  d. Save the query as **Top20Percent**, display it in Datasheet View to view the top seven records with the greatest number of CallMinutes, then close the Top20Percent datasheet.

7. Create parameter queries.

  a. Create a new query in Query Design View with the FirstName and LastName fields from the Employees table, the CaseTitle field from the Cases table, and the CallMinutes field from the Calls table.

  b. Add the parameter criteria **>=[Enter minimum minutes]** in the Criteria cell for the CallMinutes field.

  c. Specify descending sort order on the CallMinutes field.

Skills Review (continued)

   d. Click the Datasheet View button, then enter **20** in the Enter Parameter Value dialog box. The query should select 16 records.

   e. Save the query as **CallMinutesParameter**, then close it.

8. Set properties in queries.

   a. Right-click the CallMinutesParameter query in the Navigation Pane, click Object Properties, then add the following description: **Prompts for a minimum CallMinutes value**.

   b. Close the CallMinutesParameter Properties dialog box, then open the CallMinutesParameter query in Query Design View.

   c. Right-click the CallMinutes field in the query grid, then click Properties on the shortcut menu to open the Property Sheet for the Field Properties. Enter **Minutes** for the Caption property, then change the Format property to **Standard**.

   d. Click the title bar of the Calls field list, then enter **Call Details** in the Alias property.

   e. Save and close the CallMinutesParameter query.

9. Find unmatched records.

   a. Start the Find Unmatched Query Wizard.

   b. Select the Employees table, then the Cases table, to indicate that you want to view the Employees records that have no related records in the Cases table.

   c. Confirm that the two tables are related by the EmployeeID field.

   d. Select all of the fields from the Employees table in the query results.

   e. Name the query **EmployeesWithoutCases**, then view the results. There should be nine records in the datasheet including the record with your name.

   f. If requested by your instructor, print the EmployeesWithoutCases query, then close it.

10. Create summary queries.

   a. Create a new select query in Query Design View using the Cases and Calls tables.

   b. Add the following fields: CaseTitle from the Cases table, and CallMinutes from the Calls table.

   c. Add the Total row to the query design grid, then change the aggregate function for the CallMinutes field from Group By to Sum.

   d. Add the CallMinutes field to the grid again, and change the aggregate function for the CallMinutes field from Group By to Avg.

   e. Add the CallMinutes field to the grid for a third time, and change the aggregate function for the CallMinutes field from Group By to Count.

   f. Save the query as **CallAnalysis**, view the datasheet, widen all columns so that all data is clearly visible as shown in **FIGURE 5-25**, then save and close the query.

11. Create crosstab queries.

   a. Use Query Design View to create a select query with the Department field from the Employees table, the Category field from the Cases table, and the CallMinutes field from the Calls table. Save the query as **CallsCrosstab**, then view the datasheet to see all 32 individual records.

   b. Return to Query Design View, then click the Crosstab button in the Query Type group on the Design tab

FIGURE 5-25

CaseTitle	SumOfCallMinutes	AvgOfCallMinutes	CountOfCallMinutes
Downloads are taking forever	7	7	1
Email attachment problem	23	11.5	2
Excel formulas are not automatically updating	3	3	1
Google doesn't look right	40	40	1
I accidentally deleted some files. Can I get them back?	5	5	1
I can't log in	10	5	2
I can't log in.	5	5	1
I can't see the comments in my Word document.	1	1	1
I keep seeing 'There is a problem with this website's security certificate'	11	11	1
My computer is too slow.	129	32.25	4
My computer shut down for no good reason.	108	36	3
My computer won't recognize my USB device.	10	10	1
My machine keeps restarting	56	28	2
My Wi-Fi keeps disconnecting	59	29.5	2
Pop-up ads are appearing on my desktop	78	39	2
Printer problems	4	4	1
The printer won't work.	8	8	1
The wireless network keeps kicking me off.	139	46.3333333333333	3
There are little black symbols on my Word document.	1	1	1
User got the blue screen of death	2	2	1

Record: ◄ ◄ 1 of 20 ► ► ► ☒ No Filter Search

Skills Review (continued)

to add the Total and Crosstab rows to the query design grid.

c. Specify Department as the crosstab Row Heading field, Category as the crosstab Column Heading field, and Sum CallMinutes as the crosstab Value field.

d. View the datasheet as shown in **FIGURE 5-26**, then save and close the CallsCrosstab query.

e. Compact and close the IL_AC_5_SupportDesk.accdb database, then exit Access.

FIGURE 5-26

Department	Computer	Internet	Local Netwo	MS Office	Printer
Accounting	108	125		23	
Executive				139	1
Human Resources	127				
Marketing				4	12
Production	12	11	10		
Purchasing	5				
Research	58		64		

Independent Challenge 1

As the manager of Riverwalk, a multispecialty health clinic, you have created a database to manage the schedules that connect each healthcare provider with the nurses that provider needs to efficiently handle patient visits. In this exercise, you will modify the tables to improve the database.

a. Start Access. Open the IL_AC_5-3.accdb database from the location where you store your Data Files and save it as **IL_AC_5_Riverwalk**. Click Enable Content if a yellow Security Warning message appears.

b. You want to add Lookup properties to the NurseNo field in the ScheduleItems table. First you will make sure it is not currently participating in any relationships as the Lookup Wizard will not work on a field that is currently used in a relationship. Open the Relationships window, right-click the existing relationship between the Nurses and ScheduleItems tables, click Delete and Yes to delete the existing relationship, then save and close the Relationships window.

c. Open the ScheduleItems table in Design View, then start the Lookup Wizard for the NurseNo field. Select all of the fields from the Nurses table and sort them ascending order on the NurseLName field. Hide the key column, enable data integrity, and use **Nurse** as the label. Click Yes when prompted to save the table. The field name changed from NurseNo to Nurse in Design View of the ScheduleItems table and in the Relationships window, and a one-to-many relationship with referential integrity was established between the Nurses and ScheduleItems tables.

d. Close the Relationships window and the ScheduleItems table. Open the Nurses table in Datasheet View and add your own name as a new record.

e. Close the Nurses table and open the ScheduleItems table in Datasheet View. Add your name to the Nurse lookup field for the first record (TransactionNo 28), then close the ScheduleItems table.

f. Open the Providers table in Design View. The DrPA field has only four valid entries: MD, DO, PA, or NP. (MD stands for medical doctor, DO for doctor of osteopathic medicine, PA for physician assistant, and NP for nurse practitioner.) You will use the Lookup Wizard to add these values to a lookup list. Start the Lookup Wizard for the DrPA field, choose the "I will type in the values that I want" option, then click Next.

g. In Col1, enter four rows as shown in **FIGURE 5-27**. Change the title to **Degree** and check the Limit to List check box.

h. Save and view the Providers table in Datasheet View. Add your own last name to the datasheet with a Degree value of **DO**, then save and close the Providers table.

i. Open the ScheduleDate table in Design view and add >=#8/26/2021# as a Validation Rule to the ScheduleDate field which requires all entries to be on or after 8/26/2021. Add the text **All entries must**

FIGURE 5-27

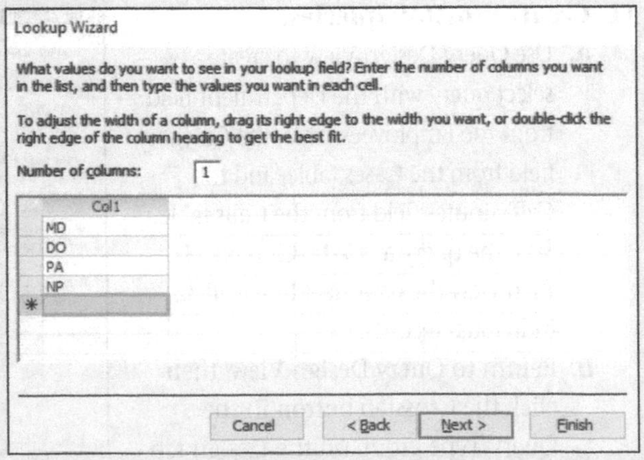

Lookup Wizard

What values do you want to see in your lookup field? Enter the number of columns you want in the list, and then type the values you want in each cell.

To adjust the width of a column, drag its right edge to the width you want, or double-click the right edge of the column heading to get the best fit.

Number of columns: 1

Col1
MD
DO
PA
NP
*

Cancel   < Back   Next >   Finish

Independent Challenge 1 (continued)

be on or after 8/26/2021 as the Validation Text property. Save and test the data, then close the ScheduleDate table.

j. Open the Nurses table in Design View and change the Indexed property to **Yes (Duplicates OK)** for the NurseLName field.

k. Add a field named **NursePhoto** with an Attachment data type and a field named **NurseEmail** with a Hyperlink data type to the end of the field list.

l. Save the Nurses table and switch to Datasheet View. In the record with your name, attach a photo of yourself or the **Support_AC_5_nurse.png** file found in your Data Files to the NursePhoto Attachment field. Add your school email address to the NurseEmail field.

m. Close the Nurses table, compact and close the IL_AC_5_Riverwalk database, then exit Access.

Independent Challenge 2

You are working for a city to coordinate a series of community-wide preparedness activities. You have created a database to track the activities and volunteers who are attending the activities. In this exercise, you will create and modify queries to analyze data.

a. Start Access, open the IL_AC_5-4.accdb database from the location where you store your Data Files, save it as **IL_AC_5_Volunteers**, then enable content if prompted.

b. Create a query in Query Design View with the LastName field from the Volunteers table, and the ActivityName and ActivityHours from the Activities table. (*Hint*: You need to add the Attendance table to Query Design View so that the Volunteers and Activities tables are joined.)

c. Use the Totals button to group the records by the ActivityName, count the LastName field, and sum the Activity-Hours field.

d. Save the query with the name **TotalActivityHours**, display it in Datasheet View as shown in FIGURE 5-28, then close the TotalActivityHours query.

e. Open the Volunteers table and add *your name* as a new record. Use your school's address for the Street field, **66215** for the Zipcode, and **1/1/89** for the Birthday field. Close the Volunteers table.

FIGURE 5-28

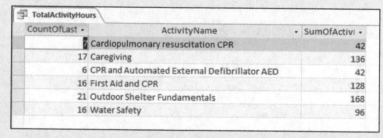

f. Start the Find Unmatched Query Wizard. Find the records in the Volunteers table that have no matching records in the Attendance table based on the common VolunteerID field. Select all of the fields from the Volunteers table, name the query **VolunteersWithoutAttendance**, view it in Datasheet View (it should contain one record, the record you entered with your own information in the previous step), then close the query.

g. Create a new query in Query Design View with the FirstName and LastName fields from the Volunteers table and the City and State fields from the Zipcodes table.

h. Add **[Enter desired state]** parameter criteria in the State field, then save the query with the name **StateParameter**.

i. Open the StateParameter query in Datasheet View using **IA** as the criterion. The query should return four records for volunteers who live in Iowa. Return to Query Design View and run the query again using **MO** as the criteria. The query should return seven records for volunteers who live in Missouri. Close the StateParameter query.

j. Compact and close the IL_AC_5_Volunteers.accdb database, then exit Access.

Visual Workshop

Open the IL_AC_5-5.accdb database from the location where you store your Data Files, save it with the name **IL_AC_5_CollegeCourses**, then enable content if prompted. Create a new query in Query Design View with the Department field from the Professors table, and the Grade and StudentID fields from the Enrollments table. (*Hint*: Add the Sections table to connect the Professors and Enrollments tables). Save the query with the name **GradesByDepartment**, view it in Datasheet View, then close it. Using the Crosstab Query Wizard, create a new crosstab query from the GradesByDepartment query. Use Department for the row heading field, Grade for the column heading field, and count the StudentID field for each row and column intersection. Accept the default name for the query, **GradesByDepartment_Crosstab**, then view it in Datasheet View as shown in **FIGURE 5-29**. Close the query, compact and close the IL_AC_5_CollegeCourses database, then exit Access.

FIGURE 5-29

Department	Total Of Stuc	A	B	C	D	F	W
ACCT	9	3	4	1	1		
BUS	9	2	4	1		1	1
CIS	22	9	9	2		1	1
ECON	3	1	1		1		
ENGR	10	3	5	2			
MATH	8		4		1	3	
MKT	11	1	7			3	

Improving Tables and Creating Advanced Queries

Creating Forms

CASE ▶ You are working with Lydia Snyder, vice president of operations at JCL Talent, to build a research database to manage industry, company, and job data. In this module, you'll create and modify forms, which are used to find, enter, and edit information.

Module Objectives

After completing this module, you will be able to:

- Add labels and text boxes
- Resize and align controls
- Create calculations on forms
- Add check boxes and toggle buttons
- Add option groups
- Add combo boxes to enter data
- Add combo boxes to find records
- Add lines and rectangles
- Add hyperlink controls
- Add command buttons
- Modify tab order
- Add images
- Create a split form
- Add subforms
- Add tab controls
- Modify form properties

Files You Will Need

IL_AC_6-1.accdb
Support_AC_6_jcl.png
Support_AC_6_confidential.jpg
Support_AC_6_man.jpg
Support_AC_6_woman.jpg
IL_AC_6-2.accdb

Support_AC_6_computer.png
Support_AC_6_draft.jpg
IL_AC_6-3.accdb
IL_AC_6-4.accdb
IL_AC_6-5.accdb

Add Labels and Text Boxes

Learning Outcomes
• Add labels to a form
• Add text boxes to a form
• Modify labels and text boxes on a form

Adding and deleting **controls**, the different individual items on a form, is a common activity. Controls can be used to enter and edit data, clarify information, or make the form easier to use. **Labels**, descriptive text that does not change as you navigate from record to record, are the most common type of unbound control. **Text boxes**, input boxes that provide a user with a location to enter and edit a field's value, are the most common type of bound control. TABLE 6-1 describes common form controls. **CASE** *Lydia Snyder asks you to improve the JobsEntry form. You add and modify labels and text boxes to handle this request.*

STEPS

1. **sam↓ Start Access, open the** IL_AC_6-1.accdb database **from the location where you store your Data Files, save it as** IL_AC_6_Jobs, **enable content if prompted, right-click the** JobsEntry form, **then click** Layout View

   You can add and modify controls in either Form Layout or Form Design View. The benefit of using Form Design View is that all form modification features are available including ruler and form section information. The benefit of using Form Layout View is that live data is displayed. The Controls group on the Design tab displays the different types of controls that you can add to a form.

2. **Click the** Text Box button 🔲 **in the Controls group, click the** form, **then use the move pointer** ⁺ᵏ **to move the new text box below the Applicants text box (which currently displays 50)**

   When you add a new text box to a form, Access automatically adds a label to the left of the text box. **Label** controls describe the data that the text box displays. You can modify a label control directly on the form or change the text using the label's **Caption property**.

3. **Double-click** Text## **in the label to select it, type** Posted, **then press** ENTER

   To bind the new text box to a field in Form Layout View, use the **Control Source** property of the text box. Recall that a **property** is a characteristic of the form or control that can be modified. All of a control's properties are stored in the control's **Property Sheet**.

4. **Click the** new text box **to select it, click the** Data tab **in the Property Sheet, click the** Control Source property list arrow, **click** FirstPosted, **click the** Default Value property, **then enter** =Date() **as shown in** FIGURE 6-1

   The **Default Value** property value is automatically entered in a field for new records using this form. =Date() is an expression that uses the built-in Access function **Date()** to return the current date. The Property Sheet shows all properties for the selected control in both Layout View and Design View.

5. **Right-click the** JobsEntry form tab, **click** Design View, **then click the** Close command button **in the Form Header section**

   The Property Sheet changes to show the properties of the selected command button.

6. **Click the** Format tab **on the ribbon, click the** Quick Styles button, **click the** Colored Fill – Blue, Accent 1 option **(second column, second row), click the** Change Shape button, **then click the** Oval shape **(second column, third row)**

   Changes you make using the ribbon are updated in the Property Sheet and vice versa.

7. **Click the** JobID text box, **double-click the** Enabled property **in the Property Sheet, click the** Fee text box, **then double-click the** Locked property **as shown in** FIGURE 6-2

   The **Enabled** property determines whether that control can have the focus in Form View. The **focus** determines where the user will enter or edit data, and is visually identified by a blinking I-beam insertion point. A user may not edit the data in an AutoNumber field, so there is no need for it to receive the focus. The **Locked** property determines whether the field can be edited, which allows a user to copy the data. When the Locked property is set to Yes, a user cannot change the data.

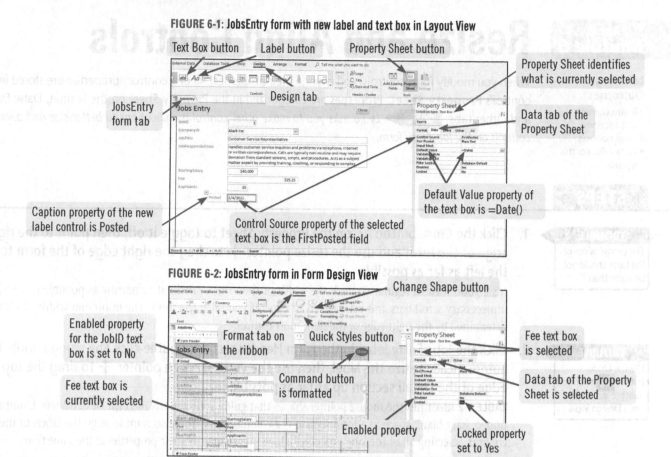

FIGURE 6-1: JobsEntry form with new label and text box in Layout View

Text Box button — Label button — Property Sheet button

JobsEntry form tab

Design tab

Property Sheet identifies what is currently selected

Data tab of the Property Sheet

Default Value property of the text box is =Date()

Caption property of the new label control is Posted

Control Source property of the selected text box is the FirstPosted field

FIGURE 6-2: JobsEntry form in Form Design View

Change Shape button

Enabled property for the JobID text box is set to No

Format tab on the ribbon

Quick Styles button

Fee text box is selected

Fee text box is currently selected

Command button is formatted

Data tab of the Property Sheet is selected

Enabled property

Locked property set to Yes

TABLE 6-1: Common form controls

name	button	used to	bound or unbound
Label	Aa	Provide consistent descriptive text as you navigate from record to record; the most common type of unbound control and can also be used as a hyperlink to another database object, external file, or webpage	Unbound
Text box	abl	Display, edit, or enter data for each record from an underlying record source; the most common type of bound control	Bound
List box		Display a list of possible data entries for a field	Bound
Combo box		Display a list of possible data entries for a field, and provide a text box for an entry from the keyboard; combines the list box and text box controls	Bound
Combo box		Find a record. (When a combo box is used to find a record versus enter or edit data, it functions as an unbound control.)	Unbound
Tab control		Create a three-dimensional aspect on a form	Unbound
Check box	☑	Display "yes" or "no" answers for a field; if the box is checked, it means "yes"	Bound
Toggle button		Display "yes" or "no" answers for a field; if the button is pressed, it means "yes"	Bound
Option button	◉	Display a value for a field within an option group	Bound
Option group	XYZ	Display and organize choices (usually presented as option buttons) for a field	Bound
Line and Rectangle		Draw lines and rectangles on the form	Unbound
Command button	XXX	Provide an easy way to initiate a command or run a macro	Unbound

Resize and Align Controls

Learning Outcomes
- Resize controls and sections
- Align controls
- Work with control layouts

When you modify form controls, you change their properties. All of a control's properties are stored in the control's **Property Sheet**. Properties are categorized in the Property Sheet on the Format, Data, Event, and Other tabs. CASE ▶ *Lydia asks you to make other control modifications to better size and align the controls on the JobsEntry form.*

STEPS

1. **Click the Close button ☒ on the Property Sheet to toggle it off, then point to the right edge of the form and use the resize pointer ↔ to drag the right edge of the form to the left as far as possible**

   It's a good idea to regularly check the width of the form to make it as narrow as possible to eliminate unnecessary scroll bars and extra sheets of paper if you print the form. The minimum width of a form is determined by the right edge of the right-most control.

2. **Click the Jobs Entry label in the Form Header section, double-click any sizing handle to automatically resize the label, then use the vertical resize pointer ↕ to drag the top edge of the Detail section up as far as possible**

   TABLE 6-2 identifies the mouse pointer shapes that guide your actions in Form Design View. Eliminating unnecessary blank space in a form section is a common task. You also want to align the labels in the first column. Selecting all of the labels together allows you to modify their properties at the same time.

3. **Click the JobID label in the first column, press and hold CTRL, click each of the other labels in the first column to select them together, release CTRL, click the Format tab on the ribbon, click the Align Right button ≣ in the Font group, click the Arrange tab on the ribbon, click the Align button, then click Right as shown in FIGURE 6-3**

   The **Align Right button** ≣ right-aligns the text *within* the control whereas the **Right command** on the Align menu right-aligns the right *edges* of the selected controls. Many other options on the Arrange tab of the ribbon control the positioning of controls on the form, as described in **TABLE 6-3**.

   When you create new forms or add controls to the form in Layout View, they are often organized in a **layout**, an invisible grid that aligns and sizes controls within the layout. See **TABLE 6-4** for more information on layouts. The Posted label and FirstPosted text box are in a layout.

4. **Click the layout selector ⊞ in the upper-left corner of the Posted label to select the layout, then click the Remove Layout button in the Table group on the Arrange tab**

   With the layout removed, you can modify the individual controls within the layout.

5. **Click the StartingSalary text box, press and hold CTRL, click the Fee text box, click the Applicants text box, click the FirstPosted text box, release CTRL, click the Size/Space button on the Arrange tab, then click To Narrowest**

   The four text boxes have been resized to the narrowest of the four.

6. **Click the Save button ▣ on the Quick Access Toolbar, right-click the JobsEntry form tab, then click Form View**

FIGURE 6-3: Resizing and aligning controls on the JobsEntry form

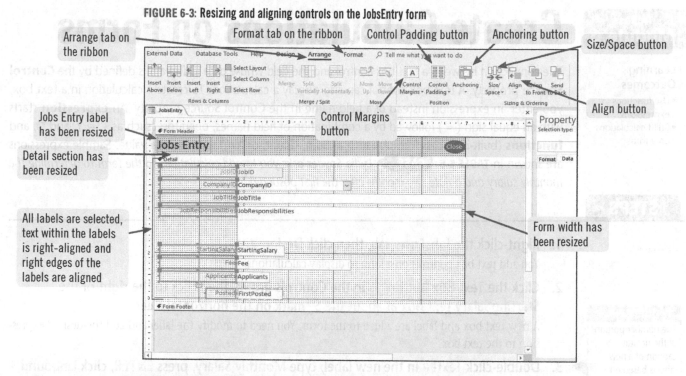

TABLE 6-2: Mouse pointer shapes in Form Design View

shape	when does this shape appear?	action
⌖	When you point to any unselected control on the form (the default mouse pointer)	Single-clicking with this mouse pointer selects a control
✛	When you point to the upper-left corner or edge of a selected control in Form Design View or the middle of the control in Form Layout View	Dragging with this mouse pointer moves the selected control(s)
↕ ↔ ⤡ ⤢	When you point to any sizing handle (except the larger one in the upper-left corner in Form Design View)	Dragging with one of these mouse pointers resizes the control

TABLE 6-3: Features that help position controls

button name	icon	description
Control Margins	🅰	Determines the **margin** of selected controls, the space between the content inside the control and the outside border of the control
Control Padding	▦	Determines the **padding** between selected controls, the space between the outside borders of the controls
Anchoring	▤	Determines the **anchor** position of selected controls, the position of the controls with respect to the edge or corner of the form
Size/Space	⧉	**Sizes** selected controls to options such as the tallest, shortest, widest, or narrowest control. **Spaces** selected controls with options such as giving them equal, more or less horizontal or vertical space Also includes options to position controls to a grid or to **group** controls together so they move, resize, and format as a single control
Align	▣	Aligns the top, right, bottom, or left edges of selected controls

TABLE 6-4: Control layouts

layout	description
Tabular	Controls are arranged in rows and columns like a spreadsheet, with labels across the top
Stacked	Controls are arranged vertically as on a paper form, with a label to the left of each control

Create Calculations on Forms

The connection between a text box control and the field whose data it displays is defined by the **Control Source** property. A text box control can also display a calculation. To create a calculation in a text box, you enter an expression instead of a field name in the Control Source property. An **expression** starts with an equal sign (=) followed by a combination of field names, operators (such as +, −, /, and *), and **functions** (built-in Access formulas such as Sum, Count, or Avg) that return a value. Sample expressions are shown in **TABLE 6-5**. **CASE** *Lydia Snyder asks you to add calculations to the form to determine the monthly salary and a date two months after the first posting date.*

STEPS

1. **Right-click the** JobsEntry **tab, then click** Design View
   You add text box controls on a form to display calculations.

2. **Click the** Text Box button ⎆ **in the Controls group, then click to the** right of the StartingSalary text box at about the 5" mark **on the horizontal ruler**
   A new text box and label are added to the form. You need to modify the label and add the desired expression to the text box.

3. **Double-click** Text## **in the new label, type** Monthly Salary, **press** ENTER, **click** Unbound **in the new text box, type** =[StartingSalary]/12, **then press** ENTER
   All expressions start with an equal sign (=). When referencing a field name within an expression, [square brackets]—(not parentheses) and not {curly braces}—surround the field name. In an expression, you must type the field name exactly as it was created in Table Design View, but you do not need to match the capitalization.

4. **Click** ⎆ **in the Controls group, click to the** right of the FirstPosted text box at about the 5" mark **on the horizontal ruler, double-click** Text## **in the new label, type** 2 Months Later, **press** ENTER, **click** Unbound **in the new text box, type** =[FirstPosted]+60, **then press** ENTER
   To calculate the number of days between the current date and the FirstPosted date, the expression would be =Date()-[FirstPosted]. Recall that **Date()** is a built-in Access function that returns the current date.

5. **Use the horizontal resize pointer** ↔ **to widen the text boxes that contain expressions to display the entire expression as shown in** FIGURE 6-4
   With the expressions in place, you are ready to view the data in Form View.

6. **Click the** Save button 🖫 **on the Quick Access Toolbar, right-click the** JobsEntry **form tab, click** Form View, **navigate to the second record for JobID 3 as shown in** FIGURE 6-5, **then close the** JobsEntry **form**

Bound versus unbound controls

Recall that controls are either bound or unbound. **Bound controls** such as text boxes display values from a field and are used to enter data. **Unbound controls** describe data, enhance the appearance of the form, or make the form easier to use.

Labels are the most common type of unbound control, but other unbound controls include lines, images, tabs, command buttons, and combo boxes used to find records. Bound controls can also be bound to an expression.

FIGURE 6-4: Creating calculations in Form Design View

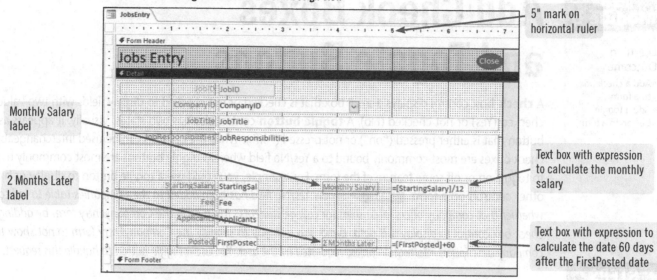

Monthly Salary label

2 Months Later label

5" mark on horizontal ruler

Text box with expression to calculate the monthly salary

Text box with expression to calculate the date 60 days after the FirstPosted date

FIGURE 6-5: Viewing calculations in Form View

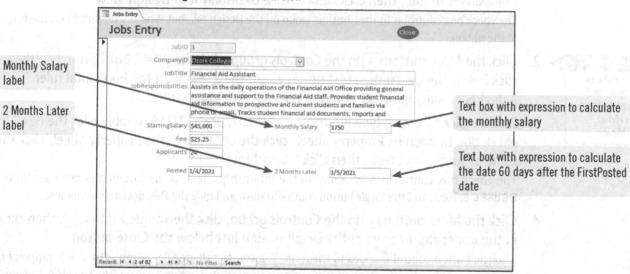

Monthly Salary label

2 Months Later label

Text box with expression to calculate the monthly salary

Text box with expression to calculate the date 60 days after the FirstPosted date

TABLE 6-5: Sample expressions

sample expression	description
=Sum([Salary])	Uses the **Sum function** to add the values in the Salary field
=[Price] * 1.05	Multiplies the Price field by 1.05 (adds 5% to the Price field)
=[Subtotal] + [Shipping]	Adds the value of the Subtotal field to the value of the Shipping field
=Avg([Freight])	Uses the **Avg function** to display an average of the values in the Freight field
=Date()	Uses the **Date function** to display the current date in the form of mm-dd-yy
="Page" &[Page]	Displays the word Page, a space, and the result of the **Page field**, a built-in Access field that contains the current page number
=[FirstName]& " " &[LastName]	Displays the value of the FirstName and LastName fields in one control, separated by a space
=Left([ProductNumber],2)	Uses the **Left function** to display the first two characters in the ProductNumber field

Add Check Boxes and Toggle Buttons

**Learning
Outcomes**
- Add a check box
  to a form
- Add a toggle
  button to a form

A **check box** control displays a small box that is checked or not checked to display fields with two values: checked (Yes) or not checked (No). A **toggle button** control also has two states. Visually, it appears as a button that is either pressed ("on") or not pressed ("off"). While the controls can be used interchangeably, check boxes are most commonly bound to a Yes/No field whereas toggle buttons are most commonly used to toggle on or off some feature of the form. For example, you could use a toggle button to display or hide other controls on a form. **CASE** *A new Yes/No field has been added to the Companies table to indicate whether that company offers internships for college students. You modify the CompanyEntry form by adding a check box control to display this data. Lydia also asks you to simplify the CompanyEntry form to not show the company description information unless requested by the user. You use a toggle button to handle this request.*

STEPS

1. **Double-click the** CompanyEntry form **to view it in Form View, right-click the** CompanyEntry tab, **then click** Design View **to display it in Design View**

   The check box control is in the Controls group on the Design tab, but typically doesn't fit on the first row of the ribbon.

QUICK TIP
You can also add
check boxes and
other controls to
forms in Form
Layout View.

2. **Click the** More button ⬇ **in the Controls group, click the** Check Box button ✅, **then click** below the Description text box at about the 2" mark **on the horizontal ruler**

   A check box control and an accompanying label have been added to the form.

3. **Double-click** Check##, **type** Internships offered?, **press** ENTER, **double-click the** new check box **to open its Property Sheet, click the** Data tab **in the Property Sheet, click the** Control Source list arrow, **then click** Internships

   The check box control is now bound to the Internships field in the Companies table as shown in **FIGURE 6-6**. Next, add the toggle button control to show and hide the Description information.

4. **Click the** More button ⬇ **in the Controls group, click the** Toggle Button 🔲, **then click** in the upper-right corner of the Detail section **just below the Close button**

   A toggle button control is added to the form. You connect the toggle button's **On Click** property to a macro named ShowHideDescription that was previously created in this database. The ShowHideDescription macro contains the instructions to show or hide the Description information.

5. **Click the** Event tab **in the Property Sheet, click the** On Click list arrow, **click** ShowHideDescription, **click the** Format tab **in the Property Sheet, click the** Caption property, **type** More, **then press** ENTER **as shown in** FIGURE 6-7

   With both the check box and toggle controls in place, you view and test them in Form View.

6. **Click the** Save button 🖫 **on the Quick Access Toolbar, right-click the** CompanyEntry tab, **click** Form View, **navigate to the second record, click the** Internships offered? check box, **then click the** More toggle button **several times**

   Clicking the More toggle button alternatively shows or hides the Description label and Description text box. The toggle button also changes appearance when it is "on" and "off." In a later module, you will learn how to create macros.

7. **Right-click the** CompanyEntry tab, **then click** Close

FIGURE 6-6: Adding a check box to a form

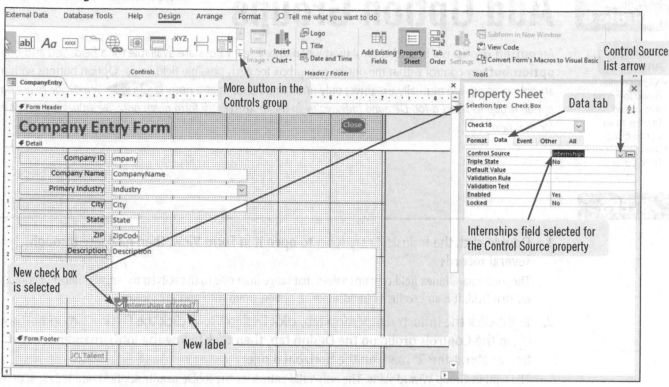

FIGURE 6-7: Adding a toggle button to a form

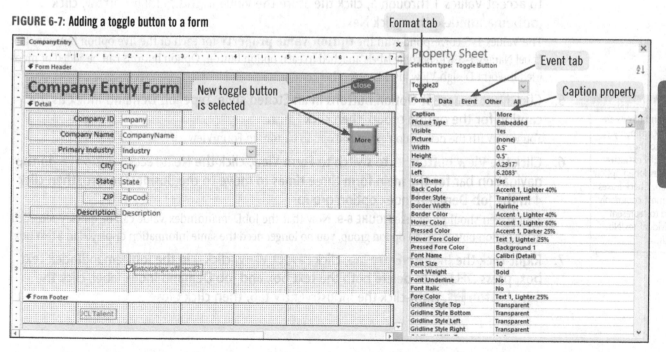

Add Option Groups

Learning Outcomes
- Add an option group to a form
- Add option buttons to an option group
- Use option buttons to edit data

An **option group** is a bound control used when only a few values are available for a field. You add one **option button** control within the option group box for each possible field value. Option buttons within an option group are mutually exclusive; only one can be chosen at a time. **CASE** *You decide to use an option group to select a Job Demand Index value in the IndustryEntry form given only five values are possible for that field.*

STEPS

1. **Double-click the** IndustryEntry form **to open it in Form View, then navigate through several records**

   The JobDemandIndex field contains values that range from one to five. Given the small number of choices for that field, it is an excellent candidate for an option group with option buttons.

2. **Right-click the** IndustryEntry form tab, **click** Design View, **click the** Option Group button **in the Controls group on the Design tab, then click** below the JobDemandIndex text box at about the 2" mark **on the horizontal ruler**

   The Option Group Wizard starts. The only valid entries for the JobDemandIndex fields are 1, 2, 3, 4, or 5. You will use these values as the label names.

3. **Type** 1, **press** TAB, **type** 2, **press** TAB, **type** 3, **press** TAB, **type** 4, **press** TAB, **then type** 5 **as shown in FIGURE 6-8**

   The Option Group Wizard walks you through the process of creating both the option group and option buttons within the group.

4. **Click** Next, **click the** No, I don't want a default option button, **click** Next, **click** Next **to accept Values 1 through 5, click the** Store the Value in this field: list arrow, **click** JobDemandIndex, **then click** Next

   The Values 1–5 correspond with the **Option Value property** for each of the five option buttons. The Label Names 1–5 will become labels attached to each option button. Option buttons can be added or modified in Form Design View just like any other control.

5. **Click** Next **to accept Option buttons in an Etched style, type** Job Demand Index **as the caption for the option group, then click** Finish

   You work with the new option group and option buttons in Form View.

6. **Click the** View button **to switch to Form View, click the** Next record button **in the navigation bar for the main form three times to move to the Business record, then click 4 in the Job Demand Index option group**

   Your screen should look like **FIGURE 6-9**. Now that the JobDemandIndex value can be quickly recorded using option buttons in an option group, you no longer need the same information displayed in a text box.

7. **Right-click the** IndustryEntry tab, **click** Layout View, **click** 4 in the JobDemandIndex text box, **press** DELETE **to delete both the text box and Job Demand Index label, click the** Save button **, right-click the** IndustryEntry tab, **then click** Close

FIGURE 6-8: Building an option group with the Option Group Wizard

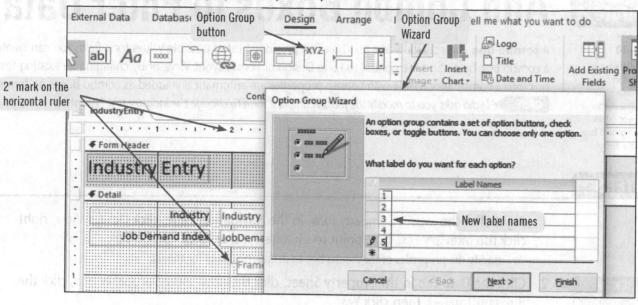

FIGURE 6-9: Using an option group in Form View

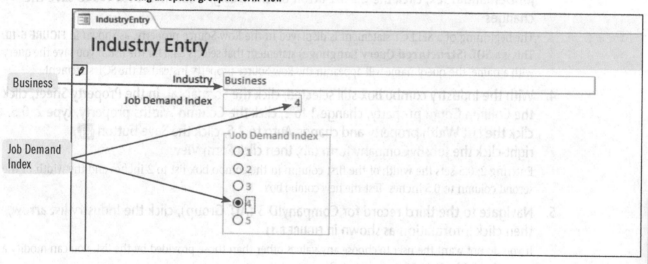

Add Combo Boxes to Enter Data

**Learning
Outcomes**
• Add a combo box
to a form
• Modify combo
box properties
• Use a combo box
for data entry

A **combo box** control works as a text box that provides a list of possible values for a field. You can create a combo box by adding the control to Form Design or Form Layout View, or by changing an existing text box into a combo box. Fields with Lookup properties are automatically added as combo boxes on forms.

CASE ▸ *Lydia asks you to modify the JobsByCompany form to change the Industry text box into a combo box.*

STEPS

1. **Right-click the** JobsByCompany form **in the Navigation Pane, click** Design View, **right-click the** Industry text box, **point to** Change To, **then click** Combo Box

   You modify the properties of the combo box to define the values for the list.

QUICK TIP
A brief description of
the property appears
in the status bar.

2. **Click the** Data tab **in the Property Sheet, click the** Row Source property box, **click the** Build button ⸬, **then click** Yes

   Clicking the Build button for the **Row Source property** opens the Query Builder window, which allows you to select the field values you want to display in the combo box list. You want to select the Industry and JobDemandIndex fields for the list from the Industries table.

3. **Double-click** Industry **in the Industries field list to add it to the query grid, double-click** JobDemandIndex, **click the** Close button **on the Design tab, then click** Yes **to save the changes**

   The beginning of a SELECT statement is displayed in the Row Source property, as shown in **FIGURE 6-10**. This is a **SQL (Structured Query Language)** statement that selects data for the list. If you save the query with a name, the query name will appear in the Row Source property instead of the SQL statement.

4. **With the Industry combo box still selected, click the** Format tab **in the Property Sheet, click the** Column Count property, **change 1 to** 2, **click the** Column Widths property, **type** 2; 0.5, **click the** List Width property **and change Auto to** 2.5, **click the** Save button 🖫, **right-click the** JobsByCompany form tab, **then click** Form View

   Entering 2; 0.5 sets the width of the first column in the combo box list to 2 inches and the width of the second column to 0.5 inches. Test the new combo box.

5. **Navigate to the third record for CompanyID 3 (AIT Group), click the** Industry list arrow, **then click** Information **as shown in FIGURE 6-11**

   If you do not want the user to choose any values other than those provided by the list, you can modify a combo box's **Limit to List** property to Yes.

FIGURE 6-10: Adding a combo box in Form Design View

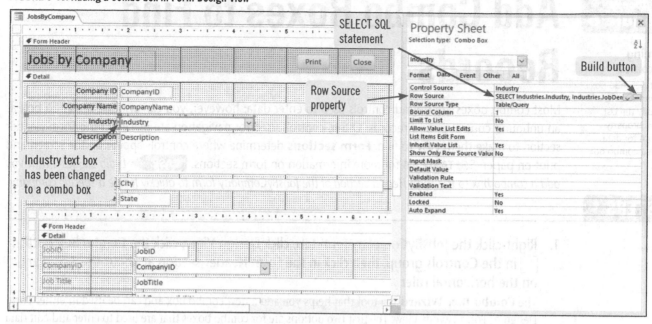

FIGURE 6-11: Using a combo box to change data in Form View

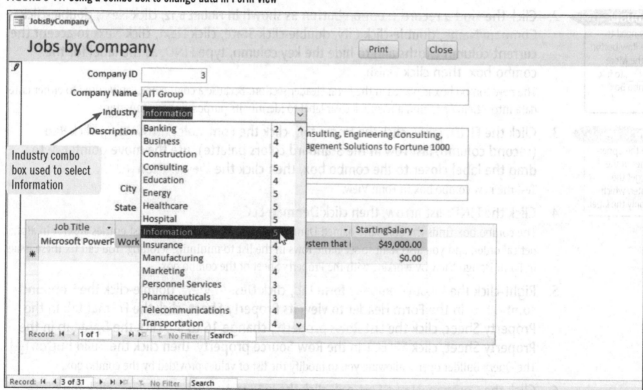

Choosing between a combo box and a list box

The list box and combo box controls are very similar, but the combo box is more popular for two reasons. While both provide a list of values from which the user can choose to make an entry in a field, the combo box also functions as a text box allowing

users to make an entry that is not on the list (unless the Limit To List property for the combo box is set to Yes). More important, however, is that most users like the drop-down list action of the combo box.

Access

Add Combo Boxes to Find Records

Learning
Outcomes
• Add a combo box
to find records
• Modify the List
Rows property
• Search for data
with a combo box

Most combo boxes are bound controls used to enter data; however, you can also use a combo box as an unbound control to find records. Often, controls used for navigation are placed in the Form Header section to make them easy to find. **Form sections** determine where controls appear on the screen and print on paper. See **TABLE 6-6** for more information on form sections. **CASE** *Lydia suggests that you add a combo box to the Form Header section of the JobsByCompany form to quickly locate a specific company.*

STEPS

1. **Right-click the** JobsByCompany form tab, **click** Design View, **click the** Combo Box button **in the Controls group, then click in the** Form Header section at about the 3.5" mark **on the horizontal ruler**

   The **Combo Box Wizard** is a tool that helps you add a new combo box and can be used in either Form Design or Form Layout View. The first two options are for combo boxes that are used to enter and edit data in a field. The difference between the first two options is where the drop-down list gets its values. The third option creates an unbound combo box that is used to find records.

TROUBLE
You may need to
click the Row button
▼ or the More
button ⥥ to find
the Combo Box
button.

2. **Click the** Find a record... option button **as shown in FIGURE 6-12, click** Next, **double-click** CompanyName, **double-click** City, **double-click** State, **click** Next, **click** Next **to accept the current column widths and to hide the key column, type** FIND: **as the label for the combo box, then click** Finish

   The new combo box is placed in the Form Header section. Because a combo box can be used to either enter data into a field or to find a record, a clear label to identify its purpose is very important.

QUICK TIP
Point to the upper-
left corner of the
label to get the
 pointer, which
moves only the label.

3. **Click the** FIND: label, **click the** Home tab, **click the** Font Color arrow , **click** Red **(second column, last row in the Standard colors palette), use the move pointer to drag the label closer to the combo box, then click the** View button

   Test the new combo box in Form View.

4. **Click the** FIND: list arrow, **then click** Denman LLC

   The combo box finds the company named Denman LLC, but the combo box list entries are not in alphabetical order, and you also want to see more rows in the list to minimize scrolling. You can fix these issues in Form Design View by working with the Property Sheet of the combo box.

5. **Right-click the** JobsByCompany form tab, **click** Design View, **double-click the** Unbound combo box **in the Form Header to view its Property Sheet, click the** Format tab **in the Property Sheet, click the** List Rows property, **change 16 to 30, click the** Data tab **in the Property Sheet, click** SELECT **in the Row Source property, then click the** Build button

   The Query Builder opens, allowing you to modify the list of values provided by the combo box.

6. **Click the** CompanyName Sort cell, **click the** list arrow, **click** Ascending, **click the** Close button **on the Design tab, click** Yes **when prompted to save changes, click the** View button , **then click the** FIND: list arrow

   This time, the combo box list is sorted in ascending order by company name, and 30 versus 16 rows are displayed, as shown in **FIGURE 6-13**.

7. **Click** Cross Team **to find the Cross Team company record, click the** Save button **on the Quick Access Toolbar, right-click the** JobsByCompany form tab, **then click** Close

FIGURE 6-12: Combo Box Wizard

Combo Box button   Row button

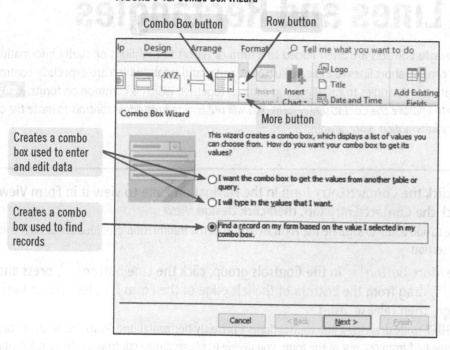

Creates a combo box used to enter and edit data

Creates a combo box used to find records

More button

FIGURE 6-13: Using a combo box to find records

Rows are sorted in ascending order by CompanyName

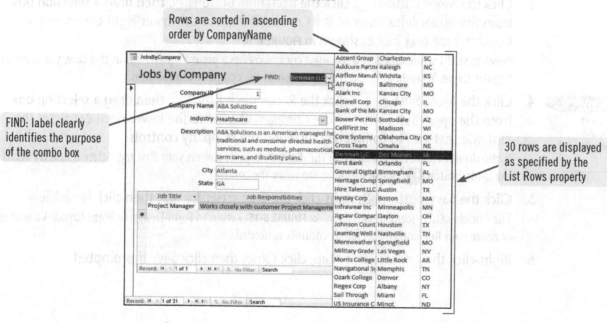

FIND: label clearly identifies the purpose of the combo box

30 rows are displayed as specified by the List Rows property

TABLE 6-6: Form sections

section	description
Detail	Appears once for every record
Form Header	Appears at the top of the form and often contains command buttons or a label with the title of the form
Form Footer	Appears at the bottom of the form and often contains command buttons or a label with instructions on how to use the form
Page Header	Appears at the top of a printed form with information such as page numbers or dates
Page Footer	Appears at the bottom of a printed form with information such as page numbers or dates

Access

Add Lines and Rectangles

Learning
Outcomes
• Add lines to a
  form
• Add rectangles to
  a form

Line or **rectangle** controls are often added to a form or report to highlight or clarify information. For example, you can use short lines to indicate subtotals and grand totals, which are especially common on reports. You can use rectangles to visually group controls together, which is common on forms. **CASE ▶** *Lydia asks you to improve the ContactsEntry form. You will use line and rectangle controls to make the contact versus company information more obvious.*

STEPS

1. **Double-click the** ContactsEntry form **in the Navigation Pane to view it in Form View, right-click the** ContactsEntry tab, **then click** Design View

   You decide to add a line to separate the Form Header from the information provided about each contact in the Detail section.

2. **Click the** More button ⬇ **in the Controls group, click the** Line button ◹, **press and hold** SHIFT, **drag from the** bottom of the left edge of the Form Header section to the right edge, **then release** SHIFT

   Pressing SHIFT while dragging a line control draws a perfectly horizontal line. With the header information visually separated from the rest of the form, you decide to use rectangle controls to clarify the contact versus the company information.

3. **Click the** More button ⬇, **click the** Rectangle button ▢, **then drag a selection box from the** upper-left corner of the ContactID label to the lower-right corner of the ContactEmail text box **as shown in FIGURE 6-14**

   Pressing SHIFT while dragging a rectangle control creates a perfect square, but in this case, you want a rectangular shape. You add a second rectangle around the company information.

QUICK TIP
Adding lines and
rectangles works
the same way for
reports.

4. **Click the** More button ⬇, **click the** Rectangle button ▢, **then drag a selection box from the** upper-left corner of the CompanyID label to the lower-right corner of the ZipCode text box **to completely surround the company controls**

   If you do not create the rectangle in the desired shape or size on your first try, delete it and try again, use the Undo button ↩, or use the mouse to resize the control.

5. **Click the** Save button 🖫, **right-click the** ContactsEntry tab, **then click** Form View

   The ContactsEntry form should look like **FIGURE 6-15**. Return to Form Design or Form Layout View to move or resize your line and two rectangle controls as needed.

6. **Right-click the** ContactsEntry tab, **click** Close, **then click** Save **if prompted**

FIGURE 6-14: Creating line and rectangle controls in Form Design View

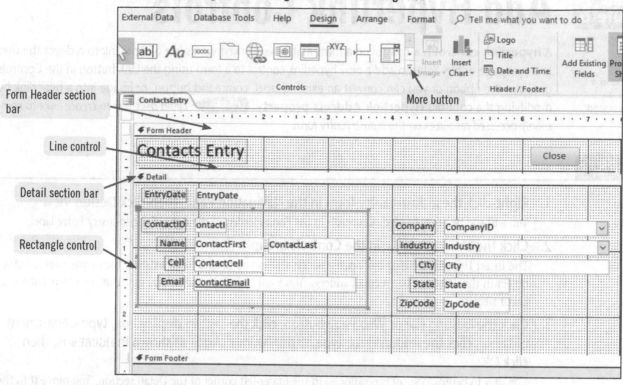

- Form Header section bar
- Line control
- Detail section bar
- Rectangle control
- More button

FIGURE 6-15: Viewing line and rectangle controls in Form View

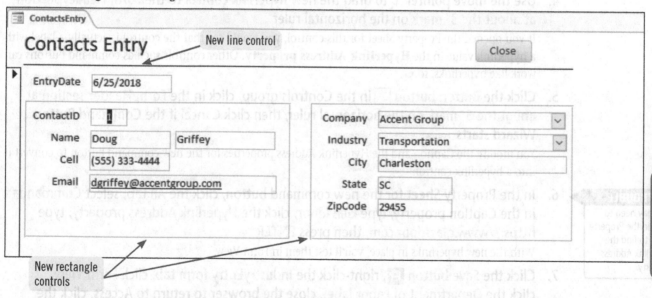

- New line control
- New rectangle controls

Line troubles

Sometimes lines are difficult to find in Form or Report Design View because they are placed against the edge of a section or the edge of other controls. To find lines that are positioned next to the edge of a section, drag the section bar to expand the section and expose the line. To draw a perfectly horizontal or vertical line, you hold SHIFT while creating or resizing the line. Also, it is easy to accidentally widen a line beyond the form or report margins, thus creating extra unwanted pages in a printout. To fix this problem, narrow any controls that extend beyond the margins of the printout, and drag the right edge of the form or report to the left. Note that the default left and right margins for an 8.5 × 11-inch sheet of paper are often 0.25 inches each, so a form or report in portrait orientation must be no wider than 8 inches. In landscape orientation they must be no wider than 10.5 inches.

Access

Add Hyperlink Controls

Learning
Outcomes
• Add a label as a
  hyperlink
• Add a command
  button as a
  hyperlink

A **hyperlink control** is a control on a form that when clicked works like a hyperlink to redirect the user to a webpage or file. You can add a new hyperlink control to a form using the Link button in the Controls group of the ribbon or you can convert an existing label, command button, or image into a hyperlink by modifying the control's **Hyperlink Address property**. **CASE** ▶ *Lydia asks you to create links to commonly accessed resources on the IndustryEntry form.*

STEPS

1. **Right-click the** IndustryEntry form **in the Navigation Pane, then click** Design View

   You will add two new hyperlink controls in the Form Header, to the right of the Industry Entry label.

2. **Click the** Link button 🌐 **in the Controls group**

   The Insert Hyperlink dialog box opens, which allows you to link to an existing file or webpage, another object in the database, or an email address. You want to link to the federal government's Department of Labor website.

3. **Click the** Existing File or Web Page button, **click the** Text to display box, **type** Department of Labor, **click the** Address box, **type** https://www.dol.gov **as shown in** FIGURE 6-16, **then click** OK

   The new hyperlink control is positioned in the upper-left corner of the Detail section. You move it to the Form Header section.

4. **Use the move pointer** ⬚ **to drag the** new hyperlink control **to the** Form Header section **at about the 3" mark** **on the horizontal ruler**

   If you opened the Property Sheet for this control, you would see that the control is actually a label with a hyperlink value in the **Hyperlink Address property**. Other controls such as command buttons can work like hyperlinks, too.

5. **Click the** Button button ▭ **in the Controls group, click in the** Form Header section at **about the 5" mark** **on the horizontal ruler, then click** Cancel **if the Command Button Wizard starts**

   You modify the Caption and the Hyperlink Address properties for the new command button to convert it into a hyperlink control.

6. **In the Property Sheet for the new command button, click the** All tab, **select** Command## **in the Caption property, type** Glassdoor, **click the** Hyperlink Address property, **type** https://www.glassdoor.com, **then press** ENTER

   With the new hyperlinks in place, you'll test them in Form View.

7. **Click the** Save button 🖫 , **right-click the** IndustryEntry form tab, **click** Form View, **click the** Department of Labor label, **close the browser to return to Access, click the** Glassdoor command button, **close your browser to return to the IndustryEntry form as shown in** FIGURE 6-17, **then close the IndustryEntry form**

FIGURE 6-16: Insert Hyperlink dialog box

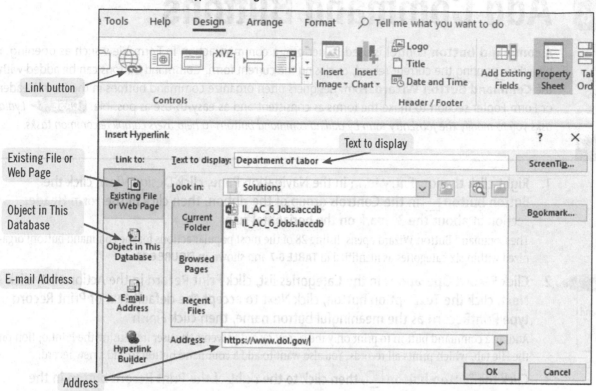

- Link button
- Existing File or Web Page
- Object in This Database
- E-mail Address
- Address
- Text to display

FIGURE 6-17: IndustryEntry form with two hyperlink controls

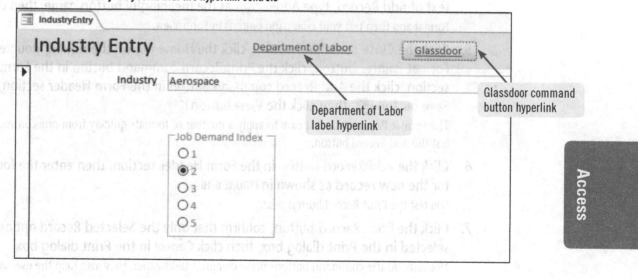

- Department of Labor label hyperlink
- Glassdoor command button hyperlink

Add Command Buttons

Learning
Outcome
• Add a command
button to a form

A **command button** control is used to perform a common action in Form View such as opening a hyperlink, printing the current record, or closing the current form. Command buttons can be added with the **Command Button Wizard**. Form designers often organize command buttons in the Form Header or Form Footer section to make the forms as consistent and as easy-to-use as possible. **CASE** ▶ *Lydia asks you to modify the JobsEntry form by adding command buttons to help users complete common tasks.*

STEPS

1. **Right-click the** JobsEntry form **in the Navigation Pane, click** Design View, **click the** Button button 🔲 **in the Controls group of the ribbon, then click in the** Form Header section at about the 3" mark **on the horizontal ruler**

   The Command Button Wizard opens, listing 28 of the most popular actions for the command button, organized within six categories as identified in **TABLE 6-7** and shown in **FIGURE 6-18**.

QUICK TIP
The meaningful
name for a command
button may not
include a space.

2. **Click** Record Operations **in the Categories list, click** Print Record **in the Actions list, click** Next, **click the** Text option button, **click** Next **to accept the default text of Print Record, type** PrintRecord **as the meaningful button name, then click** Finish

   Adding a command button to print only the *current* record prevents the user from using the Print option on the File tab, which prints all records. You also want to add a command button to add a new record.

3. **Click the** Button button 🔲, **then click to the** right of the Print Record button **in the Form Header section**

4. **Click** Record Operations **in the Categories list, confirm that** Add New Record **is selected in the Actions list, click** Next, **click the** Text option button, **click** Next **to accept the default text of Add Record, type** AddRecord **as the meaningful button name, then click** Finish

   Format and then test your command buttons in Form View.

5. **Click the** Close command button, **click the** Home tab **on the ribbon, double-click the** Format Painter button, **click the** Print Record command button **in the Form Header section, click the** Add Record command button **in the Form Header section, click the** Save button 🔲, **then click the** View button 🔲

   The Format Painter makes it easy to apply a number of formats quickly from one control to another. You test the Add Record button.

6. **Click the** Add Record button **in the Form Header section, then enter the four field values for the new record as shown in** FIGURE 6-19

   You test the Print Record button next.

7. **Click the** Print Record button, **confirm that only the Selected Record option button is selected in the Print dialog box, then click** Cancel **in the Print dialog box**

   Not only do the command buttons make common tasks easier, they also help the user avoid unintended actions such as printing all records in the form or accidentally closing the entire Access application.

FIGURE 6-18: Using the Command Button Wizard

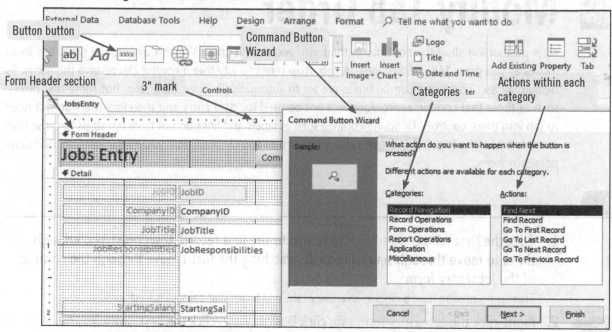

FIGURE 6-19: JobsEntry form with three command buttons

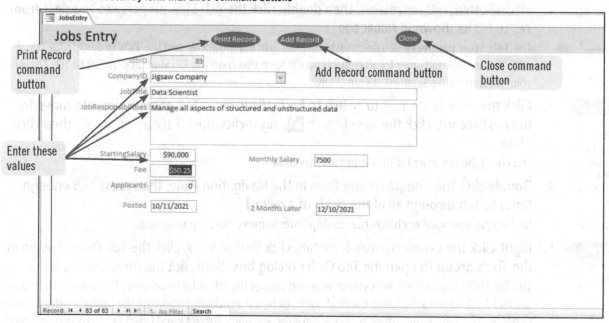

TABLE 6-7: Common actions provided by the Command Button Wizard

categories	common actions within this category
Record Navigation	Finding and navigating through records
Record Operations	Adding, deleting, copying, printing, or saving a record
Form Operations	Opening, closing, printing a form
Report Operations	Opening, emailing, printing a report
Application	Close the database and exit Access
Miscellaneous	Run a macro or open a query

Modify Tab Order

Learning
Outcome
• Modify tab order
  properties

After positioning all of the controls on the form, you should check the **tab order**, the order the focus moves as you press TAB in Form View. A **tab stop** refers to whether a control can receive the focus. By default, all text boxes and combo boxes are set to automatically have a tab stop, but some text boxes, such as those that contain expressions, will not be used for data entry and therefore users do not need to tab into those controls. Unbound controls such as labels and lines do not have tab stops because they cannot receive the focus. **CASE** *Lydia suggests that you check the tab order of the JobsEntry and CompanyEntry forms.*

STEPS

1. **Click the** First record button **to return to the first record, then press** TAB **enough times to move through several records, watching the focus move through the controls of the JobsEntry form**
   There is no need to have a tab stop in either of the text boxes that contain calculations.

QUICK TIP
You can also switch between views using the View buttons in the lower-right corner of the window.

2. **Right-click the** JobsEntry form tab, **click** Design View, **click the** text box with the =[StartingSalary]/12 expression, **click the** Other tab **in the Property Sheet, double-click the** Tab Stop property **to toggle it from Yes to No, click the** text box with the =[FirstPosted]+60 expression, **then double-click the** Tab Stop property **to toggle it from Yes to** No **as shown in FIGURE 6-20**
   The **Tab Stop property** determines whether the field accepts focus, and the **Tab Index property** indicates the numeric tab order for all controls on the form that have the Tab Stop property set to Yes. To review your tab stop changes, return to Form View.

QUICK TIP
In Form Design View, press CTRL+. (period) to switch to Form View. In Form View, press CTRL+, (comma) to switch to Form Design View.

3. **Click the** View button **to switch to Form View, press** TAB **enough times to move to the next record, click the** Save button **, right-click the** JobsEntry form tab, **then click** Close
   You check the tab order for the CompanyEntry form.

4. **Double-click the** CompanyEntry form **in the Navigation Pane, then press** TAB **enough times to tab through all of the fields of a record**
   In this case, you want to change the tab stop order to move from top to bottom.

QUICK TIP
You can also modify tab order in Form Layout View.

5. **Right-click the** CompanyEntry form tab, **click** Design View, **click the** Tab Order button **in the Tools group to open the Tab Order dialog box, then click the** Auto Order button
   The Tab Order dialog box allows you to view and change the tab order by dragging fields up or down using the **field selector** to the left of the field name, or by automatically reordering the controls with the Auto Order button. Two of the entries, however, have vague names, Toggle## and Check##. To fix this, you modify their **Name property**, which helps you to reference the control elsewhere in the database application.

6. **Click** OK **in the Tab Order dialog box to close it, click the** More toggle button, **double-click** Toggle## **in the Name property in the Property Sheet, type** MoreToggle, **click the** check box, **double-click** Check## **in the Name property, type** InternshipsCheckBox, **click the** Save button **to save your work, then click the** Tab Order button
   Your screen should look like **FIGURE 6-21**. The Tab Order dialog box now shows descriptive names for all of the controls in the Detail section that can receive the focus.

7. **Click** OK **in the Tab Order dialog box, click** **to switch to Form View, press** TAB **enough times to test the top-to-bottom order of your tab stops, then close the CompanyEntry form**

FIGURE 6-20: Changing the Tab Stop property

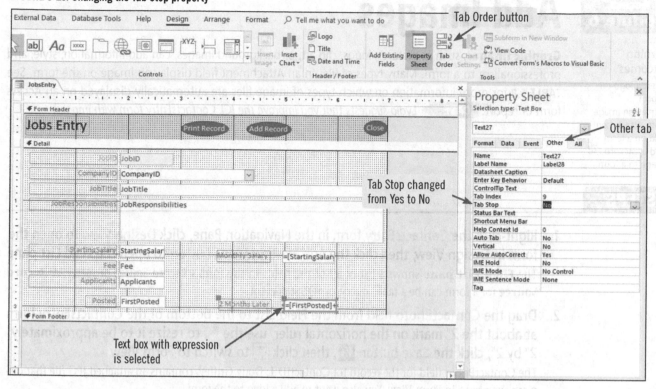

FIGURE 6-21: Modifying tab order

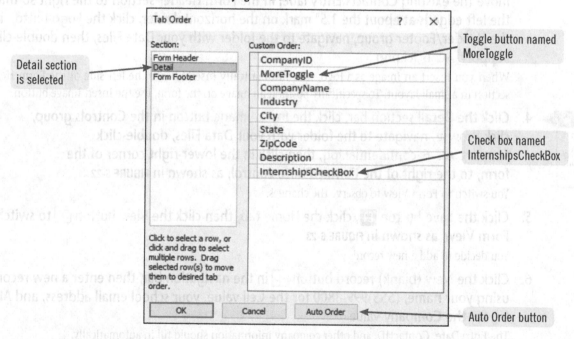

Naming conventions

Using a commonly accepted naming convention for the objects, fields, and controls in your database improves the logic and maintainability of your application. The **Leszynski/Reddick** **naming convention** uses a three-character prefix such as frm for form and txt for text box.

Access

Add Images

Learning
Outcomes
• Insert a logo on
  a form
• Display an image
  in an Attachment
  field on a form
• Add a background
  image to a form

Graphic images, such as pictures, logos, clip art, or background images, can add information, style, and professionalism to a form. Many types of files in an Attachment field display an image on the form. See **TABLE 6-8** for more information on which types of image files are automatically displayed on an Access form or report. **CASE** ▶ *Lydia suggests that you improve the JCL ContactsEntry form with images.*

STEPS

1. **Right-click the** ContactsEntry form **in the Navigation Pane, click** Design View **to open the form in Design View, then click the** Add Existing Fields button **to open the Field List pane**
   The **Field List pane** shows a list of all of the fields in the form's Record Source property. A **Record Source** for a form can be a table, query, or SQL statement.

2. **Drag the** ContactPhoto field **from the Field List to the bottom of the ContactsEntry form at about the 2" mark on the horizontal ruler, use the ↖ to resize it to be approximately 2" by 2", click the** Save button 🖫**, then click** 🖼 **to switch to Form View**
   The ContactPhoto field for the record for ContactID 1, Doug Griffey, contains an attached JPG file that displays the photo in Form View. You also want to add a logo to the form.

3. **Right-click the** ContactsEntry form tab, **click** Design View, **use the move pointer 🖑 to move the existing Contacts Entry label in the Form Header section to the right so that the left edge is at about the 1.5" mark on the horizontal ruler, click the** Logo button **in the Header/Footer group, navigate to the folder with your Data Files, then double-click** Support_AC_6_jcl.png
   When you insert an image as a logo, it is automatically inserted into the left side of the Form Header section in a small layout. To specifically position an image on the form, use the Insert Image button.

QUICK TIP
You can also add a logo or image to a form in Form Layout View.

4. **Click the** Detail section bar, **click the** Insert Image button **in the Controls group, click** Browse, **navigate to the folder with your Data Files, double-click** Support_AC_6_confidential.jpg, **then click in the lower-right corner of the form, to the right of the ContactPhoto control, as shown in** FIGURE 6-22
   You switch to Form View to observe the changes.

5. **Click the** Save button 🖫, **click the** Home tab, **then click the** View button 🖼 **to switch to Form View, as shown in** FIGURE 6-23
   You decide to add a new record.

6. **Click the** New (blank) record button ▶️ **in the navigation bar, then enter a new record using your name, (555)999-8800 for the Cell value, your school email address, and** Alark Inc **for the Company value**
   The EntryDate, ContactID, and other company information should fill in automatically.

7. **Double-click the** ContactPhoto control, **click** Add, **browse to a folder that contains a picture of yourself and double-click the picture to add it to the record or double-click the** Support_AC_6_man.jpg or Support_AC_6_woman.jpg **file supplied with your Data Files, then save and close the ContactsEntry form**

FIGURE 6-22: Adding pictures to a form

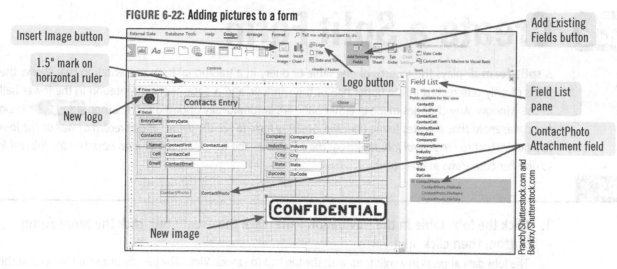

Insert Image button

1.5" mark on horizontal ruler

New logo

Logo button

New image

Add Existing Fields button

Field List pane

ContactPhoto Attachment field

Pranch/Shutterstock.com and Bankrx/Shutterstock.com

FIGURE 6-23: Final ContactsEntry form

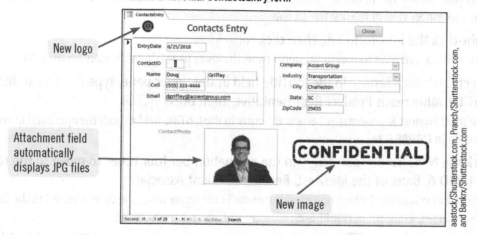

New logo

Attachment field automatically displays JPG files

New image

aastock/Shutterstock.com, Pranch/Shutterstock.com, and Bankrx/Shutterstock.com

TABLE 6-8: Image file formats that can be displayed in an Access form or report

file extension	extension description
BMP	Windows Bitmap
RLE	Run Length Encoded Bitmap
DIB	Device Independent Bitmap
GIF	Graphics Interchange Format
JPEG, JPG, JPE	Joint Photographic Experts Group
EXIF	Exchangeable File Format
PNG	Portable Network Graphics
TIFF, TIF	Tagged Image File Format
ICON, ICO	Icon
WMF	Windows Metafile
EMF	Enhanced Metafile

Applying a background image

A **background image** is an image that fills the entire form or report, appearing "behind" the other controls. A background image is

sometimes called a **watermark** image. To add a background image, use the **Picture property** for the form or report.

Access

Create a Split Form

A **split form** displays the records of one table or query in a traditional form presentation that shows the fields of only one record in the upper half of the window, and a datasheet presentation in the lower half of the window. Any changes made in either pane are automatically updated in the other. **CASE** ▶ *Lydia has commented that she likes to use both the JobsEntry form to see the details of one record as well as the Jobs table datasheet to see several Jobs records at the same time. You will create a split form based on the Jobs table to give her both views in one object.*

STEPS

1. **Click the** Jobs table **in the Navigation Pane, click the** Create tab, **click the** More Forms **button, then click** Split Form

   The Jobs data appears in a split form with the top half in Layout View. The benefit of a split form is that the upper pane allows you to display the fields of one record in any arrangement, and the lower pane maintains a datasheet view of the first few records.

2. **Right-click the** Jobs form tab, **then click** Form View

   If you edit, sort, or filter records in the upper pane, the lower pane is automatically updated, and vice versa.

3. **Select** Customer Service **in the JobTitle field in the upper pane, type** Product **so that the JobTitle value reads Product Representative, then press** ENTER

   Note that "Product Representative" is now the entry in the JobTitle field in both the upper and lower panes, as shown in **FIGURE 6-24**.

4. **Click the** Next Record button ▶ **in the navigation bar four times to move to the record for JobID 6, Bank of the Midwest, Registered Client Associate**

   Note that as you move through one record at a time in the upper pane, the current record in the datasheet is also selected, as shown in **FIGURE 6-25**.

5. **Click the** Save button 🖫 , **type** JobsSplit **as the form name, press** ENTER, **right-click the** JobsSplit form tab, **then click** Close

Creating Forms

FIGURE 6-24: Editing data in a split form

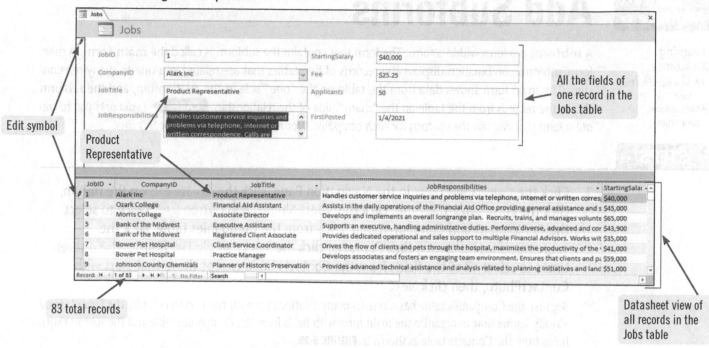

Edit symbol

Product Representative

All the fields of one record in the Jobs table

83 total records

Datasheet view of all records in the Jobs table

FIGURE 6-25: Navigating through records in a split form

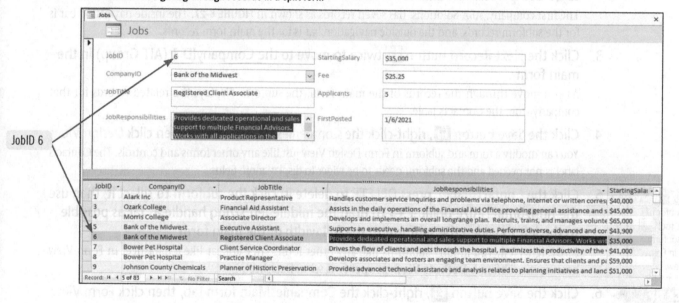

JobID 6

Add Subforms

Learning
Outcomes
• Add a subform to
a form
• Set subform
properties

A **subform** is a form within a form. The form that contains the subform is called the **main form**. A main form/subform combination displays the records of two tables that are related in a one-to-many relationship. The main form shows data from the table on the "one" side of the relationship, and the subform shows the records from the table on the "many" side of the relationship. **CASE** *Lydia asks you to create a form that displays the contacts for each company. A form/subform works well for this task.*

STEPS

1. **Click the** Companies table **in the Navigation Pane, click the** Create tab **on the ribbon, click the** Form Wizard button, **click the** Select Single Field button > **twice to select the** CompanyID **and** CompanyName fields **from the Companies table, click the** Tables/Queries list arrow, **click** Contacts, **click the** Select Single Field button > **seven times to select all of the fields from the Contacts table except those that start with** ContactPhoto, **then click** Next

   Because the Companies table has a one-to-many relationship with the Contacts table, the Form Wizard already knows how to organize the main form with fields from the Companies table and the subform with fields from the Contacts table as shown in **FIGURE 6-26**.

2. **Click** Next, **click** Next **again to accept a Datasheet layout for the subform, edit the titles to be** CompaniesMain **and** ContactsSubform, **then click** Finish

   The first company, ABA Solutions, has seven records as shown in **FIGURE 6-27**. The inside navigation bar is for the subform records, and the outside navigation bar is for the main form records.

3. **Click the** Next Record button ▶ **twice to move to the CompanyID 3 (AIT Group) in the main form**

   As you move through the records of the main form, the subform displays the related records for that company from the Contacts table.

4. **Click the** Save button 🖫, **right-click the** CompaniesMain form tab, **then click** Design View

   You can modify a form and subform in Form Design View just like any other forms and controls. The Contacts label is not needed and the subform needs to be wider to display more fields.

QUICK TIP
Use the Subform/
Subreport tool 🖾
to add a subform
to a form in Form
Design View.

5. **Click the** Contacts label, **press** DELETE **to delete it, click the** subform **to select it, then use the horizontal resize pointer ↔ to drag the middle-left sizing handle as far as possible to the left to widen the subform to the full width of the main form**

   In Design View, you modify subforms like any other form. They appear like a datasheet in Form View because the subform's **Default View property** is set to Datasheet.

QUICK TIP
Use the column
resize pointer ↔ to
resize the columns in
a subdatasheet.

6. **Click the** Save button 🖫, **right-click the** CompaniesMain form tab, **then click** Form View

   Widening the subform helps it display more fields. Note that the CompanyID field in the last column of the subform is the common field that links the main form and subform.

7. **Right-click the** CompaniesMain form tab, **then click** Close

FIGURE 6-26: Using the Form Wizard to create a form with a subform

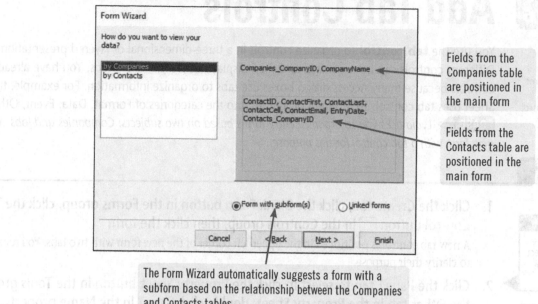

Fields from the Companies table are positioned in the main form

Fields from the Contacts table are positioned in the main form

The Form Wizard automatically suggests a form with a subform based on the relationship between the Companies and Contacts tables

FIGURE 6-27: CompaniesMain form with ContactsSubform

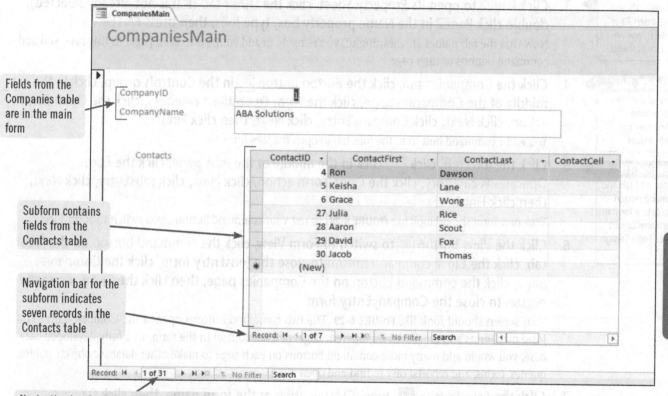

Fields from the Companies table are in the main form

Subform contains fields from the Contacts table

Navigation bar for the subform indicates seven records in the Contacts table

Navigation bar for the main form indicates 31 records in the Companies table

Linking the form and subform

If the form and subform do not appear to be correctly linked, examine the subform's Property Sheet, paying special attention to the **Link Child Fields** and **Link Master Fields** properties on the

Data tab. These properties tell you which fields serve as the link between the main form and subform.

Access

Add Tab Controls

Learning Outcomes
- Add a tab control to a form
- Modify tab control properties

You use the **tab control** to organize controls in a three-dimensional or layered presentation on a form. Different controls can be organized and then displayed by clicking the tabs. You have already used tab controls because many Access dialog boxes use tabs to organize information. For example, the Property Sheet uses tab controls to organize properties into the categories of Format, Data, Event, Other, and All.

CASE ▶ *Lydia asks you to organize entry forms based on two subjects: Companies and Jobs. You create a new form with a tab control for this purpose.*

STEPS

1. **Click the Create tab, click the Blank Form button in the Forms group, click the Tab Control button ⬚ in the Controls group, then click the form**
    A new tab control is positioned in the upper-left corner of the new form with two tabs. You rename the tabs to clarify their purpose.

2. **Click the Page1 tab to select it, click the Property Sheet button in the Tools group, click the Other tab in the Property Sheet, double-click Page1 in the Name property, type Companies, then press ENTER**
    You also give Page2 a meaningful name.

3. **Click Page2 to open its Property Sheet, click the Other tab (if it is not already selected), double-click Page2 in the Name property box, type Jobs, then press ENTER**
    Now that the tab names are meaningful, you're ready to add controls to each page. In this case, you add command buttons to each page.

4. **Click the Companies tab, click the Button button ▦ in the Controls group, click in the middle of the Companies page, click the Form Operations category, click the Open Form action, click Next, click CompanyEntry, click Next, then click Finish**
    You add a command button to the Jobs tab to open the Jobs form.

5. **Click the Jobs tab, click ▦, click in the middle of the Jobs page, click the Form Operations category, click the Open Form action, click Next, click JobsEntry, click Next, then click Finish**
    Your new form should look like **FIGURE 6-28**. To test your command buttons, you switch to Form View.

6. **Click the View button ▦ to switch to Form View, click the command button on the Jobs tab, click the Close command button to close the JobsEntry form, click the Companies page, click the command button on the Companies page, then click the Close command button to close the CompanyEntry form**
    Your screen should look like **FIGURE 6-29**. The two command buttons opened the CompanyEntry and JobsEntry forms and are placed on different pages of a tab control in the form. In a fully developed database, you would add many more command buttons on each page to make other database objects (tables, queries, forms, and reports) easy to find and open.

7. **Click the Save button ▦, type JCLNavigation as the form name, then click OK**

FIGURE 6-28: Adding command buttons to a tab control in Form Layout View

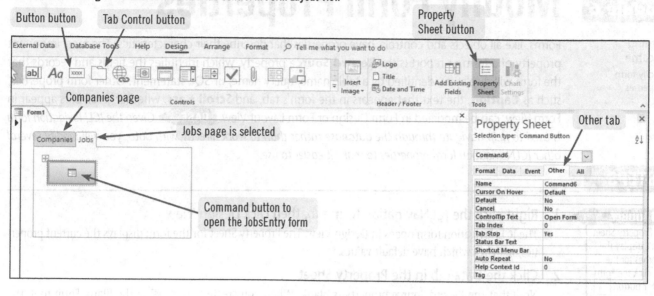

Button button   Tab Control button   Property Sheet button

Companies page   Controls   Header / Footer   Tools

Jobs page is selected   Other tab

Command button to open the JobsEntry form

FIGURE 6-29: Using a tab control in Form View

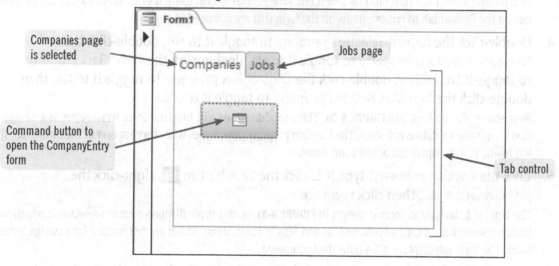

Companies page is selected   Jobs page

Command button to open the CompanyEntry form

Tab control

Create a group in the Navigation Pane

Another way to organize objects is to group them in the Navigation Pane. Right-click the Navigation Pane title bar, click Navigation Options, then click the Add Item button to add a

custom group to the Navigation pane. Objects added to custom groups are shortcuts to the actual object.

Access

Modify Form Properties

Forms, like all objects and controls, have properties that describe their characteristics. The most important property of a form or report is the **Record Source** property, which identifies the fields and records that the form will display as identified by a table name, query name, or SQL statement. Other form properties, such as **Caption**, the text that appears in the form's tab, and **Scroll Bars**, whether scroll bars appear in Form View, can be modified in Form Design or Form Layout View. **CASE** *Given the JCLNavigation form is used to help navigate through the database rather than to work directly with data, you will modify several other JCLNavigation form properties to make it easier to use.*

STEPS

TROUBLE
If the Property Sheet
doesn't display the
properties for the
form, click the Form
Selector button ▢ .

1. **Right-click the** JCLNavigation form tab, **then click** Design View

   The JCLNavigation form opens in Design View. The Property Sheet for the form displays the current properties, many of which have default values.

2. **Click the** Data tab **in the Property Sheet**

   Note that the Record Source property is blank. When you create a form using the Blank Form tool, the Record Source property is blank, but when you create a form using the Form Wizard, the Record Source property contains a table name, query name, or SQL statement that represents the fields and records you selected in the wizard.

3. **Click the** Format tab **in the Property Sheet**

   When using a form as a navigational tool such as the JCLNavigation form, it's helpful to modify the properties on the Format tab to remove items on the form that are not needed.

4. **Double-click the** Record Selectors property **to toggle it to** No, **double-click the** Navigation Buttons property **to toggle it to** No, **double-click the** Scroll Bars property **to toggle it to** Neither, **double-click the** Control Box property **to toggle it to** No, **then double-click the** Min Max Buttons property **to toggle it to** None

   Your screen should look like **FIGURE 6-30**. These modifications will help the form work better as a navigation form versus a data-entry form. The Caption property determines what text appears in the form's tab. If left blank, it will display the actual form name.

5. **Click the** Caption property, **type** JCL, **click the** Save button ▤, **right-click the** JCLNavigation tab, **then click** Form View

   The final JCLNavigation form is shown in **FIGURE 6-31**. It no longer displays a record selector, navigation buttons, scroll bars, a control box, or Min and Max buttons, items which are not needed for a navigational form. The form tab displays JCL versus the form name.

6. **sam⬆ Right-click the** JCL form tab, **click** Close, **compact and repair the database, then exit Access**

FIGURE 6-30: Modifying the JCLNavigation form's properties

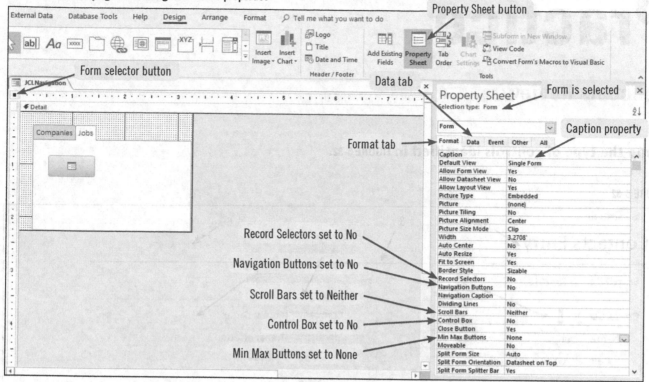

FIGURE 6-31: Final JCLNavigation form

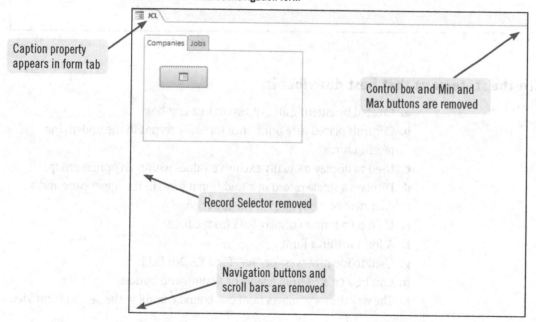

Caption property appears in form tab

Control box and Min and Max buttons are removed

Record Selector removed

Navigation buttons and scroll bars are removed

Access

Practice

Concepts Review

Name the type of controls identified in FIGURE 6-32.

FIGURE 6-32

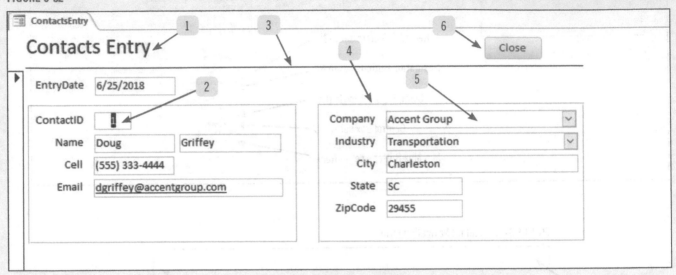

Match each term with the statement that best describes it.

7. Tab order
8. Calculated control
9. Detail section
10. Split form
11. Bound control
12. Option buttons
13. Hyperlink
14. Check Box
15. Subform

a. Created by entering an expression in a text box
b. Controls placed here print once for every record in the underlying record source
c. Used to display mutually exclusive values within an option group
d. Displays a single record in a traditional form in the upper pane and a datasheet of the records in the lower pane
e. Used on a form to display data from a field
f. A form within a form
g. Used to identify "yes" or "no" for a Yes/No field
h. Can be a created from a label or a command button
i. The way the focus moves from one bound control to the next in Form View

Select the best answer from the list of choices.

16. Every element on a form is called a(n):
   a. property.
   b. control.
   c. tool.
   d. item.

17. Which of the following is probably *not* a graphic image?
   a. Logo
   b. Calculation
   c. Clip art
   d. Picture

18. The most common bound control is the:

   a. text box.
   b. combo box.

   c. list box.
   d. label.

19. The most common unbound control is the:

   a. text box.
   b. label.

   c. combo box.
   d. command button.

20. Which form view cannot be used to view data?

   a. Design
   b. Layout

   c. Datasheet
   d. Preview

Skills Review

1. **Add labels and text boxes.**

   a. Start Access, open the IL_AC_6-2.accdb database from the location where you store your Data Files, then save it as **IL_AC_6_SupportDesk**. Enable content if prompted.

   b. Open the EmployeeMaster form in Design View, then add a text box control below the Salary text box control.

   c. Modify the Text## label to read **Dependents**. (*Hint*: You may modify the label directly on the form, or use its Caption property in the Property Sheet.)

   d. The text box should be bound to the Dependents field. (*Hint*: You may modify the text box directly on the form or use its Control Source property in the Property Sheet.)

   e. Add a second text box below the Dependents controls.

   f. Modify the Text## label to read **Emergency** and bind the text box to the **EmergencyPhone** field. (*Hint*: **FIGURE 6-33** shows the final EmployeeMaster form after Step 11.)

   g. Save the EmployeeMaster form and display it in Form View.

FIGURE 6-33

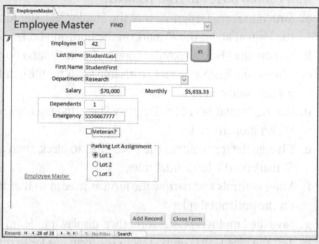

2. **Resize and align controls.**

   a. Switch to Form Design View for the EmployeeMaster form, then right-align the right edges of the labels in the first column.

   b. Left-align all of the left edges of the text boxes in the second column.

   c. Resize the EmployeeID text box and Dependents text box to be about half as wide as they currently are.

   d. Center the information within the EmployeeID and Dependents text boxes.

   e. Modify the text color for *all* controls (all labels and all text boxes) to be black.

3. **Create calculations on forms.**

   a. Add a text box to the right of the Salary text box at about the 4" mark on the horizontal ruler.

   b. Modify the Text## label to read **Monthly**, and move it closer to the text box. Modify the Control Source property of the new text box to an expression that calculates the monthly salary, **=[Salary]/12** then change the Format property for the new text box to **Currency** and the Decimal Places property to **2**.

   c. Align the top edges of the Salary label, Salary text box, Monthly label, and monthly expression text box.

   d. Set the text color for the new Monthly label and text box expression to black.

   e. Save the form, view it in Form View, and navigate through several records. Be sure the new text box correctly calculates the monthly salary.

4. Add check boxes and toggle buttons.

  a. Switch to Design View for the EmployeeMaster form and add a check box control below the EmergencyPhone text box.

  b. Modify the Control Source property for the check box to be **Veteran**.

  c. Modify the Caption property for the new label to be **Veteran?**

  d. Add a toggle button control to the upper-right corner of the Detail section of the form at about the 4.5" mark on the horizontal ruler.

  e. On the Format tab of the Property Sheet, modify the Caption property for the new toggle button to be **ID**.

  f. On the Event tab of the Property Sheet, modify the On Click property for the new toggle button to select the **ShowHideEmployeeID** macro.

  g. Save the EmployeeMaster form and display it in Form View.

  h. Click the ID button several times to test that it alternatively shows and hides the Employee ID label and text box when clicked.

5. Add combo boxes to enter data.

  a. Switch to Design View for the EmployeeMaster form, right-click the Department text box, then change it into a combo box.

  b. On the Data tab of the Property Sheet, change the Row Source property for the combo box to **Departments**.

  c. Save the EmployeeMaster form and display it in Form View.

  d. Test the combo box by changing the Department value for the first record (Employee ID 3 Aaron Cabrera) to Executive.

6. Add combo boxes to find records.

  a. Switch to Form Design View of the EmployeeMaster form then add a new combo box to the Form Header section of the form at about the 4" mark on the horizontal ruler.

  b. Choose the "Find a record..." option in the Combo Box Wizard.

  c. Choose the LastName and FirstName fields for the combo box, hide the key column, then enter **FIND** as the label for the combo box.

  d. On the Format tab of the Property Sheet, modify the List Rows property of the new combo box to be **30** and the Width property to be **2"**.

  e. Change the text color of the FIND label to black, then position the controls so that they do not extend beyond the 5" mark on the horizontal ruler.

  f. Move controls and narrow the form as needed so that the right edge of the form does not extend past the 5" mark on the horizontal ruler.

  g. Save the EmployeeMaster form then display it in Form View.

  h. Test the new FIND combo box in the form header to find the Mindi Perez record. Note that the list in the new combo box is not sorted.

  i. Return to Design View, then click the new combo box in the Form Header section.

  j. On the Data tab of the Property Sheet, click the Row Source property, then click the Build button. Add an ascending sort order to the LastName field. (*Hint*: The Combo Box Wizard automatically added the EmployeeID field back in Step c. Do not delete it.)

  k. Close and save the Query Builder, then save the form and display it in Form View.

  l. Test the updated FIND combo box in the form header to find the Samantha Wells record.

7. Add option groups.

  a. Switch to Form Design View of the EmployeeMaster form and use the Option Group Wizard to add a new option group just below the Veteran check box.

  b. The label names should be **Lot 1**, **Lot 2**, and **Lot 3**.

  c. The default choice should be Lot 1, and the values of **1**, **2**, and **3** should correspond to the three parking lots.

Skills Review (continued)

    d. Store the value in the ParkingLot field using option buttons and an etched style.

    e. The caption for the group should be **Parking Lot Assignment**.

    f. Change the font color for all labels to black.

    g. Save the EmployeeMaster form and display it in Form View.

8. Add lines and rectangles.

    a. Return to Form Design View and add a rectangle control around the four Dependents and Emergency controls (two labels and two text boxes).

    b. Add a horizontal line control across the width of the form at the bottom of the Form Header section.

    c. Save the form and display it in Form View.

9. Add hyperlink controls.

    a. Return to Design View of the EmployeeMaster form, then add a label control to the lower-left corner of the form at about the 0.5" mark on the horizontal ruler.

    b. Modify the Caption property of the new label to be **Employee Master**.

    c. Change the font color to black.

    d. On the Format tab of the Property Sheet for the label, click the Build button for the Hyperlink Address property to open the Insert Hyperlink dialog box.

    e. Click the Object in this Database button on the left, then click the expand button for Reports to show the existing reports in the database.

    f. Click the EmployeeMasterList report, then click OK in the Insert Hyperlink dialog box.

    g. Save the EmployeeMaster form then display it in Form View.

    h. Test the Employee Master hyperlink label by clicking it, then close the EmployeeMasterList report to return to the EmployeeMaster form.

10. Add command buttons.

    a. Switch to Form Design View of the EmployeeMaster form, then drag the bottom edge of the Form Footer section down about 0.5" to open it.

    b. Use the Command Button Wizard to add a new command button to the Form Footer section at about the 3" mark on the horizontal ruler.

    c. In the Record Operations category, choose the Add New Record action. Select the Text option using **Add Record** as the text, then give the button the meaningful name of **AddRecord**.

    d. Use the Command Button Wizard to add a second command button to the Form Footer section at about the 4" mark on the horizontal ruler.

    e. In the Form Operations category, choose the Close Form action. Select the Text option button with **Close Form** as the text, then give the button the meaningful name of **CloseForm**.

    f. Align the top edges of the two command buttons in the Form Footer section.

    g. Save the EmployeeMaster form then display it in Form View.

    h. Test the Add Record command button by clicking it, then pressing TAB several times to move through the controls on the form. Notice that the tab order is illogical.

    i. Without entering a new record, click the Close Form command button.

11. Modify tab order.

    a. Reopen the EmployeeMaster form in Form Design View, then open the Tab Order dialog box.

    b. Click the Auto Order button, then click OK in the Tab Order dialog box to close it.

    c. Click the EmployeeID text box to select it, then set its Tab Stop property on the Other tab of the Property Sheet to **No**.

    d. Click the ID toggle button to select it, then set its Tab Stop property to **No**.

    e. Click the text box with the =[Salary]/12 expression to select it, then set its Tab Stop property to **No**.

    f. Save the EmployeeMaster form then open it in Form View.

g. Click the Add Record command button to add a new record with your name in the Last Name and First Name boxes. Note that the Employee ID field is an AutoNumber field that is automatically incremented as you enter your first and last names. Enter **Research** for your department, **$70,000** for your salary, **1** for dependents, and your school's telephone number for the emergency value. Click the Veteran? check box if you are a veteran, then accept the default Parking Lot Assignment value of 1 as shown in **FIGURE 6-33**.

h. Click the Close Form command button to close the EmployeeMaster form.

12. Add images.

a. Open the EmployeesByDepartment form in Form Design View, then add the Support_AC_6_computer.png image provided with your Data Files as a logo to the form.

b. Open the Field List, then add the Photo field directly under the FirstName text box. Resize the Photo control to be about 2" by 2".

c. Because this form is a work in progress, below the Photo control, insert an image with the Support_AC_6_draft.jpg file provided with your Data Files. Resize the Support_AC_6_draft.jpg photo to be about 1" tall by about 3" wide and change its Size Mode property to Stretch.

d. Save the form, display it in Form View, find the record with your name, double-click the Photo control, navigate to a folder that contains your picture, double-click your picture file, or navigate to the location of your Data Files, then double-click the Support_AC_6_man.jpg or Support_AC_6_woman.jpg file to attach it to that record.

e. Close the EmployeesByDepartment form.

13. Create a split form.

a. Click the CaseListing query in the Navigation Pane, click the Create tab, click the More Forms button, then click Split Form.

b. Close the Property Sheet if it opens, then switch to Form View.

c. Drag the split bar between the upper and lower portions up, to view as many records in the lower pane as possible without covering up any of the controls in the upper pane.

d. Click the CaseTitle value for Record 5 in the datasheet and modify the entry to be **Email attachment problem with large video file**. Note that the upper pane automatically displays that record.

e. Save the form with the name **CaseListingSplit** then close the form.

14. Add subforms.

a. Use the Form Wizard to create a form with the EmployeeID, FirstName, and LastName fields from the Employees table, all of the fields from the Cases table, and all of the fields from the Calls table.

b. View the data by Employees, which presents two subforms given one employee can be related to many cases in the first subform and one case can be related to many calls in the second subform.

c. Use a Datasheet layout for both subforms.

d. Title the forms **EmployeesMain**, **CasesSubform**, and **CallsSubform**.

e. Switch to Form Design View, then delete the Cases and Calls labels to the left of their respective subforms.

f. Widen the two subforms to start at the left edge of the main form and stop at the 8" mark on the horizontal ruler.

g. Save the forms then switch to Form View.

h. EmployeeID 3, Aaron Cabrera, has two records in the Cases subform. The first case is selected and displays one call in the Calls subform.

i. Click the CaseID 2 record in the subform. Notice that the Calls subform changes to display two calls for the second case.

j. Close the EmployeesMain form.

15. Add tab controls.

a. Use the Blank Form tool to create a new, blank form.

b. In Design View, add a tab control.

c. Change the Name property for the Page1 tab to **Queries**.

d. Change the Name property for the Page2 tab to **Forms**.

Skills Review (continued)

e. Right-click the Forms tab on the tab control, click Insert Page, then change the Name property for the Page# tab to **Reports**.

f. On the Queries tab, use the Command Button Wizard to add a command button to the page. From the Miscellaneous category, choose the Run Query action and the CaseDetails query. Choose the Text option button with **Case Details** as the text. Name the button **CaseDetails**.

g. On the Forms page, use the Command Button Wizard to add a command button to the page. From the Form Operations category, choose the Open Form action and the EmployeeMaster form. Open the form to show all the records, choose the Text option with the **Employee Master** as the text, and **EmployeeMaster** as the meaningful name.

h. On the Reports page, use the Command Button Wizard to add a command button to the page. From the Report Operations category, choose the Preview Report action and the CallLog report. Choose the Text option with the **Call Log** as the text and **CallLog** as the meaningful name.

i. Save the form with the name **Nav** then switch to Form view. Test all three command buttons then close all open objects.

16. Modify form properties.

a. Open the Nav form in Form Design View.

b. Open the Property Sheet for the Nav form and change the following properties on the Format tab of the Property Sheet:

Caption: **Navigation**
Record Selectors: **No**
Navigation Buttons: **No**
Scroll Bars: **Neither**
Control Box: **No**
Min Max Buttons: **None**

c. Save the Nav form then view it in Form View to review the property changes.

d. Close the Nav form, compact and close the IL_AC_6_SupportDesk database, then exit Access.

Independent Challenge 1

As the manager of Riverwalk, a multispecialty health clinic, you have created a database to manage the schedules that connect each healthcare provider with the nurses that provider needs to efficiently handle patient visits. In this exercise you will create a form that will help users find the objects (queries, forms, and reports) that they use to manage nurse and provider information.

a. Start Access, open the IL_AC_6-3.accdb database from the location where you store your Data Files, then save it as **IL_AC_6_Riverwalk**. Enable content if prompted.

b. Use the Blank Form tool to create a new, blank form.

c. In Design View, add a tab control.

d. Change the Name property for the Page1 tab to **Nurse Info**.

e. Change the Name property for the Page2 tab to **Provider Info**.

f. On the Nurse Info tab, use the Command Button Wizard to add two command buttons, side by side in the middle of the page to do the following:

- Open the NurseEntry form to show all of the records. Use the MS Access Form picture and a meaningful name of **NurseEntryForm**.
- Preview the ScheduleByNurse report. Use the Preview picture and a meaningful name of **PreviewScheduleByNurseReport**.
- Align the tops of the command buttons.

Access

Independent Challenge 1 (continued)

g. On the Provider Info tab, use the Command Button Wizard to add two command buttons side by side in the middle of the page to do the following:
- Open the ProviderEntry form to show all of the records. Use the MS Access Form picture and a meaningful name of **ProviderEntryForm**.
- Preview the Schedule report. Use the Preview picture and a meaningful name of **PreviewScheduleReport**.
- Align the tops of the command buttons.

h. Save the form with the name **Switchboard** then switch to Form view. Test all four command buttons then close all open objects.

i. Open the Switchboard form in Form Design View.

j. Open the Property Sheet for the Switchboard form and change the following properties on the Format tab of the Property Sheet:

Record Selectors: **No**

Navigation Buttons: **No**

Scroll Bars: **Neither**

Control Box: **No**

Min Max Buttons: **None**

k. Save the Switchboard form then view it in Form View to review the property changes, as shown in **FIGURE 6-34**. Close the Switchboard form, compact and close the IL_AC_6_SupportDesk database, then exit Access.

FIGURE 6-34

Independent Challenge 2

You are working for a city to coordinate a series of community-wide preparedness activities. You have created a database to track the activities and volunteers who are attending the activities. In this exercise you will create a form/subform to provide information about the volunteers who worked at each activity.

a. Start Access, open the IL_AC_6-4.accdb database from the location where you store your Data Files, then save it as **IL_AC_6_Volunteers**. Enable content if prompted.

b. Using the Form Wizard, create a form based on all of the fields of the Volunteers and Activities tables.

c. When asked how you want to view the data, click by Activities, click by Volunteers, then click by Activities again. Note that with both options, the Form Wizard wants to create a main form/subform using the data selected. This is because both the Activities and Volunteers tables have a one-to-many relationship with the same junction table, Attendance. One volunteer can attend many activities. One activity can have many volunteers. So the decision on which table to use for the main form and which for the subform is based on how you want to view the data. Click by Activities.

d. Choose a Datasheet layout for the subform, then enter **ActivitiesMain** as the title of the main form and **VolunteersSubform** for the subform.

e. Delete, move, and edit the labels, text boxes, and subform as shown in **FIGURE 6-35**.

f. Use the column resize pointer to resize the columns of the subform as shown in **FIGURE 6-35**.

Independent Challenge 2 (continued)

FIGURE 6-35

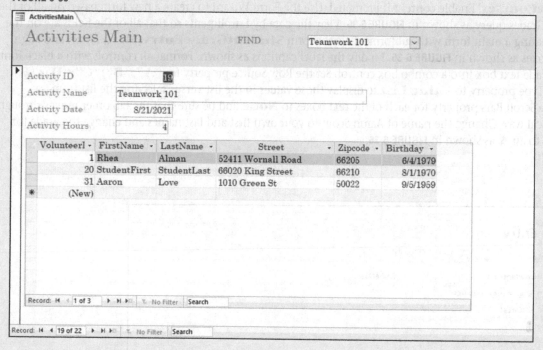

g. Save the form and in Form Design View, add a combo box in the Form Header section at about the 5" mark to find records. Select the ActivityName field for the list, hide the key column, and use **FIND** for the label.

h. Modify the properties of the new combo box to make the Column Widths **0"**; **2"**, the List Width **2"**, and Width **2"**.

i. Modify the Row Source property so that the list is sorted in ascending order based on the ActivityName field.

j. Save the form, display it in Form View, then use the new combo box to find the record for Teamwork 101.

k. Change the name of Katrina Margolis to your own name in the subform. Close the ActivitiesMain form, compact and close the IL_AC_6_Volunteers database, then exit Access.

Visual Workshop

Start Access, open the IL_AC_6-5.accdb database from the location where you store your Data Files, then save it as **IL_AC_6_CollegeCourses**. Enable content if prompted. Use the Form Wizard to create a new form based on all of the fields in the StudentGrades query as shown in **FIGURE 6-36**. View the data by Enrollments so that all of the fields are on the main form versus creating a main form with subforms. Title the form **StudentGradeEntry**. Move, resize, and align the labels and text boxes as shown in **FIGURE 6-36**. Modify the label captions as shown. Format all controls with a black font color. Change the Grade text box into a combo box control. Set the Row Source property to: *"A";"B";"C";"D";"F"* and the Row Source Type property to **Value List** to display those values in the list versus selecting the list from an existing table. Set the Scroll Bars property for each of the text boxes to **None** and be sure that the tab order moves through the controls in a logical way. Change the name of Aaron Scout to your own first and last names and change the grade for the ENGR131 course to an **A** as shown in **FIGURE 6-36**.

FIGURE 6-36

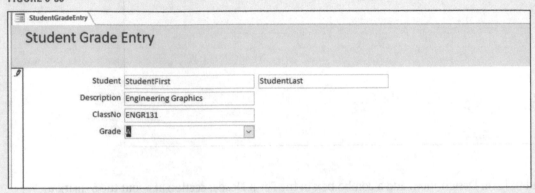

Creating Reports

CASE You are working with Lydia Snyder, vice president of operations at JCL Talent, to build a research database to manage industry, company, and job data. In this module, you'll create and modify reports that are used to analyze, subtotal, and interact with information.

Module Objectives

After completing this module, you will be able to:

- Create and preview a report
- Modify report layout
- Add fields and lines
- Group and sort records
- Add calculations and subtotals
- Resize and align controls
- Modify report sections
- Create multicolumn reports
- Add a subreport
- Add command buttons

Files You Will Need

IL_AC_7-1.accdb   IL_AC_7-4.accdb

IL_AC_7-2.accdb   IL_AC_7-5.accdb

IL_AC_7-3.accdb

Create and Preview a Report

Reports are used to subtotal, analyze, and distribute information. Both reports and forms use label controls for descriptive text and text box controls to display data. See **TABLE 7-1** for more information on common report controls. A big difference between a form and report, however, is that you use forms for data entry, whereas report data is **read-only**. You cannot enter or edit data on a report. **CASE** ▶ *Lydia Snyder asks you to create a report to display company information. You create the report using Report Design View and preview it in Print Preview.*

STEPS

QUICK TIP
If you use the Report Wizard, the Record Source property is automatically added to the report.

1. **sam̄** ↓ **Start Access, open the** IL_AC_7-1.accdb database **from the location where you store your Data Files, save it as** IL_AC_7_Jobs, **enable content if prompted, click the Create tab, then click the** Report Design button

   You can create a new report from scratch in Report Design or Report Layout View. The benefit of using Report Design View is that all report modification features are available, including ruler and report section information. The benefit of using Report Layout View is that it displays live data as you are building the report. Regardless of the view, the first task in creating a report from scratch is setting the **Record Source** property that identifies the table, query, or SQL statement that selects the fields and records for the report.

QUICK TIP
In Design View, and in other views if the object does not have a Caption property, the object's name appears in the tab.

2. **Click the** Property Sheet button **in the Tools group, click the** Data tab **in the Property Sheet, click the** Record Source list arrow, **then click** Companies

   The Record Source property can be a table, query, or SQL statement. If you use the Build button [⋯], you use the Query Builder to build an SQL statement using Query Design View. You also want to set the **Caption** property for the report, the text that will appear in the report tab when the report is opened a view other than Design View.

3. **Save the report as** CompanyInfo, **click the** Format tab **in the Property Sheet, click the** Caption property box, **type** Company Information, **then press** ENTER

   You next add the fields from the Companies table to the report.

4. **Click the** Add Existing Fields button, **click the** CompanyID field **in the Field List, drag it to the Detail section at about the 2" mark on the horizontal ruler, then drag each of the other fields to the report Detail section, as shown in** FIGURE 7-1

   Next, add the date and time to the report, then save and preview it.

5. **Click the** Date and Time button **in the Header/Footer group, click** OK **in the Date and Time dialog box, right-click the** CompanyInfo report tab, **then click** Print Preview

   Print Preview shows you how the report will look if printed, including page breaks, margins, and headers and footers.

QUICK TIP
To quickly move to a specific page, enter a number in the Current Page box.

6. **Click the** Next Page button [▶] **in the navigation bar, click the** Previous Page button [◀], **click the** Last Page button [▶|], **then click the** First Page button [|◀]

   By navigating through several pages of a report in Print Preview, you can see exactly how the report will look if printed or distributed. You can change the report margins in Print Preview.

7. **Click the** Margins button, **click the** Narrow option **(if it is not already selected) as shown in** FIGURE 7-2, **right-click the** Company Information report tab, **click** Close, **then click** Yes **to save the report**

FIGURE 7-1: Creating a report in Report Design View

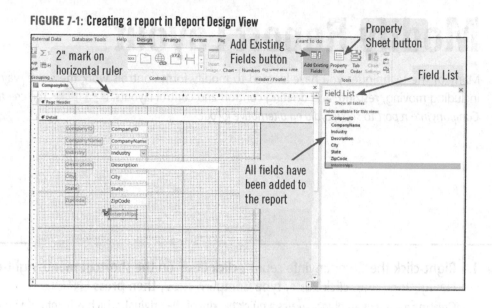

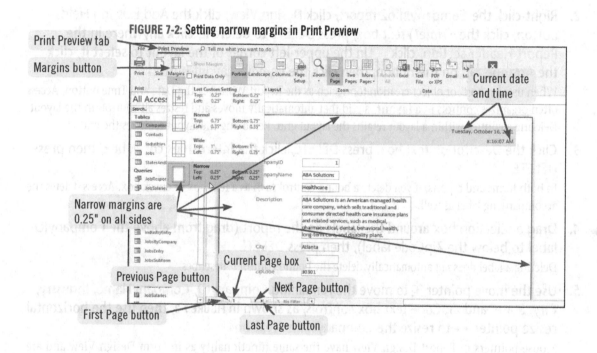

TABLE 7-1: Common report controls

name	button	used to	bound or unbound
Label	Aa	Provide consistent descriptive text; the most common type of unbound control on a report	Unbound
Text box	abl	Display data or a calculation; the most common type of bound control on a report	Bound
Line		Draw lines, used to indicate subtotals and grand totals	Unbound
Command button	xxxx	Provide an easy way to initiate a command or run a macro in Report View	Unbound

Modify Report Layout

Learning
Outcomes
• Copy and paste a
report
• Work with control
layouts
• Delete, resize, and
move controls

Many of the techniques you have learned to modify form controls work the same way with reports, including moving, resizing, and deleting controls and control layouts. **CASE** ▸ *You create a copy of the CompanyInfo report to show Lydia an alternative layout.*

STEPS

QUICK TIP
Right-click an object
to cut or delete it.
Both options remove
the object, but the
Cut option also
places a copy on the
Clipboard.

1. **Right-click the** CompanyInfo report, **click** Copy **on the shortcut menu, right-click in the** Navigation Pane, **click** Paste, **type** CompanyInfo2, **then press** ENTER

   Creating a copy of an object creates a quick backup of the original, which is helpful if you want to experiment with the copy.

2. **Right-click the** CompanyInfo2 report, **click** Design View, **click the** Add Existing Fields **button, click the** =Time() text box, **press** DELETE **to delete it, click anywhere in the** Report Header section, **click** ⊞ **in the upper-left corner of the layout to select it, click the** Arrange tab **on the ribbon, then click the** Remove Layout button

   When using report- or object-creation tools such as the Report Wizard or the Date and Time button, Access often organizes controls in a **layout**, a grid that automatically moves and resizes all controls in the layout. Deleting a control within a layout retains the layout grid. Removing the layout removes the grid.

3. **Click the** Description text box, **press** DELETE, **click the** Internships check box, **then press** DELETE

   In both forms and reports, if you delete a bound control such as a text box or check box, Access deletes the accompanying label as well.

TROUBLE
If you make a
mistake, use the
Undo button ↶
and Redo button
↷ as needed.

4. **Drag a** selection box **around the labels on the report (drag from above the CompanyID label to below the ZipCode label), then press** DELETE

   Deleting a label does *not* automatically delete the bound control it describes.

5. **Use the move pointer** ⇖ **to move the remaining** CompanyID, CompanyName, Industry, City, State, **and** ZipCode text box controls, **as shown in FIGURE 7-3, then use the horizontal resize pointer** ↔ **to resize the** CompanyName text box

   Mouse pointers in Report Design View have the same functionality as in Form Design View and are described in **TABLE 7-2**.

6. **Use the vertical resize pointer** ↕ **to drag the** top edge of the Page Footer section **up to the text boxes, right-click the** CompanyInfo2 report tab, **then click** Print Preview

   A portion of the first page of the new report, which now presents the data in a horizontal versus vertical layout, is shown in **FIGURE 7-4**. The horizontal layout of each record's data reduces the number of pages in the report to one or two pages depending on the height of the Detail section.

7. **Click the** Save button 🖫 **on the Quick Access Toolbar, right-click the** Company Information report tab, **then click** Close

FIGURE 7-3: Moving and resizing controls in Report Design View

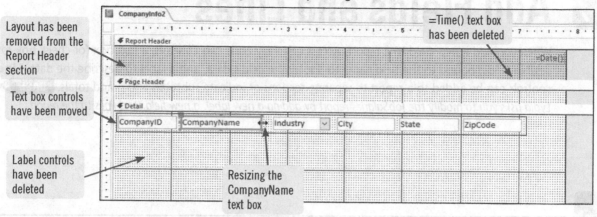

Layout has been removed from the Report Header section

=Time() text box has been deleted

Text box controls have been moved

Label controls have been deleted

Resizing the CompanyName text box

FIGURE 7-4: Previewing the new report layout

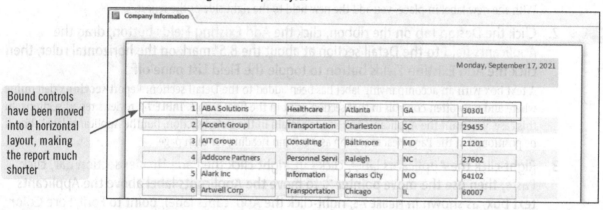

Bound controls have been moved into a horizontal layout, making the report much shorter

TABLE 7-2: Mouse pointer shapes in Report Design View

shape	when does this shape appear?	action
⌖	When you point to any unselected control on the report (the default mouse pointer)	Single-clicking with this mouse pointer selects a control. Dragging with this pointer selects all controls in the selection box.
✣	When you point to the upper-left corner or edge of a selected control in Report Design View or the middle of the control in Report Layout View	Dragging with this mouse pointer moves the selected control(s).
↕ ↔ ↖ ↗	When you point to any sizing handle (except the larger one in the upper-left corner in Report Design View)	Dragging with one of these mouse pointers resizes the control.
╪	When you point to the top edge of any report section or the bottom edge of the report	Dragging with this mouse pointer resizes the section above it.
↔	When you point to the right edge of the report	Dragging with this mouse pointer resizes the width of the report.

Add Fields and Lines

Learning Outcomes
- Add a field to a report
- Add a label to a report
- Add lines to a report

When you add a new field to a report, Access generally adds two controls, a text box (or check box for Yes/No fields) bound to the field name to display the field's data, and a label to describe the data. **Line** controls can be added to a report to separate sections or indicate subtotals and grand totals. **CASE** *Lydia asks you to modify the JobSalaries report by adding a new label, a new field, and lines to the report.*

STEPS

1. **Right-click the** JobSalaries report **in the Navigation Pane, click** Design View, **click the** Label button [Aa] **in the Controls group, click in the** Report Header section at about the 5" mark **on the horizontal ruler, type** JCL Internal Use Only, **press** ENTER, **click the** Format tab **on the ribbon, click the** Font Color list arrow [A ▾], **then click** Automatic (black)

   With the new label in place, you add the new field to the right side of the report.

   > **QUICK TIP**
   > If the Field List is wider than desired, use the ⟺ to narrow it.

2. **Click the** Design tab **on the ribbon, click the** Add Existing Fields button, **drag the** Applicants field **to the Detail section at about the 8.5" mark on the horizontal ruler, then click the** Add Existing Fields button **to toggle the Field List pane off**

   A text box with an accompanying label has been added to the Detail section. Report **sections** determine where and how often controls in that section print in the final report. **TABLE 7-3** reviews report sections. In this case, you want the Applicants text box to remain in the Detail section, but the Applicants label should be positioned in the Page Header section as a column heading for each page.

3. **Right-click the** Applicants label, **click** Cut, **right-click the** Page Header section bar, **click** Paste, **then use the move pointer** ⁺ᵏ **to move the Applicants label above the Applicants text box, as shown in FIGURE 7-5, right-click the** Applicants label, **point to** Font/Fore Color **on the shortcut menu, then click the** black sample box **(first row, second column)**

   With the new field including the bound text box and descriptive label positioned correctly, you decide to add a line above the text box that contains the =Count(*) expression in the Report Footer to indicate a total.

4. **Click the** More button [▾] **in the Controls group, click the** Line button [◻], **press and hold** SHIFT, **drag a line from above the left edge of the text box in the Report Footer section to the right edge of the text box, then release** SHIFT

   Pressing SHIFT while dragging a line control creates a perfectly horizontal or vertical line.

5. **Click the** Save button [▤] **on the Quick Access Toolbar, right-click the** JobSalaries report tab, **click** Print Preview, **then click the** Last Page button [▸ı]

   The last page of the report should look like **FIGURE 7-6**.

FIGURE 7-5: Adding labels and fields to a report

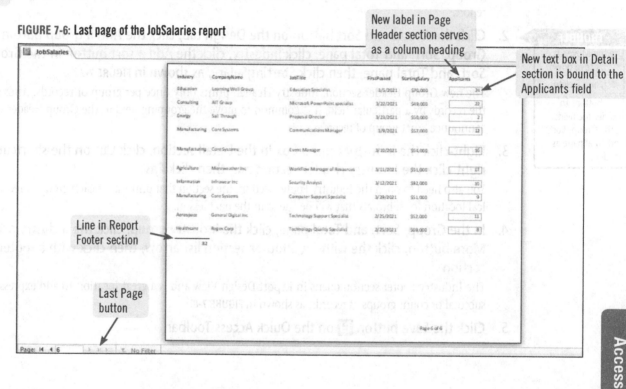

FIGURE 7-6: Last page of the JobSalaries report

TABLE 7-3: Report sections

section	where does this section print?
Report Header	At the top of the first page
Page Header	At the top of every page (but below the Report Header on the first page)
Group Header	Before every group of records
Detail	Once for every record
Group Footer	After every group of records
Page Footer	At the bottom of every page
Report Footer	At the end of the last page of the report

Group and Sort Records

You use the Group, Sort, and Total pane to identify the way the records on a report will be grouped and sorted. **Sorting** means to place the records in ascending or descending order based on the value of a field. **Grouping** means to sort records in a particular order plus provide a report section above or below that group of records. Fields that have a common value in several records are good candidates to use as a grouping field. After grouping records, it is common to further sort the records within each group.

CASE ▸ *Lydia Snyder asks you to organize the information in the JobSalaries report by industry and salary. You decide to group the records by Industry, then further sort them by StartingSalary.*

STEPS

1. **Right-click the JobSalaries tab, then click Design View**

   Grouping both sorts the records and provides a Group Header or Group Footer section before and after each group of records. The word *Group* is generic; it is replaced by the field name that is used for grouping on the report.

2. **Click the Group and Sort button on the Design tab, click the Add a group button in the Group, Sort, and Total pane, click Industry, click the Add a sort button in the Group, Sort, and Total pane, then click StartingSalary, as shown in FIGURE 7-7**

   The new Group Header section, Industry Header, prints only once per group of records. After grouping the records by a particular field, it is common to move the grouping field to the Group Header section to "announce" that group of records.

3. **Right-click the Industry combo box in the Detail section, click Cut on the shortcut menu, right-click the Industry Header section bar, then click Paste**

   You also need to open the Industry Footer section, the section that prints after each group of records, a logical location for subtotals that will be added in the next lesson.

4. **In the Group, Sort, and Total pane, click the Industry group, click the Industry group More button, click the without a footer section list arrow, then click with a footer section**

   The Industry Footer section opens in Report Design View and is a great location to add expressions that subtotal or count groups of records, as shown in FIGURE 7-8.

5. **Click the Save button 🖫 on the Quick Access Toolbar**

FIGURE 7-7: Grouping and sorting records in Report Design View

Group & Sort button

New Industry Header section

Industry combo box

New line

Group, Sort, and Total pane

Group on Industry

Sort by StartingSalary

More button for StartingSalary field

Move down button

Move up button

Delete button

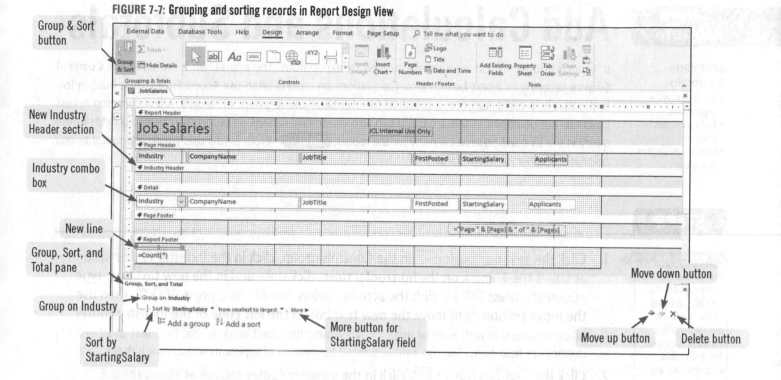

FIGURE 7-8: Opening the Group Footer section

Industry combo box moved to Industry Header section

Industry Footer section opened

with a header section

with a footer section

More button becomes the Less button for the Industry grouping field

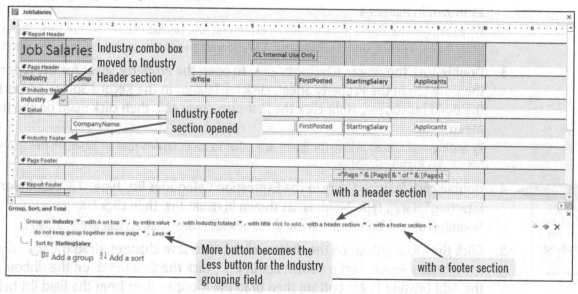

Combo boxes versus text boxes on a report

If a field has been defined with Lookup properties in Table Design View, it will automatically be added as a combo box control to a form or report. But given that the data on a report is read-only, users cannot interact with a combo box control on a report to enter or edit data. Therefore, the combo box and text box controls function the same way on a report.

Add Calculations and Subtotals

In reports and forms, calculations are created by expressions. The expression is stored in the **Control Source** property of a text box control. Calculations on reports often use Access **functions**, built-in formulas that help build common expressions to subtotal or count groups of records. A few common Access functions are described in **TABLE 7-4**. You can also create calculations on reports as calculated fields in the query in the **Record Source** property for the report. **CASE** ▶ *Lydia Snyder asks you to add subtotals and calculations to the JobSalaries report.*

STEPS

1. **Click the** Text Box button ⌑ **in the Controls group, click in the** Industry Footer section **at about the 1" mark** on the horizontal ruler, click Unbound **in the new text box, type** =Count(*), press ENTER, **click the accompanying** Text## label, **press** DELETE, **then use the move pointer** ⬈ **to move the new text box to the left edge of the Industry Footer**

   All expressions start with an equal sign (=). When using the Count function, you can insert an asterisk (*) in place of a field name. You also want to subtotal the number of applicants within each industry.

2. **Click the** Text Box button ⌑, **click in the** Industry Footer section **at about the 8.5" mark** on the horizontal ruler, double-click Text## **in the new label, type** Subtotal, **press** ENTER, **click** Unbound **in the new text box, type** =Sum([Applicants]), **then press** ENTER, **as shown in** FIGURE 7-9

   When referencing a field name within an expression, use [square brackets]—(not parentheses) and not {curly braces}—to surround the field name. You also want to add the monthly salary to the report.

3. **Double-click the** report selector box ▪ **to open the Property Sheet for the report, click the** Data tab **in the Property Sheet, click** JobSalaries **in the Record Source property, click the** Build button ⋯, **right-click the** first blank field cell, **then click** Build **on the shortcut menu**

   By adding a calculated field to the query, any other forms or reports that are based on this query will also have access to this calculation.

4. **Double-click** StartingSalary **in the Expression Categories list, type** /12, **click before** [StartingSalary], **type** Monthly: **as shown in** FIGURE 7-10, **then click** OK

   Monthly is the new calculated field name. The new field name is always followed by a colon.

5. **Click the** Close button **on the ribbon, click** Yes **to save changes, drag the** top edge of the Industry Footer section **down about 0.5", click the** Design tab **on the ribbon, click the** Add Existing Fields button, **then drag the** Monthly field **from the field list below the** StartingSalary field **in the Detail section**

   Any field added to the JobSalaries query is available to the report, including calculated fields. You format the Monthly field to display its values as currency with no digits to the right of the decimal point.

6. **Click the** Monthly text box, **click the** Property Sheet button **on the Design tab, click the** Format tab **in the Property Sheet, click the** Format property list arrow, **click** Currency, **click** Auto **in the Decimal Places property, click the** Decimal Places list arrow, **then click** 0

7. **Click the** Save button 🖫, **right-click the** JobSalaries report tab, **click** Report View, **then scroll down to see the entire Consulting group, as shown in** FIGURE 7-11

   Report View shows the entire report in one long view without page breaks. The basic information, subtotals, and calculations are now on the report.

FIGURE 7-9: Adding counts and subtotals to a report

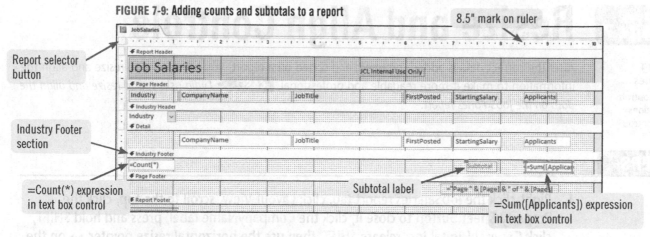

- Report selector button
- Industry Footer section
- =Count(*) expression in text box control
- 8.5" mark on ruler
- Subtotal label
- =Sum([Applicants]) expression in text box control

FIGURE 7-10: Using the Expression Builder

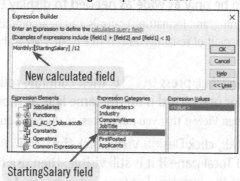

- New calculated field
- StartingSalary field

FIGURE 7-11: Previewing subtotals, counts, and calculations

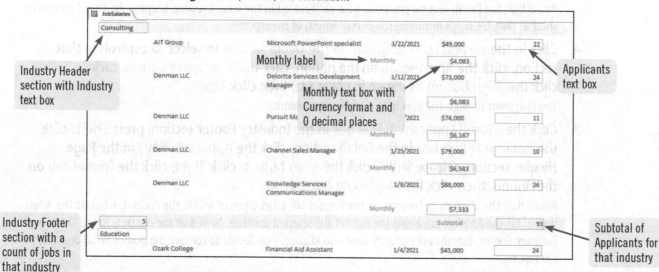

- Industry Header section with Industry text box
- Industry Footer section with a count of jobs in that industry
- Monthly label
- Monthly text box with Currency format and 0 decimal places
- Applicants text box
- Subtotal of Applicants for that industry

TABLE 7-4: Sample expressions using common Access functions

sample expression	function description
=Sum([Salary])	Uses the **Sum function** to add the values in the Salary field
=Avg([Freight])	Uses the **Avg function** to display an average of the values in the Freight field
=Date()	Uses the **Date function** to display the current date in the form of mm-dd-yy
=Left([ProductNumber],2)	Uses the **Left function** to display the first two characters in the ProductNumber field
=Count(*)	Uses the **Count function** to count the records

Resize and Align Controls

After the correct data is added, grouped, and sorted on a report, you often want to resize and align the information to make it more readable and professional. **CASE** ▶ *Lydia asks you to resize and align the data on the JobSalaries report.*

STEPS

1. **Right-click the** JobSalaries report tab, **click** Layout View, **scroll to the top, click the** Property Sheet button **to close it, click the** CompanyName label, **press and hold** SHIFT, **click** General Digital Inc, **release** SHIFT, **then use the horizontal resize pointer ↔ on the right side to narrow the column to be only as wide as needed to display the data**

   Most modifications, such as resizing, aligning, and formatting controls, can be accomplished the same way in both Design and Layout Views. The benefit of resizing controls in Layout View is that you can see the data as you are modifying the controls.

2. **Click any occurrence of the** Monthly label, **press** DELETE, **then continue resizing and moving controls until all the data for one record is on the same line, as shown in** FIGURE 7-12

   The benefit of modifying controls in Design View is that you have access to the rulers and section bars.

3. **Right-click the** JobSalaries report tab, **click** Design View, **click the** Group & Sort button **to toggle off the Group, Sort, and Total pane if it is still visible, then use the resize pointer ╪ to drag the** top edge of the Industry Footer section bar **up to remove the extra vertical space in the Detail section**

   Recall that the Detail section prints once for each record in the record source. Keeping the Detail section as short as possible helps minimize the overall length of the report.

4. **Click in the** vertical ruler to the left of the Detail section **to select all controls in that section, click the** Arrange tab **on the ribbon, click the** Size/Space button, **click** To Tallest, **click the** Align button **as shown in** FIGURE 7-13, **then click** Top

   You also want to align the data in the Applicants column.

5. **Click the** =Sum([Applicants]) text box **in the Industry Footer section, press** SHIFT, **click the** Applicants text box **in the Detail section, click the** Applicants label **in the Page Header section, release** SHIFT, **click the** Align button, **click** Right, **click the** Format tab **on the ribbon, then click the** Align Right button ▤

   Recall that the alignment buttons on the Format tab align content *within* the control, whereas the Align button on the Arrange tab aligns the *edges* of the selected controls. Now that the controls in the Detail and Industry Footer sections are perfectly sized and aligned, you decide to remove the border on all controls in the report.

6. **Press** CTRL+A **to select all controls on the report, click the** Shape Outline button **in the Control Formatting group, click** Transparent, **click the** Report Footer section bar, **click the** line control **in the Report Footer section to select it by itself, click the** Shape Outline button, **then click** Automatic (black)

   Save and preview your changes.

7. **Click the** Save button ▤, **right-click the** JobSalaries report tab, **then click** Print Preview

   The report is much shorter and more professional now that all the controls in the Detail and Report Footer sections are aligned and resized.

FIGURE 7-12: Resizing and moving controls in Report Layout View

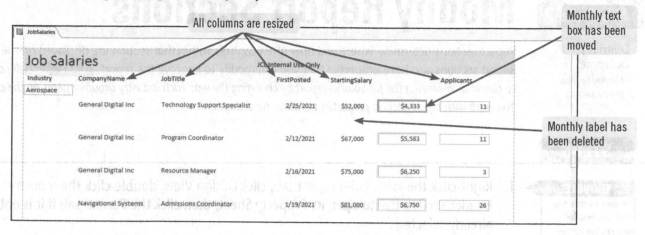

All columns are resized

Monthly text box has been moved

Monthly label has been deleted

Job Salaries

Industry	CompanyName	JobTitle	FirstPosted	StartingSalary		Applicants
Aerospace						
	General Digital Inc	Technology Support Specialist	2/25/2021	$52,000	$4,333	11
	General Digital Inc	Program Coordinator	2/12/2021	$67,000	$5,583	11
	General Digital Inc	Resource Manager	2/16/2021	$75,000	$6,250	3
	Navigational Systems	Admissions Coordinator	1/19/2021	$81,000	$6,750	26

JCL Internal Use Only

FIGURE 7-13: Aligning controls in Report Design View

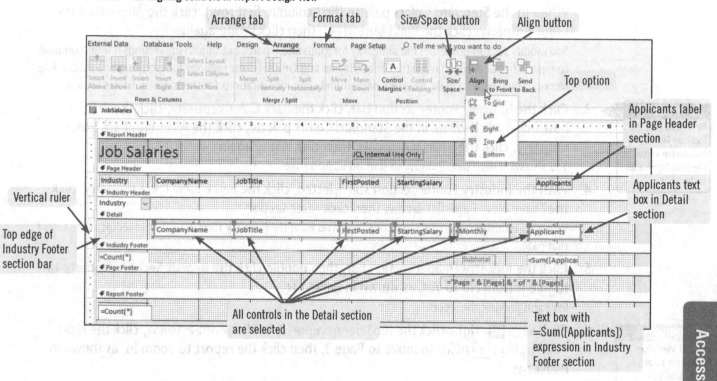

Arrange tab

Format tab

Size/Space button

Align button

Top option

Applicants label in Page Header section

Applicants text box in Detail section

Vertical ruler

Top edge of Industry Footer section bar

All controls in the Detail section are selected

Text box with =Sum([Applicants]) expression in Industry Footer section

Access

Modify Report Sections

Learning Outcome
• Modify section properties

Report sections determine where and how often controls within that section are displayed on the report. Report sections also have properties that you can modify to improve the report. **CASE** *Lydia asks you to continue improving the JobSalaries report by changing the way each industry group appears on the printout. You work with report section properties to make the changes.*

STEPS

TROUBLE
Be sure to click the Industry Header section bar versus the Industry Footer section bar.

1. **Right-click the** JobSalaries report tab, **click** Design View, **double-click the** Industry Header section bar **to open its Property Sheet, then click the** Format tab **if it is not already selected**

   The **Back Color** and **Alternate Back Color** properties determine the background color for every other Industry Header section. You change this to white for every Industry Header.

2. **Click the** Back Color property **in the Property Sheet, click the** Build button ⬚, **click** White **in the Standard Colors palette (first column, first row), click the** Alternate Back Color property, **click the** Build button ⬚, **then click** White **again**

   You modify section properties the same way for forms and reports, but modifying sections is more common in reports because they have extra Group Header and Group Footer sections for grouping and subtotaling records. You decide to make the same background color modifications for the Industry Footer section.

TROUBLE
Be sure to click the Industry Footer section bar versus the Industry Header section bar.

3. **Click the** Industry Footer section bar, **click the** Back Color property, **click the** Build button ⬚, **click** White **in the Standard Colors palette, click the** Alternate Back Color property, **click the** Build button ⬚, **then click** White **again**

   You also want each new Industry to start on its own page.

4. **With the Industry Footer section still selected, click the** Force New Page property, **click the** Force New Page list arrow, **then click** After section

   When an Industry spans more than one page, you want the Industry Header section to repeat at the top of that page.

5. **Click the** Industry Header section bar, **then double-click the** Repeat Section property **to toggle it from No to Yes, as shown in** FIGURE 7-14

   Save and preview the report.

QUICK TIP
Report View does not show page breaks, so you cannot test the Repeat Section or Force New Page section properties in Report View, only in Print Preview.

6. **Click** Save 🖫, **right-click the** JobSalaries report tab, **click** Print Preview, **click the** Next Page button ▶ **twice to move to Page 3, then click the report to zoom in, as shown in** FIGURE 7-15

   No industries have enough records to span more than one page yet, but as the database grows, this report will repeat the Industry Header section as needed and start each industry at the top of a new page.

7. **Right-click the** JobSalaries report tab, **then click** Close

FIGURE 7-14: Modifying section properties

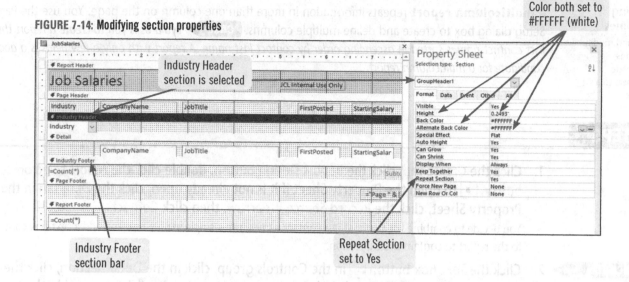

Industry Header section is selected

Industry Footer section bar

Repeat Section set to Yes

FIGURE 7-15: Previewing the final JobSalaries report

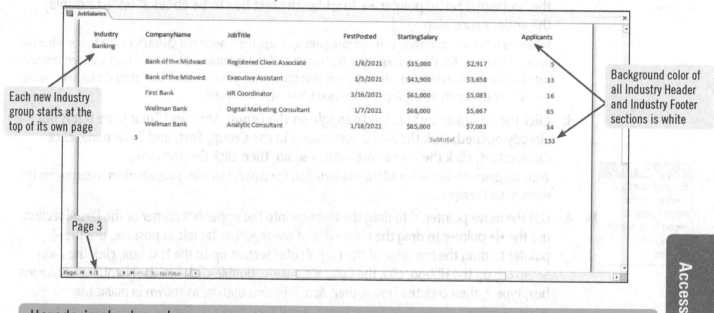

Each new Industry group starts at the top of its own page

Page 3

Background color of all Industry Header and Industry Footer sections is white

Hexadecimal color values

Hexadecimal color values are six-digit representations of color using two digits for each of the three colors of light: red, green, and blue (also sometimes called **RGB values** for red-green-blue). Each digit ranges from 0–9, then A–F for a total of 16 different values for each digit. #000000 represents no color in each of the three color positions, which yields black. #FFFFFF represents maximum amounts of red, green, and blue light, which represents white. #FF0000 represents maximum red, no green, and no blue, which defines red, and so forth. An equal mix of red, green, and blue such as #D8D8D8 is a shade of gray.

Inserting page breaks

If you want to force a page break at a certain point in a form or report, use the **Insert Page Break button** to insert a **page break control**, which forces any content after the control to start at the top of a new page when the form or report is previewed or printed.

Create Multicolumn Reports

Learning
Outcomes
• Add and modify
  columns
• Add page
  numbers to a
  report

A **multicolumn report** repeats information in more than one column on the page. You use the Page Setup dialog box to create and define multiple columns. **CASE** ▸ *Lydia asks you to create a report that lists contact names sorted in ascending order by contact last name. A report with only a few fields is a good candidate for a multicolumn report.*

STEPS

1. **Click the** Create tab, **click the** Report Design button, **double-click the** report selector button ▪ **to open the Property Sheet if it is not already open, click the** Data tab **in the Property Sheet, click the** Record Source list arrow, **then click** Contacts

   You decide to combine the first and last contact names into a single expression. You add a text box control to the report to contain the expression.

   > **QUICK TIP**
   > Be sure to insert a space after the comma in the new expression.

2. **Click the** Text Box button ▦ **in the Controls group, click in the** Detail section, **click the** Text## label, **press** DELETE, **click the new** text box **to select it, click** Unbound **in the text box, type the expression** =[ContactLast] & ", " & [ContactFirst], **press** ENTER, **then use the horizontal resize pointer ↔ to widen the text box to be about 3" wide to display the entire expression**

   When building an expression that concatenates text, use the ampersand character (&) to combine the parts. In this case, the ContactLast value is concatenated to a comma and a space, which are then concatenated to the ContactFirst value. To make sure that the records sort in ContactLast, then ContactFirst order, you will set the report sort options in the Group, Sort, and Total pane.

3. **Click the** Group & Sort button **to toggle on the Group, Sort, and Total pane if it is not already opened, click the** Add a sort button **in the Group, Sort, and Total pane, click** ContactLast, **click the** Add a sort button **again, then click** ContactFirst

   With the desired information added and sorted on the report, you turn your attention to setting up the columns for the report.

   > **QUICK TIP**
   > You must use Print Preview to view report columns. Report View doesn't display multiple columns.

4. **Use the move pointer ⌖ to drag the** text box **into the upper-left corner of the Detail section, use the ↔ pointer to drag the** right edge of the report **as far left as possible, use the ┿ pointer to drag the** top edge of the Page Footer section **up to the text box, click the** Page Setup tab **on the ribbon, click the** Columns button, **double-click 1 in the Number of Columns box, type** 2, **then click the** Down, **then** Across option button, **as shown in** FIGURE 7-16

   When designing a multicolumn report, Report Design View should display the width of only the first column. The Columns tab of the Page Setup dialog box provides options to change column settings. You also want this report to have page numbers.

   > **TROUBLE**
   > If your data doesn't look like FIGURE 7-17, return to Report Design View and check your expression and sort orders.

5. **Click** OK **in the Page Setup dialog box, click the** Design tab **on the ribbon, click the** Page Numbers button, **click the** Page N of M option button, **click the** Alignment list arrow, **click** Right, **then click** OK **in the Page Numbers dialog box**

   The page number expression was added in a text box control to the right side of the Page Header section.

6. **Right-click the** Report1 report tab, **then click** Print Preview, **as shown in** FIGURE 7-17

   Contact names are now set in two columns, sorted by the ContactLast, then by the ContactFirst fields.

7. **Click the** Save button ▦, **type** ContactList, **click** OK **in the Save as dialog box, right-click the** ContactList report tab, **then click** Close

FIGURE 7-16: Setting column properties

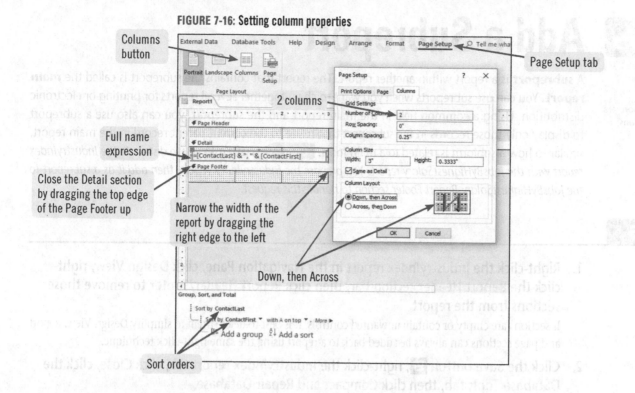

FIGURE 7-17: Previewing a multicolumn report

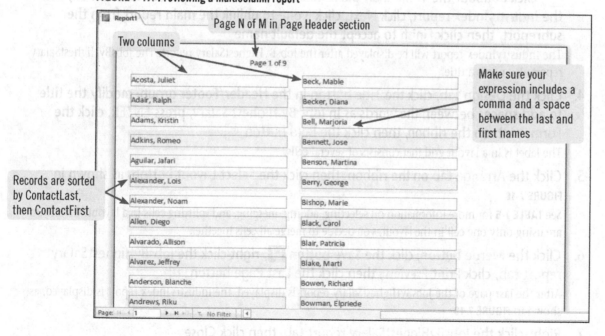

Access

Add a Subreport

Learning
Outcomes
• Add a subreport
• Remove sections
• Add a title

A **subreport** is a report within another report. The report that contains the subreport is called the **main report**. You can use subreports when you want to chain together several reports for printing or electronic distribution. Using a common field in the main report and the subreport, you can also use a subreport to display only those records in the subreport that relate to the current parent record in the main report, similar to how a subform is related to a main form. **CASE** ▸ *Lydia asks you to distribute the IndustryIndex report with the JobsByHighestSalary report. You prepare the IndustryIndex report, then add it as a subreport to the JobsByHighestSalary Report Footer section to handle this request.*

STEPS

1. **Right-click the** IndustryIndex report **in the Navigation Pane, click** Design View, **right-click the** Report Header **section bar, then click** Report Header/Footer **to remove those sections from the report**

   If sections are empty or contain unwanted controls, it is best to delete them to simplify Design View. Report and page sections can always be added back to a report using the same right-click technique.

2. **Click the** Save button 🖫, **right-click the** IndustryIndex report tab, **click** Close, **click the** Database Tools tab, **then click** Compact and Repair Database

   Compacting and repairing your database at regular intervals helps it stay organized. Next, add the Industry-Index report as a subreport to the JobsByHighestSalary report. The subreport and subform controls share the same button in the Controls group of the Design tab.

3. **Right-click the** JobsByHighestSalary report **in the Navigation Pane, click** Design View, **click the** More button ⊽ **in the Controls group, click the** Subform/Subreport button 🖼, **click at about the 1" mark on the horizontal ruler in the Report Footer section, click the** IndustryIndex report, **click** Next, **click** None **to unlink the main report from the subreport, then click** Finish **to accept the default name**

   The IndustryIndex report will be displayed after the JobsByHighestSalary report. The JobsByHighestSalary report also needs a title.

4. **Click the** Design tab, **click the** Title button **in the Header/Footer group, modify the title to add spaces between the words as in** Jobs By Highest Salary, **press ENTER, click the** Format tab **on the ribbon, then click the** Bold button Ⓑ

   The label is in a layout grid that consists of several cells.

5. **Click the** Arrange tab **on the ribbon, then click the** Select Layout button, **as shown in FIGURE 7-18**

   See **TABLE 7-5** for more information on selecting, adding, merging, and splitting cells in a layout. Given you are using only one cell in the layout, you decide to merge all cells together.

6. **Click the** Merge button, **click the** Save button 🖫, **right-click the** JobsByHighestSalary report tab, **click** Print Preview, **then click the** Last Page button ▶|

   After the last page of the JobsByHighestSalary report is displayed, the IndustryIndex report is displayed, as shown in **FIGURE 7-19**.

7. **Right-click the** JobsByHighestSalary report tab, **then click** Close

FIGURE 7-18: Main report with subreport

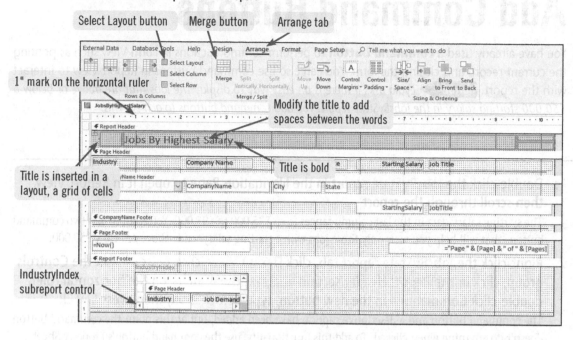

- Select Layout button
- Merge button
- Arrange tab
- 1" mark on the horizontal ruler
- Modify the title to add spaces between the words
- Title is inserted in a layout, a grid of cells
- Title is bold
- IndustryIndex subreport control

FIGURE 7-19: Previewing a subreport

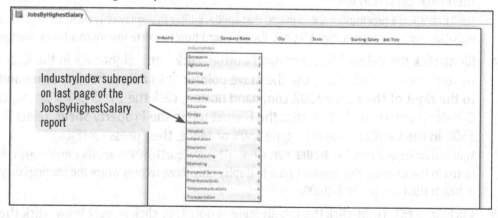

- IndustryIndex subreport on last page of the JobsByHighestSalary report

TABLE 7-5: Modifying cells in a layout

button	description
	Inserts a row cell above or below the layout
	Inserts a column cell to the left or right of the layout
	Selects all cells in the layout
	Selects all cells in the current column or row
	Merges selected cells
	Splits selected cells into two cells vertically or horizontally

Access

Add Command Buttons

Learning
Outcome
• Add a command
  button to a report

You have already used a **command button** to perform common actions in Form View such as printing the current record and closing the form. You can also use command buttons in Report View to interact with the report. **CASE** ▸ *Lydia asks if there is an easy way to display the jobs that are above or below a $50,000 starting salary in the JobsByState report. You add command buttons to achieve this.*

STEPS

1. **Double-click the** JobsByState report **in the Navigation Pane to open it in Report View, then scroll through the report**

   The starting salary data in the last column ranges from $35,000 to $95,000. You want to add two command buttons that will help you view only those jobs with a starting salary value above or below $50,000.

2. **Right-click the** JobsByState report tab, **click** Design View, **click** Button ▦ **in the Controls group, click in the** Report Header section at about the 4" mark **on the horizontal ruler, double-click** Command## **in the new button, type** Below $50K, **then press** ENTER

   The command button and a descriptive caption have been added, but at this point the command button doesn't do anything when clicked. To add this functionality, use the command button's Property Sheet.

3. **With the command button still selected, click the** Property Sheet button **to open it if it isn't already open, click the** Event tab **in the Property Sheet, click the** On Click list arrow, **then click** LessThan50K

   LessThan50K is a previously created macro that applies a filter to display only those records where the StartingSalary field value is less than $50,000. You will learn how to create macros in a future module.

4. **Right-click the** Below $50K command button, **click** Copy, **right-click in the** Report Header section, **click** Paste, **use the move pointer** ⁺⟐ **to move the new command button to the right of the Below $50K command button, click the** On Click list arrow, **click** GreaterThanOrEqualTo50K, **click the** Format tab **in the Property Sheet, select** Below $50K **in the** Caption property, **type** $50K or More, **then press** ENTER

   Your screen should look like **FIGURE 7-20**. GreaterThanOrEqualTo50K is another previously created macro stored in the database that applies a filter to display only those records where the StartingSalary field value is greater than or equal to $50,000.

5. **Click Save** 🖫, **right-click the** JobsByState report tab, **click** Report View, **click the** Below $50K command button, **then click the** $50K or More command button, **as shown in FIGURE 7-21**

   Command buttons make a report flexible and interactive.

6. **Right-click the** JobsByState report tab, **click** Close, **double-click the** Contacts table **to open it in Datasheet View, add your name as a new record with a CompanyID value of 1, then close the Contacts table**

7. **sam⬆ Compact and repair the database, then close the IL_AC_7_Jobs.accdb database and exit Access**

FIGURE 7-20: Adding command buttons to a report

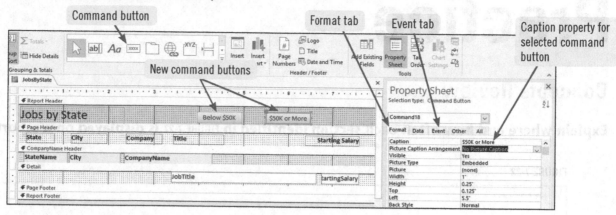

FIGURE 7-21: Filtering the records on a report with a command button

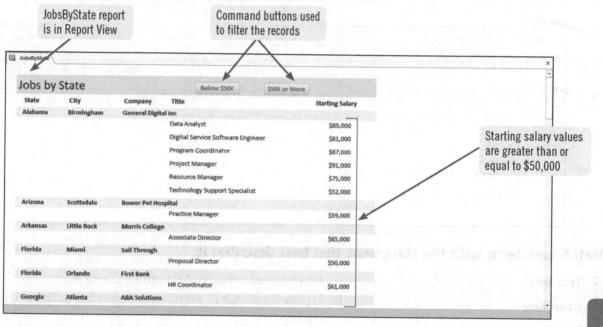

Rich Text formatting

By default every text box on a form or report has a **Text Format property** of **Plain Text**, which stores only text, not formatting instructions. The **Rich Text** value for the Text Format property allows you to mix formatting for the content of one text box using **HTML (HyperText Markup Language)** tags such as <b> for bold and <i> for italic. If you need to format the content of one text box in multiple ways, explore the capabilities of Rich Text.

Practice

Concepts Review

Explain where and how often each section identified in FIGURE 7-22 is displayed on a report.

FIGURE 7-22

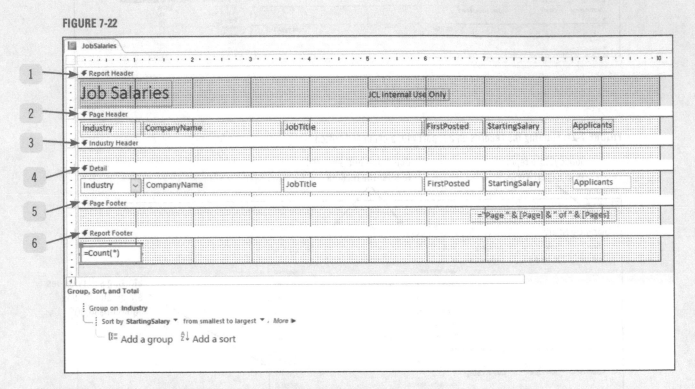

Match each term with the statement that best describes it.

7. Text box

8. Grouping

9. Sorting

10. Record Source

11. Label

12. Read-only

13. Control Source

14. Layout

15. Main report

a. A control used to display descriptive text on a report

b. To place the records in ascending or descending order based on the value of a field

c. A grid that automatically moves and resizes the controls it contains

d. To sort records in a particular order, plus provide a report section above and/or below the group of records

e. A control used to display data or a calculation on a report

f. A text box property where expressions are stored

g. A report that contains the subreport

h. A property that identifies the table, query, or SQL statement that selects the fields and records for the report

i. Not used for data entry or edits

Select the best answer from the list of choices.

16. Which report view allows you to click a command button to execute an action?

   a. Design View

   b. Layout View

   c. Print Preview

   d. Report View

17. **Which report view displays data and allows you to resize controls?**
    a. Design View
    b. Layout View
    c. Print Preview
    d. Report View

18. **Which report view displays rulers and section bars?**
    a. Design View
    b. Layout View
    c. Print Preview
    d. Report View

19. **Which report view shows margins and page breaks?**
    a. Design View
    b. Layout View
    c. Print Preview
    d. Report View

20. **Which of the following expressions would subtotal a field named Cost?**
    a. =Sum([Cost])
    b. =Subtotal{Cost}
    c. =Sub[Cost]
    d. =Total(Cost)

Skills Review

1. **Create and preview a report.**
   a. Start Access, open the IL_AC_7-2.accdb database from the location where you store your Data Files, then save it as **IL_AC_7_SupportDesk**. Enable content if prompted.
   b. Use the Report Design button to create a blank report in Report Design View. Set the report's Record Source property to the **EmployeeCalls** query and enter **Employee Calls** for the report's Caption property.
   c. Select the four fields LastName, FirstName, CaseTitle, and CallDateTime in the Field List, then drag them as a group or one at a time to the top of the Detail section at about the 1" mark on the horizontal ruler.
   d. Use the Date and Time button to add the current date and time to the report using a 30-Sep-21 format for the date and a 10:24 AM format for the time.
   e. Drag the top edge of the Page Footer section up to the text boxes in the Detail section, then save the report with the name **EmployeeCalls**.
   f. Switch to Print Preview, confirm that the report's margins are set to Narrow, then navigate through each of the report's pages to observe the length of the report.
   g. Close the EmployeeCalls report.

2. **Modify report layout.**
   a. Copy the EmployeeCalls report and paste it in the Navigation Pane with the name **EmployeeCalls2**.
   b. Open the EmployeeCalls2 report in Design View, then move, edit, and format the labels, as shown in **FIGURE 7-23**. The labels are positioned in the Page Header section, their captions have been edited to include spaces between words, and the labels have a bold and black font color.
   c. Move and format the text boxes, as shown in **FIGURE 7-23**. Note that the text boxes are positioned horizontally in the Detail section and that the CaseTitle text box has been widened to display more information.
   d. Drag the top edge of the Page Footer section up to the text boxes to remove vertical space in the Detail section.
   e. Remove the control layout from the controls in the Report Header section, then narrow and move the =Date() and =Time() text boxes side by side, as shown in **FIGURE 7-23**.
   f. Add a label to the Report Header section with **Employee Call List**, format it with bold, black font color, and 14-point font size, as shown in **FIGURE 7-23**.
   g. Save the report and preview all pages in Print Preview to make sure all information is clearly displayed, as shown in **FIGURE 7-23**. Note the difference in report page size between the EmployeeCalls report and EmployeeCalls2 report.
   h. Close the EmployeeCalls2 report.

Access

Skills Review (continued)

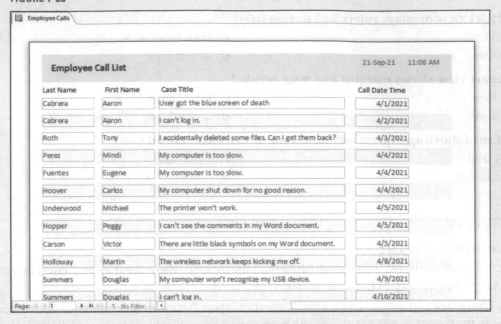

3. **Add fields and lines.**

   a. Open the CaseInfo report in Design View, then delete the EmployeeID label and EmployeeID text box.

   b. Open the Field List and add the LastName field to the report.

   c. Move the LastName label to the Page Header section between the CaseID and OpenedDate labels and modify it to be **Last Name**. Use the Format Painter to copy the formatting from the CaseID label to the Last Name label. Widen the Last Name label as needed to clearly display the entire label.

   d. Move the LastName text box in the Detail section between the existing CaseID and OpenedDate text boxes. Use the Format Painter to copy the formatting from the CaseID text box to the LastName text box and widen the LastName text box to fill the available space.

   e. Expand the height of the Report Footer section enough to move the =Count(*) text box down about 0.25", then add a horizontal line above the =Count(*) text box to indicate a total.

   f. Resize the Detail section to eliminate any extra blank space, then save the CaseInfo report, noting that the final report is shown in **FIGURE 7-24**.

FIGURE 7-24

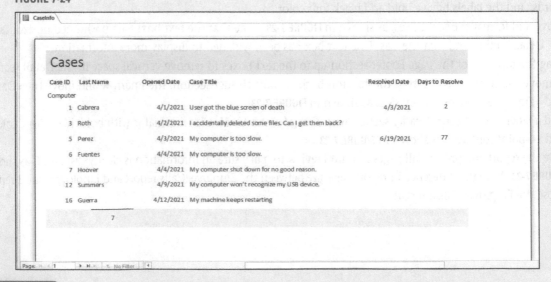

Skills Review (continued)

4. Group and sort records.

a. Open the Group, Sort, and Total pane for the CaseInfo report. Add Category as a grouping field and OpenedDate as a sort field in that order.

b. Move the Category text box to the left side of the Category Header section and delete the Category label in the Page Header section.

c. Open the Category Footer section.

d. Save the CaseInfo report.

5. Add calculations and subtotals.

a. Copy the line and the =Count(*) text box from the Report Footer section, then paste the two controls into the Category Footer section.

b. Move the Resolved Date and Days to Resolve labels in the Page Header section to the left, beside the Case Title label.

c. Move the ResolvedDate text box in the Detail section to the left next to the CaseTitle text box.

d. Add a text box control to the right of the ResolvedDate text box with the expression **=[ResolvedDate]-[OpenedDate]** to calculate the number of days between the date the case was opened and the date it was resolved.

e. Delete the accompanying Text## label, then right-align the content within the =[ResolvedDate]-[OpenedDate] text box.

f. Move and resize the =[ResolvedDate]-[OpenedDate] text box to make sure that it is positioned under the Days to Resolve label and to the left of the 10" mark on the horizontal ruler. Drag the right edge of the report to the left to make sure the report is not wider than the 10" mark on the horizontal ruler.

g. Save and preview the CaseInfo report.

6. Resize and align controls.

a. Return to Design View of the CaseInfo report, then size all the labels in the Page Header section to the Tallest and align their Top edges.

b. Size all the text boxes in the Detail section to the Tallest, and align their Top edges.

c. In the Report Footer section, align the left edges of the two controls (the line and the =Count(*) text box) with the left edges of the two controls in the Category Footer section.

d. Select all controls and use the Shape Outline button to set the border to Transparent. Select the two line controls and use the Shape Outline button to set the border to black.

e. Save and preview the CaseInfo report.

7. Modify report sections.

a. Return to Design View of the CaseInfo report, then change the Back Color and Alternate Back Color to white (**#FFFFFF**) for the Category Header section.

b. Change the Back Color and Alternate Back Color to white (**#FFFFFF**) for the Detail section.

c. Change the Back Color and Alternate Back Color to Light Gray 1 (**#ECECEC**) for the Category Footer section.

d. Set the Repeat Section property of the Category Header section to **Yes**.

e. Set the Force New Page property of the Category Footer section to **After Section**.

f. Save and preview the CaseInfo report, the first page of which is shown in FIGURE 7-24, then close the CaseInfo report.

8. Create multicolumn reports.

a. Create a new report in Report Design View and set the Record Source property to the Employees table.

b. Add page numbers using the Page N of M format to the left side of the Page Footer.

c. Add a text box to the Detail section with the expression **=[LastName]&", "&[FirstName]** as the Control Source property. Be careful to include both a comma (,) and a space between the quotation marks so that the expression produces Cabrera, Aaron versus Cabrera,Aaron on the report.

Skills Review (continued)

   d. Resize the text box to be about 2" wide. Delete the accompanying label and move the text box to the upper-left corner of the Detail section.

   e. Drag the top edge of the Page Footer section up to the bottom of the text box in the Detail section.

   f. Drag the right edge of the report as far as possible to the left so that the report is no wider than 2.5".

   g. Save the report with the name **EmployeeList**, then display it in Print Preview.

   h. Change the columns to **3** in an Across, then Down format.

   i. Save, then close the EmployeeList report.

9. Add a subreport.

   a. Open the CallLog report in Report Design View and use the Group, Sort, and Total Pane to remove the Department Header section. (*Hint*: Use the More button to specify "without a header section" for the Department group field.)

   b. Open the Report Footer section by dragging the bottom edge of the Report Footer section bar down about 0.5", then add the EmployeeList report as a subreport at the far-left edge of the Report Footer section using the None option for the link.

   c. Delete the label that accompanies the subreport control, and widen the subreport to be as wide as the report, but do not push out the right edge of the main report beyond 8".

   d. Delete the label in the Report Header section, then use the Title button to add a title to the report. Modify the title to read **Call Log**.

   e. Save and preview the CallLog report, then close it.

10. Add command buttons.

   a. Double-click the EmployeeMasterList report to open it in Report View, then test the four command buttons in the Report Header section.

   b. Open the EmployeeMasterList report in Report Design View, then add two new command buttons to the right of the Human Resources command button.

   c. Change the new command button captions to be **Marketing** and **Production**.

   d. The On Click event property of the Marketing button should be the **FilterMarketing** macro and the On Click event property of the Production button should be the **FilterProduction** macro.

   e. Make sure that all command buttons are wide enough to clearly read their captions but not so wide as to push out the right edge of the report beyond the 10" mark on the horizontal ruler. Resize and move the command buttons as necessary to keep the report width at 10" or less.

   f. Size the command buttons to the shortest button, then align the top edges of all the command buttons in the Report Header section.

   g. Save the EmployeeMasterList report, then view it in Report View. Test the new Marketing and Production command buttons, then close the EmployeeMasterList report.

   h. Double-click the Employees table, add *your name* as a new record, **9876** as the PhoneExtension field value, then complete the rest of the record with fictitious yet realistic data. Close the Employees table.

   i. Compact and repair then close the IL_AC_7_SupportDesk.accdb database and exit Access 2019.

Independent Challenge 1

As the manager of Riverwalk, a multispecialty health clinic, you have created a database to manage nurse and doctor schedules to efficiently handle patient visits. In this exercise, you will create a report that will analyze nurse schedules at the different clinic locations.

   a. Start Access, open the IL_AC_7-3.accdb database from the location where you store your Data Files, then save it as **IL_AC_7_Riverwalk**. Enable content if prompted.

   b. Use the Report Wizard to create a new report on the ScheduleDetails query. Use all the fields and view the records by LocationNo.

c. Do not add any more grouping levels, then sort the records by ScheduleDate.

d. Use a Stepped layout and a portrait orientation, and title the report **Schedule by Location**.

e. In Layout View, delete the LocationNo label and text box as well as the DoctorNo label and text box. Note that the final report is shown in **FIGURE 7-25**.

f. Save the report and switch to Design View. Add NurseName as second sort order below the LocationNo grouping field and ScheduleDate sort field.

g. Open the LocationNo Footer section and add a text box at about the 1" mark on the horizontal ruler. Add **=Count(*)** as the Control Source property and use **Count** as the Caption for the Text## label.

h. Open the ScheduleDate Header and Footer sections, move the ScheduleDate text box directly up into the ScheduleDate Header section, then copy and align the controls from the LocationNo Footer section in the ScheduleDate Footer section so that both sections count the number of records in that group.

i. Select all controls, then apply a transparent border and black font color.

j. Modify the labels in the Page Header section, as shown in **FIGURE 7-25**.

k. Save the Schedule By Location report, then view it in Report View, as shown in **FIGURE 7-25**.

l. Close the Schedule By Location report, right-click it, and rename it to be **ScheduleByLocation** to be consistent with the other objects in the database.

m. Double-click the Providers table, add *your last name* as a new record with the DrPA field value of MD, then close the Providers table.

n. Compact and close the IL_AC_7_Riverwalk.accdb and exit Access 2019.

FIGURE 7-25

Schedule by Location			
Location	Schedule Date	Nurse	Doctor
North			
	8/26/2021		
		Dana Washington	Samuelson
		Dawn Wu	Anderson
		Jennifer McCully	Samuelson
		Joyce Johnson	Fletcher
		Lydia Hemmer	Fletcher
		Mary Tharp	Agri
		Michele Blago	Northy
		Rebecca Rivera	Samuelson
		Sam Fredrick	Northy
		Tina Buck	Northy
Count	10		
	8/27/2021		
		Amberley Stein	Gold
		Dawn Wu	Northy
		Jan Regan	Gold
		Joyce Johnson	Fletcher
		Liz Ducy	Gold
		Lydia Hemmer	Fletcher

Independent Challenge 2

You are working for a city to coordinate a series of community-wide preparedness activities. You have created a database to track the activities and volunteers who are attending the activities. In this exercise, you will create a report to calculate information about the total number of volunteer hours at each activity.

a. Start Access, open the IL_AC_7-4.accdb database from the location where you store your Data Files, then save it as **IL_AC_7_Volunteers**. Enable content if prompted.

b. Create a new report in Report Design View. Set the Record Source property to the ActivityList query.

c. Group the report by ActivityName, then sort it by LastName.

d. Add the ActivityName and ActivityDate fields to the ActivityName Header section, as shown in **FIGURE 7-26**. Note that no labels are needed to describe these fields.

e. Add the LastName and ActivityHours fields to the Detail section, as shown in **FIGURE 7-26**. Note that no labels are needed to describe these fields.

f. Open the ActivityName Footer section and add a text box to subtotal (not count) the number of ActivityHours within each activity using the **=Sum([ActivityHours])** expression. Delete the accompanying Text## label.

g. Close the Page Header and Page Footer sections, then open the Report Header and Report Footer sections.

h. Copy the text box that subtotals the ActivityHours from the ActivityName Footer section to the Report Footer section and right-align the edges of the two controls plus the ActivityHours text box in the Detail section.

i. Right-align the content within the ActivityHours text box in the Detail section and the two text boxes that contain the expressions to sum the ActivityHours.

j. Add a title to the report with the text **Activity Totals**, merge all cells in the layout in the Report Header section, then save the report with the name **ActivityData**.

k. Select all controls, apply a transparent outline, then move, resize, and modify controls and section heights as needed to match **FIGURE 7-26**.

l. Add a short subtotal line above each of the two text boxes that contain the =Sum([ActivityHours]) expressions, then preview the report in Report View, as shown in **FIGURE 7-26**.

m. Open the Volunteers table, then add a new record with *your name*. Use **66215** for the Zipcode field value and fill in the rest of the record with fictitious yet realistic values. Close the Volunteers table.

n. Close the ActivityData report, compact and close the IL_AC_7_Volunteers.accdb database, and exit Access 2019.

FIGURE 7-26

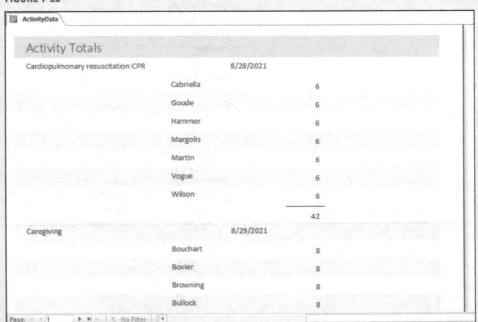

Visual Workshop

Start Access, open the IL_AC_7-5.accdb database from the location where you store your Data Files, then save it as **IL_AC_7_CollegeCourses**. Enable content if prompted. In Design View of the StudentGradeListing report, add four command buttons in the Report Header section with the captions shown in **FIGURE 7-27**. Use the On Click event of each command button to attach the command button to the corresponding macro. Size and align the command buttons as shown. Save the report and test your command buttons in Report View to filter the records for grade of A or B, C, D or F, and All, as shown in **FIGURE 7-27**. Close the StudentGradeListing report. Open the Students table and add your name as a new record with the StudentID value of **999**. Use fictitious yet realistic data for the other field values. Compact and close the IL_AC_7_CollegeCourses.accdb database and exit Access 2019.

FIGURE 7-27

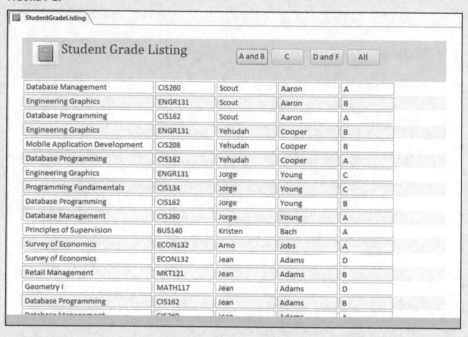

Importing and Exporting Data

CASE › You are working with Lydia Snyder, vice president of operations at JCL Talent, to build a research database to manage industry, company, and job data. In this module, you'll learn how to import and export data with other Access databases and file formats. You will build charts to better visualize information, and you will explore database templates.

Module Objectives

After completing this module, you will be able to:

- Import Access objects
- Import or export text files
- Export to Excel
- Export to PDF
- Export to HTML or XML

- Merge to Word
- Create charts
- Modify charts
- Use a database template
- Use Application Parts

Files You Will Need

IL_AC_8-1.accdb

Support_AC_8_JCL_Development.accdb

Support_AC_8_Jobs.txt

IL_AC_8-2.accdb

Support_AC_8_SupportDesk_Dev.accdb

Support_AC_8_Employees.txt

IL_AC_8-3.accdb

IL_AC_8-4.accdb

IL_AC_8-5.accdb

Import Access Objects

Access gives you the ability to import and export Access objects from one database to another. **Importing** means to copy an object *into* the current database. **Exporting** means to copy an object *from* the current database to another database. Importing and exporting Access objects is especially helpful for a database developer. The developer can build and test objects in a development database and when ready, copy them into the production database. **CASE** ➤ *You have been working with a development copy of the JCL database to create two new reports. Lydia has reviewed and approved the reports, and has asked you to add them to the production database.*

STEPS

QUICK TIP
You can also right-
click in the table
section of the
Navigation Pane,
point to Import,
then click Access
Database.

1. **sanf ↓ Start Access, open the IL_AC_8-1.accdb database from the location where you store your Data Files, save it as IL_AC_8_Jobs, enable content if prompted, click the External Data tab, click the New Data Source button, point to From Database, then click Access**

   The Get External Data – Access Database dialog box opens, prompting you for the location of the development database that contains the objects you want to import into the current database.

2. **Click the Browse button, navigate to the location where you store your Data Files, click Support_AC_8_JCL_Development.accdb, click Open, then click OK**

   The Import Objects dialog box opens. Each tab displays a list of that type of object from the selected database. You want to import two reports. You also need to import the two queries that support the reports referenced in the Record Source property for the reports.

3. **Click the Queries tab, click the ContactsByCompany query, click the JobsByCompany query, click the Reports tab, click the ContactsByCompany report, click the JobsByCompany report as shown in FIGURE 8-1, then click OK**

   As a final step, the Get External Data – Access Database dialog box prompts you to save the import steps. If you needed to repeat this import process on a regular basis, it would be a good idea to save the import steps to complete the next import process faster. In this case, you do not need to save the import steps.

4. **Click Close in the Get External Data – Access Database dialog box, double-click the ContactsByCompany report, then double-click the JobsByCompany report**

   The two imported reports open in Report View, as shown in FIGURE 8-2. In this case, the queries that served as the Record Source property for the reports were given the same name as their corresponding report, but that is not required.

5. **Right-click the JobsByCompany report tab, click Close, right-click the ContactsByCompany report tab, then click Close**

   A second way to share objects between two databases is to open both at the same time and work in the Navigation Pane to copy and paste objects between the two databases. An object must be closed before it can be cut, copied, renamed, or deleted.

   Yet a third way to share objects between two databases is to right-click the object in the Navigation Pane, point to Export, click Access, then follow the prompts provided by the Export – Access Database dialog boxes to export any object from one database to another.

FIGURE 8-1: Import Objects dialog box

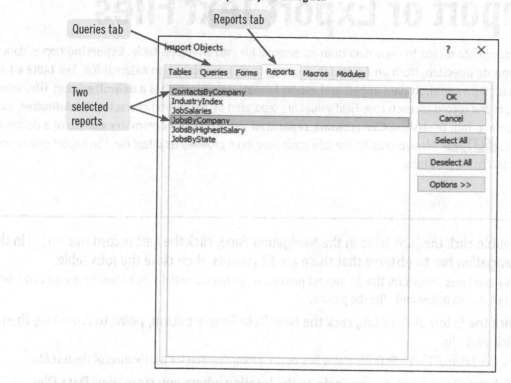

Queries tab

Reports tab

Two selected reports

FIGURE 8-2: Imported queries and reports

New reports opened in Report View

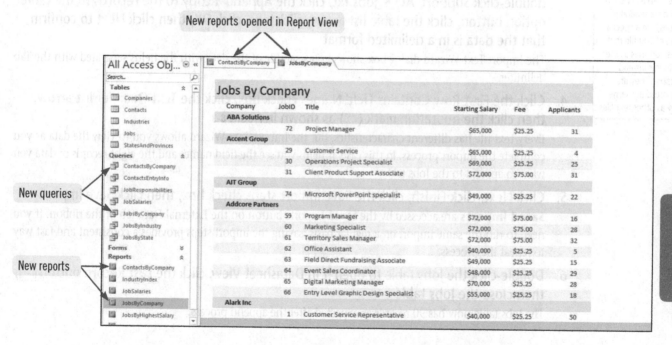

New queries

New reports

Import or Export Text Files

Learning Outcomes
- Append data from a text file
- Review data import, link, and export file formats

Importing data means to copy data from an external file into an Access table. **Exporting** copies data in the opposite direction, from an Access table, query, form, or report to an external file. See TABLE 8-1 for information on common data import and export formats, one of which is a **delimited text file**, which organizes one record on each row. Field values are separated by a common character, the **delimiter**, such as a comma, tab, or dash. A **CSV (comma-separated value)** file is a common example of a delimited text file. **CASE** ▶ *New records for the Jobs table have been provided as a text file. You import and append the records to the Jobs table.*

STEPS

1. **Double-click the** Jobs table **in the Navigation Pane, click the** Last record button ▶ **in the navigation bar to observe that there are 82 records, then close the Jobs table**

   It's a good idea to confirm that an append process completed successfully by reviewing the data and number of records before and after the process.

2. **Click the** External Data tab, **click the** New Data Source button, **point to** From File, **then click** Text File

   The Get External Data – Text File dialog box opens, prompting you for the location of the text file.

QUICK TIP

Files with a csv suffix (comma separated values) are a special type of text file that uses commas as the delimiter instead of tabs. They are imported the same way as other text files.

3. **Click the** Browse button, **navigate to the location where you store your Data Files, double-click** Support_AC_8_Jobs.txt, **click the** Append a copy to the records to the table option button, **click the** table list arrow, **click** Jobs, **click** OK, **then click** Next **to confirm that the data is in a delimited format**

   The Import Text Wizard dialog box shows you a sample of the data with the fields separated with the Tab delimiter.

4. **Click the** First Row Contains Field Names check box, **click the** Text Qualifier list arrow, **then click the** quotation mark (") **as shown in** FIGURE 8-3

   Every text file has different characteristics, but the Import Text Wizard allows you to view the data as you complete the import process. In this case, it helps you see the field names and the eight records of data you want to append to the Jobs table.

5. **Click** Next, **click** Finish, **click the** Save import steps check box, **then click** Save Import

   Saved imports are accessed by the Saved Imports button on the External Data tab of the ribbon. If you need to run the same import on a regular basis, saving the import steps provides a consistent and fast way to repeat the process.

6. **Double-click the** Jobs table **to open it in Datasheet View, click the** Last Record button ▶, **then close the Jobs table**

   The Jobs table now has 90 records as expected after the append process.

FIGURE 8-3: Import Text Wizard dialog box

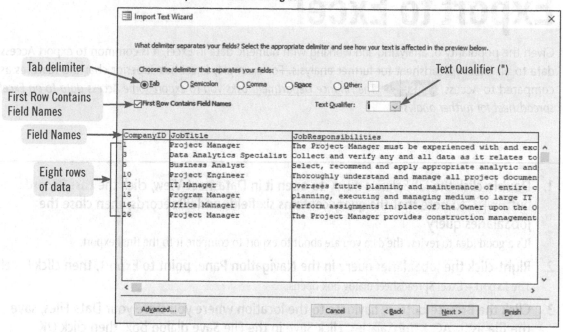

TABLE 8-1: File formats that Access can import, link, and export

category	file format	import	link	export
Microsoft Office	Excel	•	•	•
	Word			•
	Outlook address book		•	•
	Access	•	•	•
Online services	SharePoint	•	•	•
	Dynamics 365	•	•	•
	SalesForce	•	•	•
Database Management Software (DBMS)	SQL Server	•	•	•
	dBASE	•	•	•
	Azure Database	•		
	ODBC (Open Database Connectivity) Database	•	•	•
Other	Email file attachments			•
	HTML document	•	•	•
	PDF or XPS file			•
	Delimited text file such as CSV file	•	•	•
	XML file	•		•

Imported data must be structured

Before data can be imported into a new Access table, it must be structured properly. For example, before data can be appended to an existing Access table, its field names and data types must match those in the existing table. It is common to **scrub** data, which means to fix errors and inconsistencies by working with a text file in Excel before that data can be successfully imported into Access.

Export to Excel

Learning
Outcomes
• Export data to
  Excel
• Save export steps

Given the popularity of analyzing and working with numeric data in Excel, it is common to export Access data to an Excel spreadsheet for further analysis. For example, Excel has superior charting features as compared to Access. **CASE** *The Finance Department asks you to export some Access data to an Excel spreadsheet for further analysis.*

STEPS

1. **Double-click the** JobSalaries query **to open it in Datasheet View, click the** Last Record **button** ▶ **to note that the query contains six fields and 90 records, then close the JobSalaries query**

   It's a good idea to review the data you are about to export to compare it to the final export.

QUICK TIP
You can also use the
Excel button in the
Export group of the
External Data tab on
the ribbon to export
the data from a
selected table, query,
form, or report to
Excel.

2. **Right-click the** JobSalaries query **in the Navigation Pane, point to** Export**, then click** Excel

   The Export – Excel Spreadsheet dialog box opens.

3. **Click the** Browse button**, navigate to the location where you store your Data Files, save the file as** IL_AC_8_JobSalaries**, click** Save **in the File Save dialog box, then click** OK

   To quickly repeat any export process, you can save the export steps with a name, then run the export using the Saved Exports button on the External Data tab of the ribbon.

4. **Click the** Save export steps check box**, edit the Save as description to be** Export-JobSalaries to Excel**, then click** Save Export

   You access and run a **saved export** using the Saved Exports button on the External Data tab. Saving the export steps provides a fast and consistent way to repeat an export process.

   To view the data, start Excel and open the exported JobSalaries.xlsx file.

TROUBLE
Some of the columns
display ########,
but that is easily
resolved by widening
the column.

5. **Start** Excel**, click the** File tab **on the ribbon, click** Open**, click** Browse**, navigate to the location where you store your Data Files, then double-click** IL_AC_8_JobSalaries.xlsx

   The IL_AC_8_JobSalaries.xlsx file opens, as shown in **FIGURE 8-4**, where you can further analyze, chart, and manipulate the data. Note that the Excel file contains six fields and that the first row contains field names.

6. **Scroll to the bottom of the data to note that the spreadsheet contains 91 total rows, then close the** IL_AC_8_JobSalaries.xlsx file, **close Excel, and return to Access**

   You can export the data from any Access table, query, form, or report to Excel using these steps.

FIGURE 8-4: IL_AC_8_JobSalaries.xlsx workbook

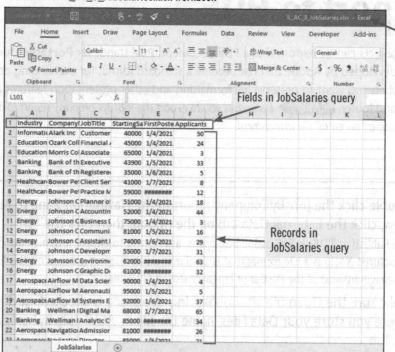

JobSalaries query exported
as an Excel file

Fields in JobSalaries query

Records in
JobSalaries query

Export to PDF

Learning Outcomes
- Export a report to PDF
- Export other objects to PDF

Access objects can be exported to a PDF document. **PDF** stands for **Portable Document Format**, a file format developed by Adobe that has become a standard format for exchanging documents. PDF files are useful when you want to preserve full formatting and other presentation features of an object such as its header and footer. **CASE** *Lydia asks you to export the JobsByCompany report to a PDF document for later distribution as an email file attachment.*

STEPS

1. **Double-click the** JobsByCompany report **in the Navigation Pane to review it in Report View, click the** External Data tab **on the ribbon, then click the** PDF or XPS button

   The Publish as PDF or XPS dialog box opens, asking you to choose a name and location for the file. **XPS** (structured XML) is a file format that is similar to a PDF file but is based on the **XML** (Extensible Markup Language) instead of the PostScript language used by PDF files.

2. **Make sure the** Open file after publishing check box **is checked, navigate to the location where you store your Data Files, name the file** IL_AC_8_JobsByCompany, **then click** Publish

   The PDF opens in the program on your computer that is associated with PDF files. Several programs, including browsers such as Chrome, Firefox, and Edge as well as Adobe Reader, can open PDF files so the program that automatically opens the JobsByCompany.pdf file will vary from computer to computer and you may be asked to choose from more than one program that can open PDF files. The main thing to notice is that the PDF file is formatted and the data is arranged exactly as it looked in the Access report, as shown in **FIGURE 8-5**.

3. **Close the** PDF window, **return to Access, click the** Save export steps check box, **modify the Save as text to be** Export-JobsByCompany to PDF, **click** Save Export, **then close the** JobsByCompany report

   The IL_AC_8_JobsByCompany.pdf file is now available for you to distribute. For example, you could attach it to an email. Because it is a PDF file, users can open, view, and print the formatted report even if they don't have Access on their computers.

   Export to Excel when you want to give users the ability to further analyze and manipulate the data. Export to PDF when you do not want to allow users to manipulate the data but want to retain the formatting, layout, and style of the report.

FIGURE 8-5: Previewing the IL_AC_8_JobsByCompany.pdf file

IL_AC_8_
JobsByCompany.pdf
file is formatted like
the JobsByCompany
report in Access

Jobs By Company

Company	JobID	Title	Starting Salary	Fee	Applicants
ABA Solutions					
	72	Project Manager	$65,000	$25.25	31
	83	Project Manager	$65,000	$50.25	0
Accent Group					
	29	Customer Service	$65,000	$25.25	4
	30	Operations Project Specialist	$69,000	$25.25	25
	31	Client Product Support Associate	$72,000	$75.00	31
AIT Group					
	74	Microsoft PowerPoint specialist	$49,000	$25.25	22
	84	Data Analytics Specialist	$52,000	$50.25	0
Addcore Partners					
	59	Program Manager	$72,000	$75.00	16
	60	Marketing Specialist	$72,000	$75.00	28
	61	Territory Sales Manager	$72,000	$75.00	32
	62	Office Assistant	$40,000	$25.25	5
	63	Field Direct Fundraising Associate	$49,000	$25.25	15
	64	Event Sales Coordinator	$48,000	$25.25	29
	65	Digital Marketing Manager	$70,000	$25.25	28
	66	Entry Level Graphic Design Specialist	$55,000	$25.25	18
Alark Inc					
	1	Customer Service Representative	$40,000	$25.25	50
	85	Business Analyst	$55,000	$50.25	0
Artwell Corp					

Emailing an Access report

Another way to email an Access report (or any other Access object) as a PDF file is to click the report in the Navigation Pane, then click the Email button in the Export group of the External Data tab on the ribbon. You are presented with the Send Object As dialog box, which allows you to choose the desired file format, such as .xlsx, .pdf, .htm, or .rtf, for the report as shown in **FIGURE 8-6**. After you select the desired file format and click OK, Outlook opens with the report attached to the email in the chosen file format. You must have Microsoft Outlook installed and configured to use this option.

FIGURE 8-6: Emailing an Access report

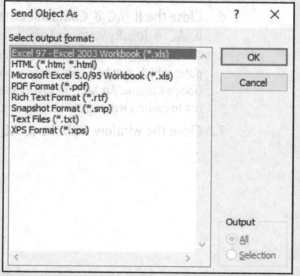

Access

Export to HTML or XML

Learning
Outcomes
• Export an object
to an HTML file
• Export an object
to an XML file
• Understand saved
exports

You can export an Access object to an **HTML (HyperText Markup Language)** or **XML (eXtensible Markup Language)** file, which are both common for sharing information over the Internet. An XML file precisely defines data using descriptive tags to mark up the beginning and end of rows (records) and columns (fields), so it is often used to send only data across the Internet. If you want a person to be able to view the data in a browser like a regular webpage, use an HTML file. **CASE** *Lydia asks you to export the Companies table as an HTML file and the JobsByState query as an XML file.*

STEPS

1. **Right-click the** Companies table, **point to** Export, **then click** HTML Document

   The Export – HTML Document dialog box opens, prompting you for a location for the exported HTML file.

2. **Click the** Browse button, **navigate to the location where you store your Data Files, save the file as** IL_AC_8_Companies, **click** Save, **click** OK, **click the** Save export steps check box, **modify the Save as text to be** Export-Companies to HTML, **then click** Save Export

   Next, export the JobsByState query as an XML file.

3. **Right-click the** JobsByState query, **point to** Export, **then click** XML File

   The Export – XML Document dialog box opens, prompting you for a location for the exported XML file.

4. **Click the** Browse button, **navigate to the location where you store your Data Files, save the file as** IL_AC_8_JobsByState, **click** Save, **click** OK, **click** OK to export the data XML and schema XSD files, **click the** Save export steps check box, **modify the Save as text to be** Export-JobsByState to XML, **then click** Save Export

   The **XSD (XML Schema Definition)** file further describes how the individual pieces of data in the XML file are defined. To confirm that the HTML and XML files were exported successfully, view them in a browser.

5. **Open** File Explorer, **navigate to the location where you store your Data Files, then double-click the** IL_AC_8_Companies.html file

   The IL_AC_8_Companies.html file opens in whatever program is associated with HTML files on your computer, probably a browser such as Google Chrome, Firefox, or Microsoft Edge. The records from the Companies table appear as an HTML table in a regular webpage, as shown in **FIGURE 8-7**.

6. **Close the** IL_AC_8_Companies.html file, **return to** File Explorer, **then double-click the** IL_AC_8_JobsByState.xml file

   The IL_AC_8_JobsByState.xml file opens in whatever program is associated with XML files on your computer, which may be a code editor or browser. **FIGURE 8-8** shows the IL_AC_8_JobsByState.xml file open in Google Chrome. An XML file's purpose is to describe and successfully transfer the data to another program, not to create a webpage that is easy for a human to read.

7. **Close the window with the** IL_AC_8_JobsByState.xml file and return to Access

FIGURE 8-7: Companies table exported to HTML

IL_AC_8_Companies.html

The path to your file will be different

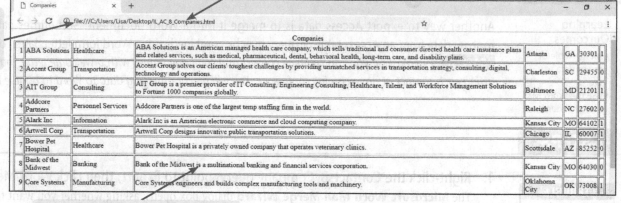

Data from the Companies table is formatted as a table in a regular webpage to share information with a human

FIGURE 8-8: JobsByState query exported to XML

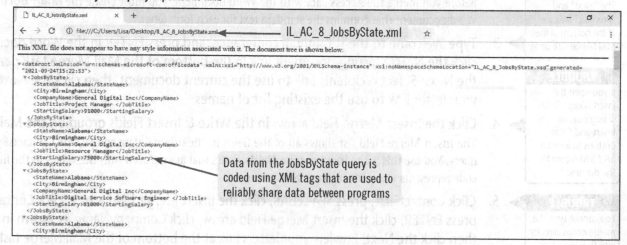

IL_AC_8_JobsByState.xml

Data from the JobsByState query is coded using XML tags that are used to reliably share data between programs

Access

Merge to Word

**Learning
Outcomes**
• Merge table or
query data to
Word
• Use the Word Mail
Merge Wizard

Another way to export Access data is to merge it into a Word document. Sometimes called a **mail merge**, data from an Access table or query may be combined with a Word form letter, label, or envelope. **CASE** ▶ *Lydia asks if you can combine contact and company names with a welcome letter that JCL will be giving each contact at an upcoming conference. You will practice merging data to Word to handle her request.*

STEPS

> **TROUBLE**
> Click the Word
> button ⊞ on
> the taskbar if
> Word doesn't
> automatically open.

1. **Right-click the** ContactsByCompany query, **point to** Export, **then click** Word Merge
   The **Microsoft Word Mail Merge Wizard** dialog box opens, asking whether you want to link to an existing document or create a new one. The Word merge process works the same way whether you export a table or query object.

> **QUICK TIP**
> The "Next" and
> "Previous" links are
> at the bottom of the
> Mail Merge task pane.

2. **Click the** Create a new document and then link the data to it **option button, then click** OK
   Word starts and opens the **Mail Merge task pane**, which steps you through the mail-merge process. Before you merge the Access data with the Word document, you must create the **main document**, the Word document that contains the standard text for each form letter.

3. **Type** Welcome to the JCL annual conference! **and press** ENTER **in the Word document, click the** Next: Starting document **link in the bottom of the Mail Merge task pane, click the** Next: Select recipients **link to use the current document, then click the** Next: Write your letter **link to use the existing list of names**

> **TROUBLE**
> If you open the
> Insert Merge Field
> dialog box, use the
> Insert and Close
> buttons to insert a
> field and return to
> the document.

4. **Click the** Insert Merge Field **arrow in the Write & Insert Fields group on the Mailings tab**
   The Insert Merge Field list shows all of the fields in the original data source, the ContactsByCompany query. You use this list to insert **merge fields**, codes that are replaced with the values in the field that the code represents when the mail merge is processed.

> **TROUBLE**
> You cannot type the
> merge codes directly
> into the document.
> You must use the
> Insert Merge Field
> button.

5. **Click** ContactFirst, **press** SPACEBAR, **click the** Insert Merge Field **arrow, click** ContactLast, **press** ENTER, **click the** Insert Merge Field **arrow, click** CompanyName **as shown in** FIGURE 8-9, **then click the** Next: Preview your letters **link at the bottom of the Mail Merge task pane**
   You are ready to complete the mail merge.

6. **Click the** Next: Complete the merge **link, click the** Edit individual letters **link in the middle of the Mail Merge task pane to view the letters on the screen, then click** OK **to merge all records, as shown in** FIGURE 8-10
   The mail-merge process combines the ContactFirst, ContactLast, and CompanyName field values from the ContactsByCompany query with the main document, creating a 443-page document using section breaks between pages.

> **QUICK TIP**
> The total number
> of pages in the
> document is
> displayed in the
> lower-left corner of
> the Word window.

7. **Press** PAGE DOWN **several times to view several pages of the merged document, then close the merged document (currently named Letters1) without saving it**
   You generally don't need to save the final merged document. Saving the one-page *main document*, however, is a good idea in case you want to make a change and remerge it (versus starting the merge process of creating a main document from scratch).

8. **Click the** Save **button** ⊞ **on the Quick Access Toolbar, click the** Browse **button, navigate to the location where you store your Data Files, enter** IL_AC_8_Welcome **in the File name text box, click** Save, **then close Word**

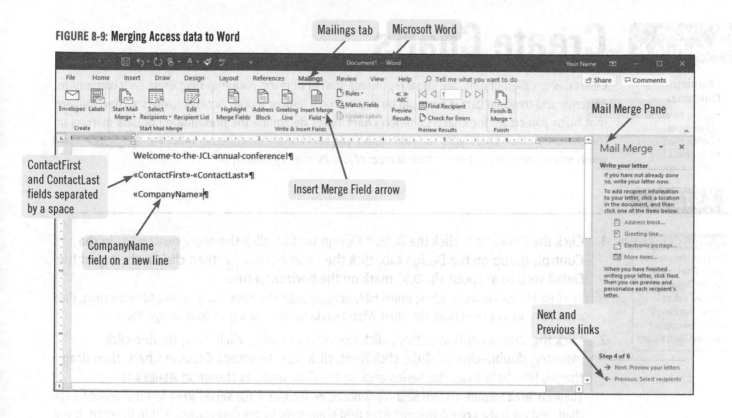

FIGURE 8-9: Merging Access data to Word

Mailings tab — Microsoft Word

ContactFirst and ContactLast fields separated by a space

Insert Merge Field arrow

CompanyName field on a new line

Welcome·to·the·JCL·annual·conference!¶

«ContactFirst»·«ContactLast»¶

«CompanyName»¶

Mail Merge Pane

Mail Merge

Write your letter

If you have not already done so, write your letter now.

To add recipient information to your letter, click a location in the document, and then click one of the items below.

Address block...
Greeting line...
Electronic postage...
More items...

When you have finished writing your letter, click Next. Then you can preview and personalize each recipient's letter.

Step 4 of 6

Next: Preview your letters
Previous: Select recipients

Next and Previous links

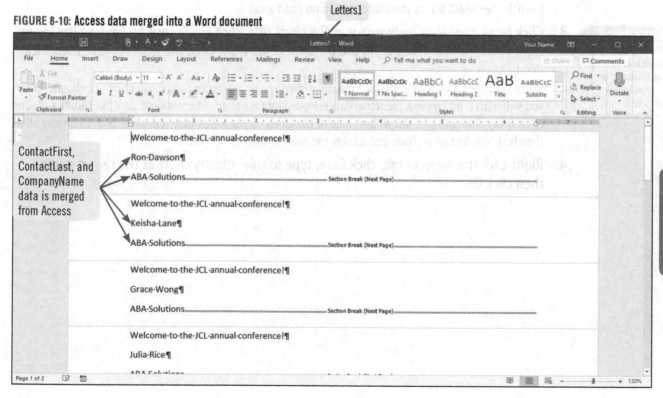

FIGURE 8-10: Access data merged into a Word document

Letters1

ContactFirst, ContactLast, and CompanyName data is merged from Access

Welcome·to·the·JCL·annual·conference!¶

Ron·Dawson¶

ABA·Solutions ——————————— Section Break (Next Page) ———

Welcome·to·the·JCL·annual·conference!¶

Keisha·Lane¶

ABA·Solutions ——————————— Section Break (Next Page) ———

Welcome·to·the·JCL·annual·conference!¶

Grace·Wong¶

ABA·Solutions ——————————— Section Break (Next Page) ———

Welcome·to·the·JCL·annual·conference!¶

Julia·Rice¶

ABA·Solutions

Create Charts

Charts, also called graphs, are visual representations of numeric data that help users see comparisons, patterns, and trends in data. Charts can be inserted on a form or report. Access provides a **Chart Wizard** that helps you create the chart. Common **chart types** determine the presentation of data markers on the chart. Common chart types such as column, pie, and line are described in **TABLE 8-2**. **CASE** *Lydia wants you to create a chart of the total number of jobs by industry for a report.*

STEPS

1. **Click the** Create tab, **click the** Report Design button, **click the** More button ▼ **in the Controls group on the Design tab, click the** Chart button 📊, **then click in the top of the Detail section at about the 0.5" mark on the horizontal ruler**

   The Chart Wizard starts by asking which table or query holds the fields you want to add to the chart, then asks you to select a chart type. The Chart Wizard works in the same way in Form Design View.

2. **Click the** Queries option button, **click** Query: JobSalaries, **click** Next, **double-click** Industry, **double-click** JobTitle, **click** Next, **click** Next **to accept Column Chart, then drag the** JobTitle field from the Series area to the Data area, **as shown in FIGURE 8-11**

   The **Axis area** identifies which field is positioned on the x-axis, the **Series area** sets the legend for the chart, and the **Data area** determines what field is measured by the data markers within the chart. If you drag a Number or Currency field to the Data area, the Chart Wizard automatically sums the values in the field. For Text or AutoNumber fields (such as JobTitle), the Chart Wizard automatically counts the values in the field. See **TABLE 8-3** for more information on chart areas.

3. **Click** Next, **type** Jobs by Industry **as the chart title, click** Finish, **use** 🖉 **to drag the lower-right corner of the chart to fill the Detail section, right-click the** Report1 tab, **then click** Print Preview

   When charts are displayed in Design View, they often appear as a generic Microsoft chart placeholder. When you switch to Print Preview, the actual data is loaded into the chart, which should look like **FIGURE 8-12**. The chart is beginning to take shape, but some of the labels on the x-axis may not have room to display all of their text. You fix this problem and modify the chart in the next lesson.

4. **Right-click the** Report1 tab, **click** Save, **type** JobsByIndustryChart **as the report name, then click** OK

FIGURE 8-11: Using the Chart Wizard to add a chart to a report

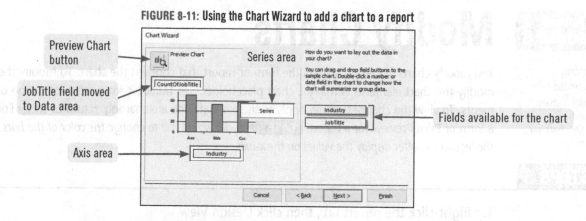

Preview Chart button

JobTitle field moved to Data area

Series area

Axis area

Fields available for the chart

FIGURE 8-12: Previewing a column chart

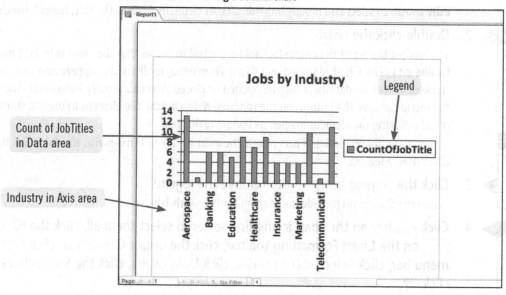

Count of JobTitles in Data area

Industry in Axis area

Legend

TABLE 8-2: Common chart types

chart type	chart icon	commonly used to show	example
Column		Comparisons of values (vertical bars)	Each vertical bar represents the sales for a different product.
Bar		Comparisons of values (horizontal bars)	Each horizontal bar represents the sales for a different product.
Line		Trends over time	Each point on the line represents monthly sales for one product.
Pie		Parts of a whole	Each slice represents quarterly sales for the entire company.
Area		Cumulative totals	Each section represents monthly sales by product, stacked to show the cumulative total sales effort.

TABLE 8-3: Chart areas

chart area	description
Data	Determines what field the data markers on the chart represent
Axis	The x-axis (horizontal axis) or y-axis (vertical axis) on the chart
Series	Displays the legend when multiple series of data are charted

Modify Charts

Learning
Outcomes
• Modify a chart
  legend
• Modify chart bar
  colors

You modify charts in Design View of the form or report that contains the chart. To modify the chart, you modify the chart elements within the chart placeholder. See **TABLE 8-4** for more information on chart elements. To view the changes as they apply to the real data you are charting, return to either Form View for a form or Print Preview for a report. **CASE** ▶ *Lydia wants you to change the color of the bars and remove the legend to better display the values on the x-axis.*

STEPS

1. **Right-click the** report tab, **then click** Design View
   To make changes to chart elements, you first must open the chart in Edit mode by double-clicking it. Use **Edit mode** to select and modify individual chart elements, such as the title, legend, bars, or axes.

QUICK TIP
To change the chart type, use the Chart Type button 📊 on the Chart Standard toolbar.

2. **Double-click the** chart
   The hashed border of the chart placeholder control indicates that the chart is in Edit mode, as shown in **FIGURE 8-13**. The Chart Standard and Chart Formatting toolbars also appear and may be on one row or stacked. The chart datasheet may be opened or closed. You can modify individual chart elements using the menu options, the buttons on the toolbars, right-clicking the element to use the shortcut menu, or by double-clicking the element to open its Format dialog box.
   Because only one series of bars counts the industries, you can describe the data with the chart title and don't need a legend.

TROUBLE
If you make a mistake, use the Undo button ↩ on the Chart Standard toolbar.

3. **Click the** Legend button 🗒 **to remove the legend**
   Removing the legend provides more room for the x-axis labels.

TROUBLE
Be careful to select all data markers versus a single data marker.

4. **Click** any bar **on the chart in the first series to select them all, click the** Fill Color arrow 🎨 **on the Chart Formatting toolbar, click the** Bright Green box, **click** Format **on the menu bar, click** Selected Data series, **click** Data Labels, **click the** Value check box, **then click** OK
   Clicking any bar selects all bars in that data series, as evidenced by the sizing handle in each of the bars. The bars change to bright green in the chart placeholder, and data labels showing the value of the bar appear above each bar.
   You also decide to modify the labels on the x-axis so they fit better.

5. **Double-click** any label on the x-axis **to open the Format Axis dialog box, click the** Font tab, **click** 8 **in the Size area, then click** OK
   Preview the updated chart.

TROUBLE
If your report doesn't look like FIGURE 8-14, return to Design View and resize it. Your report should also contain only one page.

6. **Click** outside the hashed border **to return to Report Design View, click the** Save button 💾 **on the Quick Access toolbar, right-click the** JobsByIndustryChart tab, **then click** Print Preview
   The final chart is shown in **FIGURE 8-14**.

7. **samf⬆ Close the** JobsByIndustryChart report, **double-click the** Contacts table, **add your name at CompanyID 1 as a new record, close the Contacts table, compact and close the IL_AC_8_Jobs.accdb database, then exit Access**

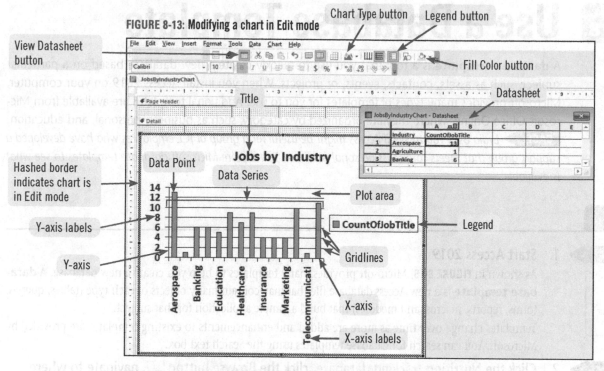

FIGURE 8-13: Modifying a chart in Edit mode

View Datasheet button

Chart Type button — Legend button

Fill Color button

Title — Datasheet

Hashed border indicates chart is in Edit mode

Data Point

Data Series

Jobs by Industry

Plot area

Y-axis labels

CountOfJobTitle — Legend

Gridlines

Y-axis

X-axis

X-axis labels

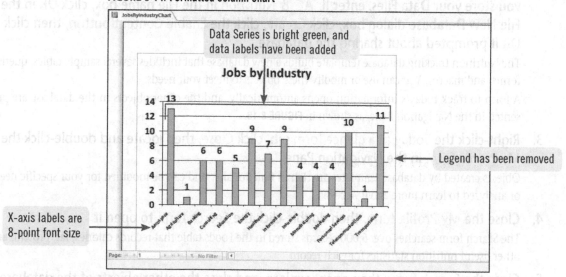

FIGURE 8-14: Formatted column chart

Data Series is bright green, and data labels have been added

Jobs by Industry

Legend has been removed

X-axis labels are 8-point font size

TABLE 8-4: Chart elements

chart element	description
Chart title	Determines what field the bars (lines, wedges, etc.) on the chart represent
X-axis	On a column chart, the horizontal axis
Y-axis	On a column chart, the vertical axis
Legend	Displays a color sample for each series of data markers
Data markers	The bars, wedges, points, or other symbol used to represent the data in the chart
Data labels	Optional values or text that describe each data marker
Data point	An individual bar, wedge, point, or symbol used to identify one data marker on the chart
Gridlines	On a column chart, the horizontal bars that help indicate where the data markers are in relationship to the y-axis
Plot area	On a column chart, the rectangle defined by the x-axis and y-axis behind the data markers

Access

Use a Database Template

Learning
Outcome
• Explore Access
  database
  templates

A **database template** is a tool that you use to quickly create a new database based on a particular subject, such as assets, contacts, events, or projects. When you install Access 2019 on your computer, Microsoft provides many types of templates for you to use. Additional templates are available from Microsoft Office Online, where they are organized by category, such as business, personal, and education.

CASE ▸ *Lydia asks you to see if Access might be useful for a group of JCL employees who have developed a support group that meets to discuss personal nutrition. You explore Microsoft database templates to see what is available.*

STEPS

QUICK TIP
One way to start
Access is to type
Access in the
search box on your
Windows taskbar.

1. **Start Access 2019**

   As shown in **FIGURE 8-15**, Microsoft provides many templates to help you create a new database. A **database template** is a new Access database file that may contain many objects of each type (tables, queries, forms, reports, macros, and modules) that build a sample application for that subject.

   Templates change over time as more are added and enhancements to existing templates are provided by Microsoft. You can search for database templates using the Search text box.

TROUBLE
Templates are
constantly changing,
so if you cannot
find the Nutrition
database or if it has
changed, explore
other templates and
forms of your choice.

2. **Click the** Nutrition tracking database, **click the** Browse button 📁, **navigate to where you store your Data Files, enter** IL_AC_8_Nutrition **in the File name box, click OK in the File New Database dialog box, click** Create, **click the** Enable Content button, **then click OK if prompted about sharing the database**

   The Nutrition tracking database template builds a new database that includes several sample tables, queries, forms, and macros. You can use or modify these objects to meet your needs.

   A form to track today's information opens automatically, and the other objects in the database are presented in the Navigation Pane, as shown in **FIGURE 8-16**.

3. **Right-click the** Today at a glance form tab, **click** Close, **then locate and double-click the** My Profile form **in the Navigation Pane**

   Objects created by database templates are rich in functionality and can be modified for your specific needs or analyzed to learn more about Access.

4. **Close the** My Profile form, **then double-click the** Search form **to open it**

   The Search form searches over 6,000 records stored in the Foods table that records calories, fat, protein, and other useful nutrition statistics for each record.

5. **Close the** Search form, **then open, explore, and close the other objects of the database**

   The Foods and Tips tables contain many records, and the other objects create the full application. You can learn a great deal about Access by exploring database templates. You will continue using this sample database to learn about Application Parts.

FIGURE 8-15: Access database templates

Search

Featured templates

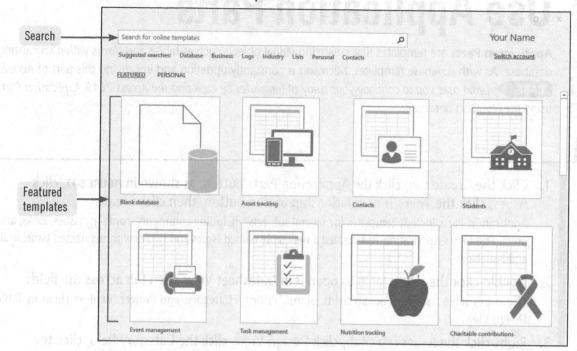

FIGURE 8-16: A sample form in the IL_AC_8_Nutrition.accdb database

Template forms

Template macros

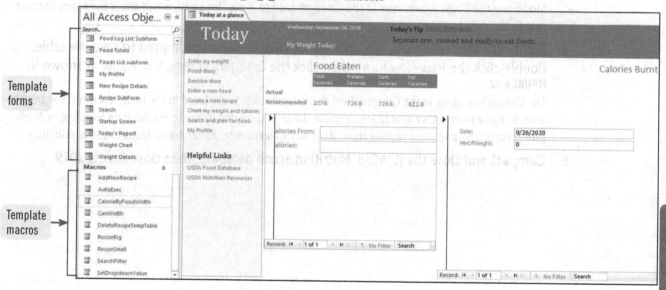

Use Application Parts

Application Parts are templates that create individual objects such as tables and forms *within* an existing database. As with database templates, Microsoft is constantly updating and improving this part of Access.

CASE ▸ *Lydia asks you to continue your study of templates by exploring the Access 2019 Application Parts using the Nutrition database.*

STEPS

1. **Click the** Create tab, **click the** Application Parts button, **as shown in** FIGURE 8-17, **click** Issues, **click the** There is no relationship option button, **then click** Create

   Application Parts include templates for several subjects, including comments, contacts, issues, tasks, and users. The Issues Application Part created a new table named Issues and two new forms named IssueDetail and IssueNew.

2. **Double-click the** Issues table **to open it in Datasheet View, then tab across the fields**

   The Issues table has four Lookup fields: Status, Priority, Category, and Project. Explore them in Table Design View.

3. **Right-click the** Issues table tab, **click** Design View, **click the** Category field, **click the** Lookup tab, **then modify the Row Source property to be** "Health";"Food";"Exercise" **as shown in** FIGURE 8-18

   Modifying the Lookup properties of the Category field in Table Design View will affect the forms that use that field.

4. **Right-click the** Issues table tab, **click** Close, **click** Yes **when prompted to save the table, double-click the** IssueNew form, **then click the** Category combo box arrow **as shown in** FIGURE 8-19

   The change you made to the Category field in the Issues table is displayed in the IssueNew form. You might want to make many other modifications to use the objects created by an Access database template or Application Parts. These features provide an exciting way to learn more about Access features and possibilities.

5. **Compact and close the IL_AC_8_Nutrition.accdb database, then close Access 2019**

FIGURE 8-17: Exploring Application Parts

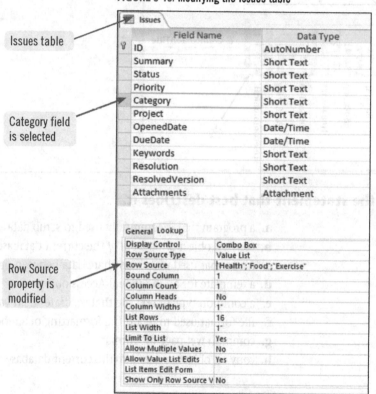

Application Parts

Issues

FIGURE 8-19: Exploring the IssueNew form

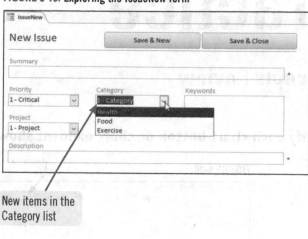

New items in the Category list

FIGURE 8-18: Modifying the Issues table

Issues table

Category field is selected

Row Source property is modified

Field Name	Data Type
ID	AutoNumber
Summary	Short Text
Status	Short Text
Priority	Short Text
Category	Short Text
Project	Short Text
OpenedDate	Date/Time
DueDate	Date/Time
Keywords	Short Text
Resolution	Short Text
ResolvedVersion	Short Text
Attachments	Attachment

General | **Lookup**

Display Control	Combo Box
Row Source Type	Value List
Row Source	"Health";"Food";"Exercise"
Bound Column	1
Column Count	1
Column Heads	No
Column Widths	1"
List Rows	16
List Width	1"
Limit To List	Yes
Allow Multiple Values	No
Allow Value List Edits	Yes
List Items Edit Form	
Show Only Row Source V	No

Creating custom Application Parts

To create a custom Application Part from the objects of an existing database, click the File tab on the ribbon, click Save As, click Template, then click the Save As button. The Create New Template from Database dialog box provides options to describe your new Application Part including its name, description, icon, and other details.

Access

Practice

Concepts Review

Identify each chart button or chart element shown in FIGURE 8-20.

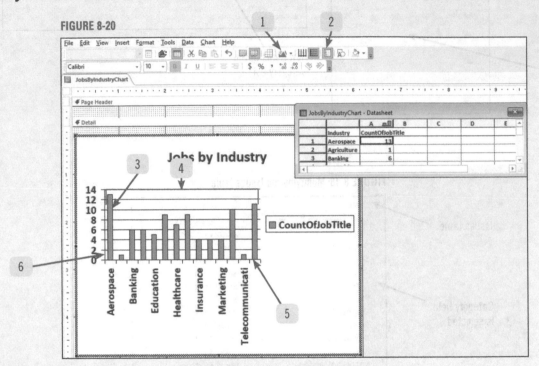

FIGURE 8-20

Match each term with the statement that best describes it.

7. **Application Part**	**a.** a program that is commonly used to scrub data
8. **HTML**	**b.** copy an object or data *out of* the current database
9. **export**	**c.** file format used mainly to share data between programs on the web
10. **PDF**	**d.** a template for an individual Access object
11. **XML**	**e.** a common type of text file that separates field values with commas
12. **import**	**f.** file format used to retain the formatting of a report
13. **Excel**	**g.** common webpage file format
14. **CSV**	**h.** copy an object or data *into* the current database

Select the best answer from the list of choices.

15. **Which chart type is commonly used to show trends over time?**
   a. Pie
   b. Line
   c. Gantt
   d. Scatter

16. **Which chart type is commonly used to show cumulative values?**
   a. Bar
   b. Line
   c. Pareto
   d. Area

17. **Which chart element contains color samples for each series of data markers?**
   a. Legend
   b. X-axis
   c. Y-axis
   d. Plot area

18. **Why would you use an Application Part?**
   a. to quickly create new objects
   b. to import and export data
   c. to email a report
   d. to start the Chart Wizard

19. **When a table or query is exported to an HTML file, how is the data presented on the page?**
   a. as an ordered single column
   b. using XML markup tags
   c. as an HTML table
   d. as an unordered list

20. **Which of the following types of objects may *not* be copied between two Access databases?**
   a. tables
   b. queries
   c. forms
   d. Every type of Access object can be copied between two databases.

Skills Review

1. **Import Access objects.**
   a. Start Access, open the IL_AC_8-2.accdb database from the location where you store your Data Files, then save it as **IL_AC_8_SupportDesk**. Enable content if prompted.
   b. Import the 50States table and the StateEntry form from the Support_AC_8_SupportDesk_Dev.accdb database in the location where you store your Data Files. Do not save the import steps.
   c. Verify that the 50States table and StateEntry form have been successfully imported into your database by opening them. Both should show 50 records.
   d. Close the 50States table and StateEntry form.

2. **Import or export text files.**
   a. Open the Employees table, then note the total number of records, 26. Close the Employees table.
   b. Import the Support_AC_8_Employees.txt file from the location where you store your Data Files, then append the records to the Employees table. Note that the data is tab delimited, that the first row contains field names, and that there are five data records. Do not save the import steps.
   c. Open the Employees table to confirm that there are now 31 records, add a new record with **your name**, Department value of **Information Systems**, Salary value of **$80,000**, and Dependents value of **1**, then close the table.

3. **Export to Excel.**
   a. Open the CaseInfo report in Report View to scroll through and view the data, noting that it contains 22 total records, then close the report.
   b. Export the CaseInfo report to Excel using the file name of **IL_AC_8_CaseInfo** in the location where you store your Data Files.
   c. Open the IL_AC_8_CaseInfo.xls file in Excel, confirm that the Excel file contains 23 rows of data (the first row will contain column headings), then save and close Excel and return to the IL_AC_8_SupportDesk.accdb database in Access.
   d. Save the export steps with the name **Export-CaseInfo to Excel**.

4. **Export to PDF.**
   a. Open the EmployeeMasterList report to review the information, then close the report.
   b. Export the EmployeeMasterList report to PDF using the file name of **IL_AC_8_EmployeeMasterList** in the location where you store your Data Files.
   c. Review the PDF file, then close it and return to Access.
   d. Save the export steps with the name **Export-EmployeeMasterList to PDF**.

Skills Review (continued)

5. Export to HTML or XML.

   a. Open the Cases table to review the fields and records, then close the table.

   b. Export the Cases table to XML using the file name of **IL_AC_8_Cases** in the location where you store your Data Files. Export both the XML and XSD files.

   c. Save the export steps with the name **Export-Cases to XML**.

   d. Export the Employees table to HTML using the file name of **IL_AC_8_Employees** in the location where you store your Data Files. Do not include formatting.

   e. Save the export steps with the name **Export-Employees to HTML**.

6. Merge to Word.

   a. Merge the Employees table to a new document in Word.

   b. Create the main document in Word with the merge fields and text as shown in **FIGURE 8-21**. Be careful to add a space between the FirstName and LastName merge fields.

   c. Complete the merge process. Close the Letters1 document, which is the final merged result with 32 pages, without saving it.

   d. Save the main document with the name **IL_AC_8_TuitionMemo** in the location where you store your Data Files, then close Word and return to Access.

FIGURE 8-21

To: → «FirstName» «LastName»¶

Re: → New Employee Benefits¶

Date: → (Insert current date)¶

Today we are pleased to announce a new employee tuition reimbursement plan! Call Chris Guerra in Human Resources for details!¶

7. Create charts.

   a. Open the EmployeeMasterList report in Design view, then add a chart control using the Chart button in the Controls group to the top of the Report Footer section at about the 0.5" mark on the horizontal ruler.

   b. Select the EmployeesByDepartment query, the Department field, and the LastName field for the chart.

   c. Choose a column chart with the Department in the Axis area and move the LastName to the Data area. The LastName field will be counted in the Data area.

   d. Choose <No Field> for both the Report and Chart fields.

   e. Accept the default title and do not display a legend on the chart.

   f. Save the report and preview the chart on the last page returning to Design View as necessary to resize the chart so that all of the labels on the x-axis are clearly visible.

8. Modify charts.

   a. Return to Design View of the EmployeeMasterList report, double-click the chart to edit it, then modify the title to be **Employees By Department**.

   b. Change the bar color of the first set of bars to blue.

   c. Save the report, then preview the chart on the last page as shown in **FIGURE 8-22**.

   d. Compact and close the IL_AC_8_SupportDesk.accdb database, then close Access.

FIGURE 8-22

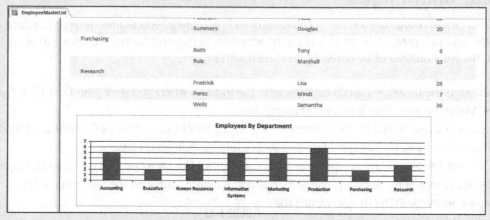

9. Use a database template.

a. Start Access and build a new database based on the Charitable Contributions template. (If that template is not available, choose another.)

b. Save the database with the name **IL_AC_8_Charity** in the location where you store your Data Files.

c. Enable content, press F11 to open the Navigation Pane, then notice that the objects are organized by subject instead of by object type.

d. Right-click the Navigation Pane title bar, point to Category, then click Object type.

e. Enter your name in the Last Name and First Name fields of the Contributors table, then explore the rest of the objects in the database and be ready to discuss something new that you learned about Access in class.

10. Use Application Parts.

a. If you cannot see the ribbon in the IL_AC_8_Charity database, close it, press SHIFT, reopen the IL_AC_8_Charity database and do not release SHIFT until the database is open. (*Hint*: Pressing SHIFT overrides startup options such as custom toolbars and hiding the Navigation Pane.)

b. On the Create tab of the ribbon, use the Application Parts button to add a Comments table. There is no relationship to the new Comments table.

c. Open the Comments table to review the fields, then close it.

d. Compact and repair then close the IL_AC_8_Charity.accdb database and exit Access 2019.

Independent Challenge 1

As the manager of Riverwalk, a multispecialty health clinic, you have created a database to manage nurse and doctor schedules to efficiently handle patient visits. In this exercise you will export Access data to three common file formats in order to discuss the reasons you may need or want to use each format.

a. Start Access, open the IL_AC_8-3.accdb database from the location where you store your Data Files, then save it as **IL_AC_8_Riverwalk**. Enable content if prompted.

b. Add your last name and a DrPA field value of **MD** to the Providers table.

c. Export the Providers table to Excel using the file name of **IL_AC_8_Providers** in the location where you store your Data Files. Do not include formatting. Save the export with the name **Export-Providers to Excel**.

d. Export the Providers table to HTML using the file name of **IL_AC_8_Providers** in the location where you store your Data Files. Do not include formatting. Save the export with the name **Export-Providers to HTML**.

e. Export the Providers table to PDF using the file name of **IL_AC_8_Providers** in the location where you store your Data Files. Do not include formatting. Save the export with the name **Export-Providers to PDF**.

f. Open and review the data in each of the three exported files. Be prepared to give a reason you would choose to export data to each of these three different file formats.

g. Close all open exported files, then compact and close the IL_AC_8_Riverwalk.accdb and Access 2019.

Independent Challenge 2

You are working for a city to coordinate a series of community-wide preparedness activities. You have created a database to track the activities and volunteers who are attending the activities. In this exercise you will create a report to calculate information about the total number of volunteer hours at each activity.

a. Start Access, open the IL_AC_8-4.accdb database from the location where you store your Data Files, then save it as **IL_AC_8_Volunteers**. Enable content if prompted.

b. Add your name as a new record in the Volunteers table with a Street value of **12345 College Blvd**, a Zipcode value of **66215**, and a Birthday value of **1/1/1991**. Close the Volunteers table.

c. In Design View of the VolunteerList report, use the Chart control from the Controls group on the ribbon to add a chart to the upper area of the Report Footer section at about the 0.5" mark on the horizontal ruler.

d. Base the report on the ActivityList query using the ActivityName and ActivityHours fields.

e. Use a column chart with the ActivityName in the Axis area and the ActivityHours (which will be summed) in the Data area.

f. Choose <No Field> for the Report and Chart Fields and use **Hours by Activity** for the chart title. Do not display a legend.

g. Resize the chart, change the data markers fill color to red, change the x-axis label font size to **8** point, and add the **value** as the data labels as shown in FIGURE 8-23.

h. Save and close the VolunteerList report.

i. Compact and close the IL_AC_8_Volunteers.accdb database, then close Access 2019.

FIGURE 8-23

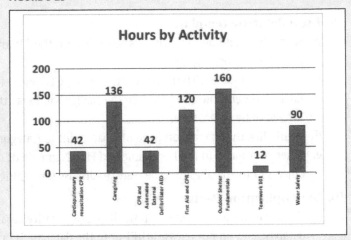

Visual Workshop

Start Access, open the IL_AC_8-5.accdb database from the location where you store your Data Files, then save it as **IL_AC_8_CollegeCourses**. Enable content if prompted. Add your name to the Students table as a new record using **999** as the StudentID, your own first and last names, and other fictitious but realistic data. Add a chart to the upper-left corner of the Report Footer section of the StudentGradeListing report based on the StudentGrades query. Include the ClassNo and PassOrFail fields. Use a column chart, then add the PassOrFail field to the Data area, where it will be counted. (Note that the PassOrFail field is used in both the Data and Series areas.) Choose <No Field> when asked to link the Report and Chart fields, title the chart **Pass or Fail by Class**, and display a legend. Format the first series (fail) with a red fill color and the second series (pass) with a blue fill color as shown in **FIGURE 8-24**. Widen the chart and change the font size to **10** point for the x axis (category axis) so that all of the ClassNo field values are clearly visible as shown in **FIGURE 8-24**. Save and close the StudentGradeListing report. Compact and close the IL_AC_8_CollegeCourses.accdb database, then exit Access 2019.

FIGURE 8-24

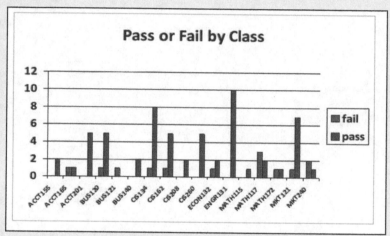

Access

Creating Action Queries

CASE You are working with Lydia Snyder, vice president of operations at JCL Talent, to build a research database to manage industry, company, and job data. In this module, you'll work with action queries to back up and modify data. You will also learn how to modify join properties in a query to answer questions about the relationships between the tables.

Module Objectives

After completing this module, you will be able to:

- Create a Make Table query
- Create an Append query
- Create a Delete query
- Create an Update Query
- Create an outer join
- Apply an outer join
- Create a self join

Files You Will Need

IL_AC_9-1.accdb
IL_AC_9-2.accdb
IL_AC_9-3.accdb
IL_AC_9-4.accdb
IL_AC_9-5.accdb

Create a Make Table Query

Learning
Outcomes
• Define action
  queries
• Create a Make
  Table query

All the queries you have created prior to this module are Select queries. A **Select query** starts with the SQL keyword **SELECT** to select fields and records that match specific criteria. When you **run** a select query in Access, a datasheet of the selected fields and records is produced. An **action query** not only selects, but also *changes* all the selected data when it is run. Access provides four types of action queries: Make Table, Append, Delete, and Update. See **TABLE 9-1** for more information on action queries. A **Make Table query** is a type of action query that creates a new table of data. The location of the new table can be the current database or another Access database. **CASE** > *Lydia Snyder asks you to archive the first month's jobs for the year 2021 that are currently stored in the Jobs table. A Make Table query will handle this request.*

STEPS

1. **san** ↓ **Start Access, open the** IL_AC_9-1.accdb database **from the location where you store your Data Files, save it as** IL_AC_9_Jobs, **enable content if prompted, click the** Create tab **on the ribbon, click the** Query Design button, **double-click** Jobs **in the Show Table dialog box, then click** Close

   All action queries start out as select queries.

2. **Double-click the * (asterisk) at the top of the Jobs field list**

   Adding the asterisk to the query design grid adds all the fields in that table to the grid. Later, if you add new fields to the Jobs table, they are automatically included in this query.

3. **Use ↕ to resize the field list to see all fields, double-click the** FirstPosted field **to add it to the second column of the query grid, click the** FirstPosted field Criteria cell, **type** >=1/1/21 and <=1/31/21, **click the** FirstPosted field Show check box **to uncheck it, then use the ↔ resize pointer to widen the FirstPosted column to view the entire Criteria entry, as shown in** FIGURE 9-1

   Before changing this Select query into a Make Table query, it is always a good idea to run the query as a Select query to view the selected data.

4. **Click the** View button ▦ **to switch to Datasheet View, click any entry in the** FirstPosted field, **then click the** Descending button **in the Sort & Filter group**

   Sorting the records in descending order based on the values in the FirstPosted field allows you to confirm that only records in January of 2021 appear in the datasheet.

5. **Click the** View button ▧ **to return to Design View, click the** Make Table button **in the Query Type group, type** Jan2021 **in the Table Name box, then click** OK

   The Make Table query is ready, but action queries do not change data until you click the Run button. All action query icons display an exclamation point to remind you that they change data only when you run them. To prevent running an action query accidentally, use the Datasheet View button to view the selected records for an action query. Use the Run button only when you are ready to run the action.

6. **Click the** View button ▦ **to double-check the records you have selected, click the** View button ▧ **to return to Query Design View, click the** Run button **to execute the action, click** Yes **when prompted that you are about to paste 39 rows, save the query with the name** MakeJan2021, **then close it**

   When you run an action query, Access prompts you with an "Are you sure?" message before actually updating the data. The Undo button cannot undo changes made by action queries.

7. **Double-click the** Jan2021 table **in the Navigation Pane to view the new table's datasheet, as shown in** FIGURE 9-2, **then close the** Jan2021 table

Creating Action Queries

FIGURE 9-1: Creating a Make Table query

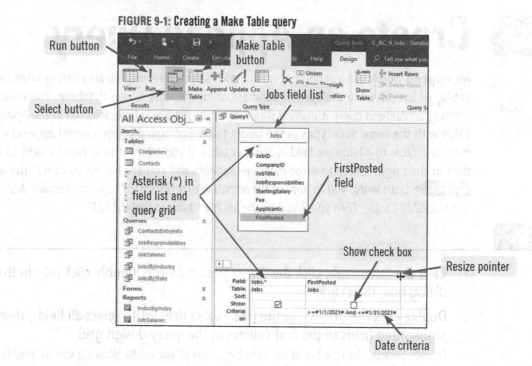

Run button

Make Table button

Select button

Jobs field list

FirstPosted field

Asterisk (*) in field list and query grid

Show check box

Resize pointer

Date criteria

FIGURE 9-2: Jan2021 table datasheet

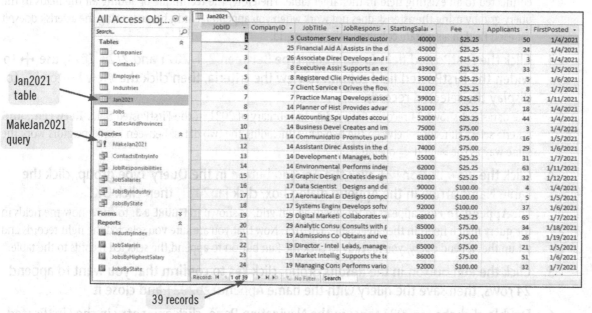

Jan2021 table

MakeJan2021 query

39 records

TABLE 9-1: Action queries

action query	query icon	description	example
Make Table		Creates a new table from data in one or more tables	Make a backup copy of employee data in the same or another database
Append		Adds a group of records from one or more tables to the end of another table	Append the records of an employee table from one division of the company to the employee table from another division
Update		Updates the value of a field	Raise prices by 10 percent for selected products in the Products table
Delete		Deletes a group of records from one or more tables	Remove products that are discontinued from a Products table

Access

Create an Append Query

Learning
Outcome
• Create an Append
query

An **Append query** is an action query that adds selected records to an existing table called the **target table**, which can be in the current database or in any other Access database. The most difficult part of creating an Append query is making sure that all the fields you have selected in the Append query match fields with the same data types in the target table. For example, you cannot append a Short Text field from one table to a Number field in another table. If you attempt to append a field to an incompatible field in the target table, an error message appears and you are forced to cancel the append process.

CASE ▸ *Lydia wants you to append the records with a FirstPosted value in February 2021 in the Jobs table to the Jan2021 table. Then you'll rename the Jan2021 table to JanFeb2021.*

STEPS

1. **Click the** Create tab, **click the** Query Design button, **double-click** Jobs **in the Show Table dialog box, then click** Close

2. **Double-click the** title bar **in the Jobs table's field list to select all fields, then drag the highlighted fields to the first column of the query design grid**

   Double-clicking the title bar of the field list selects all the fields, allowing you to quickly add them to the query grid. To successfully append records to a table, you need to identify how each field in the query is connected to an existing field in the target table. Therefore, the technique of adding all the fields to the query grid by using the asterisk does not work when you append records, because using the asterisk doesn't list each field in a separate column in the query grid.

3. **Click the** FirstPosted field Criteria cell, **type** Between 2/1/2021 and 2/28/2021, **use** ✛ **to widen the FirstPosted field column to view the criteria, then click the** View button ⊞ **to display the selected records**

   The datasheet shows 24 records with a date in February of 2021 in the FirstPosted field. **Between...and** criteria select all records between the two dates, including the two dates. Between...and operators work the same way as the >= and <= operators.

4. **Click the** View button ⊠, **click the** Append button **in the Query Type group, click the** Table Name arrow **in the Append dialog box, click** Jan2021, **then click** OK

   The **Append To row** appears in the query design grid, as shown in **FIGURE 9-3**, to show how the fields in the query match fields in the target table, Jan2021. Now that you are sure you selected the right records and set up the Append query, you're ready to click the Run button to append the selected records to the table.

5. **Click the** Run button **in the Results group, click** Yes **to confirm that you want to append 24 rows, then save the query with the name** AppendFeb2021 **and close it**

6. **Double-click the** Jan2021 table **in the Navigation Pane, click any entry in the** FirstPosted field, **then click the** Descending button **in the Sort & Filter group**

   The 24 February records are appended to the Jan2021 table, which previously had 39 records for a new total of 63 records, as shown in **FIGURE 9-4**.

7. **Save and close the** Jan2021 table, **right-click the** Jan2021 table, **click** Rename, **type** JanFeb2021, **then press** ENTER

FIGURE 9-3: Creating an Append query

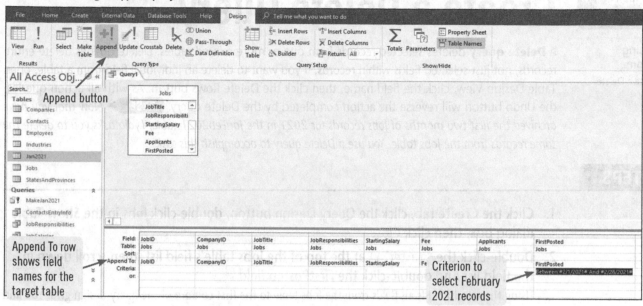

Append button

Append To row shows field names for the target table

Criterion to select February 2021 records

FIGURE 9-4: Jan2021 table with appended records

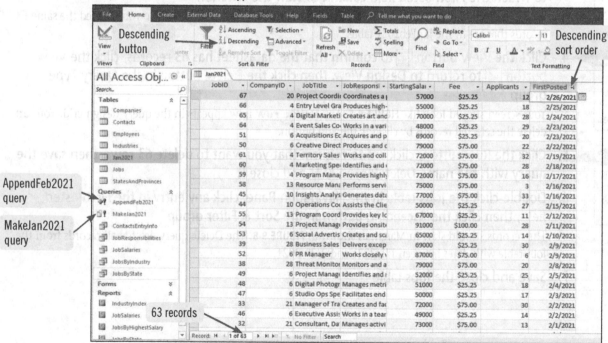

Descending button

Descending sort order

AppendFeb2021 query

MakeJan2021 query

63 records

1900 versus 2000 dates

If you type only two digits of a date, Access assumes that the digits 00 through 29 are for the years 2000 through 2029. If you type 30 through 99, Access assumes the years refer to 1930 through 1999.

If you want to specify years outside these ranges, you must type all four digits of the year.

Create a Delete Query

A **Delete query** deletes selected records from one or more related tables. Delete queries delete entire records, not just selected fields within records. If you want to delete an individual field from a table, open Table Design View, click the field name, then click the Delete Rows button. As with all action queries, the Undo button will reverse the action completed by the Delete query. **CASE** ▸ *Now that you have archived the first two months of Jobs records for 2021 in the JanFeb2021 table, Lydia asks you to delete the same records from the Jobs table. You use a Delete query to accomplish this task.*

STEPS

1. **Click the** Create tab, **click the** Query Design button, **double-click** Jobs **in the Show Table dialog box, then click** Close

2. **Double-click the** * (asterisk) **at the top of the Jobs table's field list, then scroll down in the field list and double-click the** FirstPosted field

   Using the asterisk adds all fields from the Jobs table to the first column of the query design grid. You add the FirstPosted field to the second column of the query design grid so you can enter limiting criteria for this field.

3. **Click the** FirstPosted field Criteria cell, **type** Between 1/1/21 and 2/28/21, **then use** ↔ **to widen the FirstPosted field column to view the criterion**

   Before you run a Delete query, be sure to check the selected records to make sure you selected the same 63 records that are in the JanFeb2021 table.

4. **Click the** View button **to confirm that the datasheet has 63 records, click the** View button **to return to Design View, then click the** Delete button **in the Query Type group**

   Your screen should look like **FIGURE 9-5**. The **Delete row** now appears in the query design grid. You can delete the selected records by clicking the Run button.

5. **Click the** Run button, **click** Yes **to confirm that you want to delete 63 rows, then save the query with the name** DeleteJanFeb2021 **and close it**

6. **Double-click the** Jobs table **in the Navigation Pane, click any entry in the** FirstPosted field, **then click the** Ascending button **in the Sort & Filter group**

   The records should start in March, as shown in **FIGURE 9-6**. The Delete query deleted all records from the Jobs table with dates between 1/1/2021 and 2/28/2021.

7. **Save and close the Jobs table**

FIGURE 9-5: Creating a Delete query

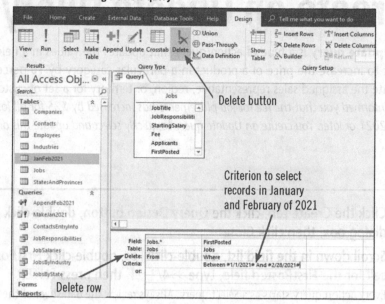

Delete button

Criterion to select records in January and February of 2021

Delete row

Field:	Jobs.*	FirstPosted
Table:	Jobs	Jobs
Delete:	From	Where
Criteria:		Between #1/1/2021# And #2/28/2021#
or:		

FIGURE 9-6: Final Jobs table

Ascending button

Ascending sort order

Delete query

19 records

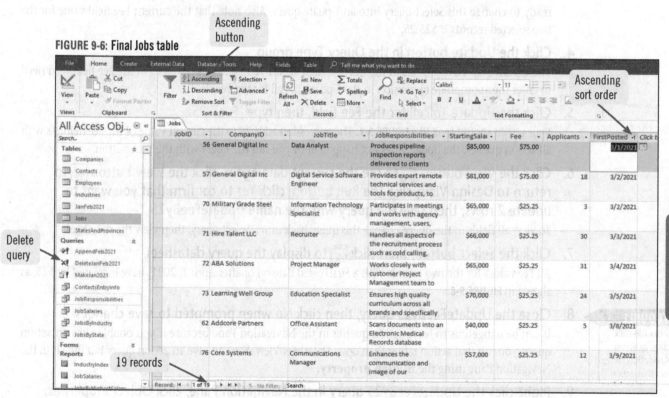

JobID	CompanyID	JobTitle	JobResponsibilities	StartingSalar	Fee	Applicants	FirstPosted	Click t
56	General Digital Inc	Data Analyst	Produces pipeline inspection reports delivered to clients	$85,000	$75.00		3/1/2021	
57	General Digital Inc	Digital Service Software Engineer	Provides expert remote technical services and tools for products, to	$81,000	$75.00	18	3/2/2021	
70	Military Grade Steel	Information Technology Specialist	Participates in meetings and works with agency management, users,	$65,000	$25.25	3	3/2/2021	
71	Hire Talent LLC	Recruiter	Handles all aspects of the recruitment process such as cold calling,	$66,000	$25.25	30	3/3/2021	
72	ABA Solutions	Project Manager	Works closely with customer Project Management team to	$65,000	$25.25	31	3/4/2021	
73	Learning Well Group	Education Specialist	Ensures high quality curriculum across all brands and specifically	$70,000	$25.25	24	3/5/2021	
62	Addcore Partners	Office Assistant	Scans documents into an Electronic Medical Records database	$40,000	$25.25	5	3/8/2021	
76	Core Systems	Communications Manager	Enhances the communication and image of our	$57,000	$25.25	12	3/9/2021	

Record: 1 of 19   No Filter   Search

Create an Update Query

Learning
Outcomes
• Create an Update
  query
• Hide an object in
  the Navigation
  Pane

An **Update query** is a type of action query that updates the values in a field. For example, you might want to increase the price of a product in a particular category by 10 percent. Or you might want to update the assigned sales representative, region, or territory for a set of customers. **CASE** *Lydia has just informed you that the fee for job placements has increased by $25 for all jobs with a FirstPosted date of 4/1/2021 or later. You create an Update query to quickly select and update this data.*

STEPS

1. **Click the** Create tab, **click the** Query Design button, **double-click** Jobs **in the Show Table dialog box, then click** Close

2. **Scroll down in the field list, double-click** Fee, **double-click** FirstPosted, **click the** Criteria **cell for the FirstPosted field, type** >=4/1/21, **then press** ENTER

   Every action query starts as a Select query. Always review the datasheet of the Select query before initiating any action that changes data to double-check which records are affected.

3. **Click the** View button 🔲 **to display the query datasheet and observe the FirstPosted values and number of records, then click the** View button 🔲 **to return to Design View**

   After confirming that you are selecting only records with a FirstPosted value of April 1, 2021, or later, you're ready to change this Select query into an Update query. Also note that the current Fee field value for the two selected records is $25.25.

4. **Click the** Update button **in the Query Type group**

   The **Update To row** appears in the query design grid. To add $25 to the values in the Fee field, you need to enter the appropriate expression in the Update To cell for the Fee field.

5. **Click the** Update To cell **for the Fee field, then type** [Fee]+25

   Your screen should look like **FIGURE 9-7**. The expression adds 25 to the current value of the Fee field. As with all action queries, the update does not happen until you run the query with the Run button.

6. **Click the** View button 🔲 **to see the current data again, click the** View button 🔲 **to return to Design View, click the** Run button, **click** Yes **to confirm that you want to update 2 rows, then save the query with the name** UpdateFeeBy25

   To view all fields in the query, change this query back into a Select query, then view the datasheet.

7. **Click the** Select button, **then click** 🔲 **to display the query datasheet**

   All Fee values for the two records with a FirstPosted date on or after April 1, 2021, have increased by $25, as shown in **FIGURE 9-8**.

TROUBLE
If you double-click
an action query in
the Navigation Pane,
you run that action.

8. **Close the UpdateFeeBy25 query, then click** No **when prompted to save changes**

   It can be dangerous to leave action queries in the Navigation Pane because if you double-click an action query, you run that action rather than open Datasheet View. You can save an action query but hide it in the Navigation Pane using the **Hidden property**.

9. **Right-click the** UpdateFeeBy25 **query in the Navigation Pane, click** Object Properties, **click the** Hidden check box, **then click** OK

FIGURE 9-7: Creating an Update query

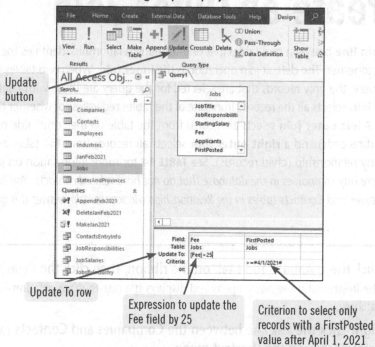

Update button

Update To row

Expression to update the Fee field by 25

Criterion to select only records with a FirstPosted value after April 1, 2021

FIGURE 9-8: Viewing updated Fee values

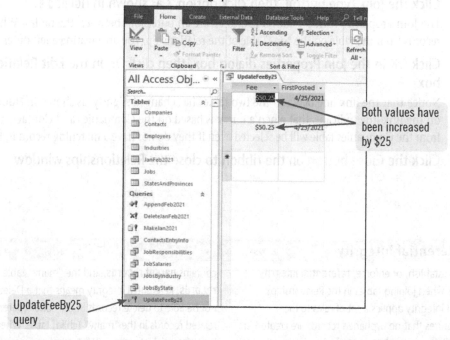

UpdateFeeBy25 query

Both values have been increased by $25

Access

Create an Outer Join

Learning
Outcomes
• Modify a join in
the Relationships
window
• Understand join
operations

The **join line** between two tables in a one-to-many relationship identifies the common field that links the tables together. The default join operation is the **inner join.** When two tables are related with an inner join in a query, the only records that are selected for the query are those with related records in each table. An **outer join** selects all the records from one of the tables regardless of whether there is a related record in the other. A **left outer join** selects all records from the table on the "one" side of a one-to-many relationship (parent records) and a **right outer join** selects all records from the table on the "many" side of a one-to-many relationship (child records). See TABLE 9-2 for more information on joins. **CASE** *Lydia asks if there are any companies in the database that do not have related contacts. You build an outer join between the Companies and Contacts tables in the Relationships window to help answer this question.*

STEPS

1. **Click the** Database Tools tab **on the ribbon, then click the** Relationships button

   The Relationships window opens and displays the one-to-many relationships between the tables in the database.

2. **Right-click the** link line **between the Companies and Contacts table, then click** Edit Relationship **on the shortcut menu**

   The Edit Relationships dialog box opens and displays information about the one-to-many relationship between the Companies and Contacts table. The CompanyID field in each table is used as the linking field.

3. **Click the** Join Type button, **then click option** 2 **as shown in** FIGURE 9-9

   The Join Properties window allows you to create an outer join between the tables. When you select ALL records from the table on the "one" side of the relationship, you are creating a left outer join.

4. **Click** OK **in the Join Properties dialog box, then click** OK **in the Edit Relationships dialog box**

   Notice that the link line between the two tables has changed slightly, as shown in FIGURE 9-10. The arrow on the link line indicates that when a query is based on the Companies and Contacts tables, ALL records from the Companies table will be selected even if they do not have a matching record in the Contacts table.

5. **Click the** Close button **on the ribbon to close the Relationships window**

Reviewing referential integrity

Recall that you can establish, or enforce, **referential integrity** between two tables when joining tables in the Relationships window. Referential integrity applies a set of rules to the relationship that ensures that no orphaned records are created in the database. A table has an **orphan record** when information in the foreign key field of the "many" table doesn't have a matching entry in the primary key field of the "one" table. The term *orphan* comes from the analogy that the "one" table contains **parent records**, and the "many" table contains **child records**. Referential integrity means that a Delete query would not be able to delete records in the "one" (parent) table that has related records in the "many" (child) table. When a relationship has referential integrity, a "1" symbol appears on the field on the "one" side of the relationship, and an infinity symbol appears on the field on the "many" side of the relationship.

FIGURE 9-9: Modifying join properties in the Relationships window

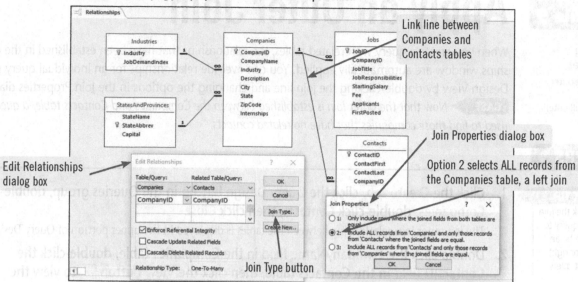

Edit Relationships dialog box

Join Type button

Link line between Companies and Contacts tables

Join Properties dialog box

Option 2 selects ALL records from the Companies table, a left join

FIGURE 9-10: Relationships window with outer join

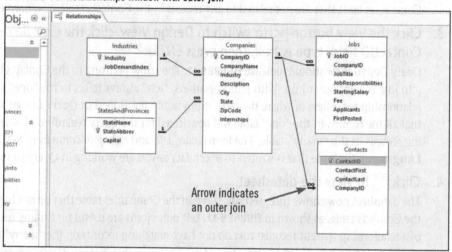

Arrow indicates an outer join

TABLE 9-2: Join operations

join operation	description	example based on a one-to-many relationship between the Customers and Sales tables
inner	Default join; selects records from two related tables in a query that have matching values in the linking field of both tables	Each record from the Customers table must have one or more related records in the Sales table to be selected for the query.
left outer	Selects all the records from the left table (the "one" table in a one-to-many relationship) even if the "one" (parent) table doesn't have matching records in the related "many" (child) table	Select records from the Customers table that have no related records in the Sales table.
right outer	Selects all the records from the right table (the "many" table in a one-to-many relationship) even if the "many" (child) table doesn't have matching records in the related "one" (parent) table	Select orphan records in the Sales table that have no related records in the Customers table. (*Note:* Enforcing referential integrity on a relationship prevents orphan records from being entered into a relational database.)
self	Relates a table to itself	Relate an Employee table to itself using two fields in the same table to identify the relationship between employees and supervisors.

Apply an Outer Join

When you create a query with related tables, the relationships that have been established in the Relation-ships window are automatically applied. You can override relationships for an individual query in Query Design View by double-clicking the join line and changing the options in the Join Properties dialog box.

CASE ▸ *Now that the outer join is established between the Companies and Contacts table, a query can be used to find those companies that have no related contacts.*

STEPS

1. **Click the Create tab, click the Query Design button in the Queries group, double-click Companies, double-click Contacts, then click Close**

   The left outer join relationship between the tables is displayed in the upper portion of Query Design View.

2. **Double-click the CompanyName field in the Companies table, double-click the ContactID field in the Contacts table, then click the View button ▦ to view the datasheet**

   This query selects 446 records using the left outer join between the tables. To find only those records in the Companies table that are not related to any records in the Contacts table, you need to add criteria.

3. **Click the View button ☑ to switch to Design View, click the Criteria cell for the ContactID field, type Is Null, then press ENTER**

   Query Design View should look like **FIGURE 9-11**. The arrow pointing to the Contacts table indicates that the join line is a left outer join. With join operations, "left" always refers to the "one" table of a one-to-many relationship regardless of where the table is physically positioned in Query Design View. A left join means that all the records in the "one" table will be selected for the query regardless of whether they have match-ing records in the "many" table. The terms *inner*, *left*, and *right join* come from **SQL (Structured Query Language)**, the code that is written to select data as you are working in Query Design View.

4. **Click ▦ to view the datasheet**

   The datasheet now shows three records, those in the Companies table that do not have matching records in the Contacts table, as shown in **FIGURE 9-12**. Left outer joins are useful for finding records on the "one" side of a relationship (parent records) that do not have matching records on the "many" side (child records).

   When referential integrity is enforced on a relationship before data is entered, you cannot create new records on the "many" side of a relationship that do not have matching records on the "one" side. Although a right outer join helps you find orphan records in a poorly designed database, it would not be very useful in the JCL jobs database because referential integrity was applied on all relationships before any records were entered.

5. **Close the query and save it with the name CompaniesWithoutContacts**

FIGURE 9-11: Using Is Null criteria

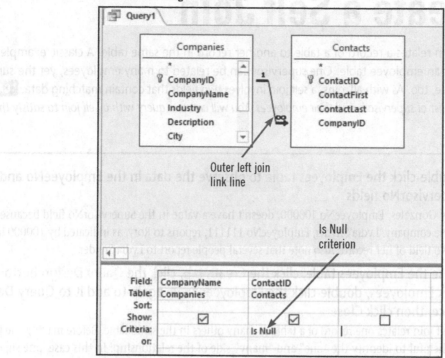

Outer left join
link line

Is Null
criterion

FIGURE 9-12: Companies without contacts

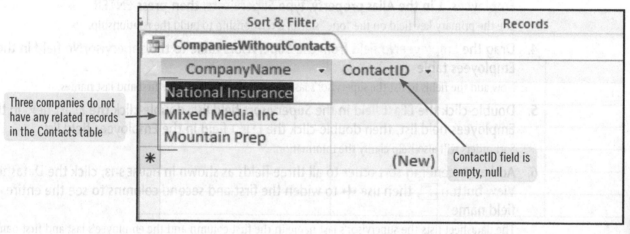

Three companies do not
have any related records
in the Contacts table

ContactID field is
empty, null

Null versus zero-length string values

The term **null** describes a field value that does not exist because it has never been entered. In a datasheet, null values look the same as a zero-length string value but have a different purpose. A **zero-length string** value is a deliberate entry that contains no characters. You enter a zero-length string by typing two quotation marks ("") with no space between them. A null value, on the other hand, indicates unknown data. By using null and

zero-length string values appropriately, you can later query for the records that match one or the other condition. To query for zero-length string values, enter two quotation marks ("") as the criterion. To query for null values, use **Is Null** as the criterion. To query for any value other than a null value, use **Is Not Null** as the criterion.

Access

Create a Self Join

A self join relates a record of a table to another record in the same table. A classic example of a self join involves an employee table. One supervisor can be related to many employees, yet the supervisor is an employee, too. As with all joins, a self join involves two fields that contain matching data. **CASE** ▶ *Lydia needs a list of supervisors and their employees. You will create a query with a self join to satisfy this request.*

STEPS

1. **Double-click the Employees table to observe the data in the EmployeeNo and SupervisorNo fields**

   Rory Gonzales, EmployeeNo 100000, doesn't have a value in the SupervisorNo field because he's the CEO of the company. Lydia Snyder, EmployeeNo 111111, reports to Rory, as indicated by 100000 in the SupervisorNo field of her record. Also note that several people report to Lydia Snyder.

2. **Close the Employees table, click the Create tab, click the Query Design button, double-click Employees, double-click the Employees table again to add it to Query Design View twice, then click Close**

   A self join relates one record of a table to many others in the same table. Before making the join, however, it's helpful to identify the "one" and "many" side of the relationship. In this case, one supervisor can be related to many employees.

3. **Right-click the Employees_1 field list, click Properties on the shortcut menu, select Employees_1 in the Alias property, type Supervisors, then press ENTER**

   Use the primary key field on the "one" side of a relationship to build the relationship.

4. **Drag the EmployeeNo field from the Supervisors table to the SupervisorNo field in the Employees table**

   Now add the fields to list the supervisor's last name and the employee's first and last names.

5. **Double-click the ELast field in the Supervisors field list, double-click the ELast field in the Employees field list, then double-click the EFirst field in the Employees field list**

   Sort orders will also help clarify the information.

6. **Add an Ascending sort order to all three fields as shown in FIGURE 9-13, click the Datasheet View button ▦, then use ↔ to widen the first and second columns to see the entire field name**

   The datasheet lists the supervisor's last name in the first column and the employee's last and first names, as shown in **FIGURE 9-14**. Given you selected the ELast field twice, it is further qualified with the table name prefix. Also note that Lydia Snyder is listed as an employee once, reporting to Gonzalez, but that her last name is listed many times because many employees report to her.

7. **Close the query and save it with the name SupervisorList**

8. **sam↑ Open the Employees table, add your name as a new record with the EmployeeNo value of 727272 and a SupervisorNo value of 100000, close the Employees table, compact and close the IL_AC_9_Jobs.accdb database, then close Access**

FIGURE 9-13: Creating a self join

Employees table is the "many" table

SupervisorNo field is the foreign key field in this relationship

Table row

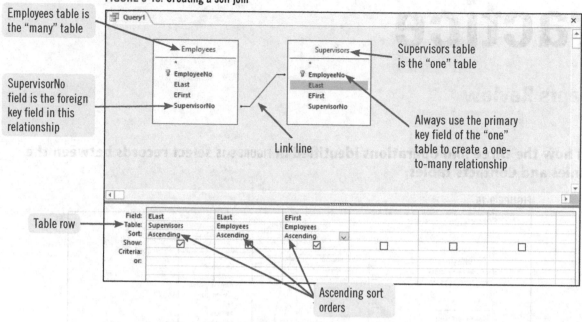

Supervisors table is the "one" table

Always use the primary key field of the "one" table to create a one-to-many relationship

Link line

Ascending sort orders

FIGURE 9-14: Datasheet for SupervisorList query

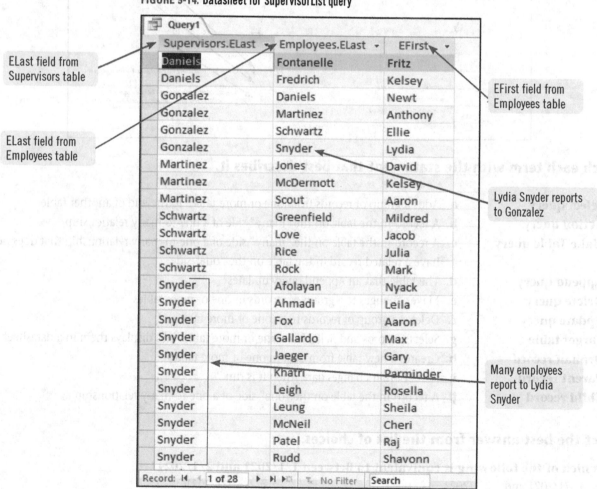

ELast field from Supervisors table

ELast field from Employees table

EFirst field from Employees table

Lydia Snyder reports to Gonzalez

Many employees report to Lydia Snyder

Practice

Concepts Review

Explain how the three join operations identified in FIGURE 9-15 **select records between the Companies and Contacts tables.**

FIGURE 9-15

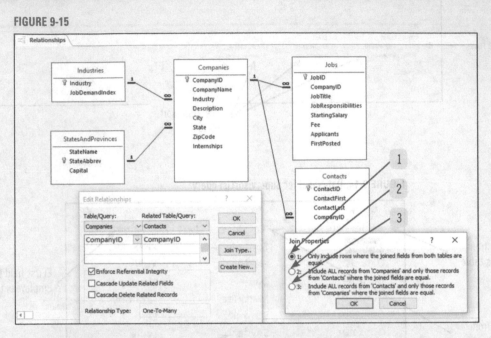

Match each term with the statement that best describes it.

4. **Select query**
5. **Action query**
6. **Make Table query**

7. **Append query**
8. **Delete query**
9. **Update query**
10. **Target table**
11. **Orphan record**
12. **Parent record**
13. **Child record**

a. Adds a group of records from one or more tables to the end of another table
b. A record in the table on the "many" side of a one-to-many relationship
c. A record in the table on the "many" side of a one-to-many relationship that does not have a related record in the table on the "one" side
d. The table that an Append query updates
e. Makes changes to a group of records in one or more tables
f. Deletes a group of records from one or more tables
g. Selects records and fields from one or more tables and displays them in a datasheet
h. Creates a new table from data in one or more tables
i. A query that changes data when it is run
j. A record in the table on the "one" side of a one-to-many relationship

Select the best answer from the list of choices.

14. **Which of the following is equivalent to Between 1/1/2021 and 2/1/2021?**
   a. > 1/1/2021 and < 2/1/2021
   b. >= 1/1/2021 and <= 2/1/2021
   c. >= 1/1/2021
   d. <= 2/1/2021

Creating Action Queries

15. What happens when you double-click an action query in the Navigation Pane?
a. You open its datasheet.
b. You open it in Design View.
c. You run the query.
d. You rename the query.

16. In Query Design View, which button do you click to initiate the process that an action query takes?
a. Datasheet View
b. Design View
c. Update
d. Run

17. If you want to find records in the table on the "one" side of a one-to-many relationship that do not have related records in the "many" side, which join do you use?
a. Inner
b. Left outer
c. Right outer
d. Self

18. If you want to select records in the table on the "many" side of a one-to-many relationship that do not have related records in the "one" side, which join do you use?
a. Inner
b. Left outer
c. Right outer
d. Self

19. If you want to select records that have related records in both the "one" and "many" sides of a one-to-many relationship, which join do you use?
a. Inner
b. Left outer
c. Right outer
d. Self

20. If you want to select records that have no value in a field, which criterion do you use?
a. Is Null
b. Is Not Null
c. "" (two quotation marks)
d. " " (two quotation marks with a space between them)

Skills Review

1. Create a Make Table query.

a. Start Access, open the IL_AC_9-2.accdb database from the location where you store your Data Files, then save it as **IL_AC_9_SupportDesk**. Enable content if prompted.

b. Create a new query in Query Design View based on the Calls table.

c. Select all fields from the Calls table using the asterisk (*), then add the CallDate field a second time and add criteria to select only those calls in April of 2021. (*Hint*: There are several ways to select all the records in a single month, but using the asterisk as a wildcard, as in **4/*/2021**, is one of the shortest.)

d. Uncheck the Show check box for the CallDate field, then display the datasheet to make sure you've selected the correct records. The datasheet should have eight records.

e. Return to Design View and change the query into a Make Table query using the name **April2021** for the new table, then run the query.

f. Save the query with the name **MakeApril2021**, then close it.

g. Open the April2021 table to make sure that it has eight records with a CallDate value in April of 2021, then close it.

2. Create an Append query.

a. Create a new query in Query Design View based on the Calls table. Add all the fields to the query grid *except* for the CallID field.

b. Add criteria to the CallDate field to select only those records from May of 2021, then display the datasheet. It should have seven records.

c. Return to Design View and change the query into an Append query to append the records to the April2021 table.

d. Run the query to append the seven records, save it with the name **AppendMay2021**, then close the query.

e. Open the April2021 table to make sure it now has 15 records, close it, then rename it to be **AprilMay2021**.

3. Create a Delete query.

a. Create a new query in Query Design View based on the Cases table.

b. Select all fields from the Cases table using the asterisk (*), then add the ResolvedDate field a second time. Add criteria to select only those records where the ResolvedDate field has a value using the criterion of **Is Not Null**.

c. Uncheck the Show check box for the ResolvedDate field, then display the datasheet to make sure you've selected the correct records. The datasheet should have six records.

d. Return to Design View and change the query into a Delete query.

e. Run the query to delete six records, save it with the name **DeleteResolvedCases**, then close it.

4. Create an Update query.

a. Start a new query in Query Design View with the Employees table.

b. Add the Department field and the Salary field to the query grid.

c. Add criteria to select all employees in the **Production** department, then sort the records in descending order on the Salary field.

d. Display the datasheet and note that six records are selected with Salary field values ranging from $55,000 to $52,000.

e. Return to Design View and change the query into an Update query.

f. Add the expression **[Salary]*1.1** to the Update To cell of the Salary field to represent a 10% increase.

g. Run the query to update the six records, then view the datasheet to view the updated values that should now range from $60,500 to $57,200.

h. Save the query with the name **UpdateProductionSalaries**, then close it.

i. Hide the UpdateProductionSalaries query in the Navigation Pane.

5. Create an outer join.

a. Open the Relationships window, then double-click the join line between the Employees and Cases table.

b. Click the Join Type button and select option 2 to include ALL records from the Employees table even if there are no related records in the Cases table.

c. Save and close the Relationships window.

6. Use an outer join.

a. Create a new query in Query Design View using the Employees and Cases tables.

b. Select the FirstName and LastName fields from the Employees table and the CaseID field from the Cases table.

c. Add **Is Null** criteria to the CaseID field, then display the datasheet, which should show 12 records.

d. Save the query with the name **EmployeesWithoutCases**, then close it.

7. Create a self join.

a. Start a new query in Query Design View and add the Employees table twice.

b. Change the Alias property of the Employees_1 table to **Managers**.

c. Link the tables by dragging the EmployeeID field from the Managers table to the ManagerID field in the Employees table.

d. Add the LastName field from the Managers table, and the Department, LastName, and FirstName fields from the Employees table in that order to the grid.

e. Add an ascending sort order to the Department, LastName, and FirstName fields from the Employees table, then view the datasheet and widen all columns to view the field names, as shown in **FIGURE 9-16**.

Skills Review (continued)

FIGURE 9-16

FIGURE 9-16

Managers.LastName	Department	Employees.LastName	FirstName
Hoover	Accounting	Calderon	Sean
Hoover	Accounting	Rivas	Philip
Hoover	Accounting	Serrano	Craig
Hoover	Accounting	West	Jeffrey
Holloway	Executive	Holloway	Martin
Fuentes	Human Resources	Guerra	Chris
Fuentes	Human Resources	James	Kayla
Underwood	Marketing	Carey	Alan
Underwood	Marketing	Hopper	Peggy
Underwood	Marketing	Mckenzie	Jesse
Underwood	Marketing	Windsor	Romeo
Cabrera	Production	Bryant	Pauline
Cabrera	Production	Bryant	Phillip
Cabrera	Production	Clayton	Shawn
Cabrera	Production	Petersen	Todd
Cabrera	Production	Summers	Douglas
Roth	Purchasing	Ruiz	Marshall
Perez	Research	Fredrick	Lisa
Perez	Research	Wells	Samantha

f. Save the query with the name **ManagerList**, then close it.

g. Add your name as a new record to the Employees table with reasonable Salary and Dependents values, **Information Systems** as the Department, and **3** for the ManagerID value, then close the Employees table.

h. Compact and close the IL_AC_9_ SupportDesk.accdb database, then close Access.

Independent Challenge 1

As the manager of Riverwalk, a multispecialty health clinic, you have created a database to manage nurse and doctor schedules to efficiently handle patient visits. In this exercise, you will create left outer joins to query for nurses and providers who have not been assigned to the schedule.

a. Start Access, open the IL_AC_9-3.accdb database from the location where you store your Data Files, then save it as **IL_AC_9_Riverwalk**. Enable content if prompted.

b. Open the Relationships window and change the relationship between the Nurses and ScheduleItems tables to be a left outer join that includes ALL records from the Nurses table even if there are no related records in the ScheduleItems table, as shown in **FIGURE 9-17**.

FIGURE 9-17

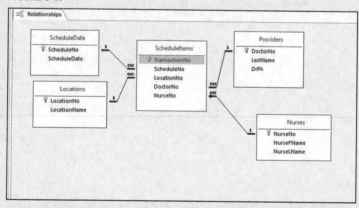

Independent Challenge 1 (continued)

   c. Save and close the Relationships window, then start a new query in Query Design view using the Nurses and ScheduleItems tables.

   d. Add the NurseFName and NurseLName fields from the Nurses table and the TransactionNo field from the ScheduleItems table.

   e. Add **Is Null** criteria to the TransactionNo field, then view the query. It should select one record.

   f. Save the query with the name **NursesWithoutScheduleItems**, then close it.

   g. Add your name as a new record in the Providers table with the DrPA value of **MD**, then start a new query in Query Design View using the ScheduleItems and Providers tables.

   h. Modify the join line to be a left outer join to select ALL records from the Providers table even if there are no related records in the ScheduleItems table.

   i. Select the LastName from the Providers table and the TransactionNo field from the ScheduleItems table.

   j. Add **Is Null** criteria to the TransactionNo field, then view the query. It should select two records, one of which contains your last name.

   k. Save the query with the name **ProvidersWithoutScheduleItems**, then close it.

   l. Consider the difference between specifying a left outer join between two tables in the Relationships window versus specifying a left outer join between tables in Query Design View, and be prepared to discuss the difference in class.

   m. Compact and close the IL_AC_9_Riverwalk.accdb database, then close Access.

Independent Challenge 2

You are working for a city to coordinate a series of community-wide preparedness activities. You have created a database to track the activities and volunteers who are attending the activities. In this exercise, you will create a left outer join to identify those activities that have been planned but for which no volunteer attendance has been recorded.

   a. Start Access, open the IL_AC_9-4.accdb database from the location where you store your Data Files, then save it as **IL_AC_9_Volunteers**. Enable content if prompted.

   b. In the Relationships window, modify the relationship between the Activities table and the Attendance table to be a left outer join to include ALL records in the Activities table even if there are no related records in the Attendance table, as shown in **FIGURE 9-18**.

FIGURE 9-18

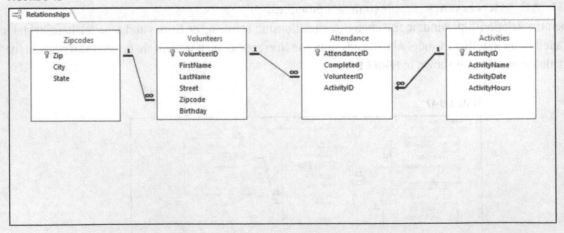

Creating Action Queries

Independent Challenge 2 (continued)

c. In the Edit Relationships dialog box of the relationship between the Activities and Attendance tables, consider the Cascade Update Related Fields and Cascade Delete Related Records options on the one-to-many relationship, as compared to the Update and Delete action queries. Be prepared to discuss how these features are similar and different in class.

d. Save and close the Relationships window.

e. Start a new query in Query Design View with the Attendance and Activities tables.

f. Add the AttendanceID field from the Attendance table and the ActivityName field from the Activities table.

g. Add **Is Null** criteria to the AttendanceID field, then display the datasheet. It should have 15 records.

h. Save the query with the name **ActivitiesWithoutAttendance**, then close it.

i. Add your name as a new record to the Volunteers table. Use realistic but fictitious data for the other fields of the record and use **66210** for the Zipcode.

j. Compact and close the IL_AC_9_Volunteers.accdb database, then exit Access 2019.

Visual Workshop

Start Access, open the IL_AC_9-5.accdb database from the location where you store your Data Files, then save it as **IL_AC_9_CollegeCourses**. Enable content if prompted. Add your name as a new record to the Students table using a StudentID of **777** and fictitious but realistic data for the rest of the record. Close the Students table. Create a new query in Query Design View using the Students and Enrollments table. Create a left outer join on the join line to select ALL students even if there are no related records in the Enrollments table. Select all the fields from the Students table and the EnrollmentID field from the Enrollments table. Use **Is Null** criteria in the EnrollmentID field, save the query with the name **StudentsWithoutEnrollments**, display it in Datasheet View, then widen all columns to show all data, as shown in **FIGURE 9-19**. Close the StudentsWithoutEnrollments query, compact and close the IL_AC_9_CollegeCourses.accdb database, then close Access 2019.

FIGURE 9-19

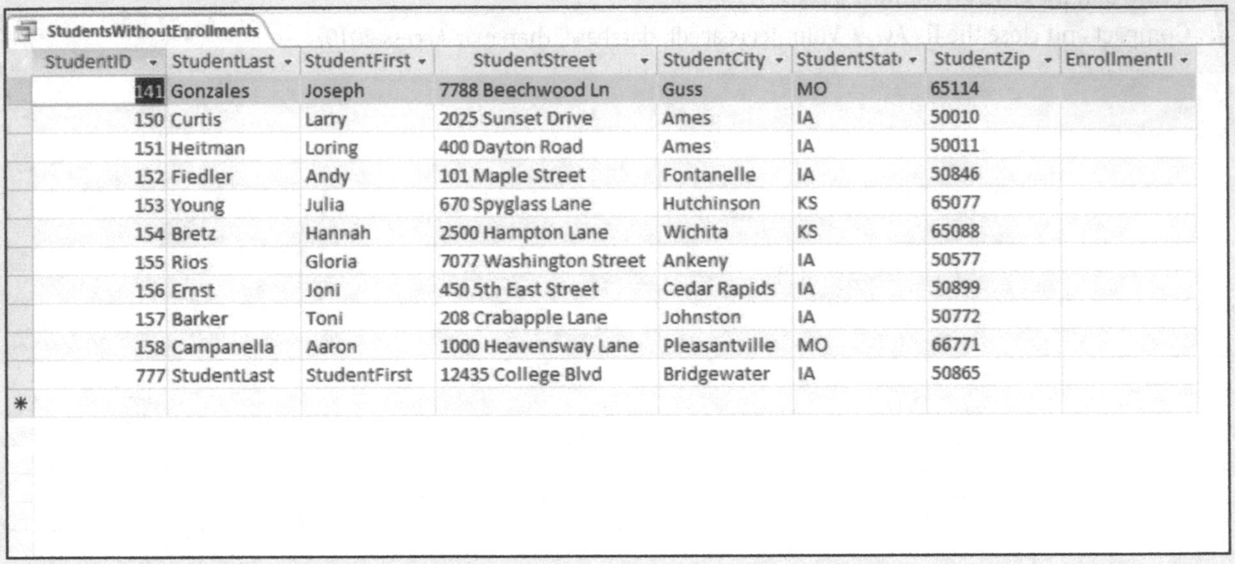

StudentID	StudentLast	StudentFirst	StudentStreet	StudentCity	StudentStat	StudentZip	EnrollmentI
141 Gonzales	Joseph	7788 Beechwood Ln	Guss	MO	65114	
150 Curtis	Larry	2025 Sunset Drive	Ames	IA	50010	
151 Heitman	Loring	400 Dayton Road	Ames	IA	50011	
152 Fiedler	Andy	101 Maple Street	Fontanelle	IA	50846	
153 Young	Julia	670 Spyglass Lane	Hutchinson	KS	65077	
154 Bretz	Hannah	2500 Hampton Lane	Wichita	KS	65088	
155 Rios	Gloria	7077 Washington Street	Ankeny	IA	50577	
156 Ernst	Joni	450 5th East Street	Cedar Rapids	IA	50899	
157 Barker	Toni	208 Crabapple Lane	Johnston	IA	50772	
158 Campanella	Aaron	1000 Heavensway Lane	Pleasantville	MO	66771	
777 StudentLast	StudentFirst	12435 College Blvd	Bridgewater	IA	50865	

Creating Macros

CASE You are working with Lydia Snyder, vice president of operations at JCL Talent, to build a research database to manage industry, company, and job data. In this module, you'll create and modify macros that make the database application easier to use and automate repetitive tasks.

Module Objectives

After completing this module, you will be able to:

- Understand macros
- Create a macro
- Modify actions and arguments
- Assign a macro to a command button
- Use Macro If statements
- Use the Macro Else clause
- Create a data macro
- Troubleshoot macros

Files You Will Need

IL_AC_10-1.accdb

IL_AC_10-2.accdb

IL_AC_10-3.accdb

IL_AC_10-4.accdb

IL_AC_10-5.accdb

Understand Macros

Learning
Outcomes
• Describe the
benefits of macros
• Define macro
terminology
• Describe Macro
Design View
components

A **macro** is a database object that stores actions to complete Access tasks. Repetitive Access tasks, such as printing several reports or opening and maximizing a form, are good candidates for a macro. Automating routine tasks by using macros builds efficiency, accuracy, and flexibility into your database. **CASE** ▶ *Lydia Snyder encourages you to study the major benefits of using macros, macro terminology, and the components of Macro Design View before building your first macro.*

DETAILS

The major benefits of using macros include the following:
- Saving time by automating routine tasks
- Increasing accuracy by ensuring that tasks are executed consistently
- Improving the functionality and ease of use of forms by using macros connected to command buttons
- Ensuring data accuracy in forms by using macros to respond to data entry errors
- Automating data transfers such as collecting data from Excel
- Helping users by responding to their interactions within a form

Macro terminology:
- A **macro** is an Access object that stores a series of actions to perform one or more tasks.
- **Macro Design View** is the window in which you create a macro. **FIGURE 10-1** shows Macro Design View with an OpenForm action. See **TABLE 10-1** for a description of the Macro Design View components.
- Each task that you want the macro to perform is called an **action**. A macro may contain one or more actions.
- **Arguments** are properties of an action that provide additional information on how the action should execute.
- A **conditional expression** is an expression resulting in either a true or a false answer that determines whether a macro action will execute. Conditional expressions are used in **If statements**.
- An **event** is something that happens to a form, window, toolbar, or control—such as the click of a command button or an entry in a field—that can be used to initiate the execution of a macro.
- A **submacro** is a collection of actions within a macro object that allows you to name and create multiple, separate macros within a single macro object. Submacros are referenced in macro lists using a Macroname.Submacroname syntax.

FIGURE 10-1: Macro Design View with OpenForm action

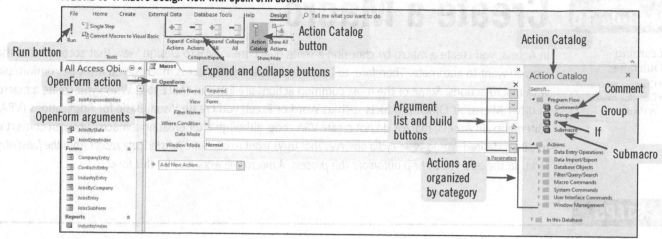

TABLE 10-1: Macro Design View components

component	description
Action Catalog	Lists all available macro actions organized by category. Use the Search box to narrow the number of macro actions to a particular subject.
Program Flow	Contains useful tools to comment and organize your code, including Comment, Group, If, and Submacro.
Comment	Provides a way to document the macro with explanatory text.
Group	Allows for actions and program flow to be grouped in a named, collapsible block that is not executed.
If	Provides a way to add a conditional expression that is evaluated as either true or false to a macro. If true, the macro action is executed. If false, the macro action is skipped. If statements in Access 2019 may contain Else If and Else clauses.
Submacro	Allows for a named collection of macro actions that are executed using the RunMacro or OnError macro actions.
Arguments	Lists required and optional arguments for the selected action.
Run button	Runs the selected macro.
Expand and Collapse buttons	Allows you to expand or collapse the macro actions to show or hide their arguments.

Create a Macro

In Access, you create a macro by choosing a series of actions in Macro Design View that accomplishes the job you want to automate. Therefore, to become proficient with Access macros, you must be comfortable with macro actions. Some of the most common actions are listed in **TABLE 10-2**. When you create a macro in other Microsoft Office products such as Word or Excel, you create Visual Basic for Applications (VBA) statements. In Access, macros do not create VBA code, although after creating a macro, you can convert it to VBA if desired. **CASE** *Lydia observes that users want to open the JobsByState report from the JobsEntry form, so she asks you to help automate this process. A macro will work well for this task.*

STEPS

TROUBLE
If you do not enable
content, your
macros will not run.

1. **sam↓ Start Access, open the IL_AC_10-1.accdb database from the location where you store your Data Files, save it as IL_AC_10_Jobs, enable content if prompted, click the Create tab, then click the Macro button**

   Macro Design View opens, ready for you to choose your first action.

TROUBLE
If you choose the
wrong macro action,
click the Delete
button ☒ in the
upper-right corner
of the macro action
block and try again.

2. **Click the Action list arrow, then scroll and click OpenReport**

   The OpenReport action is now the first action in the macro, and the arguments that further define the OpenReport action appear in the action block. The **action block** organizes all the arguments for a current action and is visually highlighted with a rectangle and gray background. You can expand or collapse the action block to view or hide details by clicking the Collapse/Expand button to the left of the action name or the Expand and Collapse buttons on the Design tab in Macro Design View.

   The **OpenReport action** has three required arguments: Report Name, View, and Window Mode. View and Window Mode have default values. If you start working with the OpenReport action's arguments but do not select a Report Name, the word *Required* is shown, indicating that you must select a choice for that argument. The Filter Name and Where Condition arguments are optional as indicated by their blank boxes.

QUICK TIP
Hover over any
macro action or
argument to see
a ScreenTip of
information about
that item.

3. **Click the Report Name argument list arrow, then click JobsByState**

   All the report objects in the current database appear in the Report Name argument list, making it easy to choose the report you want.

4. **Click the View argument list arrow, then click Report if it is not already selected**

   Your screen should look like **FIGURE 10-2**. Macros can contain one or many actions. In this case, the macro has only one action.

5. **Click the Save button 🖫 on the Quick Access toolbar, type OpenJobsByStateReport in the Macro Name text box, click OK, right-click the OpenJobsByStateReport macro tab, then click Close**

   The Navigation Pane lists the OpenJobsByStateReport object in the Macros group.

QUICK TIP
To print a macro
from Macro Design
View, click the File
tab, click Print, click
the Print button,
then click OK.

6. **Double-click the OpenJobsByStateReport macro in the Navigation Pane to run the macro**

   The JobsByState report opens in Report View.

7. **Close the JobsByState report**

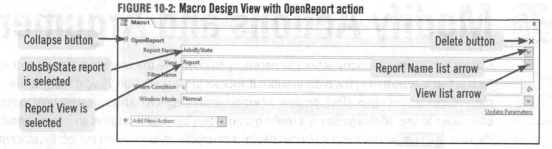

FIGURE 10-2: Macro Design View with OpenReport action

- Collapse button
- JobsByState report is selected
- Report View is selected
- Delete button
- Report Name list arrow
- View list arrow

TABLE 10-2: Common macro actions

subject area	macro action	description
Data Entry Operations	DeleteRecord	Deletes the current record
	SaveRecord	Saves the current record
Data Import/Export	EMailDatabaseObject	Sends the specified database object through Outlook with specified email settings
	ImportExportSpreadsheet*	Imports or exports the spreadsheet you specify
	ImportExportText*	Imports or exports the text file you specify
Database Objects	GoToControl	Moves the focus (where you are currently typing or clicking) to a specific field or control
	GoToRecord	Makes a specified record the current record
	OpenForm	Opens a form in Form View, Design View, Print Preview, or Datasheet View
	OpenReport	Opens a report in Report View, Design View, or Print Preview, or prints the report
	OpenTable	Opens a table in Datasheet View, Design View, or Print Preview
	SetValue*	Sets the value of a field, control, or property
Filter/Query/Search	ApplyFilter	Restricts the number of records that appear in the resulting form or report by applying limiting criteria
	FindRecord	Finds the first record that meets the criteria
	OpenQuery	Opens a select or crosstab query; runs an action query
Macro Commands	RunCode	Runs a Visual Basic function (a series of programming statements that does a calculation or comparison and returns a value)
	RunMacro	Runs a macro or attaches a macro to a custom menu command
	StopMacro	Stops the currently running macro
System Commands	Beep	Sounds a beep tone through the computer's speaker
	PrintOut*	Prints the active object, such as a datasheet, report, form, or module
	SendKeys*	Sends keystrokes directly to Microsoft Access or to an active Windows application
User Interface Commands	MessageBox	Displays a message box containing a warning or an informational message
	ShowToolbar*	Displays or hides a given toolbar
Window Management	CloseWindow	Closes a window
	MaximizeWindow	Enlarges the active window to fill the Access window

*You must click the Show All Actions button on the ribbon for these actions to appear.

Modify Actions and Arguments

Macros can contain as many actions as necessary to complete the process that you want to automate. Each action is evaluated in the order in which it appears in Macro Design View, starting at the top. Whereas some macro actions open, close, preview, or export data or objects, others are used only to make the database easier to use. **MessageBox** is a useful macro action because it displays an informational message to the user. **CASE** ▶ *Lydia asks if you can display a descriptive message when the JobsByState report opens to explain how the data is sorted. The MessageBox macro action will handle this request.*

STEPS

1. **Right-click the** OpenJobsByStateReport macro **in the Navigation Pane, then click** Design View **on the shortcut menu**

   The OpenJobsByStateReport macro opens in Macro Design View.

2. **Click the** Add New Action list arrow, **scroll, then click** MessageBox

   Each action has its own arguments that further clarify what the action does.

3. **Click the** Message argument box **in the action block, then type** sorted by state, city, company, and starting salary

   The Message argument determines what text appears in the message box. By default, the Beep argument is set to "Yes" and the Type argument is set to "None."

4. **Click the** Type argument list arrow **in the action block, then click** Information

   The Type argument determines which icon appears in the dialog box the MessageBox action creates.

5. **Click the** Title argument box **in the action block, then type** Sort information...

   Your screen should look like **FIGURE 10-3**. The Title argument specifies what text is displayed in the title bar of the resulting dialog box. If you leave the Title argument blank, the title bar of the resulting dialog box displays "Microsoft Access."

6. **Save the macro, then click the** Run button **in the Tools group**

   If your speakers are turned on, you should hear a beep, then the message box appears, as shown in **FIGURE 10-4**.

7. **Click** OK **in the dialog box, close the** JobsByState report, **then save and close Macro Design View**

FIGURE 10-3: Adding the MessageBox action

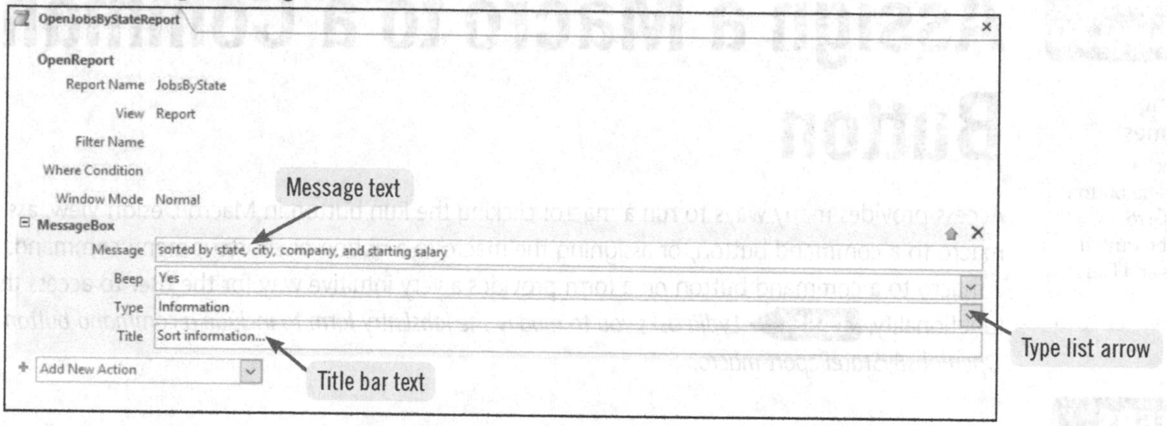

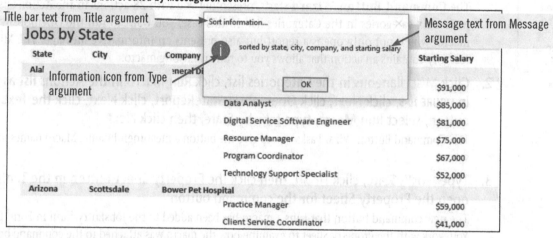

FIGURE 10-4: Dialog box created by MessageBox action

Assigning a macro to a key combination

You can assign a key combination such as SHIFT+CTRL+L to a macro by creating a macro with the name **AutoKeys**. Enter the key combination for the submacro action's name. Use + for SHIFT, % for ALT, and ^ for CTRL. Enclose special keys such as F3 in {curly braces}. For example, to assign a macro to SHIFT+CTRL+L, use +^L as the submacro name. To assign a macro to SHIFT+F3, use +{F3} as the submacro name. Any key combination assignments you make in the AutoKeys macro override those that Access has already specified. Therefore, check the Keyboard Shortcuts information in the Microsoft Access Help system to make sure that the AutoKeys assignment you are creating doesn't override an existing Access quick keystroke that may be used for another purpose.

Assign a Macro to a Command Button

Learning
Outcomes
• Connect a
 command button
 to a macro
• Describe trusted
 folders and files

Access provides many ways to run a macro: clicking the Run button in Macro Design View, assigning the macro to a command button, or assigning the macro to a ribbon or shortcut menu command. Assigning a macro to a command button on a form provides a very intuitive way for the user to access the macro's functionality. **CASE** ▶ *Lydia asks you to modify the JobsEntry form to include a command button to run the OpenJobsByStateReport macro.*

STEPS

QUICK TIP
Be sure the Use
Control Wizards
button 📄 is
selected. To find
it, click the More
button 📄 in the
Controls group on
the Design tab.

1. **Right-click the** JobsEntry form **in the Navigation Pane, click** Design View, **use ✛ to expand the Form Footer about 0.5", click** Button 📼 **in the Controls group, then click at about the 1" mark on the horizontal ruler in the Form Footer section**

   The **Command Button Wizard** starts, presenting you with 28 actions in the Actions list organized within six categories in the Categories list. In this case, you want to run the OpenJobsByStateReport macro, which not only opens a report but also presents an informative message. The Miscellaneous category contains an action that allows you to run an existing macro.

2. **Click** Miscellaneous **in the Categories list, click** Run Macro **in the Actions list as shown in** FIGURE 10-5, **click** Next, **click** OpenJobsByStateReport, **click** Next, **click the** Text option button, **select** Run Macro, **type** Jobs by State, **then click** Next

   The Command Button Wizard asks you to give the button a meaningful name. Macro names may not have spaces.

3. **Type** JobsByState, **click** Finish, **then click the** Property Sheet button **in the Tools group to open the Property Sheet for the command button**

   The new command button that runs a macro has been added to the JobsEntry form in Form Design View. You work with the Property Sheet to examine how the macro was attached to the command button.

4. **Click the** Event tab **in the Property Sheet, then note that the On Click property contains [Embedded Macro]**

   The OpenJobsByStateReport macro was attached to the **On Click property** of this command button. In other words, the macro runs when the user clicks the command button. To make sure that the new command button works as intended, you view the form in Form View and test the command button.

5. **Close the** Property Sheet, **click the** View button 📧 **to switch to Form View, click the** Jobs by State command button **in the Form Footer section, click** OK **in the message box, then close the** JobsByState report

   The JobsEntry form with the new command button should look like FIGURE 10-6. It's common to put command buttons in the Form Footer so that users have a consistent location to find them.

6. **Save and close the** JobsEntry form

FIGURE 10-5: Adding a command button to run a macro

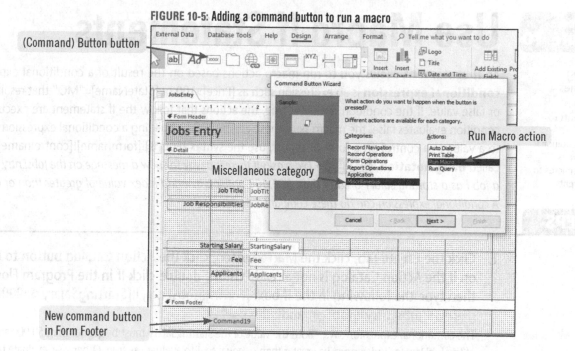

(Command) Button button

Miscellaneous category

Run Macro action

New command button in Form Footer

FIGURE 10-6: JobsEntry form with new command button

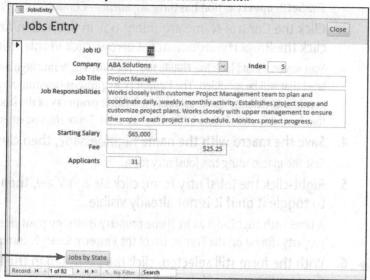

New command button in Form Footer

Using a trusted database and setting up a trusted folder

A **trusted database** allows you to run macros and Visual Basic for Applications code (VBA). By default, a database is not trusted. To trust a database, click the Enable Content button on the Security Warning bar each time you open a database. To permanently trust a database, store the database in a **trusted folder**. To create a trusted folder, open the Options dialog box from the File tab, click the Trust Center, click the Trust Center Settings button, click the Trusted Locations option, click the Add new location button, then browse to and choose the folder you want to trust.

Use Macro If Statements

Learning Outcomes
• Apply If statements to macros
• Enter conditional expressions
• Attach macros to form events

An **If statement** allows you to run macro actions based on the result of a conditional expression. A **conditional expression** is an expression such as [Price]>100 or [StateName]="MO" that results in a true or false value. If the condition evaluates true, the actions that follow the If statement are executed. If the condition evaluates false, the macro skips those actions. When building a conditional expression that refers to a value in a control on a form or report, use the syntax [Forms]![formname]![controlname], which is called **bang notation.** **CASE** ▸ *Lydia asks if there is a way to show a message on the JobsEntry form when a job has a starting salary greater than $50,000 and job demand index value of greater than or equal to 4. A conditional expression can do these comparisons.*

STEPS

1. **Click the Create tab, click the Macro button, click the Action Catalog button to toggle it on if the Action Catalog is not already visible, double-click If in the Program Flow area, then type the following in the If box: [Forms]![JobsEntry]![StartingSalary]>50000 And [Forms]![JobsEntry]![JobDemandIndex]>=4**

   The conditional expression says, "Both the value of the StartingSalary must be greater than 50,000 and the value of the JobDemandIndex must be greater than or equal to 4 to evaluate as true. Otherwise, evaluate false." Given the expression is built with the **And operator**, both parts must be true for any actions nested within the If statement to run. Using the **Or operator** would mean that only one part of the expression would have to be true.

2. **Click the Add New Action list arrow in the If block, then scroll and click SetProperty**

   The **SetProperty** action has three arguments—Control Name, Property, and Value.

3. **Click the Control Name argument box in the Action Arguments pane, type HighLabel, click the Property argument list arrow, click Visible, click the Value box, then type True**

   Your screen should look like **FIGURE 10-7**. The **Control Name** argument must match the **Name property** of the label that will be modified. The **Property argument** determines what property is being modified. The **Value argument** determines the value of the **Visible property** of the label. For properties such as the Visible property that have only two choices in the Property Sheet, Yes or No, you enter a value of False for No and True for Yes.

4. **Save the macro with the name HighMessage, then close Macro Design View**

   Test the macro using the JobsEntry form.

5. **Right-click the JobsEntry form, click Design View, then click the Property Sheet button to toggle it on if it is not already visible**

   A label with HighLabel as its Name property is already positioned in the Form Header section. Its Visible property (found on the Format tab of the Property Sheet) is currently set to No.

6. **With the form still selected, click the Event tab in the Property Sheet, click the On Current list arrow, then click HighMessage**

   An **event** is a specific activity that occurs within the database, such as clicking a command button, moving from record to record, editing data, or opening or closing a form. The **On Current** event of the form occurs when focus moves from one record to another. By attaching the HighMessage macro to the form's On Current event, the macro will run every time you move to a new record in the form.

7. **Save the form, switch to Form View, then navigate to the second record**

   The macro runs twice, for the first record where the starting salary value of $45,000 evaluates false, and also for the second record where the starting salary of $65,000 and job demand index value of 4 evaluate true, which displays the High Wage / High Demand! label as shown in **FIGURE 10-8**.

8. **Navigate through five more records, observing the label, Index value, and Starting Salary value**

   You need to modify the macro so that the label's Visible property is set back to False when the Index value is less than 4 or the Starting Salary value is less than or equal to $50,000. You complete that task in the next lesson.

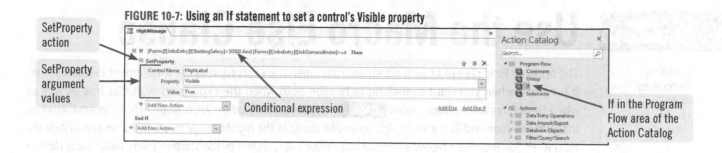

FIGURE 10-7: Using an If statement to set a control's Visible property

SetProperty action

SetProperty argument values

Conditional expression

If in the Program Flow area of the Action Catalog

FIGURE 10-8: Running the HighMessage macro

HighLabel

High Wage / High Demand!

Job demand index value is >= 4

Jobs Entry

Job ID	31
Company	Accent Group
	Index	4
Job Title	Customer Service
Job Responsibilities	Checks and reports quality findings to internal client as appropriate. Interfaces with multiple functional areas to investigate cases and acquire information. Interprets evidence from multiple tools and systems to determine legitimacy of customer behavior across multiple products.
Starting Salary	$65,000
Fee	$25.25
Applicants	4

Starting salary value is >$50,000

Close

Access

Use the Macro Else Clause

The optional **Else clause** of an If statement runs when the expression in the If statement evaluates false. It is helpful when you want something to happen both when the expression evaluates true as well as when the expression evaluates false. **CASE** *Lydia has reviewed the High Wage / High Demand! label on the JobsEntry form and likes it so far. Adding an Else clause to the HighMessage macro will allow you to hide the label when you move to a record where the Index value is less than 4 or the Starting Salary value is less than or equal to $50,000.*

STEPS

1. **Right-click the HighMessage macro in the Navigation Pane, click Design View on the shortcut menu, click anywhere in the If block to activate it, then click the Add Else link in the lower-right corner of the If block**

   The **Else** portion of an If statement allows you to run a different set of macro actions if the conditional expression evaluates False. In this case, you want to set the Value of the Visible property of the HighLabel control to False if either part of the conditional expression evaluates False.

QUICK TIP
Use the Move up
and Move down
buttons as necessary
to move macro
actions in Macro
Design View.

2. **Add the same SetProperty action and arguments to the Else block, but enter False for the Value argument, as shown in FIGURE 10-9**

   With the second action edited, the macro will now turn the label's Visible property to True (Yes) or False (No), depending on how the expression evaluates. Note that the entire If – Then – Else block is included between the If and End If statements in the macro.

3. **Save and close the HighMessage macro**

   You are ready to test the updated macro.

4. **Click the First record button ◄ in the JobsEntry form, then click the Next record button ▶ to navigate through 17 records**

   The HighMessage macro runs each time you move from record to record. The macro evaluates the values in the StartingSalary and JobDemandIndex text boxes because you attached it to the On Current event of the form. Other common event properties are shown in **TABLE 10-3**. All event properties are found on the Event tab of the Property Sheet for the selected object or control.

5. **Save and close the JobsEntry form**

FIGURE 10-9: Adding an Else portion to an If block

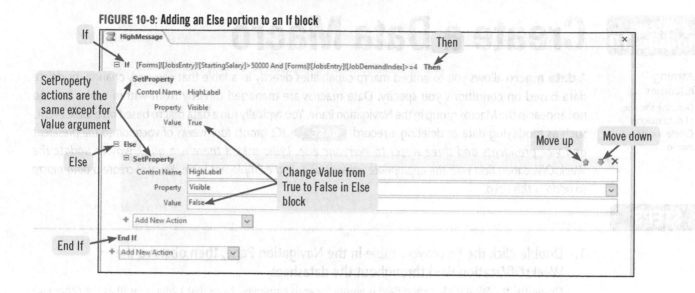

TABLE 10-3: Common event properties

item	event property	runs...
Form	On Current	when the focus moves from record to record
Form, report	On Load	when a form or report is initially loaded
Form, report, control	On Click	when a form, report, or control is clicked
Form, bound control	Before Update	before a record (form) or field is updated
Form, bound control	After Update	after a record (form) or field value is updated
Form, bound control	On Dirty	when the contents of the specified control change
Form, bound control	On Got Focus	when a form or control gets the focus
Form, report	On Close	when the form or report closes

Create a Data Macro

A **data macro** allows you to embed macro capabilities directly in a table that can add, change, or delete data based on conditions you specify. Data macros are managed directly from within tables and do not appear in the Macros group in the Navigation Pane. You typically run a data macro based on a table event, such as modifying data or deleting a record. **CASE** *JCL grants four weeks of vacation to the president and vice presidents and three weeks to everyone else. Lydia asks if there is a quick way to update the WeeksOfVacation field with the appropriate value, 3 or 4, in the Employees table. You will create a data macro to address this need.*

STEPS

1. **Double-click the** Employees table **in the Navigation Pane, then observe the WeeksOfVacation field throughout the datasheet**

   Currently, the WeeksOfVacation field is empty for each employee. Note that Lydia (as well as the other vice presidents of the company) reports to SupervisorNo 100000, who is Rory Gonzales, the CEO of JCL.

2. **Right-click the** Employees table tab, **click** Design View **on the shortcut menu, click the Create Data Macros button in the Field, Record & Table Events group, click** After Insert, **then click the** Action Catalog button **in the Show/Hide group if it is not already open**

   In this case, you chose the After Insert event, which runs after a new record is entered. See **TABLE 10-4** for more information on table events. Creating a data macro is very similar to creating a regular macro. You add the logic and macro actions needed to complete the task at hand.

3. **Double-click the** ForEachRecord data block **in the Action Catalog, click the** For Each Record In **list arrow, click** Employees **in the list, click the** Where Condition **text box, type** [SupervisorNo]<>"100000", **double-click the** EditRecord data block **in the Action Catalog, double-click the** SetField data action **in the Action Catalog, click the** Name box **in the SetField block, type** WeeksOfVacation, **click the** Value box **in the SetField block, then type** 3, **as shown in FIGURE 10-10**

   The <> symbols mean "is not equal to" so all employees who do not directly report to Rory Gonzales, EmployeeNo 100000, should be assigned three weeks of vacation. The EmployeeNo field is defined with a Short Text, not a Number data type, so "quotation marks" are used to surround the field value of "100000". Test the new data macro by adding a new record.

4. **Click the** Save button 🖫, **click the** Close button **on the ribbon, click the** View button 🎛 **to display the datasheet, click** Yes **to save the table, click the** New button **in the Records group, enter a new record as shown in FIGURE 10-11 with your name, then press TAB to move to a new record**

   The macro is triggered by the After Insert event of the table, and the WeeksOfVacation field is automatically updated to 3 for the new record and all other records with a SupervisorNo not equal to "100000", as shown in **FIGURE 10-11**.

5. **Right-click the** Employees table tab, **then click** Close **on the shortcut menu**

   New or edited data is automatically saved when you move from record to record or close a database object.

FIGURE 10-10: Creating a data macro

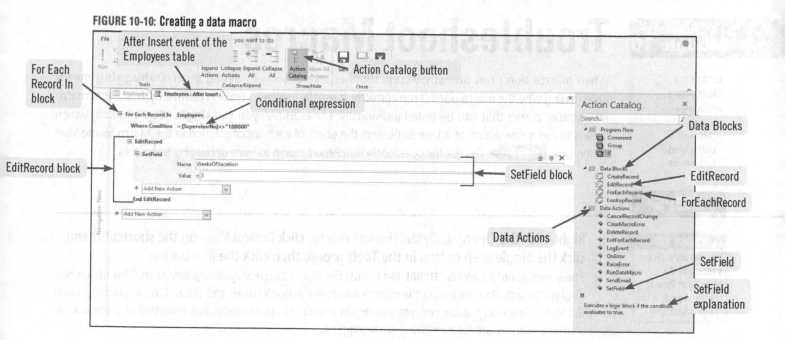

For Each Record In block

After Insert event of the Employees table

Action Catalog button

Conditional expression

EditRecord block

SetField block

Data Blocks

Data Actions

EditRecord

ForEachRecord

SetField

SetField explanation

FIGURE 10-11: Running a data macro

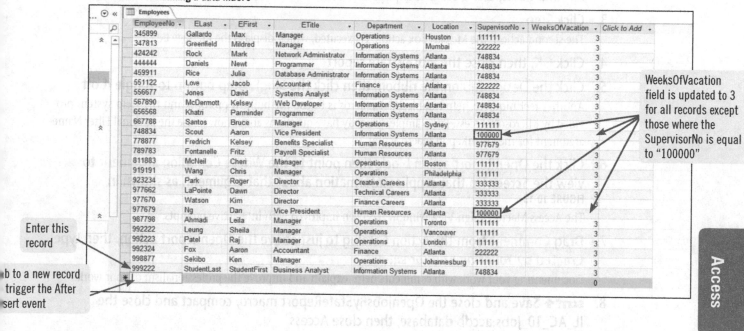

Enter this record

Tab to a new record to trigger the After Insert event

WeeksOfVacation field is updated to 3 for all records except those where the SupervisorNo is equal to "100000"

TABLE 10-4: Table events

table event	runs...
After Insert	after a new record has been inserted into the table
After Update	after an existing record has been changed
After Delete	after an existing record has been deleted
Before Delete	before a record is deleted, to help the user validate or cancel the deletion
Before Change	before a record is changed, to help the user validate or cancel the edits

Troubleshoot Macros

Learning
Outcomes
• Single step a
  macro
• Describe
  debugging
  techniques

When macros don't run properly, Access supplies several tools to debug them. **Debugging** means determining why the macro doesn't run correctly. It usually involves breaking down a dysfunctional macro into smaller pieces that can be tested individually. For example, you can **single step** a macro, which means to run it one action at a time to observe the effect of each specific action in the Macro Single Step dialog box. **CASE** *You use the OpenJobsByStateReport macro to learn debugging techniques.*

STEPS

QUICK TIP
You can right-click
a macro in the
Navigation Pane to
copy and paste it to
create a backup.

1. **Right-click the** OpenJobsByStateReport macro, **click** Design View **on the shortcut menu, click the** Single Step button **in the Tools group, then click the** Run button

   The screen should look like **FIGURE 10-12**, with the Macro Single Step dialog box open. This dialog box displays information, including the macro's name, the action's name, and the action's arguments. From the Macro Single Step dialog box, you can step into the next macro action, halt execution of the macro, or continue running the macro without single stepping.

2. **Click** Step **in the Macro Single Step dialog box**

   Stepping into the second action lets the first action run and pauses the macro at the second action. The Macro Single Step dialog box now displays information about the second action.

3. **Click** Step

   The second action, the MessageBox action, is executed, which displays the message box.

4. **Click** OK, **then close the** JobsByState **report**

5. **Click the** Design tab **on the ribbon, then click the** Single Step button **to toggle it off**

   Another technique to help troubleshoot macros is to use the built-in prompts and the Help system provided by Microsoft Access. For example, you may have questions about how to use the optional Filter Name argument for the OpenReport macro action.

6. **Click the** OpenReport action block, **then point to the** Where Condition argument **to view the ScreenTip that supplies information about that argument, as shown in** FIGURE 10-13

   The Access Macro Design View window has been improved with interactive prompts.

7. **Drag** Comment **from the Action Catalog to just above the OpenReport action, then type** Created by *Your Name* on *current date*

   Documenting your work with comments helps explain and improve the professionalism of your work.

8. **sam↑ Save and close the** OpenJobsByStateReport macro, **compact and close the** IL_AC_10_Jobs.accdb database, **then close Access**

FIGURE 10-12: Single stepping through a macro

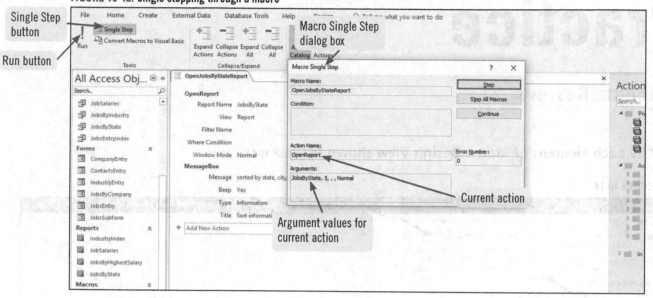

Single Step button

Run button

Macro Single Step dialog box

Current action

Argument values for current action

FIGURE 10-13: Viewing ScreenTips

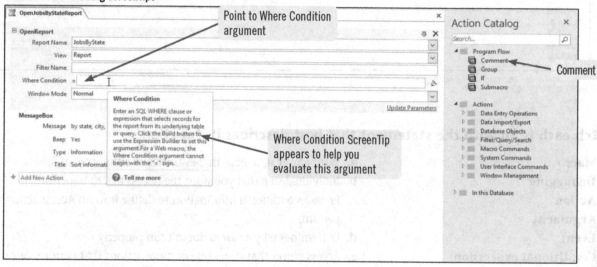

Point to Where Condition argument

Comment

Where Condition ScreenTip appears to help you evaluate this argument

Practice

Concepts Review

Identify each element of Macro Design View shown in FIGURE 10-14.

FIGURE 10-14

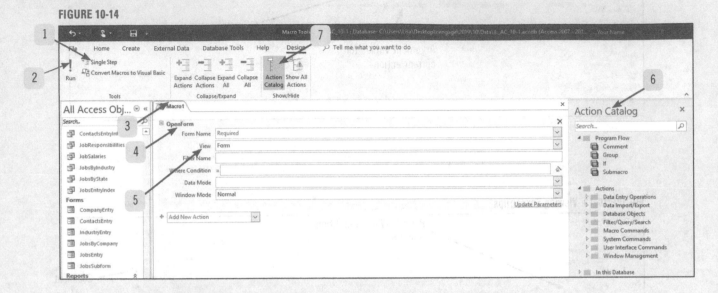

Match each term with the statement that best describes its function.

8. Macro
9. Debugging
10. Action
11. Argument
12. Event
13. Conditional expression

a. Part of an If statement that evaluates as either true or false
b. Individual step that you want the Access macro to perform
c. Provides additional information to define how an Access action will perform
d. Determines why a macro doesn't run properly
e. Access object that stores one or more actions that perform one or more tasks
f. Specific action that occurs within the database, such as clicking a button or opening a form

Select the best answer from the list of choices.

14. Which of the following is *not* a major benefit of using a macro?
    a. To save time by automating routine tasks
    b. To ensure consistency in executing routine or complex tasks
    c. To redesign the relationships among the tables of the database
    d. To make the database more flexible or easy to use

15. Which of the following best describes the process of creating an Access macro?

a. Open Macro Design View and add actions, arguments, and If statements to accomplish the desired task.

b. Use the single step recorder to record clicks and keystrokes as you complete a task.

c. Use the Macro Wizard to determine which tasks are done most frequently.

d. Use the macro recorder to record clicks and keystrokes as you complete a task.

16. Which of the following would *not* be a way to run a macro?

a. Double-click a macro action within the Macro Design View window.

b. Assign the macro to an event of a control on a form.

c. Assign the macro to a command button on a form.

d. Click the Run Macro button on the Database Tools tab.

17. Which of the following is *not* a reason to run a macro in single step mode?

a. You want to change the arguments of a macro while it runs.

b. You want to run only a few of the actions of a macro.

c. You want to observe the effect of each macro action individually.

d. You want to debug a macro that isn't working properly.

18. Which of the following is *not* true of conditional expressions in If statements in macros?

a. Conditional expressions give the macro more power and flexibility.

b. Macro If statements provide for Else and Else If clauses.

c. More macro actions are available when you are also using conditional expressions.

d. Conditional expressions allow you to skip over actions when the expression evaluates as false.

19. Which example illustrates the proper syntax to refer to a specific control on a form?

a. (Forms) ! (formname) ! (controlname)

b. {Forms} ! {formname} ! (controlname)

c. [Forms] ! [formname] ! [controlname]

d. Forms ! formname. controlname

20. Which event is executed every time you move from record to record in a form?

a. New Record

b. On Current

c. On Move

d. Next Record

Skills Review

1. Understand macros.

a. Start Access, open the IL_AC_10-2.accdb database from the location where you store your Data Files, then save it as **IL_AC_10_SupportDesk**. Enable content if prompted.

b. Open the ViewReports macro in Macro Design View, then record your answers to the following questions:
   - How many macro actions are in the macro?
   - What arguments does the first action contain?
   - What values were chosen for the arguments of the first macro action?

c. Close Macro Design View for the ViewReports macro.

2. Create a macro.

a. Start a new macro in Macro Design View.

b. Add the OpenQuery action.

c. Select EmployeesByDepartment as the value for the Query Name argument.

d. Select Datasheet for the View argument.

e. Select Edit for the Data Mode argument.

f. Save the macro using **ViewEmployees** as the name.

g. Run the macro to make sure it works, close the EmployeesByDepartment query, then close the ViewEmployees macro.

3. Modify actions and arguments.

 a. Open the ViewEmployees macro in Macro Design View.

 b. Add a MessageBox action as the second action of the query.

 c. Type **Sorted by last name within department** for the Message argument.

 d. Select No for the Beep argument.

 e. Select Information for the Type argument.

 f. Type **Employee list information** for the Title argument.

 g. Save the macro, then run it to make sure the MessageBox action works as intended.

 h. Click OK in the dialog box created by the MessageBox action, close the EmployeesByDepartment query, then save and close the ViewEmployees macro.

 i. Open the ViewReports macro object in Design View.

 j. Modify the View argument for the OpenReport action for the EmployeeMasterList report from Report to **Print Preview**.

 k. Save and close the ViewReports macro.

4. Assign a macro to a command button.

 a. In Design View of the EmployeesByDepartment form, expand the height of the Form Footer section to be about 0.5" tall.

 b. Use the Command Button Wizard to add a new command button to the Form Footer section at about the 0.5" mark on the horizontal ruler. The new button should run the ViewEmployees macro.

 c. The text on the button should read **View Employees by Department**.

 d. The meaningful name for the button should be **ViewEmployees**.

 e. Save the form, then test the command button in Form View.

 f. Click OK in the message box, then close the EmployeesByDepartment query.

 g. Save and close the EmployeesByDepartment form.

5. Use Macro If Statements.

 a. Start a new macro in Macro Design View, then open the Action Catalog window if it is not already open.

 b. Double-click If in the Action Catalog pane to add an If block to the macro.

 c. Enter the following condition in the If box that tests whether the Salary value in the EmployeeMaster form is greater than or equal to $70,000: **[Forms]![EmployeeMaster]![Salary]>=70000**

 d. Add the SetProperty action to the If block.

 e. Type **BenefitLabel** in the Control Name box for the SetProperty action.

 f. Select Visible for the Property argument for the SetProperty action.

 g. Enter **True** for the Value argument, and save the macro with the name **BenefitMessage**.

6. Use the Macro Else clause.

 a. With the BenefitMessage macro still open in Design View, click the Add Else link in the lower-right corner of the If block.

 b. Enter the same SetProperty action from the If statement under the Else clause with the same values for the Control Name and Property arguments, but modify the Value property from True to **False**.

 c. Save the macro and compare it with **FIGURE 10-15** to make any necessary adjustments.

FIGURE 10-15

Skills Review (continued)

d. Add a comment to the top of the macro with your name and today's date, then close and save Macro Design View.

e. Open the EmployeeMaster form in Design View then attach the BenefitMessage macro to the On Current event property of the form.

f. Save the form and open it in Form View. Navigate through several records to test whether the label appears based on the value in the Salary text box. The label should only appear when the Salary value is greater than or equal to $70,000.

g. Close the EmployeeMaster form.

7. Create a data macro.

a. Open the Cases table in Table Design View.

b. Add a field named **DaysToResolve** with a Number data type and the following Description: **The number of days between the OpenedDate and the ResolvedDate**.

c. Delete 0 in the Default Value property of the new DaysToResolve field so that new records will not automatically have the value of 0 in this field, save the Cases table, then switch to Datasheet View to note that the DaysToResolve field is blank for every record.

d. Switch back to Table Design View, then create a data macro based on the Before Change event.

e. Insert an If block, then specify **IsNull([ResolvedDate])** for the expression, which will test to see if the ResolvedDate field has an entry. If the ResolvedDate field is empty (null), the expression will evaluate true. If the ResolvedDate field contains a value, the expression will evaluate false.

f. Click the Add Else link. Add a SetField data action and set the Name argument to **DaysToResolve** and the Value to **[ResolvedDate]-[OpenedDate]** to calculate the number of days between these dates, as shown in **FIGURE 10-16**.

g. Save and close the data macro, save the Cases table, switch to Datasheet View, then test the new data macro by entering a ResolvedDate value of **4/2/2021** in the first record (CaseID 1) and **4/3/2021** in the second record (CaseID 2).

h. Close the Cases table.

FIGURE 10-16

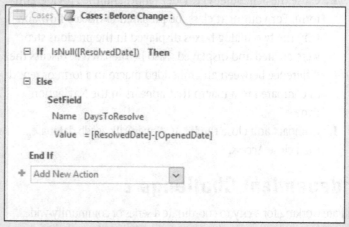

8. Troubleshoot macros.

a. Open the ViewReports macro in Macro Design View.

b. Click the Single Step button, then click the Run button.

c. Click Step three times to step through the three actions of the macro, then close all three reports.

d. Return to Macro Design View of the ViewReports macro then click the Single Step button on the Design tab to toggle off this feature.

e. Add a comment to the top of the macro with your name and today's date, then save and close the ViewReports macro.

f. Compact and close the IL_AC_10_SupportDesk.accdb database, then close Access 2019.

Independent Challenge 1

As the manager of Riverwalk, a multispecialty health clinic, you have created a database to manage nurse and doctor schedules to efficiently handle patient visits. In this exercise, you will create macros to help automate the application.

a. Start Access, open the IL_AC_10-3.accdb database from the location where you store your Data Files, then save it as **IL_AC_10_Riverwalk**. Enable content if prompted.

b. Open the ProviderEntry form in Form Design View, then expand the Form Footer to be about 0.5" in height.

c. Add a command button to the Form Footer section at about the 1" mark on the horizontal ruler. Use the Command Button Wizard, and select the Preview Report action from the Report Operations category.

d. Select the ScheduleByProvider report.

e. Use the text **Preview Schedule Report** on the command button and the meaningful name of **ScheduleReport**.

f. Select the command button and open the Property Sheet. Note that the On Click property on the Event tab of the Property Sheet shows that an [Embedded Macro] is attached to that event. Click the Build button for the On Click property to open Macro Design View for the embedded macro.

g. Modify the View property from Print Preview to Report.

h. Add a MessageBox action with the argument values shown in **FIGURE 10-17**.

FIGURE 10-17

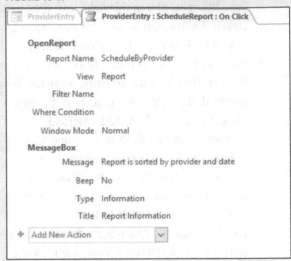

i. Save and close the embedded macro, then save the ProviderEntry form and display it in Form View.

j. Click the Preview Schedule Report button, enter **12/1/21** in the Enter Parameter Prompt dialog box, then click OK in the Report Information dialog box to display the ScheduleByProvider report.

k. Close the ScheduleByProvider report and the ProviderEntry form. For your next class, be prepared to discuss how and why the two dialog boxes displayed in the previous step were created and displayed. Also be prepared to discuss the difference between an embedded macro in a form or report as compared to a macro that appears in the Navigation Pane.

l. Compact and close the IL_AC_Riverwalk.accdb database, then close Access.

Independent Challenge 2

You are working for a city to coordinate a series of community-wide preparedness activities. You have created a database to track the activities and volunteers who are attending the activities. In this exercise, you will create macros to help automate the application.

a. Start Access, open the IL_AC_10-4.accdb database from the location where you store your Data Files, then save it as **IL_AC_10_Volunteers**. Enable content if prompted.

b. Open the Volunteers table in Design View and add a new field named **Team** with a Short Text data type.

c. Add a data macro on the After Insert event to the table that determines which value to automatically insert into the Team field based on the value in the Birthday field, as shown in **FIGURE 10-18**.
The expression **[Birthday]<(Date()-60*365.25)** determines if the person has an age greater than 60. If so, the Team value will be Gold. Date() returns the number of days

FIGURE 10-18

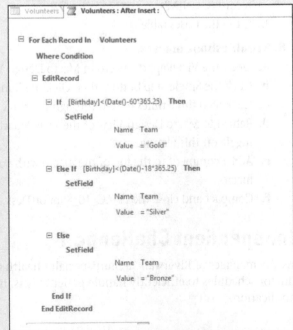

between 1/1/1900 and today (around 44,000). The expression 60*365.25 returns a value that represents the number of days in 60 years (21,915). The complete expression Date()-60*365.25 returns the difference between those two values. If the [Birthday] value (the number of days between 1/1/1900 and the Birthday) is less than the difference, the person is older than 60 years old.

The Else If clause only runs when the If clause evaluates false.

The expression **[Birthday]<(Date()-18*365.25)** determines if the person is older than 18. If so, the Team value will be Silver.

The Else clause only runs when both the If and the Else If clauses evaluate false. Birthdays that do not evaluate true for ages greater than 60 or greater than 18 are minors and are assigned a Team value of Bronze.

d. Save the data macro then switch to Datasheet View of the Volunteers table. Add your name, the school's street address, the Zipcode of **66215**, and today's date for the Birthday value, then press TAB to add a new record. All Team values should automatically update.

e. Sort the records in descending order based on the Birthday field (which should put your record on top), then scroll through the records to observe when the Team value changes from Bronze (under 18) to Silver (18 to 59 years old) and Silver to Gold (60 and over).

f. Save and close the Volunteers table.

g. Compact and close the IL_AC_10_Volunteers.accdb database, then close Access.

Visual Workshop

Start Access, open the IL_AC_10-5.accdb database from the location where you store your Data Files, then save it as **IL_AC_10_CollegeCourses**. Enable content if prompted. Develop a new macro called **GradeFilters** with the four submacros, actions, and argument values shown in **FIGURE 10-19**. Add a comment with your name and the current date to the top of the GradeFilters macro, then save and close the GradeFilters macro. Open the StudentGradeListing report in Design View and attach these submacros to the On Click event of their associated command buttons:

- **GradeFilters.GradeAorB** to the command button with the caption of A and B
- **GradeFilters.GradeC** to the command button with the caption of C
- **GradeFilters.GradeDorF** to the command button with the caption of D and F
- **GradeFilters.GradeAll** to the command button with the caption of All

Save the StudentGradeListing report and display it in Report View. Test the command buttons, close the report, compact and close the IL_AC_10_CollegeCourses.accdb database, then close Access.

FIGURE 10-19

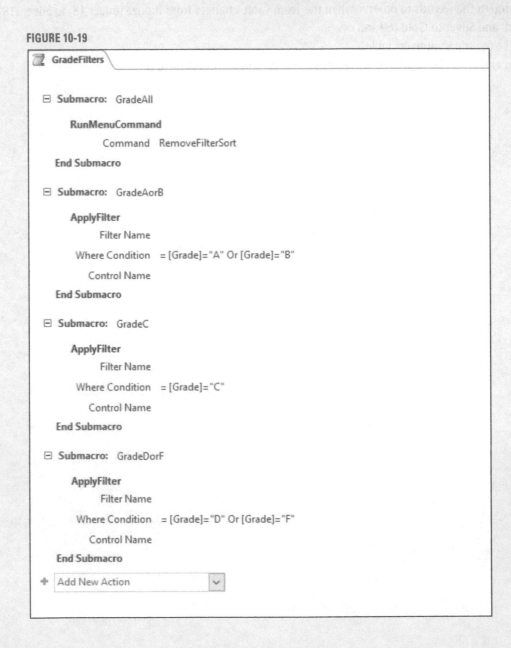

Creating Modules and VBA

CASE You are working with Lydia Snyder, vice president of operations at JCL Talent, to build a research database to manage industry, company, and job data. In this module, you create and modify modules and VBA to make the database application easier to use and to extend its capabilities.

Module Objectives

After completing this module, you will be able to:

- Understand modules and VBA
- Compare macros and modules
- Create functions
- Use VBA If statements
- Document procedures
- Build class modules
- Modify procedures
- Troubleshoot VBA

Files You Will Need

IL_AC_11-1.accdb
IL_AC_11-2.accdb
IL_AC_11-3.accdb

IL_AC_11-4.accdb
IL_AC_11-5.accdb

Understand Modules and VBA

Learning
Outcomes
• Define VBA terms
• Describe Visual
  Basic Editor
  components

Access is a robust relational database program for small applications. Access also provides user-friendly tools, such as wizards and Design Views, to help users quickly create reports and forms that previously took programmers many hours to build. You may, however, want to automate a task or create a new function that goes beyond the capabilities of the built-in Access features. Within each program of the Microsoft Office suite, a programming language called **Visual Basic for Applications (VBA)** is provided to help you extend the program's capabilities. In Access, VBA is stored within modules. A **module** is an Access object that stores Visual Basic for Applications (VBA) programming code. VBA is written in the **Visual Basic Editor (VBE)**, shown in FIGURE 11-1. The components and text colors of the VBE are described in TABLE 11-1. An Access database has two kinds of modules. **Standard modules** contain global code that can be executed from anywhere in the database. Standard modules are displayed as module objects in the Navigation Pane. **Class modules** are stored within a form or report object for use within that individual form or report. **CASE** ▸ *You ask some questions about VBA.*

DETAILS

The following questions and answers introduce the basics of Access modules:

• **What does a module contain?**

   A module contains VBA programming code organized in procedures. **Standard modules** are stored in the Navigation Pane and contain procedures available to all other objects. **Class modules** are stored in an individual form or report.

• **What is a procedure?**

   A **procedure** performs an operation or calculates an answer with one or several lines of code, each of which is called a **statement**. VBA has two types of procedures: functions and subs. **Declaration statements** precede procedure statements and help set rules for how the statements in the module are processed.

• **What is a function?**

   A **function** is a procedure that returns a value. Access supplies many **built-in functions**, such as Sum, Count, Pmt, and Now, that can be used in an expression in a query, form, or report to calculate and return a value. You might want to create a custom function, however, to calculate answers using formulas unique to your business.

• **What is a sub?**

   A **sub** (also called **sub procedure**) performs a series of VBA statements to manipulate data, controls, and objects. Subs are generally executed when an event occurs, such as when a command button is clicked or a form is opened.

• **What are arguments?**

   Arguments are constants, variables, or expressions passed to a procedure that the procedure needs to execute. For example, the full syntax for the Sum function is Sum(*expr*), where *expr* represents the argument for the Sum function, typically the field that is being summed. In VBA, arguments are declared in the first line of the procedure immediately after a procedure's name and are enclosed in parentheses. Multiple arguments are separated by commas.

• **What is an object?**

   In VBA, an **object** is any item that can be used or manipulated, including the traditional Access objects (table, query, form, report, macro, and module), as well as form controls and sections, existing procedures, and built-in VBA objects that provide functionality to your code.

• **What is a method?**

   A **method** is an action that an object can perform. Procedures are often written to invoke methods in response to user actions. For example, you could invoke the GoToControl method to move the focus to a specific control on a form in response to the user clicking a command button.

FIGURE 11-1: Visual Basic Editor (VBE) window for a standard module

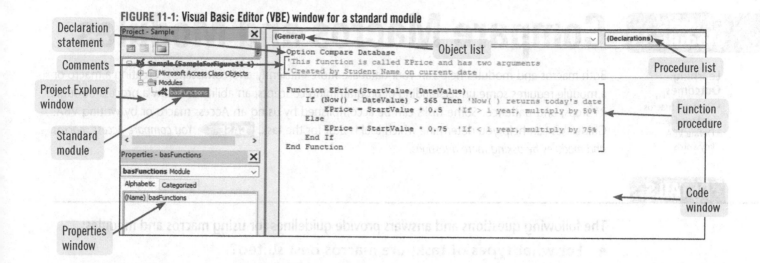

TABLE 11-1: Components and text colors for the Visual Basic Editor window

component or color	description
Visual Basic Editor (VBE)	Comprises the entire Microsoft Visual Basic program window that contains smaller windows, including the Code window and Project Explorer window
Code window	Contains the VBA for the project selected in the Project Explorer window
Project Explorer window	Displays a hierarchical list of the projects in the database; a project can be a module object or a form or report object that contains a class module
Declaration statements	Includes statements that apply to every procedure in the module, such as declarations for variables, constants, user-defined data types, and external procedures in a dynamic-link library
Object list	In a class module, lists the objects associated with the current form or report
Procedure list	In a standard module, lists the procedures in the module; in a class module, lists events (such as Click or Dblclick)
Blue	Indicates a VBA keyword; blue words are reserved by VBA and are already assigned specific meanings
Black	Indicates normal text; black text is the unique VBA code created by the developer
Red	Indicates syntax error; a red statement indicates that it will not execute correctly because of a syntax error (perhaps a missing parenthesis or a keyword spelling error)
Green	Indicates comment text; any text after an apostrophe is considered a comment, and is therefore ignored in the execution of the procedure

Converting macros to VBA

You can convert a form or report's embedded macros to VBA by opening the form or report in Design View, then clicking the Convert Form's (Report's) Macros to Visual Basic button in the Tools group. The VBA is inserted as a class module within the form or report and can be viewed by clicking the View Code button in the Tools group in Form or Report Design View.

You can also convert global macros found in the Navigation Pane to VBA by opening the macro in Macro Design View, and then clicking the Convert Macros to Visual Basic button in the Tools group. The VBA is stored in a standard module located in the Navigation Pane and identified with a name that starts with "Converted Macro."

Compare Macros and Modules

Learning
Outcomes
• Contrast macros
  and modules
• Define VBA
  keywords

Both macros and modules help run your database more efficiently and consistently. Creating a macro or a module requires some understanding of programming concepts, an ability to follow a process through its steps, and patience. Some tasks can be accomplished by using an Access macro or by writing VBA. Guidelines can help you determine which tool is best for the task. **CASE** *You compare Access macros and modules by asking more questions.*

DETAILS

The following questions and answers provide guidelines for using macros and modules:

- **For what types of tasks are macros best suited?**

  Macros are an easy way to handle common, repetitive, and simple tasks such as opening and closing forms and reports, applying filters, and printing reports.

- **Which is easier to create, a macro or a module, and why?**

  Macros are generally easier to create because Macro Design View is more structured than the VBE. The hardest part of creating a macro is choosing the correct macro action. But once the action is selected, the arguments associated with that macro action are displayed, eliminating the need to learn any special programming syntax. To create a module, however, you must know a robust programming language, VBA, as well as the correct **syntax** (rules) for each VBA statement. In a nutshell, macros are simpler to create, but VBA is more powerful.

- **When must I use a macro?**

  You must use macros to make global, shortcut key assignments. **AutoExec** is a special macro name that automatically executes when the database first opens.

- **When must I use a module?**

  1. You must use modules to create unique functions. For instance, you might want to create a function called Commission that calculates the appropriate commission using your company's unique commission formula.
  2. Access error messages can be confusing to the user. However, by using VBA procedures, you can detect the error when it occurs and display your own message.
  3. Although Access macros have recently been enhanced to include more powerful If-Then logic, VBA is still more robust in the area of programming flow statements with tools such as nested If statements, Case statements, and multiple looping structures. Some of the most common VBA keywords, including If...Then, are shown in **TABLE 11-2**. VBA keywords appear in blue in the VBE code window.
  4. VBA code may declare **variables**, which store data that can be used, modified, or displayed during the execution of the procedure.
  5. VBA may be used in conjunction with **SQL (Structured Query Language)** to select, update, append, and delete data.

  Like macros, modules can be accessed through the Navigation Pane or embedded directly within a form or report. When embedded in a form or report object, the module is called a **class module**, like the one shown in **FIGURE 11-2**. If you develop forms and reports in one database and copy them to another, the class modules automatically travel with the object that stores it. Use class modules for code that is unique to that form or report. Use standard modules (also called **global modules**) to store code that will be reused in many places in the database application.

FIGURE 11-2: Visual Basic Editor window for a class module

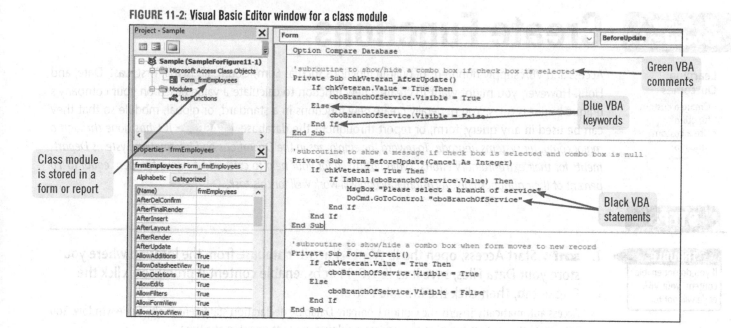

Class module is stored in a form or report

Green VBA comments

Blue VBA keywords

Black VBA statements

TABLE 11-2: Common VBA keywords

statement	explanation
Function	Declares the name and arguments that create a new function procedure
End Function	When defining a new function, the End Function statement is required as the last statement to mark the end of the VBA code that defines the function
Sub	Declares the name for a new Sub procedure; Private Sub indicates that the Sub is accessible only to other procedures in the module where it is declared
End Sub	When defining a new sub, the End Sub statement is required as the last statement to mark the end of the VBA code that defines the sub
If...Then	Executes code (the code follows the Then statement) when the value of an expression is true (the expression follows the If statement)
End If	When creating an If...Then...Else clause, the End If statement is required as the last statement
Const	Declares the name and value of a constant, an item that retains a constant value throughout the execution of the code
Option Compare Database	A declaration statement that determines the way string values (text) will be sorted
Option Explicit	A declaration statement that specifies that you must explicitly declare all variables used in all procedures; if you attempt to use an undeclared variable name, an error occurs at compile time, the period during which source code is translated to executable code
Dim	Declares a variable, a named storage location that contains data that can be modified during program execution
On Error GoTo	Upon an error in the execution of a procedure, specifies the location (the statement) where the procedure should continue
Select Case	Executes one of several groups of statements called a Case depending on the value of an expression; using the Select Case statement is an alternative to using ElseIf in If...Then...Else statements when comparing one expression with several different values
End Select	When defining a new Select Case group of statements, the End Select statement is required as the last statement to mark the end of the VBA code

Access

Create Functions

Learning
Outcomes
• Create a custom
function
• Use a custom
function

Access and VBA supply hundreds of built-in functions such as Sum, Count, Iif, IsNull, First, Last, Date, and Hour. However, you might want to create a new function to calculate a value based on your company's unique business rules. You generally create new functions in a standard, or global, module so that they can be used in any query, form, or report throughout the database. **CASE** ▶ *JCL has gone through a major computer systems upgrade. To reward the employees in the Operations and Information Systems Departments for their extraordinary efforts, Lydia has asked for your help to calculate a bonus for them equal to 10 percent of their annual salary. A custom function will work well for this task.*

STEPS

TROUBLE
If you do not enable
content, your VBA
code will not run.

1. **sam↓ Start Access, open the IL_AC_11-1.accdb database from the location where you store your Data Files, save it as IL_AC_11_Jobs, enable content if prompted, click the Create tab, then click the Module button**

   Access automatically inserts the Option Compare Database declaration statement in the Code window. You will create the custom function to calculate employee bonuses one step at a time.

QUICK TIP
The Option Explicit
statement appears if
the Require Variable
Declaration option
is checked in the
VBA Options dialog
box. To view the
default settings, click
Tools on the VBA
menu bar, then click
Options.

2. **Type function Bonus(Salary), then press ENTER**

   This statement creates a new function named Bonus, which uses one argument, Salary. The VBE automatically capitalized Function and added the **End Function** statement, a required statement to mark the end of the function. VBA keywords are blue.

3. **Press TAB, type Bonus = Salary * 0.1, then press ENTER**

   Your screen should look like **FIGURE 11-3**. The Bonus = statement explains how the Bonus function will calculate a value and what value it will return. The function will multiply the Salary by 0.1 and return the result.

   It is not necessary to indent statements, but indenting code between matching Function/End Function, Sub/End Sub, or If/End If statements enhances the program's readability. When you press ENTER at the end of a VBA statement, the VBE automatically adds spaces as appropriate to enhance the readability of the statement.

4. **Click the Save button 🔲 on the Standard toolbar, type basFunctions in the Save As dialog box, click OK, then click the upper Close button ✕ in the upper-right corner of the VBE window to close the Visual Basic Editor**

   It is common for VBA programmers to use three-character prefixes to name objects and controls. This makes it easier to identify that object or control in expressions and modules. The prefix **bas** is short for (Visual) Basic and applies to standard (global) modules. Naming conventions for other objects and controls are listed in **TABLE 11-3** and are used throughout the IL_AC_11_Jobs.accdb database. You can use the new function, Bonus, in a query, form, or report.

5. **Click the Create tab, click the Query Design button, double-click tblEmployees, then click Close in the Show Table dialog box**

   You use the new Bonus function in the query to calculate the 10 percent bonus.

QUICK TIP
Field names used in
expressions are not
case sensitive, but
they must exactly
match the spelling
of the field name
as defined in Table
Design View.

6. **Double-click EFirst, double-click ELast, double-click Department, double-click AnnualSalary, click the blank Field cell to the right of the AnnualSalary field, type BonusPay:Bonus([AnnualSalary]), then click the View button 🔳 as shown in FIGURE 11-4**

   You created a new field called BonusPay that uses the custom Bonus function that calculates and returns 10 percent of the AnnualSalary.

7. **Save the query with the name qryBonus, then close it**

Creating Modules and VBA

FIGURE 11-3: Creating the Bonus function

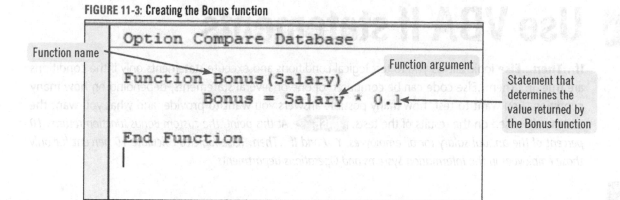

Function name →

Function argument →

Statement that determines the value returned by the Bonus function →

```
Option Compare Database


Function Bonus(Salary)
    Bonus = Salary * 0.1


End Function
```

FIGURE 11-4: Using the Bonus function in a query

EFirst	ELast	Department	AnnualSalary	BonusPay
Rory	Gonzalez	Executive	$340,000.00	34000
Lydia	Snyder	Operations	$175,000.00	17500
Ellie	Schwartz	Finance	$155,000.00	15500
Nyack	Afolayan	Operations	$89,000.00	8900
Shavonn	Rudd	Operations	$90,000.00	9000
Rosella	Leigh	Operations	$88,000.00	8800
Anthony	Martinez	Sales and Marketing	$165,000.00	16500
Gary	Jaeger	Operations	$91,500.00	9150
Sophie	Tan	Operations	$90,000.00	9000
Max	Gallardo	Operations	$91,000.00	9100
Mildred	Greenfield	Operations	$87,000.00	8700
Mark	Rock	Information Systems	$81,000.00	8100
Newt	Daniels	Information Systems	$75,000.00	7500
Julia	Rice	Information Systems	$76,000.00	7600
Jacob	Love	Finance	$73,000.00	7300
David	Jones	Information Systems	$70,500.00	7050
Kelsey	McDermott	Information Systems	$65,000.00	6500

qryBonus

Calculated field, BonusPay, uses Bonus custom function to multiply the AnnualSalary by 0.1

TABLE 11-3: Common three-character prefix naming conventions

object or control	prefix	example
Table	tbl	tblProducts
Query	qry	qrySalesByRegion
Form	frm	frmProducts
Report	rpt	rptSalesByCategory
Macro	mcr	mcrCloseInventory
Module	bas	basRetirement
Label	lbl	lblFullName
Text Box	txt	txtLastName
Combo box	cbo	cboStates
Command button	cmd	cmdPrint

Use VBA If statements

**Learning
Outcomes**
• Use VBA If...
  Then...Else logic
• Use the Zoom
  feature

If...Then...Else logic allows you to test logical conditions and execute statements only if the conditions are true. If...Then...Else code can be composed of one or several statements, depending on how many conditions you want to test, how many possible answers you want to provide, and what you want the code to do based on the results of the tests. **CASE** ▶ *At this point, the custom Bonus function returns 10 percent of the annual salary for all employees. You add If...Then...Else logic to calculate 10 percent for only those employees in the Information Systems and Operations departments.*

STEPS

1. **Right-click the** basFunctions module **in the Navigation Pane, then click** Design View

   To determine the employee's department, the Bonus function needs another piece of information; it needs another argument.

2. **Click just before the right parenthesis in the Function statement, type** , (a comma)**, type** Dept**, then press** ↓

   Now that you established another argument named Dept, you can work with the argument in the definition of the function.

QUICK TIP
Indentation doesn't affect the way the function works, but it does make the code easier to read.

3. **Click to the right of the right parenthesis in the Function statement, press** ENTER**, press** TAB**, then type** If (Dept = "Information Systems") Then

   The expression compares the Dept argument to the string "Information Systems". If true, Bonus is calculated as Salary * 0.1.

4. **Indent and type the rest of the statements exactly as shown in** FIGURE 11-5

   The **ElseIf** statement is executed when the first If expression evaluates to false. In this case, it multiplies Salary by 0.1 if Dept is equal to "Operations." You can add as many ElseIf clauses to the statement as desired.

   The **Else** statement is executed when all If and ElseIf statements evaluate to false. In this case, the Else statement will execute if Dept is equal to anything other than "Information Systems" or "Operations."

   The **End If** statement is needed to mark the end of the If...Then...Else block of code.

TROUBLE
If a compile or syntax error appears, open the VBE window, compare your function with FIGURE 11-5, then correct any errors.

5. **Click the** Save button 🖫 **on the Standard toolbar, close the Visual Basic window, right-click the** qryBonus query**, then click** Design View

   You need to modify the calculated BonusPay field to include a value for each argument in the modified Bonus function.

6. **Right-click the** BonusPay field **in the query design grid, click** Zoom **on the shortcut menu, click** between the right square bracket and right parenthesis**, then type** ,[Department]

   Your Zoom dialog box should look like FIGURE 11-6. Both of the arguments used to define Bonus function in the VBA code are replaced with actual field names that contain the data for the argument. Commas separate multiple arguments in the function.

7. **Click** OK **in the Zoom dialog box, then click the** View button 📰 **as shown in** FIGURE 11-7

   The Bonus function now calculates one of two different results for the BonusPay field, depending on the value in the Department field.

8. **Save then close the** qryBonus query

FIGURE 11-5: If...Then...ElseIf...Then...Else

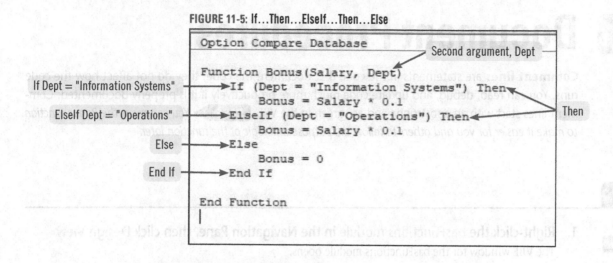

```
Option Compare Database

Function Bonus(Salary, Dept)
    If (Dept = "Information Systems") Then
        Bonus = Salary * 0.1
    ElseIf (Dept = "Operations") Then
        Bonus = Salary * 0.1
    Else
        Bonus = 0
    End If

End Function
```

Second argument, Dept
If Dept = "Information Systems"
ElseIf Dept = "Operations"
Else
End If
Then

FIGURE 11-6: Using the Zoom dialog box for long expressions

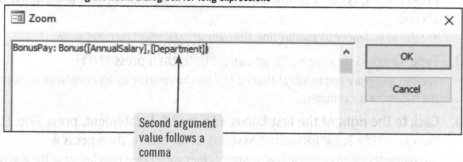

```
Zoom                                                    ×

BonusPay: Bonus([AnnualSalary],[Department])            OK

                                                        Cancel
```

Second argument value follows a comma

FIGURE 11-7: BonusPay field calculates 10% of AnnualSalary based on Department value

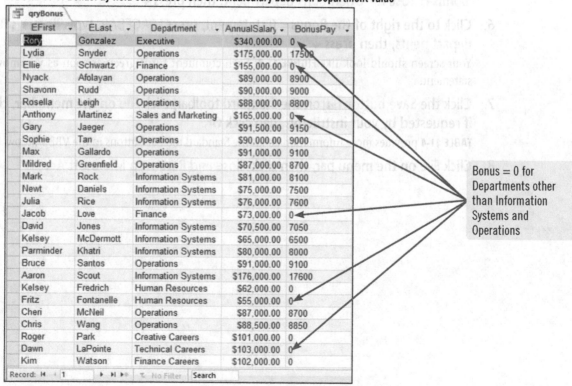

EFirst	ELast	Department	AnnualSalary	BonusPay
Rory	Gonzalez	Executive	$340,000.00	0
Lydia	Snyder	Operations	$175,000.00	17500
Ellie	Schwartz	Finance	$155,000.00	0
Nyack	Afolayan	Operations	$89,000.00	8900
Shavonn	Rudd	Operations	$90,000.00	9000
Rosella	Leigh	Operations	$88,000.00	8800
Anthony	Martinez	Sales and Marketing	$165,000.00	0
Gary	Jaeger	Operations	$91,500.00	9150
Sophie	Tan	Operations	$90,000.00	9000
Max	Gallardo	Operations	$91,000.00	9100
Mildred	Greenfield	Operations	$87,000.00	8700
Mark	Rock	Information Systems	$81,000.00	8100
Newt	Daniels	Information Systems	$75,000.00	7500
Julia	Rice	Information Systems	$76,000.00	7600
Jacob	Love	Finance	$73,000.00	0
David	Jones	Information Systems	$70,500.00	7050
Kelsey	McDermott	Information Systems	$65,000.00	6500
Parminder	Khatri	Information Systems	$80,000.00	8000
Bruce	Santos	Operations	$91,000.00	9100
Aaron	Scout	Information Systems	$176,000.00	17600
Kelsey	Fredrich	Human Resources	$62,000.00	0
Fritz	Fontanelle	Human Resources	$55,000.00	0
Cheri	McNeil	Operations	$87,000.00	8700
Chris	Wang	Operations	$88,500.00	8850
Roger	Park	Creative Careers	$101,000.00	0
Dawn	LaPointe	Technical Careers	$103,000.00	0
Kim	Watson	Finance Careers	$102,000.00	0

Record: 14 1 ▶ ▶I ▶▶ ⊤ No Filter Search

Bonus = 0 for Departments other than Information Systems and Operations

Access

Document Procedures

Learning
Outcomes
• Add VBA
 comments
• Use the VBE
 toolbar

Comment lines are statements in the code that document the code; they do not affect how the code runs. You can read, debug, and update code much more productively if it is properly documented. Comment lines start with an apostrophe and are green in the VBE. **CASE** *You comment the Bonus function to make it easier for you and others to follow the purpose and logic of the function later.*

STEPS

QUICK TIP
You can also create comments by starting the statement with the **rem** statement (short for remark).

1. **Right-click the** basFunctions module **in the Navigation Pane, then click** Design View
   The VBE window for the basFunctions module opens.

2. **Click the blank line between the Option Compare Database and Function statements, press ENTER, type** 'This function is called Bonus and has two arguments, **then press ENTER**
   As soon as you move to another line, the comment statement becomes green.

TROUBLE
Be sure to use an ' (apostrophe) and not a " (quotation mark) to begin the comment line.

3. **Type** 'Created by *your name* on *current date*, **then press** ENTER
   You can also place comments at the end of a line by entering an apostrophe to mark that the next part of the statement is a comment.

4. **Click to the right of the first Bonus = Salary * 0.1 statement, press SPACEBAR, type** 'Bonus is 10% for Information Systems department, **then press** ↓
   All comments are green, regardless of whether they are on their own line or at the end of an existing line.

5. **Click to the right of the second Bonus = Salary * 0.1 statement, press SPACEBAR, type** 'Bonus is 10% for Operations department, **then press** ↓

6. **Click to the right of the Bonus = 0 statement, press SPACEBAR, type** 'Bonus is 0 for other departments, **then press** ↓
   Your screen should look like **FIGURE 11-8**. Each comment turns green as soon as you move to a new statement.

7. **Click the** Save button 🖫 **on the Standard toolbar, click** File **on the menu bar, click** Print **if requested by your instructor, then click** OK
   TABLE 11-4 provides more information about the Standard toolbar buttons in the VBE window.

8. **Click** File **on the menu bar, then click** Close and Return to Microsoft Access

FIGURE 11-8: Adding comments to a module

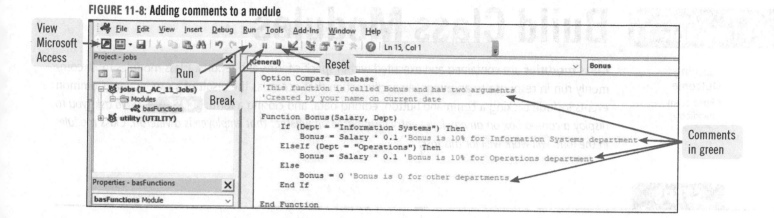

TABLE 11-4: Standard toolbar buttons in the Visual Basic window

button name	button	description
View Microsoft Access		Switches from the active Visual Basic window to the Access window
Insert Module		Opens a new module or class module Code window, or inserts a new procedure in the current Code window
Run Sub/UserForm		Runs the current procedure if the insertion point is in a procedure, or runs the UserForm if it is active
Break		Stops the execution of a program while it's running and switches to Break mode, which is the temporary suspension of program execution in which you can examine, debug, reset, step through, or continue program execution
Reset		Resets the procedure
Project Explorer		Displays the Project Explorer, which provides a hierarchical list of the currently open projects (set of modules) and their contents
Object Browser		Displays the Object Browser, which lists the defined modules and procedures as well as available methods, properties, events, constants, and other items that you can use in the code

Using comments for debugging

You can use comments to "comment out" or temporarily hide statements that you want to leave in your module but do not want to execute. "Commenting out" statements that do not work (versus editing the same broken statement(s) over and over) keeps a trail of every line of code that you have written.

This process makes development, debugging, and sharing your thought processes with other developers much more productive. When the code is working as intended, extra lines that have been "commented out" that are no longer needed for the testing or debugging process can be deleted.

Creating Modules and VBA

AC 11-11

Access

Build Class Modules

Class modules are contained and executed within specific forms and reports. Class modules most commonly run in response to an **event**, a specific action that occurs as the result of a user action. Common events include clicking a command button, editing data, and closing a form. **CASE** ▶ *Lydia asks you to display a combo box on an employee entry form based on whether that employee is a veteran. Class modules in the form will work well for this task.*

STEPS

TROUBLE
If the first line of
your procedure
is not Private
Sub chkVeteran_
AfterUpdate( ),
delete the stub, close
the VBE, and repeat
Step 2.

1. **Double-click the** frmEmployeeEntry form **in the Navigation Pane to open it in Form View, then click the** Branch of Service combo box arrow **to review the choices**

   A choice in the Branch of Service combo box only makes sense if an employee is a veteran. You'll use a class module to set the Visible property for the Branch of Service combo box to True if the Veteran check box is checked and False if the Veteran check box is not checked.

2. **Right-click the** frmEmployeeEntry tab, **click** Design View, **double-click the** Veteran check box **to open its Property Sheet, click the** Event tab **in the Property Sheet, click the** After Update property, **click the** Build button ⬚, **click** Code Builder, **then click** OK

   The class module for the frmEmployeesEntry form opens. Because you opened the VBE window from a specific event of a control on the form, the **stub**, the first and last lines of the sub procedure, was automatically created. The procedure's name, chkVeteran_AfterUpdate, contains the **Name property** of the control, and the name of the event that triggers this procedure. A procedure triggered by an event is often called an **event handler**.

QUICK TIP
Write your VBA
code in lowercase.
The VBE will
automatically correct
the case.

3. **Enter the statements shown in** FIGURE 11-9

   The If structure makes the cboBranchOfService control visible or not visible based on whether the chkVeteran control is checked (true) or unchecked (false).

QUICK TIP
The **On Current**
event of the form is
triggered when you
navigate through
records.

4. **Save the changes and close the VBE window, click the** View button ▦, **click the** Veteran check box **for the first record several times, then navigate through several records**

   Clicking the Veteran check box triggers the procedure that responds to the After Update event. However, you need the procedure to run every time you move from record to record, not just when the Veteran check box is clicked.

TROUBLE
If the Code window
appears with a
yellow line, it means
the code cannot
be run successfully.
Click the Reset
button ▣ on the
Standard toolbar,
then compare
your VBA with
FIGURE 11-10.

5. **Right-click the** frmEmployeeEntry tab, **click** Design View, **click the** Form Selector button ▣, **click the** Event tab **in the Property Sheet, click the** On Current event property, **click the** Build button ⬚, **click** Code Builder, **click** OK, **then copy or retype the If structure from the chkVeteran_AfterUpdate sub to the Form_Current sub, as shown in** FIGURE 11-10

   You have now created a second event handler in this class module. The cboBranchOfService combo box will be visible based on updating the chkVeteran check box or by moving from record to record. To test the new sub procedure, switch to Form View.

6. **Save the changes and close the VBE window, click** ▦ **to switch to Form View, then navigate through several records to test the new procedure**

   Now, as you move from record to record, the Branch of Service combo box should be visible for those employees with the Veteran check box selected and not visible if the Veteran check box is not selected.

7. **Return to the first record for Rory Gonzalez, click the** Veteran check box **(if it is not already selected), click the** Branch of Service combo box arrow, **click** Army **as shown in** FIGURE 11-11, **then save and close** frmEmployeeEntry

FIGURE 11-9: Creating an event handler procedure

chk prefix identifies a
check box

cbo prefix identifies a
combo box

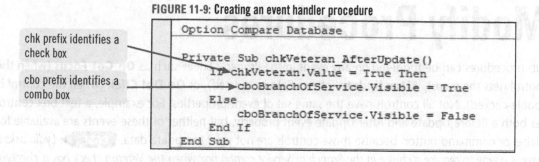

```
Option Compare Database


Private Sub chkVeteran_AfterUpdate()
    If chkVeteran.Value = True Then
        cboBranchOfService.Visible = True
    Else
        cboBranchOfService.Visible = False
    End If
End Sub
```

FIGURE 11-10: Copying the If structure to a new event handler procedure

Copy If structure
from chkVeteran_
AfterUpdate sub to
Form_Current sub

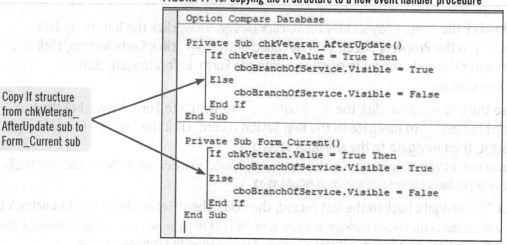

```
Option Compare Database

Private Sub chkVeteran_AfterUpdate()
    If chkVeteran.Value = True Then
        cboBranchOfService.Visible = True
    Else
        cboBranchOfService.Visible = False
    End If
End Sub

Private Sub Form_Current()
    If chkVeteran.Value = True Then
        cboBranchOfService.Visible = True
    Else
        cboBranchOfService.Visible = False
    End If
End Sub
```

FIGURE 11-11: Branch of Service combo box is visible when Veteran box is checked

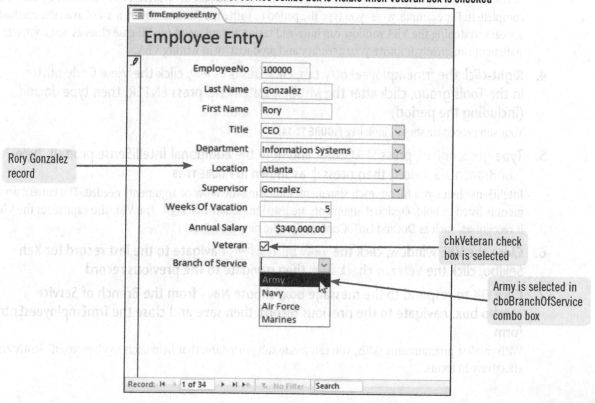

Rory Gonzalez
record

chkVeteran check
box is selected

Army is selected in
cboBranchOfService
combo box

Modify Procedures

Learning
Outcomes
• Attach procedures
  to events
• Use IntelliSense
  technology

Sub procedures can be triggered on any event in the Property Sheet such as **On Got Focus** (when the control gets the focus), **After Update** (after a field is updated), or **On Dbl Click** (when the control is double-clicked). Not all controls have the same set of event properties. For example, a text box control has both a Before Update and After Update event property, but neither of these events are available for a label or command button because those controls are not used to update data. **CASE** ▶ *Lydia asks if there is a way to require a choice in the Branch of Service combo box when the Veteran check box is checked. You modify the VBA in the form to handle this request.*

STEPS

QUICK TIP
If you select the
Always use event
procedures check
box in the Object
Designers section of
the Access Options
dialog box, you
bypass the Choose
Builder dialog box
and go directly to
the VBE.

1. **Right-click the** frmEmployeeEntry **form, click** Design View, **click the** Before Update **property in the Property Sheet, click the** Build button ⸱⸱⸱ , **click** Code Builder, **click** OK, **then enter the code shown in FIGURE 11-12 into the Form_BeforeUpdate stub**
   Test the procedure.

2. **Close the** VBE window, **click the** View button ▦ **to switch to Form View, click the** Last record button ▶❙ **to navigate to the Ken Sekibo record, click the** Veteran check box **to select it, then navigate to the previous record**
   Because the chkVeteran control is selected but the cboBranchOfService combo box is null, the MsgBox statement produces the message shown in **FIGURE 11-13**.

3. **Click** OK, **navigate back to the last record, then click the** Veteran check box **to uncheck it**
   The code produces the correct message, but you want the code to place the focus in the cboBranchOfService combo box to force the user to choose a branch of service when this condition occurs.
   DoCmd is a VBA object that supports many methods to run common Access commands, such as closing windows, opening forms, previewing reports, navigating records, setting focus, and setting the value of controls. As you write a VBA statement, visual aids that are part of **IntelliSense technology** help you complete it. For example, when you type the period (.) after the DoCmd object, a list of available methods appears. Watching the VBA window carefully and taking advantage of IntelliSense clues as you complete a statement can greatly improve your accuracy and productivity in writing VBA.

4. **Right-click the** frmEmployeeEntry **tab, click** Design View, **click the** View Code button **in the Tools group, click after the** MsgBox statement, **press** ENTER, **then type** docmd. **(including the period)**
   Your sub procedure should look like **FIGURE 11-14**.

5. **Type** gotocontrol, **press** SPACEBAR **and note the additional IntelliSense prompt, type** "cboBranchOfService", **then press ↓ as shown in FIGURE 11-15**
   IntelliSense helps you fill out each statement, indicating the order of arguments needed. The current argument is listed in bold. Optional arguments are listed in [square brackets]. The VBE also capitalizes the VBA it recognizes, such as DoCmd.GoToControl. Test the new procedure.

6. **Close the VBE window, click the** View button ▦ , **navigate to the last record for Ken Sekibo, click the** Veteran check box, **then navigate to the previous record**

7. **Click** OK **to respond to the message box, choose** Navy **from the Branch of Service combo box, navigate to the previous record, then save and close the frmEmployeesEntry form**
   With modest programming skills, you can create sub procedures that help users work more efficiently and effectively in forms.

FIGURE 11-12: Form_BeforeUpdate sub

Form_BeforeUpdate sub

```
Private Sub Form_BeforeUpdate(Cancel As Integer)
    If chkVeteran.Value = True Then
        If IsNull(cboBranchOfService.Value) Then
            MsgBox "Please select a branch of service"
        End If
    End If
End Sub
```

FIGURE 11-13: Message produced by MsgBox statement

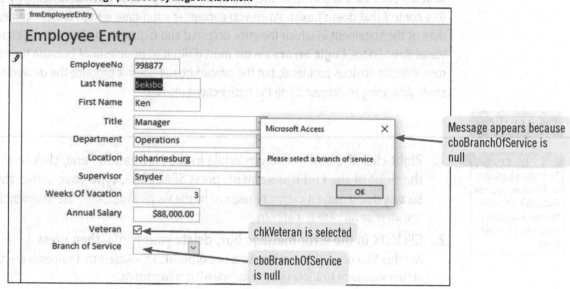

frmEmployeeEntry

Employee Entry

EmployeeNo	998877
Last Name	Sekibo
First Name	Ken
Title	Manager
Department	Operations
Location	Johannesburg
Supervisor	Snyder
Weeks Of Vacation	3
Annual Salary	$88,000.00
Veteran	☑
Branch of Service	

Microsoft Access ✕

Please select a branch of service

OK

Message appears because cboBranchOfService is null

chkVeteran is selected

cboBranchOfService is null

FIGURE 11-14: IntelliSense technology prompts

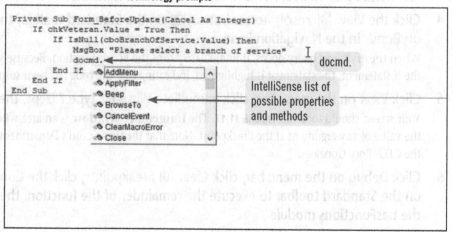

```
Private Sub Form_BeforeUpdate(Cancel As Integer)
    If chkVeteran.Value = True Then
        If IsNull(cboBranchOfService.Value) Then
            MsgBox "Please select a branch of service"
            docmd.
        End If        ⊛ AddMenu
    End If            ⊛ ApplyFilter
End Sub                ⊛ Beep
                       ⊛ BrowseTo
                       ⊛ CancelEvent
                       ⊛ ClearMacroError
                       ⊛ Close
```

docmd.

IntelliSense list of possible properties and methods

FIGURE 11-15: New DoCmd statement

```
Private Sub Form_BeforeUpdate(Cancel As Integer)
    If chkVeteran.Value = True Then
        If IsNull(cboBranchOfService.Value) Then
            MsgBox "Please select a branch of service"
            DoCmd.GoToControl "cboBranchOfService"
        End If
    End If
End Sub
```

New DoCmd statement

Access

Troubleshoot VBA

Access provides several techniques to help you **debug** (find and resolve) different types of VBA errors. A **syntax error** occurs immediately as you are writing a VBA statement that cannot be read by the Visual Basic Editor. This is the easiest type of error to identify because your code turns red when the syntax error occurs. **Compile-time errors** occur as a result of incorrectly constructed code and are detected as soon as you run your code or select the Compile option on the Debug menu. For example, you may have forgotten to insert an End If statement to finish an If structure. **Run-time errors** occur as incorrectly constructed code runs and include attempting an illegal operation such as dividing by zero or moving focus to a control that doesn't exist. When you encounter a run-time error, VBA will stop executing your procedure at the statement in which the error occurred and highlight the line with a yellow background in the Visual Basic Editor. **Logic errors** are the most difficult to troubleshoot because they occur when the code runs without obvious problems, but the procedure still doesn't produce the desired result. **CASE** *You study debugging techniques using the basFunctions module.*

STEPS

1. **Right-click the** basFunctions module **in the Navigation Pane, click** Design View, **click to the** right of the End If statement, **press** SPACEBAR, **type** your name, **then press** ↓

   Because that statement cannot be resolved by the Visual Basic Editor, the statement immediately turns red and an error message box appears.

2. **Click** OK **in the error message box, delete** your name, **then press** ↓

   Another VBA debugging tool is to set a **breakpoint**, a bookmark that suspends execution of the procedure at that statement to allow you to examine what is happening.

3. **Click the** If statement line, **click** Debug **on the menu bar, then click** Toggle Breakpoint

   Your screen should look like **FIGURE 11-16**.

4. **Click the** View Microsoft Access button 🔲 **on the Standard toolbar, then double-click** qryBonus **in the Navigation Pane**

   When the qryBonus query opens, it immediately runs the Bonus function. Because you set a breakpoint at the If statement, the statement is highlighted, indicating that the code has been suspended at that point.

5. **Click** View **on the menu bar, click** Immediate Window, **type** ? Dept, **then press** ENTER

   Your screen should look like **FIGURE 11-17**. The **Immediate window** is an area where you can determine the value of any argument at the breakpoint. Note that the first record's Department value is Executive for the CEO, Rory Gonzales.

6. **Click** Debug **on the menu bar, click** Clear All Breakpoints, **click the** Continue button ▶ **on the Standard toolbar to execute the remainder of the function, then save and close the basFunctions module**

   You return to qryBonus in Datasheet View.

7. **sam↑ Close the qryBonus datasheet, compact and close the IL_AC_11_Jobs.accdb database, then close Access**

FIGURE 11-16: Setting a breakpoint

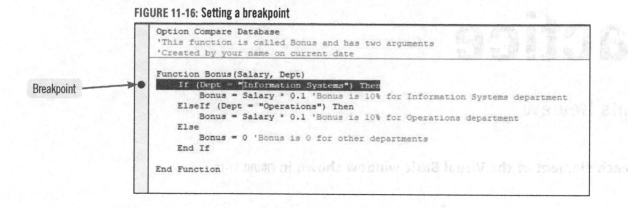

Breakpoint

```
Option Compare Database
'This function is called Bonus and has two arguments
'Created by your name on current date

Function Bonus(Salary, Dept)
    If (Dept = "Information Systems") Then
        Bonus = Salary * 0.1 'Bonus is 10% for Information Systems department
    ElseIf (Dept = "Operations") Then
        Bonus = Salary * 0.1 'Bonus is 10% for Operations department
    Else
        Bonus = 0 'Bonus is 0 for other departments
    End If

End Function
```

FIGURE 11-17: Stopping execution at a breakpoint

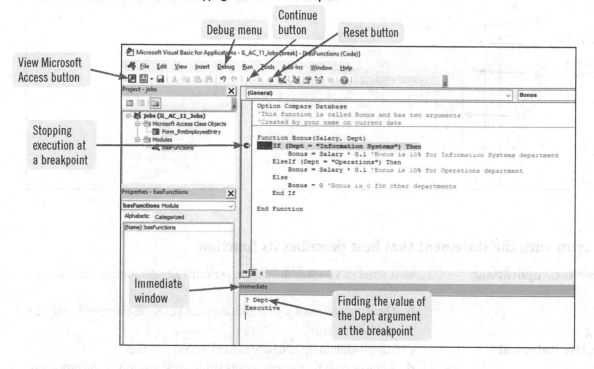

Continue button

Debug menu

Reset button

View Microsoft Access button

Stopping execution at a breakpoint

Immediate window

Finding the value of the Dept argument at the breakpoint

Debugging

Debugging is the process of finding and resolving bugs or problems in code. The term is generally attributed to Grace Hopper, a computer pioneer. Wikipedia (https://en.wikipedia.org/wiki/Debugging) states that while Grace was working at Harvard University in the 1940s, a moth was found in a relay component of the computer, which impeded operations. After the moth was removed, Grace remarked that they were "debugging" the system.

Access

Practice

Concepts Review

Identify each element of the Visual Basic window shown in FIGURE 11-18.

FIGURE 11-18

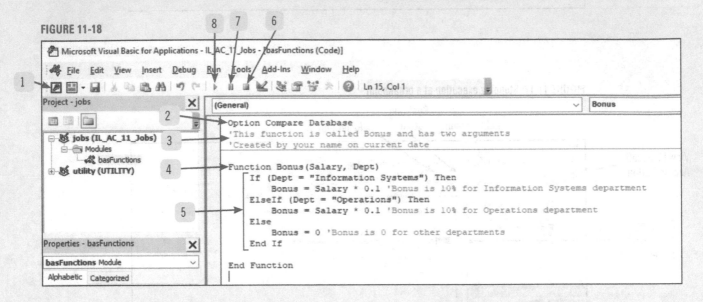

Match each term with the statement that best describes its function.

9. Visual Basic for Applications (VBA)

10. Module

11. Debugging

12. If...Then...Else statement

13. Procedure

14. Class modules

15. Breakpoint

16. Arguments

17. Function

a. A series of VBA statements that performs an operation or calculates a value

b. Allows you to test a logical condition and execute commands only if the condition is true

c. The programming language used in Access modules

d. A line of code that automatically suspends execution of the procedure

e. A process to find and resolve programming errors

f. A procedure that returns a value

g. Constants, variables, or expressions passed to a procedure to further define how it should execute

h. Stored as part of the form or report object in which they are created

i. The Access object where global VBA code is stored

18. **The term** *debugging* **is attributed to which computer science pioneer?**

a. Tim Berners-Lee

b. Grace Hopper

c. Bill Gates

d. Ida Lovelace

19. Which character is used to indicate a comment in VBA?

   a. quotation mark (")

   b. forward slash (/)

   c. exclamation point (!)

   d. apostrophe (')

20. Which of the following is a run-time error?

   a. Dividing by zero

   b. Mistyping the word *function*

   c. Forgetting an End If statement

   d. Using too many comments

Skills Review

1. Understand modules and VBA.

   a. Start Access, open the IL_AC_11-2.accdb database from the location where you store your Data Files, then save it as **IL_AC_11_SupportDesk**. Enable content if prompted.

   b. Open the VBE window for the basFunctions module.

   c. Record your answers to the following questions about this module:

     • What is the name of the function?

     • What are the names of the arguments of the function?

     • What is the purpose of the End Function statement?

     • Why are the End Function statements in blue?

     • Why are some of the lines indented?

     • What is the purpose of the Dim keyword?

2. Compare macros and modules.

   a. If not already opened, open the VBE window for the basFunctions module.

   b. Record your answers to the following questions on a sheet of paper:

     • Why was a module rather than a macro used to create these procedures?

     • Why is VBA generally more difficult to create than a macro?

     • Identify each of the VBA keywords or keyword phrases, and explain the purpose for each.

3. Create functions.

   a. If not already opened, open the VBE window for the basFunctions module.

   b. Create a function called **TutitionReimbursement** below the End Function statement of the RetireYears function by typing the VBA statements shown in **FIGURE 11-19**. The company has a tuition reimbursement policy that assists employees with college tuition if they make less than $50,000 per year and have more than one dependent. This function will help identify qualifying employees.

   c. Save the basFunctions module, then close the VBE window.

   d. Use Query Design View to create a new query using the FirstName, LastName, Salary, and Dependents fields from the tblEmployees table.

   e. Create a calculated field named **Tuition** in the next available column by carefully typing the expression as follows: **Tuition: TuitionReimbursement ([Salary],[Dependents])** (*Hint:* Use the Zoom dialog box to more easily enter long expressions.)

FIGURE 11-19

```
Function TuitionReimbursement(SalaryValue, DependentsValue)

        TuitionReimbursement = "Qualified"

        TuitionReimbursement = "Not Qualified"

End Function
```

Access

f. Create a second calculated field named **RetirementCalc** in the next available column by carefully typing the expression as follows: **RetirementCalc: RetireYears([Birthday],[StartDate])** (*Hint*: Use the Zoom dialog box to enter long expressions.)

g. View the datasheet, then widen the RetirementCalc column to view the entire field name. At this point the RetirementCalc calculation should work correctly, but the Tuition field should calculate to "Not Qualified" for all employees, which is not correct. Save the query as **qryEmployeeData**, then close it.

4. Use VBA If statements.

a. Open the VBE window for the basFunctions module, then modify the TuitionReimbursement function to add the If structure shown in **FIGURE 11-20**. The If structure tests to see if the SalaryValue is less than $50,000 and if the DependentsValue is greater than 1.

b. Save the basFunctions module, then close the VBE window.

c. Open the qryEmployeeData datasheet, then change the Dependents field value for Eugene Fuentes to **2**. His Tuition field should change from Not Qualified to Qualified.

d. Close the datasheet.

FIGURE 11-20

```
Function TuitionReimbursement(SalaryValue, DependentsValue)
    If SalaryValue < 50000 And DependentsValue > 1 Then
        TuitionReimbursement = "Qualified"
    Else
        TuitionReimbursement = "Not Qualified"
    End If
End Function
```

5. Document procedures.

a. Open the VBE window for the basFunctions module, then add the comments to the top of the module, to the RetireYears function, and to the TuitionReimbursement function, as shown in **FIGURE 11-21**. Be sure to insert your actual name and today's date.

FIGURE 11-21

```
Option Compare Database

'Created by your name on the current date
'Function RetireYears adds an employees age to the years of employment

Function RetireYears(BirthDate, HireDate)
    Dim YearsOld
    YearsOld = Int((Date - BirthDate) / 365.25)      'calculates an employees age
    Dim YearsWorked
    YearsWorked = Int((Date - HireDate) / 365.25)  'calculates full years of employment
    RetireYears = YearsOld + YearsWorked           'adds years of age to years of employment
End Function

'Function TuitionReimbursement determines if an employee is eligible for tuition benefit
Function TuitionReimbursement(SalaryValue, DependentsValue)
    If SalaryValue < 50000 And DependentsValue > 1 Then 'salary must be < $50,000 and dependents must be > 1
        TuitionReimbursement = "Qualified"
    Else
        TuitionReimbursement = "Not Qualified"
    End If
End Function
```

b. Save the changes to the basFunctions module, print the module if requested by your instructor, then close the VBE window.

6. Build class modules.

a. Open frmEmployeeMaster in Form View, then move through several records to observe the data.

b. Switch to Design View, and add a new text box control below the StartDate text box. Change the Name property of the text box to **txtRetirementCalc**, the Control Source property of the text box to **=RetireYears([txtBirthday],[txtStartDate])**, and the Tab Stop property to **No**.

c. Change the Caption property of the label to **Retirement Calculation**.

d. Below the new txtRetirementCalc text box, add another label control. Type **Eligible for Tuition Reimbursement!** in the label control. Change the Name property to **lblTuition** and the Visible property to **No**. Save the form, view it in Form View, and move through several records. At this point the txtRetirementCalc text box shows a number that is the person's age plus their years of service at the company, but the tuition reimbursement label is not visible for any record.

Skills Review (continued)

e. Switch to Form Design View, then format the new labels and txtRetirementCalc text box with a dark black font color. Resize the labels to display all of their text. Modify the After Update event of the form with a VBA procedure, as shown in **FIGURE 11-22**.

f. Save and close the Visual Basic Editor. Save the form, switch to Form View, and enter a new record as shown in **FIGURE 11-23** to make sure the message appears. The Retirement Calculation varies based on the current date.

g. Click OK in the dialog box, enter **2** in the txtDependents text box, then save and close the form.

7. Modify procedures.

a. Open the frmEmployeeMaster form in Design View, then click the Build button on the After Update event of the form to return to the same procedure in the VBE.

b. Modify the subprocedure to include another If... Then...Else block of code, as shown in **FIGURE 11-24**.

c. Copy the If...Then...Else structure that tests for the salary and dependents values from the Form_AfterUpdate sub procedure to the Form_Current procedure.

d. Save then close the VBE window. Save the frmEmployeeMaster form, then switch to Form View.

e. Navigate to the last record with your name, then edit the record to test for salary values of **$50,000** and **$49,000**, then dependent values of **null**, **1**, and finally **2** dependents.

f. After testing your code, save, then close the frmEmployeeMaster form.

8. Troubleshoot VBA.

a. Open the VBE window for the basFunctions module.

b. Click anywhere in the following statement in the TuitionReimbursement function:

If SalaryValue < 50000 And DependentsValue > 1 Then

c. Click Debug on the menu bar, then click Toggle Breakpoint to set a breakpoint at this statement.

d. Save the changes, then close the VBE window and return to Microsoft Access.

e. Open the qryEmployeeData query datasheet. This action attempts to use the TuitionReimbursement function to calculate the value for the Tuition field, which stops and highlights the statement in the VBE window where you set a breakpoint.

f. Click View on the menu bar, click Immediate Window (if not already visible), delete any previous entries in the Immediate window, type **?SalaryValue**, then press ENTER. At this point in the execution of the VBA, the SalaryValue should be 55000, the value you entered for the first record.

g. Type **?DependentsValue**, then press ENTER. At this point in the execution of the VBA code, the DependentsValue should be 3, the value for the first record. (*Hint*: You can resize the Immediate window by dragging the top edge.)

h. Click Debug on the menu bar, click Clear All Breakpoints, then click the Continue button on the Standard toolbar. Close the VBE window and close the qryEmployeeData object.

i. Compact and repair, then close the IL_AC_11_SupportDesk.accdb database and close Access 2019.

FIGURE 11-22

```
Private Sub Form_AfterUpdate()
  If IsNull(txtDependents) Then
    MsgBox ("Please enter # of dependents")
    DoCmd.GoToControl "txtDependents"
  End If
End Sub
```

FIGURE 11-23

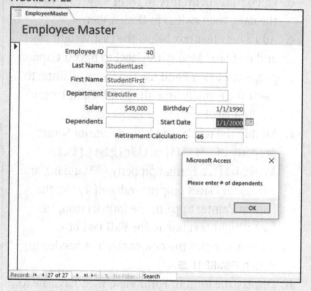

FIGURE 11-24

```
Private Sub Form_AfterUpdate()
  If IsNull(txtDependents) Then
    MsgBox ("Please enter # of dependents")
    DoCmd.GoToControl "txtDependents"
  End If
  If txtSalary.Value < 50000 And txtDependents.Value > 1 Then
    lblTuition.Visible = True
  Else
    lblTuition.Visible = False
  End If
End Sub
```

Access

Independent Challenge 1

As the manager of Riverwalk, a multispecialty health clinic, you have created a database to manage patient outcomes. In this exercise, you will create a custom function and use it on a form to help calculate body mass index.

a. Start Access, open the IL_AC_11-3.accdb database from the location where you store your Data Files, then save it as **IL_AC_11_Riverwalk**. Enable content if prompted.

b. Create a new standard module with the VBA and comments shown in **FIGURE 11-25**.

c. Save the module with the name **basFunctions**, then close the VBE window.

d. Open frmPatientEntry in Form View to review the data, then switch to Design View.

e. Add a new text box below the Last Weight label and text box. Modify the label to have a Caption property of **BMI** and use the Format Painter to paint the formats from the Last Weight label to the BMI label.

f. Modify the text box to have a Control Source property of **=BMI([txtHeight],[txtWeight])**, a Format property of Standard, and a Decimal Places property value of **1**. Use the Format Painter to paint the formats from the Last Weight text box to the BMI text box.

g. Move and resize the new controls as needed to match **FIGURE 11-26**.

h. Display the form in Form View, then navigate to the second record, as shown in **FIGURE 11-26**.

i. Compact and close the IL_AC_Riverwalk.accdb database, then close Access.

FIGURE 11-25

```
'Student name - current date
'Calculate BMI (Body Mass Index)
'A healthy BMI is 21-24.

Function BMI(HeightValue, WeightValue)
    If HeightValue = 0 Then
        BMI = 0
    Else
        BMI = (WeightValue * 0.4536) / (HeightValue * 0.0254) ^ 2
    End If

End Function
```

FIGURE 11-26

Independent Challenge 2

You are working for a city to coordinate a series of community-wide preparedness activities. You have created a database to track the activities and volunteers who are attending the activities. In this exercise, you will create a class module to help identify a requirement for minor volunteers.

a. Start Access, open the IL_AC_11-4.accdb database from the location where you store your Data Files, then save it as **IL_AC_11_Volunteers**. Enable content if prompted.

b. Open the frmVolunteerEntry form in Form View, click in the Birthday text box, click the Descending button to sort the records in descending order by Birthday, then navigate through several records. Some of the volunteers are under 18 years old, and you want the form to display a message when the volunteer is under 18 years old.

c. Switch to Form Design View, click the Birthday text box, open the Property Sheet for the Birthday text box, click the Build button for the After Update event, click the Code Builder option, then enter the code for the procedure shown in **FIGURE 11-27** as well as the comments above it.

d. Create a Form_Current() sub procedure and copy the statements from Birthday_AfterUpdate() to the Form_Current() so that the statements also run when you move from record to record.

e. Save the VBA code, close the VBE, then open the form in Form View to test the class procedures. You should be prompted with the message for the first record. Make sure the records are still sorted in descending order on the Birthday field.

f. Click OK, then modify the Birthday value for the first record (Volunteer ID 35 Taney Wilson) to be **1/1/99**. You should not be prompted with a message after entering that date.

g. Move to the second record (Volunteer ID 26 Sally Olingback) and test it with the Birthday value of **1/1/99** (no prompt) and then **11/1/08** (prompt).

h. Compact and close the IL_AC_11_Volunteers.accdb database, then close Access.

FIGURE 11-27

```
'Created by your name on current date
'Date represents today's date
'Birthday represents the value in the Birthday text box
'Date - Birthday gives the days between the two dates
'(Date - Birthday) / 365.25 produces the number of years between the two dates
'Int() produces the integer portion of the date

Private Sub Birthday_AfterUpdate()
  If Int((Date - Birthday) / 365.25) < 18 Then
       MsgBox ("Volunteer must be accompanied by adult.")
  End If
End Sub
```

Visual Workshop

Start Access, open the IL_AC_11-5.accdb database from the location where you store your Data Files, then save it as **IL_AC_11_ CollegeCourses**. Enable content if prompted. Use **FIGURE 11-28** to develop a new function named **Points** in a standard module named **basFunctions**. Include *your* name and the current date as a comment.

Modify the qryEnrollmentAndGrades query by adding two calculated fields after the Grade field. The first calculated field is named **PointsPerClass** and uses the new Points function as follows to determine the points per class based on the grade earned in that class:

PointsPerClass: Points([Grade])

The second calculated field is named QPPC (short for quality points per class), which is determined by the credits for the class multiplied by the points earned per class:

QPPC: [Credits]*[PointsPerClass]

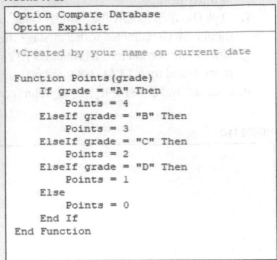

FIGURE 11-28

```
Option Compare Database
Option Explicit

'Created by your name on current date

Function Points(grade)
    If grade = "A" Then
        Points = 4
    ElseIf grade = "B" Then
        Points = 3
    ElseIf grade = "C" Then
        Points = 2
    ElseIf grade = "D" Then
        Points = 1
    Else
        Points = 0
    End If
End Function
```

Save and view the qryEnrollmentAndGrades query in Datasheet view to make sure that the PointsPerClass and QPPC calculated fields are calculating successfully. A 4-credit class with a grade of B should result in 3 PointsPerClass and 12 QPPC.

Open frmStudents in Design View and make these property modifications on the Control Source property of these text boxes. The text boxes are identified by their Name property and location:

txtQPPC in the Detail section of the subform: **QPPC**

txtSumQPPC in the Form Footer section of the subform: **=Sum([QPPC])**

txtSumCredits in the Form Footer section of the subform: **=Sum([Credits])**

txtGPA in the Detail section of the main form: **=[frmEnrollmentsSubform].[Form]![txtSumQPPC]/ [frmEnrollmentsSubform].[Form]![txtSumCredits]**

This expression divides the value in the txtSumQPPC text box in the frmEnrollmentsSubform's Form Footer section and divides it by the value in the txtSumCredits text box. Save the frmStudents form and display it in Form View, as shown in **FIGURE 11-29**. Navigate through several records to make sure all calculations are displayed correctly. Save and close frmStudents, compact and close the IL_AC_11_CollegeCourses.accdb database, then close Access.

FIGURE 11-29

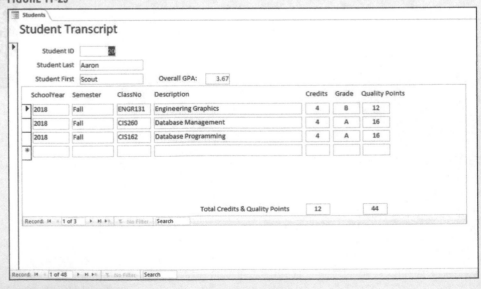

Completing the Application

CASE You are working with Lydia Snyder, vice president of operations at JCL Talent, to build a research database to manage industry, company, and job data. In this module, you'll create a navigation form. You also work with several administrative issues, such as setting passwords, changing startup options, and analyzing database performance to protect, improve, and enhance the database.

Module Objectives

After completing this module, you will be able to:

- Create a navigation form
- Set startup options
- Analyze database performance
- Secure a database
- Split a database
- Document a database

Files You Will Need

IL_AC_12-1.accdb

IL_AC_12-2.accdb

IL_AC_12-3.accdb

IL_AC_12-4.accdb

IL_AC_12-5.accdb

Create a Navigation Form

Learning
Outcomes
• Create a
  navigation form
• Add and edit
  navigation buttons

A **navigation form** is a special Access form that includes a **navigation control**, a special type of control that contains **navigation button controls** that allow a user to easily switch between the various forms and reports in your database. **CASE** ▶ *Lydia asks you to create an interface to make it easy to access the forms and reports in the JCL jobs database. A navigation form will work well for this purpose.*

STEPS

1. **Start Access, open the** IL_AC_12-1.accdb database **from the location where you store your Data Files, save it as** IL_AC_12_Jobs, **enable content if prompted, click the** Create **tab, click the** Navigation button **in the Forms group, click the** Vertical Tabs, Left option, **then close the Field List window if it opens**

   The new navigation form opens in Layout View. Vertical Tabs, Left is a **navigation system style** that determines how the navigation buttons are displayed in the navigation control on the form. Other navigation system styles include additional vertical and horizontal arrangements for the tabs.

QUICK TIP
In the Navigation Pane, click the object expand ⌄ and collapse ⌃ buttons to display or hide objects. Click the Shutter Bar Open/Close button « to open or close the entire pane.

2. **Drag the** frmEmployeeEntry form **from the Navigation Pane to the first navigation button, which displays [Add New]**

   The frmEmployeeEntry form is added as the first navigation button, as shown in **FIGURE 12-1**, and a new navigation button with [Add New] is automatically created as well. The second and third navigation buttons will contain reports.

3. **Drag the** rptJobSalaries report **from the Navigation Pane to the second navigation button, which displays [Add New], then drag the** rptJobsByState report **to the third navigation button, which also displays [Add New]**

   With the objects in place, you can rename the navigation buttons to be less technical.

QUICK TIP
You can also modify the text on a navigation button in Form Design View by modifying the navigation button's Caption property.

4. **Double-click the** frmEmployeeEntry navigation button, **edit it to read** Employees, **double-click the** rptJobSalaries navigation button, **edit it to read** Salaries, **double-click the** rptJobsByState navigation button, **then edit it to read** Jobs by State

   You can reorder the navigation buttons by dragging them to their new location.

TROUBLE
Click the Jobs by State navigation button if it is not already selected.

5. **Drag the** Jobs by State navigation button **up between the Employees and Salaries navigation buttons, then click the** Form View button 🖳 **to display the form, as shown in FIGURE 12-2**

   Test, save, and close the new navigation form.

6. **Click the** Employees navigation button **in the form, click the** Jobs by State navigation **button, click the** Salaries navigation button, **click the** Save button 🖫 **on the Quick Access Toolbar, type** frmNavigation, **click OK, then close frmNavigation**

FIGURE 12-1: Creating a navigation form

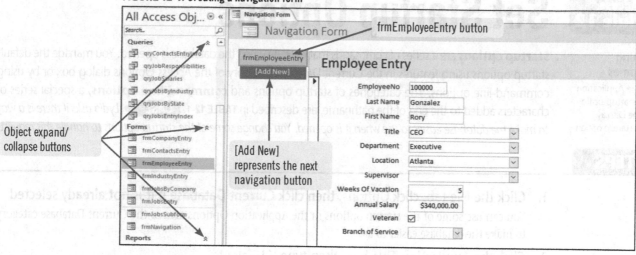

Object expand/collapse buttons

frmEmployeeEntry button

[Add New] represents the next navigation button

FIGURE 12-2: Navigation form in Form View

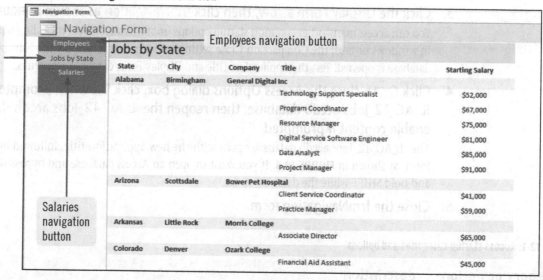

Jobs by State navigation button has been moved to the middle

Employees navigation button

Salaries navigation button

Jobs by State

State	City	Company	Title	Starting Salary
Alabama	Birmingham	General Digital Inc		
			Technology Support Specialist	$52,000
			Program Coordinator	$67,000
			Resource Manager	$75,000
			Digital Service Software Engineer	$81,000
			Data Analyst	$85,000
			Project Manager	$91,000
Arizona	Scottsdale	Bower Pet Hospital		
			Client Service Coordinator	$41,000
			Practice Manager	$59,000
Arkansas	Little Rock	Morris College		
			Associate Director	$65,000
Colorado	Denver	Ozark College		
			Financial Aid Assistant	$45,000

Setting Navigation Pane options

You can change the way the Navigation Pane appears by clicking the title bar of the Navigation Pane and choosing a different way to organize the objects (e.g., by Object Type, Created Date, or Custom Groups) in the upper portion of the menu. The lower portion of the menu lets you display only one object type (e.g., Tables, Queries, Forms, Reports, or All Access Objects). Right-click the Navigation Pane for more options on the shortcut menu, including Navigation Options, which allows you to create custom groups within the Navigation Pane.

Set Startup Options

Learning Outcomes
• Set the Application Title startup option
• Set the Display Form startup option

Startup options are a series of commands that execute when the database is opened. You manage the default startup options using features in the Current Database category of the Access Options dialog box or by using command-line options. The categories of startup options and **command-line options**, a special series of characters added to the end of the pathname, are described in TABLE 12-1. **CASE** ▶ *Lydia asks if there is a way to make the database easier to use when it is opened. You change some of the startup options to handle this request.*

STEPS

1. **Click the File tab, click Options, then click Current Database if it is not already selected**

   You can use some of the startup options in the Application Options area of the Current Database category to make the database easier to use.

2. **Click the Application Title box, then type JCL Talent**

   When filled in, the **Application Title** property value appears in the title bar instead of the database filename.

3. **Click the Display Form arrow, then click frmNavigation as shown in FIGURE 12-3**

   You can access many other common startup options from this dialog box, including whether objects appear in windows or tabs, the Compact on Close setting, and whether to display the Navigation Pane when the database is opened. Test the Application Title and Display Form database properties.

4. **Click OK to close the Access Options dialog box, click OK when prompted, close the IL_AC_12_Jobs.accdb database, then reopen the IL_AC_12_Jobs.accdb database and enable content if prompted**

   The IL_AC_12_Jobs.accdb database opens with the new application title, followed by the frmNavigation form, as shown in FIGURE 12-4. If you want to open an Access database and bypass startup options, press and hold SHIFT while the database opens.

5. **Close the frmNavigation form**

TABLE 12-1: Access startup categories and options

category or option	description
General	Sets default interface, file format, default database folder, and username options
Current Database	Provides for application changes, such as whether the windows are overlapping or tabbed, the database compacts on close, and Layout View is enabled; also provides Navigation Pane, ribbon, toolbar, and AutoCorrect options
Datasheet	Determines the default gridlines, cell effects, and fonts of datasheets
Object Designers	Determines default Design View settings for tables, queries, forms, and reports; also provides default error-checking options
Proofing	Sets AutoCorrect and Spelling options
Language	Sets Editing, Display, and Help languages
Client Settings	Sets defaults for cursor action when editing display elements, printing margins, date formatting, and advanced record management options
Customize Ribbon	Provides an easy-to-use interface to modify the buttons and tabs on the ribbon
Quick Access Toolbar	Provides an easy-to-use interface to modify the buttons on the Quick Access Toolbar
Add-ins	Provides a way to manage add-ins, software that works with Access to add or enhance functionality
Trust Center	Provides a way to manage trusted publishers, trusted locations, trusted documents, macro settings, and other privacy and security settings
/excl	Command-line option that opens the database for exclusive access, as in C:\Documents\JCL.accdb /excl
/ro	Command-line option that opens the database for read-only access, as in C:\Documents\JCL.accdb /ro

FIGURE 12-3: Setting startup options

Access Options dialog box

Current Database

Display Document Tabs

Compact on Close

Display Navigation Pane

Application Title

Display Form

Windows or Tabbed Documents

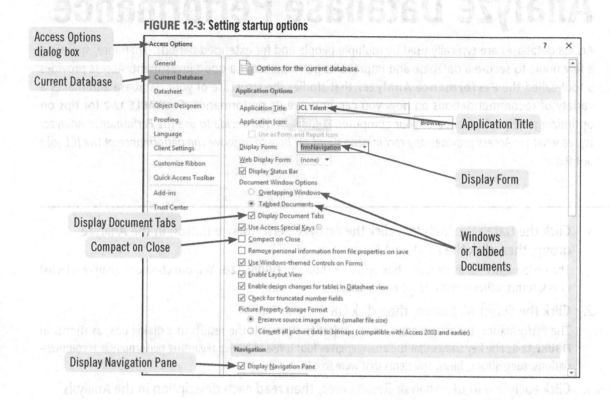

FIGURE 12-4: Display Form and Application Title startup options are in effect

Application Title

frmNavigation automatically opens

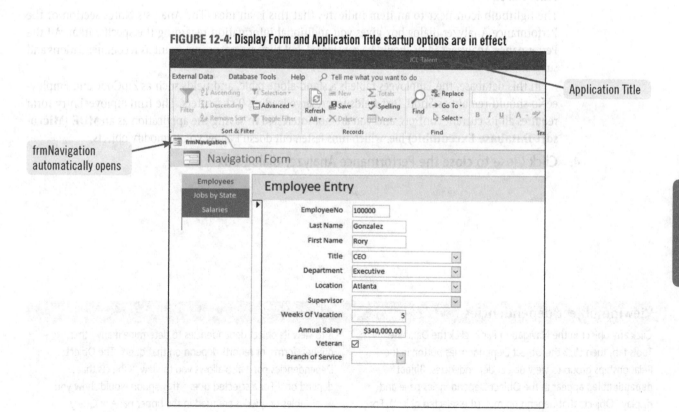

Access

Analyze Database Performance

Access databases are typically used by multiple people and for extended periods. Therefore, spending a few hours to secure a database and improve its performance is a good investment. Access provides a tool called the **Performance Analyzer** that studies the structure of your database and makes a variety of recommendations on how you can improve its performance. See **TABLE 12-2** for tips on optimizing the performance of your computer. **CASE** *You decide to use the Performance Analyzer to see whether Access provides any recommendations on how to improve the performance of the JCL jobs database.*

STEPS

1. **Click the** Database Tools tab, **click the** Analyze Performance button **in the Analyze group, then click the** All Object Types tab

   The Performance Analyzer dialog box opens, as shown in **FIGURE 12-5**. You can choose to analyze selected tables, forms, other objects, or the entire database.

2. **Click the** Select All button, **then click** OK

   The Performance Analyzer examines each object and presents the results in a dialog box, as shown in **FIGURE 12-6**. The key shows that the analyzer gives four levels of advice regarding performance: recommendations, suggestions, ideas, and items that were fixed.

3. **Click** each line in the Analysis Results area, **then read each description in the Analysis Notes area**

   The lightbulb icon next to an item indicates that this is an idea. The Analysis Notes section of the Performance Analyzer dialog box gives you additional information regarding the specific item. All the Performance Analyzer's ideas should be considered, but they are not as important as recommendations and suggestions.

   In this database, the Employees table is a stand-alone table, and fields such as ZipCode and EmployeeNo should remain as Short Text fields to preserve leading 0 characters. The frmEmployeeEntry form requires all its current controls, and you are not interested in saving the application as an **MDE (Microsoft Database Executable)** file, which runs faster, but doesn't allow you to modify objects.

4. **Click** Close **to close the Performance Analyzer dialog box**

Viewing object dependencies

Click any object in the Navigation Pane, click the Database Tools tab, then click the Object Dependencies button in the Relationships group to view object dependencies. **Object dependencies** appear in the Object Dependencies pane and display "Objects that depend on me" (the selected object). For example, before deleting a query, you might want to select it to view its object dependencies to determine if any other queries, forms, or reports depend on that query. The Object Dependencies pane also allows you to view "Objects that I depend on." For a selected query, this option would show you what tables or queries are used in the upper pane of Query Design View.

FIGURE 12-5: Performance Analyzer dialog box

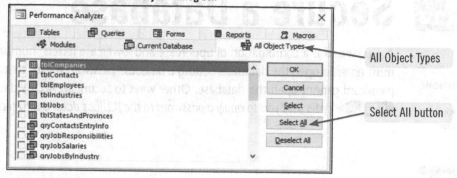

All Object Types

Select All button

FIGURE 12-6: Performance Analyzer results

Analysis Results

Key symbols

Analysis Notes for the selected item

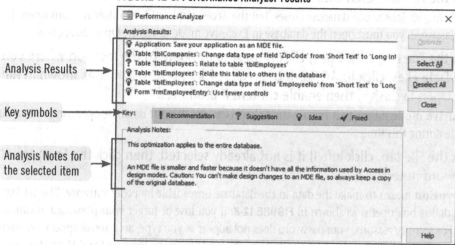

TABLE 12-2: Tips for optimizing performance

degree of difficulty	tip
Easy	Close all applications that you don't currently need
Easy	Eliminate unneeded memory-resident programs, such as complex screen savers, email alert programs, and unneeded virus checkers
Easy	If you are the only person using a database, open it in Exclusive mode
Easy	Use the Compact on Close feature
Moderate	Add more memory to your computer
Moderate	If others don't need to share the database, load it on your local hard drive instead of the network's file server (but be sure to back up local drives regularly, too)
Moderate	Split the database so that the data is stored on the file server but other database objects are stored on your local (faster) hard drive
Moderate to difficult	Move the database to an uncompressed drive
Moderate to difficult	Run Performance Analyzer on a regular basis, examining and appropriately acting on each recommendation, suggestion, and idea
Moderate to difficult	Make sure that all PCs are running the latest versions of Windows and Access
Essential	Make sure your database is normalized correctly and that appropriate one-to-many relationships are established in the Relationships window

Secure a Database

Learning Outcomes
- Open the database in Exclusive mode
- Set a password and encryption

A **password** is a combination of uppercase and lowercase letters, numbers, and symbols that the user must enter to open the database. Setting a database password means that anyone who doesn't know the password cannot open the database. Other ways to secure an Access database are listed in **TABLE 12-3**.

CASE ▶ *Lydia asks you to apply a password to the JCL jobs database to secure its data.*

STEPS

1. Click the File tab, then click Close

The IL_AC_12_Jobs.accdb database closes, but the Access application window remains open. To set a database password, you must open the database in Exclusive mode using the Open dialog box.

TROUBLE
You cannot use the Recent list to open a database in Exclusive mode.

2. Click the File tab, click Open, click Browse to navigate to the location where you store your Data Files, click IL_AC_12_Jobs.accdb, click the Open arrow as shown in FIGURE 12-7, click Open Exclusive, then enable content if prompted

Exclusive mode means that you are the only person who has the database open, and others cannot open the file during this time.

QUICK TIP
Passwords are case sensitive, so, GoJCL! and gojcl! are different passwords.

3. Click the File tab, click Info if it is not already selected, then click the Encrypt with Password button

Encryption means to make the data in the database unreadable by other software. The Set Database Password dialog box opens, as shown in **FIGURE 12-8**. If you lose or forget your password, it cannot be recovered. For security reasons, your password does not appear as you type; an asterisk appears for each keystroke instead. Therefore, you must enter the same password in both the Password and Verify text boxes to make sure you haven't made a typing error.

4. Type GoJCL!22 in the Password box, press TAB, type GoJCL!22 in the Verify box, click OK, then click OK if prompted about row level locking

Passwords should be easy to remember but not easy to guess. **Strong passwords** are longer than eight characters and use the entire keyboard, including uppercase and lowercase letters, numbers, and symbols.

5. Close, then reopen the IL_AC_12_Jobs.accdb database

The Password Required dialog box opens.

6. Type GoJCL!22, then click OK

The IL_AC_12_Jobs.accdb database opens, giving you full access to all the objects. To remove a password, you must exclusively open a database, just as you did when you set the database password.

TROUBLE
You must browse for the file to open it exclusively.

7. Click the File tab, click Close, click the File tab, click Open, click Browse to navigate to the location where you store your Data Files, single-click IL_AC_12_Jobs.accdb, click the Open arrow, click Open Exclusive, type GoJCL!22 in the Password Required dialog box, then click OK

8. Click the File tab, click Info, click the Decrypt Database button, type GoJCL!22, click OK, then close the IL_AC_12_Jobs.accdb database and exit Access

FIGURE 12-7: Opening a database in Exclusive mode

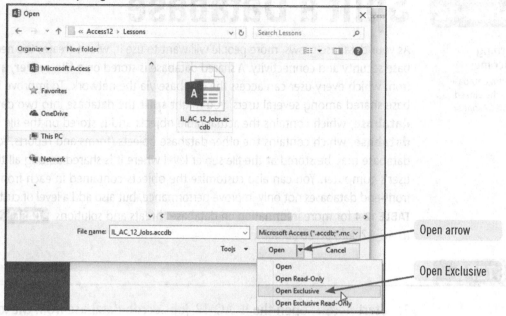

Open arrow

Open Exclusive

FIGURE 12-8: Set Database Password dialog box

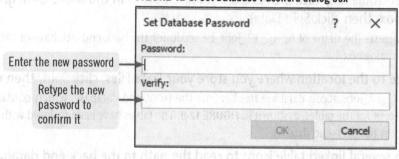

Enter the new password

Retype the new
password to
confirm it

TABLE 12-3: Methods to secure an Access database

method	description
Password	Restricts access to the database to only those who know the password
Encryption	Makes the data indecipherable to other programs when sent across a network
Startup options	Hides or disables certain functions when the database is opened
Show/hide objects	Shows or hides objects in the Navigation Pane; a simple way to prevent users from unintentionally deleting objects is to hide them in the Navigation Pane by checking the Hidden property in the object's Property Sheet
Split a database	Separates the back-end data and the front-end objects (such as forms and reports) into two databases that work together; splitting a database allows you to give each user access to only those objects they need

Trusting a database to automatically enable content

Trusting a database means to identify the database file as one that is safe to open. Trusted databases automatically enable all content, including all macros and VBA, and, therefore, do not present the Enable Content message when they are opened. To trust a database, click the File tab, click Options, click Trust Center on the left, click the Trust Center Settings button, then use the Trusted Documents or Trusted Locations options to either trust an individual database file or an entire folder. To trust the folder, click Trusted Locations, click Add new location, click Browse to locate the folder to trust, select the desired folder, click the Subfolders of this location are also trusted check box to also trust subfolders, and then click OK to move through the dialog boxes and complete the process.

Access

Split a Database

As your database grows, more people will want to use it, which creates the need for higher levels of database security and connectivity. A shared database is stored on a **file server**, a centrally located computer from which every user can access the database via the network. To improve the performance of a database shared among several users, you might **split** the database into two database files: the **back-end database**, which contains the actual table objects and is stored on the file server, and the **front-end database**, which contains the other database objects (forms and reports, for example). The front-end database may be stored at the file server level where it is shared among all the users or placed on each user's computer. You can also customize the objects contained in each front-end database. Therefore, front-end databases not only improve performance, but also add a level of customization and security. See **TABLE 12-4** for more information on database threats and solutions. **CASE** ▶ *Lydia asks you to split the IL_AC_12_Jobs.accdb database.*

STEPS

1. **Start** Access, **open the** IL_AC_12_Jobs.accdb database **from the location where you store your Data Files, enable content if prompted, close the frmNavigation form, click the** Database Tools tab, **click the** Access Database button **in the Move Data group, read the dialog box, then click** Split Database

   Access suggests the name of IL_AC_12_Jobs_be.accdb for the back-end database in the Create Back-end Database dialog box.

2. **Navigate to the location where you store your Data Files, click** Split, **then click** OK

   The IL_AC_12_Jobs.accdb database has become the front-end database, which contains all the Access objects except for the tables, as shown in **FIGURE 12-9**. The tables have been replaced with links to the physical tables in the back-end database.

TROUBLE
The path to your
back-end database
will be different.

3. **Point to several linked table icons to read the path to the back-end database, right-click any of the** linked table icons, **click** Linked Table Manager, **then click the** Expand button ⊞ **to the left of Access, as shown in** FIGURE 12-10

   The Linked Table Manager dialog box allows you to select and manually update tables. This is useful if the path to the back-end database changes and you need to reconnect the front-end and back-end database.

4. **Click** Close

   To the front-end database, a linked table functions the same as a regular table even though the data is physically stored elsewhere. To modify the structure of a linked table, you need to open the database where the table is physically stored.

   In addition to tables in another Access database, Access can link to data in several different file formats, including Excel, dBASE, SharePoint lists, HTML, and any data that can be reached with an **ODBC (Open Database Connectivity)** connection. Use the External Data tab on the ribbon along with the New Data Source button to create an individual link to an external data source.

FIGURE 12-9: Front-end database with linked tables

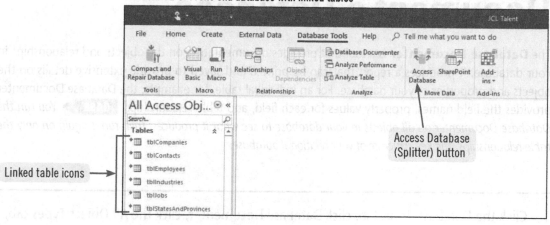

Linked table icons →

Access Database (Splitter) button

FIGURE 12-10: Linked Table Manager

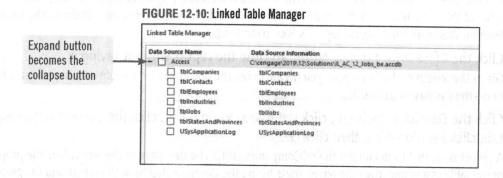

Expand button becomes the collapse button →

TABLE 12-4: Database threats and solutions

incident	what can happen	appropriate actions
Virus	Viruses can cause a wide range of harm, from profane messages to corrupted files	Install virus-checking software
Power outage	Power problems such as **brownouts** (dips in power), and **spikes** (surges in power) can damage the hardware	Purchase a **UPS (uninterruptible power supply)** and **surge protectors** (power strip with surge protection)
Theft or intentional damage	Computer thieves or other scoundrels steal or vandalize computer equipment	Physically secure the file server in a locked room, back up data in an off-site location on a daily basis, and set database passwords

Document a Database

Learning
Outcomes
• Use the Database
  Documenter
• Study one-to-
  many relationships

The **Database Documenter** is a tool that provides documentation on the objects and relationships in your database. It produces a report that can be printed and saved to provide extensive details on the objects and properties of your database. For an individual table, for example, the Database Documenter provides the field names, property values for each field, and table relationships. **CASE** *You run the Database Documenter on all objects in your database to see what it produces, then run it again on only the table relationships, the key structure of your relational database.*

STEPS

1. **Click the** Database Tools tab, **click** Database Documenter, **click the** All Object Types tab, **click the** Select All button **as shown in** FIGURE 12-11, **then click** OK

   The Database Documenter tool analyzes the selected objects and prepares a report starting with the properties of tblCompanies, the fields in tblCompanies, each of the properties of each of the fields, and so on. Even for this small database, the report is 200+ pages long.

2. **Click the** Close Print Preview button **to close the report without saving it**

   Given the length of the full report, you decide to use the documenter on a subset of important information—the database relationships.

3. **Click the** Database Tools tab, **click** Database Documenter, **click the** Current Database tab, **click** Relationships, **then click** OK

   A report is created to document the tblCompanies table. The first page of the report lists the properties of the table as a whole, then the report starts listing the Columns (fields) of the report and the properties of each.

4. **Click the** report **to zoom in to view the table relationships, as shown in** FIGURE 12-12

   The first page of the report shows you the one-to-many relationships in the database starting with these three:

   tblCompanies has a one-to-many relationship with tblContacts.

   tblCompanies has a one-to-many relationship with tblJobs.

   tblIndustries has a one-to-many relationship with tblCompanies.

5. **Click the** Close Print Preview button

   You can print reports from the Database Documenter, but they close without allowing you to save them. You can easily re-create them using the Database Documenter tool as needed.

6. **Compact and close the IL_AC_12_Jobs.accdb database, then exit Access**

FIGURE 12-11: Documenter dialog box

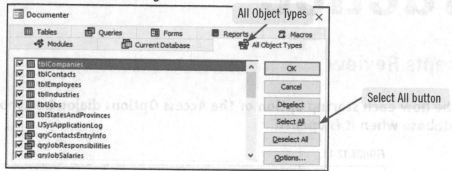

FIGURE 12-12: Database Documenter report of database relationships

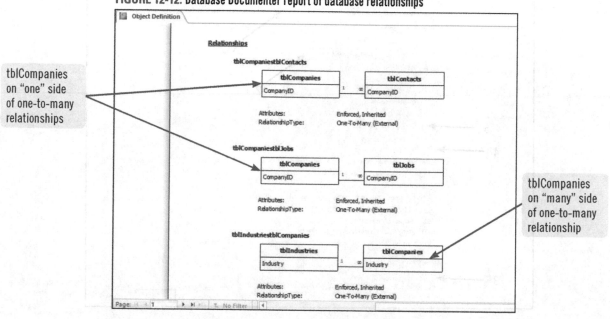

tblCompanies on "one" side of one-to-many relationships

tblCompanies on "many" side of one-to-many relationship

Access

Practice

Concepts Review

Describe how each startup option of the Access Options dialog box shown in FIGURE 12-13 **affects the database when it is opened.**

FIGURE 12-13

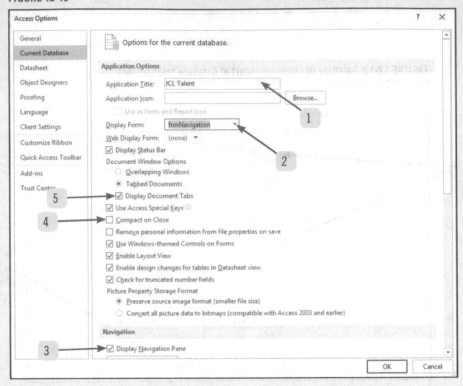

Match each term with the statement that best describes its function.

6. Database Documenter

7. Exclusive mode

8. Performance Analyzer

9. Navigation form

10. Back-end database

11. Encrypting

a. Means that no other users can have access to the database file while it's open

b. Scrambles data so that it is indecipherable when opened by another program

c. Studies the structure and size of your database and makes a variety of recommendations on how you may be able to improve its speed

d. Contains database tables

e. Provides an easy-to-use database interface

f. Provides a report on the selected objects and relationships in your database Select the best answer from the list of choices.

Select the best answer from the list of choices.

12. Which of the following is *not* true about the reports created by the Database Documenter?

a. They may be saved in the database.

b. They may be printed.

c. They document table relationships.

d. They document field property values.

13. Which is *not* a strong password?

   a. 1234$College=6789

   b. 5Matthew14?

   c. Lip44Balm*!

   d. password

14. Which character precedes a command-line option?

   a. !

   b. @

   c. ^

   d. /

15. The Application Title and Display Form startup options are found in which category in the Access Options dialog box?

   a. General

   b. Current Database

   c. Object Designers

   d. Proofing

16. Compacting and repairing a database does *not* help with which issue?

   a. Identifying unused database objects

   b. Preventing data integrity problems

   c. Eliminating wasted space

   d. Making the database as small as possible

17. How does the object dependencies feature help the database developer?

   a. It identifies performance issues based on object dependencies.

   b. It identifies naming convention issues between objects in the database.

   c. It deletes unused objects.

   d. It helps prevent the developer from deleting a query used by another object.

18. Which of the following is *not* a reason to create a backup?

   a. Protect against theft

   b. Minimize damage caused by an incident that corrupts data

   c. Improve performance of the database

   d. Safeguard information should a natural disaster destroy the database

19. Why might you split a database?

   a. To make access to the database more secure

   b. To improve performance

   c. To customize the front-end databases

   d. All of the above

20. What controls are automatically created on a navigation form?

   a. Navigation control and navigation buttons

   b. Navigation control and hyperlinks

   c. Navigation buttons and command buttons

   d. Navigation buttons and page breaks

Skills Review

1. Create a navigation form.

a. Start Access, open the IL_AC_12-2.accdb database from the location where you store your Data Files, then save it as **IL_AC_12_SupportDesk**. Enable content if prompted.

b. Create a navigation form using the Horizontal Tabs style.

c. Close the Field List if it opens.

d. Add the frmEmployeeMaster form, the rptCallLog report, the rptCaseInfo report, and the rptEmployeeMasterList report as navigation buttons.

e. Rename the navigation buttons to **Employee Entry**, **Call Log**, **Case Info**, and **Employee List**.

f. Display the form in Form View, then test each navigation button.

g. Save the form with the name **frmNavigation** as shown in **FIGURE 12-14**, then close it.

FIGURE 12-14

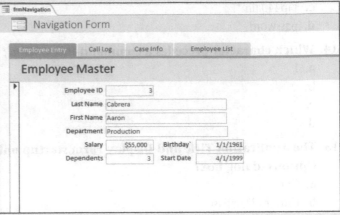

2. Set startup options.

a. Open the Access Options dialog box to the Current Database category.

b. Type **Technical Support Center** in the Application Title box, click the Display Form arrow, click the frmNavigation form, then apply the changes.

c. Close the IL_AC_12_SupportDesk.accdb database, then reopen it to check the startup options. Notice the change in the Access title bar.

d. Close the frmNavigation form that automatically opened when you opened the database.

3. Analyze database performance.

a. On the Database Tools tab, click the Analyze Performance button.

b. On the All Object Types tab, select all objects, then click OK.

c. Read each of the ideas and descriptions, then close the Performance Analyzer.

d. Open the frmEmployeeMaster form in Design View, then click the View Code button. This form contains an empty module. According to the Performance Analyzer suggestions from the previous step, removing an empty module can improve performance.

e. Close the code window, then open the Property Sheet for the form. On the Other tab, change the Has Module property from Yes to **No**, then click Yes when prompted if you are sure.

f. Save and close the frmEmployeeMaster form, then close Access.

4. Secure a database.

a. Start Access and open the IL_AC_12_SupportDesk.accdb database in Exclusive mode. (*Hint*: Remember that you must browse for a database from within Access to open it in Exclusive mode.)

b. Encrypt the database and set the password to **HelpIs#1**. (*Hint*: Check to make sure the Caps Lock key is not selected because passwords are case sensitive.) Click OK if prompted about row level locking.

c. Close the IL_AC_12_SupportDesk.accdb database, but leave Access open.

d. Reopen the IL_AC_12_SupportDesk.accdb database to test the password. Close the IL_AC_12_SupportDesk.accdb database.

e. Reopen the IL_AC_12_SupportDesk.accdb database in Exclusive mode. Type **HelpIs#1** as the password.

f. Unset the password and decrypt the database.

g. Close the frmNavigation form, then close Access.

Skills Review (continued)

5. Split a database.

   a. Start Access, open the IL_AC_12_SupportDesk.accdb database from the location where you store your Data Files, then enable content if prompted.

   b. Close the frmNavigation form.

   c. On the Database Tools tab, click the Access Database button and split the database.

   d. Name the back-end database with the default name **IL_AC_12_SupportDesk_be** and save it in the location where you store your Data Files.

   e. Point to the linked table icons to observe the path to the back-end database.

6. Document a database.

   a. Use the Database Documenter tool to document the relationships in the database.

   b. Print the one-page report, then close it.

   c. Compact and repair then close the IL_AC_12_ SupportDesk.accdb database and close Access 2019.

Independent Challenge 1

As the manager of Riverwalk, a multispecialty health clinic, you have created a database to manage patient outcomes. In this exercise, you will use the Performance Analyzer to improve the performance of the database.

   a. Start Access, open the IL_AC_12-3.accdb database from the location where you store your Data Files, and save it as **IL_AC_12_Riverwalk**. Enable content if prompted.

   b. On the Database Tools tab, click the Analyze Performance button.

   c. On the All Object Types tab, select all objects, then click OK.

   d. Read each of the ideas and descriptions, then close the Performance Analyzer.

   e. Open the frmPatientEntry form in Design View, then click the View Code button. This form contains a module with one declaration statement and one comment but without any procedures.

   f. Close the code window, then open the Property Sheet for the form. On the Other tab, change the Has Module property from Yes to **No**, then click Yes when prompted if you are sure.

   g. Save and close the frmPatientEntry form.

   h. Run the Performance Analyzer on all objects in the database again.

   i. Four of the suggestions are to change fields that have a Data Type of Short Text to a Number field with a Field Size of Long or Double Integer, as shown in **FIGURE 12-15**. Be prepared to discuss in class why those ideas should not be implemented in this database.

   j. Compact and close the IL_AC_12_Riverwalk.accdb database, then close Access.

FIGURE 12-15

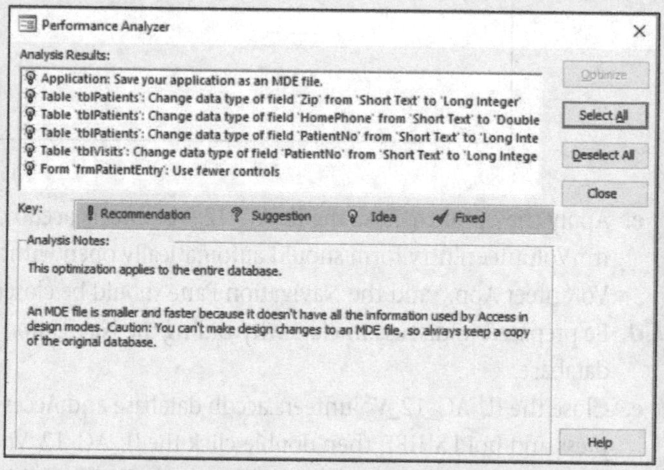

Independent Challenge 2

You are working for a city to coordinate a series of community-wide preparedness activities. You have created a database to track the activities and volunteers who are attending the activities. In this exercise, you will experiment with startup options and how to override them as the database developer.

a. Start Access, open the IL_AC_12-4.accdb database from the location where you store your Data Files, then save it as **IL_AC_12_Volunteers**. Enable content if prompted.

b. Click File on the ribbon, click Options, then click the Current Database category. Make the changes to startup options shown in **FIGURE 12-16** and listed below:

Application Title: **Community Volunteer App**

Display Form: frmVolunteerEntry

Display Document Tabs: No

Compact on Close: Yes

Display Navigation Pane: No

FIGURE 12-16

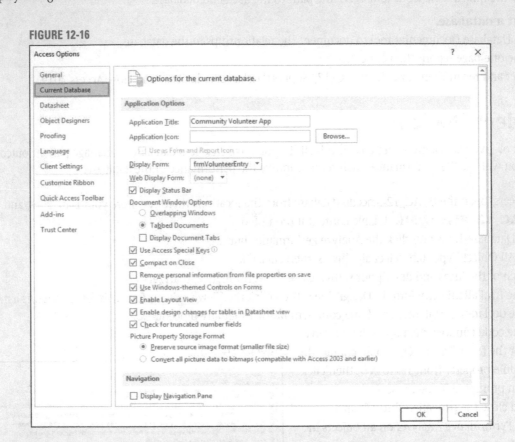

c. Apply the options, close the IL_AC_12_Volunteers.accdb database, then reopen it to observe the changes. The frmVolunteerEntry form should automatically open without a tab, the title bar should display "Community Volunteer App," and the Navigation Pane should be closed.

d. Be prepared to discuss in class why hiding the Navigation Pane and not displaying object tabs can help secure a database.

e. Close the IL_AC_12_Volunteers.accdb database and Access, navigate to the folder where you store your Data Files, press and hold SHIFT, then double-click the IL_AC_12_Volunteers.accdb database to open it. Be sure to not release SHIFT until the database is opened. Pressing SHIFT while opening an Access database file bypasses the startup options.

f. Compact and close the IL_AC_12_Volunteers.accdb database, then close Access.

Completing the Application

Visual Workshop

Start Access, open the IL_AC_12-5.accdb database from the location where you store your Data Files, then save it as **IL_AC_12_CollegeCourses**. Create a navigation form as shown in **FIGURE 12-17** using the Horizontal Tabs navigation style. Add the frmDepartments, frmProfessors, frmClasses, and frmStudentTranscript forms and modify the navigation button text as shown. Save the navigation form with the name **frmNavigation** and set frmNavigation to be the Display Form when the database opens. Close and reopen the database to make sure the startup option has been applied correctly, then close Access.

FIGURE 12-17

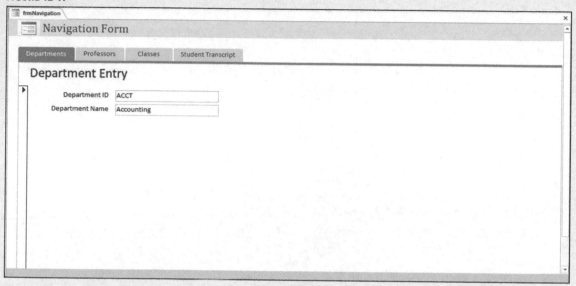

Index

file formats, AC 2-3
   that Access can import, link, and export,
      AC 8-5
file server, AC 12-10
Filter buttons, AC 3-13
Filter By Form, AC 3-12
Filter By Selection, AC 3-12
Filtered, AC 2-19
filtering data, AC 3-12–3-13
filters *vs.* queries, AC 3-13
Find and Replace dialog box, AC 3-11
Find buttons, AC 3-11
Find Unmatched Query Wizard, AC 5-18,
   AC 5-19
Firefox, AC 8-8
focus, AC 1-6
foreign key field, AC 2-14, AC 2-15
   specifying data type, AC 2-17
form(s), AC 1-4
   Access objects, AC 1-5
   adding check boxes and toggle buttons,
      AC 6-8–6-9
   adding command buttons, AC 6-20–6-21
   adding hyperlink control, AC 6-18–6-19
   adding images, AC 6-24–6-25
   adding labels and text boxes, AC 6-2–6-3
   adding lines and rectangles, AC 6-16–6-17
   adding option group, AC 6-10–6-11
   adding subforms, AC 6-28–6-29
   adding tab controls, AC 6-30–6-31
   combo boxes addition to, AC 6-12–6-13
   controls, AC 6-3
   create calculations on, AC 6-6–6-7
   creating, AC 1-16–1-17, AC 6-1–6-33
   editing existing record in, AC 1-17
   entering new record, AC 1-17
   finding records by adding combo boxes,
      AC 6-14–6-15
   in Form View, AC 4-3
   linking with subforms, AC 6-29
   modifying properties, AC 6-32–6-33
   modifying tab order, AC 6-22–6-23
   split form displays, AC 6-26–6-27
format
   Date/Time field, AC 2-10
   Short Text field property, AC 2-9
Format Painter, AC 4-15
formatted column chart, AC 8-17
formatting
   conditional, AC 4-12–4-13
   datasheet, AC 3-22–3-23
   Rich Text, AC 7-21
   using commands, AC 3-23
form creation tools, AC 4-3
Form Design View, AC 4-6–4-7, AC 6-3
   adding, moving, and aligning controls,
      AC 4-7

adding combo box in, AC 6-13
creating calculations in, AC 6-7
creating line and rectangle controls in,
   AC 6-17
mouse pointer shapes, AC 4-7
mouse pointer shapes in, AC 6-5
Form Layout View, AC 4-4–4-5
   formatting commands, AC 4-5
   modifying controls in, AC 4-5
form sections, AC 6-14, AC 6-15
Form View, AC 1-16, AC 4-2–4-3
   navigation form in, AC 12-3
Form Wizard, AC 1-16
fractional value, AC 2-5
FROM SQL keyword, AC 3-7
front-end database, AC 12-10
   with linked tables, AC 12-11
function(s), AC 3-20, AC 3-21, AC 6-6,
   AC 7-10, AC 11-2, AC 11-5. *See also*
   specific types
   aggregate, AC 5-20, AC 5-21
   built-in, AC 11-2
   creating, AC 11-6–11-7
   DATE, AC 3-21
   Date(), AC 6-2
   end, AC 11-5, AC 11-6
   LEFT, AC 3-21
   LEN, AC 3-21
   PMT, AC 3-21
   RIGHT, AC 3-21

G

Get External Data-Access Database dialog
   box, AC 8-2
Get External Data-Excel Spreadsheet
   dialog box, AC 2-2, AC 2-3
Get External Data-Text File dialog box,
   AC 8-4
global modules, AC 11-4
graphic images, AC 6-24
(greater than, >), AC 3-17
(greater than or equal to, ≥), AC 3-17
grouping
   definition of, AC 7-8
   records, AC 7-8–7-9
   records in Report Design View, AC 7-9

H

hexadecimal color values, AC 7-15
hidden object
   showing, AC 9-9
Hidden property, AC 9-8
horizontal ruler, AC 4-10

HTML (HyperText Markup Language),
   AC 7-21, AC 8-10
   companies table exported to, AC 8-11
   exporting to, AC 8-10–8-11
hyperlink, AC 1-10
Hyperlink Address property, AC 6-18
hyperlink control
   adding to forms, AC 6-18–6-19
Hyperlink data type, AC 1-11
Hyperlink dialog box, AC 6-18
Hyperlink fields, AC 5-8
   adding attachment and, AC 5-9
   creating, AC 5-8–5-9

I

If statements, AC 10-2, AC 10-10,
   AC 11-8–11-9
   conditional expressions used in, AC 10-2
   Else portion of, AC 10-12
   using, AC 10-10–10-11
   using to set control's Visible property,
      AC 10-11
If...then, AC 11-5
If...Then...Else, AC 11-8
images. *See also* watermark image
   adding, AC 6-24–6-25
   graphic, AC 6-24
Immediate window, AC 11-16
imported queries and reports, AC 8-3
importing, AC 2-2, AC 8-4
   Access objects, AC 8-2–8-3
   definition of, AC 8-2
   file formats, AC 2-3
   saved, AC 8-4
   text files, AC 8-4–8-5
Import Objects dialog box, AC 8-2–8-3
Import Spreadsheet Wizard, AC 1-23,
   AC 2-2, AC 2-3
Import Text Wizard dialog box, AC 8-4,
   AC 8-5
Indexed property, AC 5-6
infinity symbol, AC 2-16
inner join, AC 9-11
INNER JOIN ... ON SQL keyword, AC 3-7
inner line, AC 9-10
Input Mask, AC 2-8
   entering data with, AC 2-9
   modifying, AC 2-9
   Short Text field property, AC 2-9
   working with, AC 2-9
inserting, page breaks, AC 7-15
Insert Page Break button, AC 7-15
INSERT SQL keyword, AC 3-7
integer, AC 2-5, AC 2-7
IntelliSense technology, AC 11-14

Q

queries, AC 1-4, AC 3-2
  Access objects, AC 1-5
  action, AC 3-4, AC 9-2, AC 9-3
  Append, AC 9-4–9-5
  creating, AC 1-14–1-15
  crosstab, AC 5-22–5-23
  filters vs., AC 3-13
  Make Table, AC 9-2–9-3
  modifying properties in, AC 5-16–5-17
  parameter, AC 5-14–5-15
  Select, AC 1-14, AC 9-2
  sorting datasheet, AC 1-15
  summary, AC 5-20–5-21
  for Top Values, AC 5-12–5-13
query by example (QBE) grid, AC 3-4
Query Datasheet View, AC 3-2
  editing data, AC 3-3
  freezing and hiding columns, AC 3-3
  sorting, AC 3-9
  viewing Applicants field, AC 3-7
  working with, AC 3-2–3-3
query design grid, AC 3-4
Query Design View
  adding and deleting table, AC 3-5
  adding and removing fields, AC 3-5
  creating new query, AC 3-5
  with AND criteria, AC 3-17
  linking tables, AC 3-5
  with OR criteria, AC 3-19
  sorting, AC 3-9
  viewing Applicants field, AC 3-7
  working with, AC 3-4–3-5
query grid, AC 3-4
query wizards, AC 5-19

R

read-only report data, AC 7-2
read-only reports, AC 1-18
record(s), AC 1-6, AC 1-7, AC 2-14
  child, AC 9-10
  deleting in Jobs table, AC 1-9
  editing in Companies table, AC 1-9
  grouping, AC 7-8–7-9
  orphan, AC 9-10
  parent, AC 9-10
  sorting, AC 7-8–7-9
Recordset Type property, AC 5-16
record source, AC 1-18, AC 6-24
Record Source property, AC 6-32, AC 7-2, AC 7-10
rectangles controls
  adding, AC 6-16–6-17

referential integrity, AC 2-15, AC 5-19, AC 9-10
relational database, AC 1-7
  designing, AC 2-14–2-15
  purpose of, AC 2-14
  terminologies, AC 2-14–2-15
relational database software, AC 1-2
Relationship report, AC 2-16
Relationships window
  modifying join properties in, AC 9-11
  with outer join, AC 9-11
rem statement, AC 11-10
repair, AC 1-24
repetitive Access tasks, AC 10-2
report(s), AC 1-4
  Access objects, AC 1-5
  adding counts to, AC 7-11
  combo boxes versus text boxes on, AC 7-9
  create and preview, AC 7-2–7-3
  creating, AC 1-18–1-19
  creating in Report Design View, AC 7-3
  creating multicolumn, AC 7-16–7-17
  Excel and Access compared, AC 1-3
  modifying layout, AC 7-4–7-5
  modifying sections, AC 7-14–7-15
  previewing, AC 1-19
  setting grouping fields, AC 1-19
report controls, AC 7-3
report creation tools, AC 4-9
report data
  read-only, AC 7-2
Report Design View, AC 4-10–4-11
  aligning controls in, AC 7-13
  creating report in, AC 7-3
  grouping records in, AC 7-9
  mouse pointer shapes in, AC 7-5
  moving controls in, AC 7-5
  resizing controls in, AC 7-5
  sorting records in, AC 7-9
report layout
  modifying, AC 7-4–7-5
Report Layout View, AC 4-8–4-9
  moving controls in, AC 7-13
  resizing column, AC 4-9
  resizing controls in, AC 7-13
report sections, AC 4-11
  modifying, AC 7-14–7-15
report views, AC 4-9
Report Wizard, AC 1-18
Required
  Date/Time field, AC 2-10
  Short Text field property, AC 2-9
resizing
  controls, AC 6-4–6-5, AC 7-12–7-13
  controls in Report Design View, AC 7-5
  controls in Report Layout View, AC 7-13

reviewing
  referential integrity, AC 9-10
RGB values, AC 7-15
Rich Text formatting, AC 7-21
Rich Text value, AC 7-21
Right command, AC 6-4
RIGHT function, AC 3-21
right outer join, AC 9-10, AC 9-11
Row Source Lookup property, AC 5-2
Row Source property, AC 6-12
run, AC 3-4, AC 9-2
running
  data macro, AC 10-15
  HighMessage macro, AC 10-11
run-time errors, AC 11-16. See also error(s)

S

saved export, AC 8-6
saved imports, AC 8-4
Scroll Bars, AC 6-32
Scroll Lock, AC 2-19
scrubbing, AC 2-15
scrub data, AC 8-5
section bars, AC 4-10
sections, AC 4-10, AC 7-6–7-7
securing, database, AC 12-8–12-9
security
  Excel and Access compared, AC 1-3
SELECT, AC 9-2
select case, AC 11-5
select query, AC 1-14, AC 3-4, AC 9-2
SELECT SQL keyword, AC 3-6, AC 3-7
self join
  creating, AC 9-14–9-15
  definition of, AC 9-11, AC 9-14
Series area, AC 8-14, AC 8-15
SetProperty, AC 10-10
setting
  breakpoint, AC 11-17
  database password dialog box, AC 12-9
  navigation pane options, AC 12-3
  startup options, AC 12-4–12-5
Short Text, AC 1-10, AC 2-8
  field properties, AC 2-9
  modifying, AC 2-8–2-9
Short Text data type, AC 1-11
Simple Query Wizard, AC 1-14
  using, AC 1-15
Single, in Number Field Size, AC 2-7
single stepping through macro, AC 10-16–10-17
Smart Tags, AC 2-11
Snapshot, AC 5-16

sorting, AC 3-8–3-9
  definition of, AC 7-8
  query datasheet, AC 1-15
  records, AC 7-8–7-9
  records in Report Design View, AC 7-9
Sort row, AC 3-8
spikes, AC 12-11
split form displays, AC 6-26–6-27
splitting, AC 12-10
  database, AC 12-10–12-11
SQL (Structured Query Language),
  AC 6-12, AC 9-12, AC 11-4
standard modules, AC 11-2
starting
  Microsoft Access 2019, AC 1-4
startup options, AC 12-4
  application title, AC 12-5
  setting, AC 12-4–12-5
statement, AC 11-2
status bar indicators, AC 2-19
storage
  Excel and Access compared, AC 1-3
strong passwords, AC 12-8
Structured Query Language (SQL),
  AC 6-12, AC 9-12, AC 11-4
Structured Query Language (SQL) View
  adding Applicants field, AC 3-7
  working with, AC 3-6–3-7
stub, AC 11-12
sub, AC 11-2, AC 11-5
subdatasheet, AC 2-18–2-19
subforms
  adding, AC 6-28–6-29
  definition of, AC 6-28
  linking with form, AC 6-29
submacro
  definition of, AC 10-2
sub procedure, AC 11-2
subreport
  adding, AC 7-18–7-19
  definition of, AC 7-18
  main report with, AC 7-19
  previewing, AC 7-19
subtotals
  adding, AC 7-10–7-11
  previewing, AC 7-11
subtraction operator (-), AC 3-21
summary queries
  building, AC 5-20–5-21
  definition of, AC 5-20

surge protectors, AC 12-11
syntax, AC 11-4
syntax error, AC 11-16. *See also* **error(s)**

T

tab controls
  adding, AC 6-30–6-31
  definition of, AC 6-30
Tab Index property, AC 6-22
table(s), AC 1-4, AC 1-7, AC 2-14
  Access objects, AC 1-5
  child, AC 5-18
  creating, AC 1-10–1-11
  parent, AC 5-18
Table Design View, AC 2-6
table events, AC 10-15
tab order
  definition of, AC 6-22
  modifying, AC 6-22–6-23
tab stop, AC 6-22
Tab Stop property, AC 6-22
  changing, AC 6-23
target table, AC 9-4
template, AC 1-22
text boxes, AC 1-16, AC 4-2, AC 6-2,
  AC 7-9
  adding, AC 6-2–6-3
text files
  delimited, AC 8-4
  exporting, AC 8-4–8-5
  importing, AC 8-4–8-5
Text Format property, AC 7-21
themes, AC 4-15–4-16
three-character prefix naming
  conventions, AC 11-7
toggle buttons
  adding, AC 6-8–6-9
  definition of, AC 6-8
Top Values, AC 5-12
  datasheet, AC 5-13
  options, AC 5-13
  query for, AC 5-12–5-13
Total row, AC 5-20, AC 5-22
troubleshooting
  macros, AC 10-16–10-17
  VBA, AC 11-16–11-17
Trust Center Settings button,
  AC 10-9

trusted database
  definition of, AC 10-9
  using, AC 10-9
trusted folder
  creating, AC 10-9
  setting up, AC 10-9
trusting, database, AC 12-9

U

unbound controls, AC 4-7, AC 6-6
understanding, macros, AC 10-2–10-3
unmatched records
  finding, AC 5-18–5-19
Update query
  creating, AC 9-8–9-9
  definition of, AC 9-3, AC 9-8
UPDATE...SET SQL keyword, AC 3-7
Update To row, AC 9-8
UPS (uninterruptible power supply),
  AC 12-11
user, AC 4-2
using VBA If statement, AC 11-8–11-9

V

Validation Rule, AC 5-6
  expressions, AC 5-7
Validation Text field properties, AC 5-6
Validation Text message, AC 5-7
Validation Text property, AC 5-6
Value argument, AC 10-10
Value field, AC 5-22
variables, AC 11-4
viewing
  object dependencies, AC 12-6
  ScreenTips, AC 10-17
View Shortcuts, AC 2-19
virus, AC 12-11
Visible property, AC 10-10
Visual Basic Editor (VBE), AC 11-2,
  AC 11-3
Visual Basic Editor Window
  for class module, AC 11-5
  components and text color for, AC 11-3
Visual Basic for Applications (VBA)
  converting macros to, AC 11-3
  creating, AC 11-1–11-17

If statements, AC 11-8–11-9
keywords, AC 11-5
troubleshooting, AC 11-16–11-17
understanding, AC 11-2–11-3
Visual Basic for Applications code (VBA),
AC 10-9
statements, AC 10-4
Visual Basic Window
for standard module, AC 11-3
standard toolbar buttons in, AC 11-11

W

watermark image, AC 6-25
WHERE SQL keyword, AC 3-7

wildcard characters, AC 3-19
Word
merging Access data to, AC 8-13
merging to, AC 8-12–8-13

X

XML (Extensible Markup Language),
AC 2-2, AC 8-8
exporting to, AC 8-10–8-11
JobsByState
XPS (structured XML) file, AC 8-8
XSD (XML Schema Definition) file,
AC 8-10

Y

Yes/No data type, AC 1-11

Z

zero-length string value, AC 9-13